HOMER BESIDE HIMSELF

Homer Beside Himself

Para-Narratives in the Iliad

MAUREEN ALDEN

OXFORD
UNIVERSITY PRESS

OXFORD
UNIVERSITY PRESS

Great Clarendon Street, Oxford, OX2 6DP
Oxford University Press is a department of the University of Oxford.
It furthers the University's objective of excellence in research, scholarship,
and education by publishing worldwide in

Oxford New York

Athens Auckland Bangkok Bogotá Buenos Aires Calcutta
Cape Town Chennai Dar es Salaam Delhi Florence Hong Kong Istanbul
Karachi Kuala Lumpur Madrid Melbourne Mexico City Mumbai Nairobi
Paris São Paulo Shanghai Singapore Taipei Tokyo Toronto Warsaw

and associated companies in Berlin Ibadan

Oxford is a registered trade mark of Oxford University Press
in the UK and certain other countries

Published in the United States
by Oxford University Press Inc., New York

British Library Cataloguing in Publication Data

Data available

Library of Congress Cataloging in Publication Data

Data applied for

ISBN 0-19-815285-X

1 3 5 7 9 10 8 6 4 2

Typeset in Imprint
by Regent Typesetting, London
Printed in Great Britain
on acid-free paper by
Biddles Ltd., Guildford & King's Lynn

For Michael

PREFACE

THIS book attempts to explain the relationship between the main narrative of the *Iliad* and its secondary narratives and episodes in a minor key. Its main thesis is that the preoccupations of the primary narrative are explored and interpreted in the other narratives of the poem: none of the narratives of the *Iliad* is there by accident, and none is merely ornamental; the elements of each are related to some aspect of the main story. This practice is not unusual in literature. However, the extraordinary humanity and craftsmanship of the whole poem is the result of genius, perhaps like that of Shakespeare, but at any rate so rare and so far beyond the reach of most of us, that we have in the past tried to explain the poem by reductive methods, identifying the extraneous material it was supposed to have attracted over the years. This was a mistake. We should give the poem a chance as a considered unity, and examine the components of subsidiary narratives in their connection with the main narrative. The motif of requests in 'ascending scale of affection' is used in relation to three characters in the *Iliad*: it dominates the *Iliad*'s account of the story of Meleager, one of the main secondary narratives of the poem. Since the main narrative explores this motif only in connection with Achilles and Hector, I have considered in the later part of the book how it is used to compare them.

I have two institutional debts which are a pleasure to acknowledge. The British Academy very generously funded a visit to the Fondation Hardt in Geneva, where this work was begun in earnest. The Queen's University of Belfast granted me study leave during 1995–6 and again in the autumn of 1999. I am grateful also to library staff at Queen's and the Joint Library of the Hellenic and Roman Societies.

Iannis Kakridis, Malcolm Willcock, Keith Sidwell, Richard Seaford, and John Wilkins have been kind enough to discuss ideas and portions of the manuscript with me. Richard Janko provided much expert advice. Fred Williams read large portions of the manuscript and saved me from a great many foolish blunders. His erudition and congenial society are one of the pleasures of working at Queen's. Another is the company of students and colleagues who have encouraged this work. I am deeply grateful to two anonymous readers for Oxford University Press, whose constructive advice has greatly improved this book. I am grateful too to all the staff at OUP involved in the production of the volume, and especially to Hilary O'Shea and Enid Barker. For the errors remaining in the work I am alone responsible. It should not be assumed that any of the persons mentioned in this preface necessarily agrees with the views expressed in the book. The manuscript was closed in the summer of 1999, and I could not make reference to work appearing after that.

In personal terms, I am grateful to George Huxley, Richard Janko, John Dillon, Keith Sidwell, Mgr. Denis Faul, John Kremer, and Jennifer Fitzgerald for support at a difficult time. In this context I would also like to thank Linda Ballard of the Ulster Folk and Transport Museum for underpinning my researches into Homer.

Finally, no words can express my gratitude to my husband, Michael Allen, for his great forbearance while bits of this manuscript were tried out on him, and for shoring me up when things got rough. As a small token of my love and esteem, this book is dedicated to him.

M.J.A

Belfast
29 Oct. 1999

ACKNOWLEDGEMENTS

I AM indebted to the Franz Steiner Verlag for permission to include in Chapter 5 material developed from 'Genealogy as Paradigm: The Example of Bellerophon', an article first published in *Hermes*, 124 (1996).

Michael Longley very kindly allowed me to include his poem 'Ceasefire' from his book *Ghost Orchid* published in 1995 by Cape. This poem first appeared in the *Irish Times* on 3 September 1994, in the week the Northern Irish ceasefires were declared.

CONTENTS

LIST OF TABLES

ABBREVIATIONS

BM	British Museum
DK	H. Diels and W. Kranz, *Die Fragmente der Vorsokratiker*, i–iii (Berlin, 1952)
EGF	M. Davies (ed.), *Epicorum Graecorum Fragmenta* (Göttingen, 1988)
FGrH	F. Jacoby (ed.), *Fragmente der griechischen Historiker* (Berlin, 1923–58)
LfrGrE	B. Snell and H. Erbse (eds.), *Lexicon des frühgriechischen Epos* (Göttingen, 1955–)
LIMC	*Lexicon Iconographicum Mythologiae Classicae* (Zurich, 1981–)
M–W	R. Merkelbach and M. L. West, *Fragmenta Hesiodea* (Oxford, 1967)
PMG	D. L. Page (ed.), *Poetae Melici Graeci* (Oxford, 1962)
RE	A. F. W. Pauly, G. Wissowa, *et al.* (eds.), *Realencyclopädie der Classischen Altertumswissenschaft* (Stuttgart, 1893–1980)
SM	*Pindarus*, ed. B. Snell and H. Maehler, i (Leipzig, 1984); ii (Leipzig, 1975)
TGF	A. Nauck (ed.), *Tragicorum Graecorum Fragmenta* (Leipzig, 1926)
TrGF	*Tragicorum Graecorum Fragmenta*, i, ed. B. Snell (Göttingen, 1971); ii, ed. R. Kannicht (Göttingen, 1981); iv, ed. S. Radt (Göttingen, 1977)
UFTM	Ulster Folk and Transport Museum

I

Introduction

This book explores a new and very simple approach to Homeric narratives.[1] It begins from the assumption that para-narratives, by which I mean secondary narratives related by the poet's characters, and also the interludes related in the voice of the poet himself which do not advance the progress of the main narrative, will be relevant in some way either to the interpretation of their immediate context or to that of the main narrative, or to both. To read the poems in this way requires no mastery of any complicated theory or terminology. Most people would now agree that paradigms (stories which provide a pattern or example to be imitated or avoided), such as the story of Niobe who remembered to eat in spite of her grief told to the grieving Priam to encourage him to remember to eat (*Il.* 24. 602–17), relate to the situation of their addressee. A broader term than paradigm is required, however, to cover the subsidiary episodes of the primary narrative which do not advance its progress, but provide material for comparison with its major events. The idea that para-narratives are related in some way to the main narrative is not very different from Bundy's idea that an epinician ode commissioned by a patron in praise of the achievements of a victor will be encomiastic in its primary intent, and any mythical material it may contain will serve the purpose of enhancing the glory of the patron.[2] Certainly my students have found it helpful to read the poems using the para-narratives set beside the main narrative as a subtle guide to its interpretation. This book is about para-narratives in the *Iliad*, but it will do no harm to see how they work from a few examples in the *Odyssey*.

The *Iliad* and the *Odyssey* are both highly integrated and carefully composed poems which can only be explained as the work of a brilliant and insightful poet carefully shaping and

---

[1] For discussion of previous work on Homeric narratives, see Appendix A.
[2] Bundy (1986: 3; 1st pub. 1962).

polishing his work over many years. Homer is a superb poet in the oral tradition of Greek poetry. Orally composed traditional poetry makes use of formulae, type-scenes, and story shapes (sometimes called story patterns). I say more in Appendix B about the oral tradition and its relationship to the Homeric text we read today, but for the time being, let us consider story shapes. Part of the stock-in-trade of a poet in the Greek tradition is a whole range of story shapes on which he can elaborate and produce variations to suit his purposes. An example of such a story shape would be the absent hero who returns home in the nick of time to prevent the (re)marriage of his wife or sweetheart. The hero tends to be detained beyond the time previously agreed that his wife would wait for him: he receives assistance, often from a sympathetic female figure; he eventually arrives home to discover his wife or sweetheart true to him, but about to be forced into marriage with someone else. The reader will recognize the outline of the *Odyssey*, but the story shape is found in traditional storytelling all over the world. It celebrates the fidelity of the woman who withstands all pressures to be disloyal to her husband, although there are also versions where she gives in to the pressure, either through a genuine mistake, or through weakness, like Clytemnestra (*Od.* 4. 265–72), or depravity.[3]

The story of Demodocus about the love-affair of Ares and Aphrodite (*Od.* 8. 266–369) is a para-narrative related to this story shape. Its shape echoes with variation the story shape of the main narrative. One of the comic variations on the basic story shape introduced into this para-narrative is that the husband facilitates the whole episode where Aphrodite, in the (carefully contrived) absence of her husband, yields to pressure from Ares to be his partner in adultery. Of course the guilty pair are caught in bed, unable to move under the bonds Hephaestus has devised to trap them, and all the gods come along to laugh, not least at the god whose obsession with gadgets has led him to arrange for such a crime to be committed against himself. The para-narrative is amusing in itself, but it also causes the audience to think about adultery in the case of an intruder in the house while the husband is absent. In fact the suitors are intruders into the house of Odysseus in the absence

---

[3] See Alden (1997: 523–4 nn. 31, 33, 34, 35).

of the master, and their presence in such circumstances by itself raises the spectre of adultery. Moreover, the suitors have slept with the maids and exerted pressure on Penelope to marry one of them. Like Ares (*Od*. 8. 332, 355, 358), they offer compensation for their crimes (*Od*. 22. 55–9),[4] but Odysseus exercises his right to reject it and kill them (*Od*. 22. 61–4; cf. *Il*. 9. 523).

The Oresteia story is also used in the *Odyssey* as a further para-narrative illustrating the punishment of adulterers. Telemachus is repeatedly told of the vengeance taken on Aegisthus by Orestes, whose mother Aegisthus had seduced and whose father he had murdered (*Od*. 1. 298–300; 3. 304–10; 4. 543–7). Telemachus is urged to emulate Orestes and kill the suitors (*Od*. 1. 294–302), who are by implication made to correspond to Aegisthus.[5]

Another story shape used by the poet to explore the theme of intruders in a house in the absence of the master is the Cyclops story, a folk-tale of which versions have been recorded right across Europe from Greece to Ireland.[6] The hero, for one reason or another, enters the dwelling of a giant: once inside he realizes that he is trapped, since only the giant can open the door. After a while he has reason to suppose the giant wants to kill him and, usually, to eat him: he avoids this fate by blinding the giant, who has only one eye, or is afflicted by eye trouble of some kind. The hero manages to escape by deceiving the giant into letting him out, often as he clings underneath, or wears the skin of, an animal belonging to the giant. Once outside he taunts the giant, whose revenge may take one of two forms. In one family of versions the ogre's revenge takes the form of a ring which calls out 'here I am, here I am', or else causes the wearer to call out 'here I am, here I am'. The giant throws this ring to the hero who puts it on, thereby enabling the blinded giant to follow him as he runs away. Since the ring cannot be

---

[4] For the idea that it is a matter for righteous indignation (νεμεσσητόν) for the offended party to go on being angry after compensation has been offered, although his anger was perfectly reasonable before, cf. *Od*. 22. 59 and *Il*. 9. 523.

[5] See D'Arms and Hulley (1946) and Alden (1997: 519–20).

[6] See Frazer (1921: ii. 404–55): to his list add Ulster Folk and Transport Museum tape 002, *Told in Ireland: The Stories of Frank McKenna*: 'The Steed of Bells', an oral version recorded by Linda Ballard from Frank McKenna of Co. Tyrone. He had heard it from his grandfather in the 1920s.

removed, the hero is forced to avoid capture by cutting off the finger with the ring on it and throwing it to the giant. In the *Odyssey* and the stories influenced by it, the giant takes his revenge by cursing the hero when he learns his name. The curse of the Cyclops is significant: he prays to his father Poseidon that Odysseus shall never reach home, or if he does, that he shall arrive late and with the loss of all his comrades, and find πήματα (troubles)[7] in his house. This is exactly what happened to Polyphemus, who came home late and alone to cook his dinner (*Od.* 9. 233–4), only to find when he lit the fire that his cave was full of intruders (*Od.* 9. 251) in the form of Odysseus and his men who were to afflict him with troubles by robbing him of his eye. In due course Odysseus will come home late and with the loss of all his comrades, to find his house full of πήματα in the form of the suitors of his wife. He will arrive at his house at dinner-time to find the suitors with a fire lit and feasting on animals from his herds (*Od.* 17. 170–6; 269–71), just as the Cyclops had arrived at dinner-time, after Odysseus and his men had lit a fire and feasted on his cheeses (*Od.* 9. 231–4). The two references to the return of the flocks from the fields associated with Odysseus' return to his house (*Od.* 17. 170–1; 212–14) recall the arrival of the Cyclops at his cave, driving the flocks from the pastures (*Od.* 9. 237–9). These correspondences are long-range and indicate a poet who plans and controls the shape of his work as a whole.

The relationship between the Cyclops episode and the return of Odysseus to his house is not exhausted with the fulfilment of Polyphemus' curse. On his return to his house, Odysseus becomes a kind of triumphant amalgam of Odysseus and Polyphemus, assuming the role of whoever is the winner of every point in their encounter. Inside the house Odysseus will assume control of the door (*Od.* 21. 235–41), leaping onto the threshold as his rags fall away, as from a transfigured god appearing in a doorway (*Od.* 22. 2).[8] This recalls the parody of a theophany in a doorway when the blinded Cyclops sits in the doorway of his cave with arms outstretched to prevent the escape of his victims (*Od.* 9. 415–18). Compare also the

---

[7] On the name of Odysseus as a signifier of trouble, see Dimock (1963) and Schein (1970).

[8] Cf. *h. Dem.* 188–9. See Ogle (1911: 262).

association of ideas between the Cyclops's imagined revenge on Odysseus:

τῷ κέ οἱ ἐγκέφαλός γε διὰ σπέος ἄλλυδις ἄλλη
θεινομένου ῥαίοιτο⁹ πρὸς οὐδεϊ

Then his brains would be smashed in all directions through the cave
as he was dashed against the floor

(*Od.* 9. 458–9)

and Athene's prediction of the fate of the suitors:

καί τιν' ὀίω
αἵματί τ' ἐγκεφάλῳ τε παλαξέμεν ἄσπετον οὖδας
ἀνδρῶν μνηστήρων, οἵ τοι βίοτον κατέδουσιν.

and I think
the endless ground will be sprinkled with the blood and brains
of the suitors, who eat up your livelihood.

(*Od.* 13. 394–6)

There are many other parallels[10] between the two episodes: Odysseus makes the Cyclops helpless with drink, and the suitors accuse Odysseus of being drunk (*Od.* 18. 331, 391; 21. 293); the eating of forbidden food and not being able to contain it (*Od.* 9. 373–4; 18. 406–7) is found in both episodes, and the shooting of Antinous, cup in hand (*Od.* 22. 15–21)[11] seems related to the many vase paintings of the scene showing the blinding of the Cyclops as he holds the cup whose contents have made him helpless.[12]

Two stories told to Telemachus at the court of Helen and Menelaus in Sparta also function as para-narratives to encourage Telemachus to believe in Odysseus' abilities, even in adverse circumstances. The first is told by Helen, who describes how Odysseus disguised himself as a slave and entered the city of Troy, where he was recognized only by Helen, who gave him a bath and fresh clothes, and swore not to reveal that he had been in Troy until he was safely at the ships

---

[9] Euripides seems to have read ῥαίνοιτο (would be sprinkled) for ῥαίοιτο (would be smashed): see Stanford (1947: 363 ad *Od.* 9. 459).

[10] For details, with further bibliography, see Alden (1993).

[11] Cf. the death of Eurymachus (*Od.* 22. 82–7) and see Fenik (1974: 146–7) for these passages as doublets.

[12] Touchefeu-Meynier (1968: pls. II, IV, V); Hansen (1986: 61–74).

again. Odysseus killed many Trojans during his time in the city and gained much information (*Od.* 4. 244–58). The story celebrates Odysseus' ability to penetrate hostile territory in disguise and to wreak carnage on his enemies in their own territory: it looks forward to Odysseus' penetration of the hostile territory his house has become since the suitors arrived, and to the carnage Odysseus will inflict on the suitors in the territory they have made their own. The association of the two episodes is confirmed by the correspondence of Helen in the former to Eurycleia in the latter: both women offer a bath, however rudimentary, after recognizing the hero, and both women are urged to keep the hero's presence a secret.[13] The second of the two stories is told by Menelaus, who relates how Helen came with Deiphobus to the Wooden Horse when it was brought into Troy: Helen walked three times round the horse and called each of the heroes inside by name, imitating the voice of his wife in every case. The triple circumambulation and the mimicry suggest enchantment, but Odysseus is proof against it, silencing any of the the Greeks tempted to respond to Helen's calls. The story celebrates Odysseus' ability to survive even enchantment in hostile territory in circumstances where other men would succumb, and ends with a reference to his divine protectress when Athene takes Helen away (*Od.* 4. 271–89).

The first impetus to think about subsidiary narrative in Homer in this way came to me from reading Malcolm Willcock's work on the invention of details in paradigms,[14] especially the paradigm of Meleager in book 9 of the *Iliad*, to achieve a closer fit with the situation in the main narrative to which it is compared. I was also particularly intrigued by the work of Kakridis on the same paradigm,[15] and I have learned a great deal from both of these scholars, although they should not be taken to endorse anything I have said.[16] It was Kakridis who first observed that Meleager was in receipt of a string of visitors, each dearer that the last. Each of these visitors, or groups of visitors, made the same request to Meleager, to return to the fighting and save his community from the enemy.

---

[13] Bath: *Od.* 4. 252; 19. 503–5; secrecy: *Od.* 4. 253–6; 19. 500–2.
[14] Willcock (1964; 1977).
[15] Kakridis (1949: 11–42; 127–48).
[16] Kakridis did once say to me 'I am glad you went further than I did.'

The besiegers were already climbing on the fortifications and setting fire to the town, and Meleager's own chamber was under bombardment when his wife finally made the same request as the string of visitors, and Meleager yielded to her entreaties. Kakridis called this motif of the series of visitors, each dearer than the last, and all making the same request 'the ascending scale of affection'. He demonstrated that the motif was used frequently in Greek literature, and that Homer uses it not only of Meleager, but also of Achilles, who receives a series of requests to lay aside his anger and fight. Kakridis also discussed a series of approaches to Hector from women and relatives, mostly urging him not to risk his life by courting danger in pursuit of glory. My debt to this work of Kakridis will be evident throughout the following pages, but most especially in Chapter 7, where I seek to establish that the motif of the ascending scale of affection is used to contrast Hector and Achilles in terms of their responses to λιταί (prayers).

Kakridis was one of the three main exponents of Neo-analysis: the others are Schadewaldt and Kullmann.[17] Neo-analysis argues that the poems now described as the Epic Cycle, including the *Cypria*, the *Iliu persis*, and above all the *Aethiopis* attributed to Arctinus, were the sources for the *Iliad*. The *Aethiopis*, after telling the story of the Amazon queen, Penthesilea, went on to the events describing the deaths of Memnon and Achilles. Memnon was the king of the Ethiopians who entered the war in its tenth year as an ally of the Trojans. He killed Achilles' friend, Antilochus, and Achilles killed Memnon to avenge him, despite a prophecy from Thetis that he would die shortly afterwards if he fought with Memnon. Achilles died at the hands of Paris and Apollo near the Scaean gate by an arrow in his heel (recalling the incident in the *Iliad* where Diomede is shot in the foot by Paris (*Il.* 11. 373–400)). Ajax and Odysseus recovered his body, Thetis and the Nereids mourned at his funeral, and funeral games were held in Achilles' honour.[18] There is absolutely no doubt that Homer was well acquainted with the material just summarized: the

---

[17] Accessible accounts of Neo-analysis may be found in Kullmann (1984); Schein (1984: 18–19); Willcock in Morris and Powell (1997: 174–89).

[18] See Davies (1988: 47) = Bernabé (1988: 67–9, no. 12), *Aethiopis*; on Arctinus, see Davies (1988: 80) and Bernabé (1988: 66–7).

mourning of Thetis and the Nereids, for example, is mentioned
in the account of Achilles' funeral (*Od.* 24. 47–59). They also
rise out of the sea to mourn (*Il.* 18. 35–67) when Achilles lies
stretched on the ground grieving for Patroclus (*Il.* 18. 26), but
they are sent back by Thetis to take the news of Patroclus'
death to Nereus in the depths of the sea: rather an anticlimax
for the displacement of fifty-one goddesses, as indicated by
Kakridis in his discussion of the passage.[19] There are obvious
similarities between the roles of Achilles' friends, Patroclus in
the *Iliad* and Antilochus in the *Aethiopis*. Thetis' prophecy that
Achilles would die soon afterwards if he fought Memnon could
be the explanation of the possible prophecy from his mother
mentioned by Nestor and Patroclus (*Il.* 11. 794–5: cf. *Il.* 16.
36–7) that might prevent Achilles from fighting. Neo-analysis
regards the content of the Cyclic epics as more ancient than the
Homeric epics and assumes that their form was fixed before the
composition of the *Iliad*, even if they were not recorded in
writing until after the *Iliad* was composed. It is important for
us to remember that traditional poetry like the Homeric poems
does not arise from nothing, but makes use of oral sources and
models within the tradition. Homer, however, is infinitely
superior to anything we have in the fragments of the Cycle.
Griffin[20] offers a convincing demonstration of the differences
between the Homeric poems, with their restraint, decency,
and lack of sensationalism, and the Cyclic epics, with their
invulnerable heroes made immortal after death, their interest in
the romantic and the grisly, and their uninspired reporter's
style. The Homeric epics survive because of their superior
quality: the verdict of antiquity was that the poems of the Epic
Cycle did not deserve to survive. Homer is certainly aware of a
vastly greater range of mythic material than he relates, and
some of it is accessible to us only from later sources: he is
certainly familiar with all the material familiar to the poets of
the Epic Cycle, but he does not handle it in the same way.

For example, Homer tends to avoid the monstrous and the
fantastic, although comparison with other sources suggests he
is aware of this aspect of the stories he tells. When Zeus relates
to Hera the embarrassing catalogue of ladies to whom he paid
his addresses (*Il.* 14. 317–27),[21] he is made to omit all mention

[19] (1949: 66–75).   [20] (1977).   [21] See 2.4.3 below.

of his transformations which are mentioned in other accounts of these adventures. For example, the allusion (*Il.* 14. 322) to Minos and Rhadamanthys, two of the children born to Europa, daughter of Phoenix, implies knowledge of how Zeus assumed the form of a bull and carried her over the sea to Crete, where she gave birth to her children, but nothing so extraordinary as a god in the form of a bull is mentioned by Homer: Hesiod and Bacchylides were less reticent.[22] Aristotle makes the point that Homer puts things into the mouths of his characters when he does not wish to vouch for their truth himself.[23] So Glaucus is made to say his grandfather, Bellerophon, killed the Chimaera, probably the most monstrous creature in the *Iliad*. On the subject of its origins, Glaucus says only that it was of divine race, not human (*Il.* 6. 180). Hesiod gives it monstrous parents, even if he does not make absolutely clear whether it is the child of the Lernean Hydra, or her parents, Echidna and Typhon:[24] at any rate the Hesiodic creature has three heads, one of a lion, one of a goat, and one of a snake. Both the Homeric account and Hesiod agree that it is a lion in front, a snake behind, and it breathes out fire (*Il.* 6. 181–2 = Hesiod, *Th.* 323–4). Hesiod tells how Bellerophon and Pegasus killed it:[25] there is no mention of the winged horse, Pegasus, in Homer. Even though the information is conveyed through Glaucus, the *Iliad* says no more than that Bellerophon killed it θεῶν τεράεσσι πιθήσας (trusting in the portents of the gods, *Il.* 6. 183). At 5. 6 below, I argue that Homer knows about Pegasus but deliberately suppresses the information, revealing only what suits his poetic purpose.

While I accept that the material eventually fixed in the poems of the Epic Cycle was familiar to Homer, I do have trouble with the certainty in Neo-analysis that motifs in the *Iliad* and the *Odyssey* derive from fixed versions of the poems of the Epic Cycle. I would prefer to say that the Homeric motifs derive from songs in circulation in the epic tradition: some, like that of the Cyclops, may derive from traditional

---

[22] Hesiod, *Cat.* 140: Bacchylides, *fr.* 10 (Snell).

[23] Aristotle, *fr.* 163 (Rose) = Sch. A ad *Il.* 19. 108 (from Porphyry) (= Erbse (1969–88: iv. 600–1), 108b); see also Sch. T ad *Il.* 20. 234 (= Erbse (1969–88: v. 41), 234d).

[24] See M. L. West (1966: 254–5) on Hesiod, *Th.* 319; see also Kirk (1985–90: ii. 183) ad *Il.* 6. 179–83.

[25] Hesiod, *Th.* 325 and cf. *Cat.* 43a 84–7.

stories. I do not believe that these songs and stories ever
became permanently fixed without the aid of writing. We are in
a better position than we were to make judgements on the
means by which the Homeric poems came to be recorded in
writing. The evidence suggests that orally composed poetry is
recorded in writing by dictation to an amanuensis, and that
even after the recording, most people's experience of the poetry
will be through oral performance by a singer.

In the following pages I endeavour to convey how all the
narratives which do not advance the main plot of the *Iliad* are
nevertheless related to it or to an episode within it, and shed
light on its interpretation. The poet skilfully manipulates the
wealth of material available to him to shape and influence
responses to his main narrative. He is perfectly happy to introduce details into his secondary narratives so that they correspond more closely to an episode of his main narrative. I do not
think there is any conflict between a unitarian view of the
poems and the view that they were orally composed. The information we possess about poets who compose orally suggests
that the best devote considerable effort to rehearsing and planning until their poem is as they wish.[26] The minds of such
people are like libraries: their knowledge of their tradition is far
more extensive than might be supposed by someone who heard
only a single performance of one poem. Their repertoires
include many polished compositions, and they can also compose new songs appropriate to their tradition, presumably
because, in the Greek tradition, at least, the gods have endowed
them, as they endowed Demodocus, with gifts to give pleasure
in whatever way their spirit dictates (*Od.* 8. 44–5). All poets,
according to Odysseus, are worthy of respect because the Muse
teaches them and loves them (*Od.* 8. 479–81). The Ithacan
poet, Phemius, whose patronymic, $Τερπιάδης$, indicates the
poetic tradition in his family, insists that Odysseus will regret it
if he kills him and makes an end of his god-given powers (*Od.*
22. 345–9). The Homeric poems were at the core of Greek education, and the para-narratives are as clear in their communication of meaning as the parables in the New Testament, if only
we are prepared to stop reading them like children, unable to
grasp anything but the surface meaning, and open our minds to

[26] Lord (1991: 80–1).

their underlying connection with the unfolding events of the main narrative.

Earlier categorizations of Homeric narratives are discussed in Appendix A: they tend to be concerned with projections into the past, but para-narratives can be outside time, like the αἶνος of the Λιταί, which expresses an eternal truth about the consequences of heeding and rejecting prayers, and the scenes on the shield, which are outside time, and reflect the events of the *Iliad* itself as if in a mirror. Everyone knows how a shield can be used as a mirror, and how Perseus used his shield to look at the reflection of the Gorgon rather than at the reality which would have turned him to stone. My reason for writing on a subject which has already received so much attention was to show how all the narratives set beside the main narrative reflect upon its events and act as a guide to its interpretation: in this respect they are all paradigmatic and never simply ornamental. No one has ever discussed the body of para-narratives contained in the *Iliad* in this way, and some of the para-narratives here considered have received very little critical attention. I believe students and others will find in this reading of para-narratives in the *Iliad* a useful method to adopt in their reading of the poem. If this book encourages readers to look for the relevance of para-narratives to the primary narrative of the poem, it will have served its purpose.

We need a new text of Homer: fortunately, M. L. West is providing one, but the first volume appeared when most of this book was already written, and the second volume has not yet come out. The text of Allen which I have used has serious flaws: he attached too much importance to the readings of later medieval manuscripts and printed many of the post-Alexandrian plus-verses they contain. I have indicated serious difficulties with Allen's text and any departures from it where appropriate. The Alexandrian scholars Zenodotus and Aristarchus athetized[27] lines which they found linguistically odd, inconsistent, repetitive, or improper: since their atheteses rarely agree with the manuscripts and quotations in ancient authors, I have tended to ignore them. Paradoxically athetesis means the line is well attested in the manuscript tradition

---

[27] Marked with the obelus, a critical sign indicating doubts about the genuineness of the line.

known to the Alexandrians. Aristarchus also omitted lines, erroneously in the case of *Il.* 9. 458–61, where Phoenix considered killing his father, and rightly at *Il.* 18. 604–5, where the material is interpolated from *Od.* 4. 17–18 to give the dancers on the shield of Achilles a musician.[28] The translations of passages quoted from Homer are my own, and I have done my best to translate all the Greek words in my text. Where the same word is used repeatedly at very frequent intervals, I have not translated it every single time: readers without Greek should look back a little way, and should find the translation they require with very little effort.

---

[28] For discussion of textual matters see Janko (1992: 20–8), to which this brief account is heavily indebted.

2
Para-Narratives

2.1 PARA-NARRATIVES: INTRODUCTION

The *Iliad* is made up of narratives, primary and secondary. The primary narrative is told in the voice of the poet/narrator, and the secondary narratives in the voices of his characters. The main plot of the primary narrative needs no rehearsal. Everyone knows that its principal elements are the quarrel between Agamemnon and Achilles, Achilles' rejection of Agamemnon's first attempt at reconciliation, Patroclus' return to battle and his death, reconciliation between Agamemnon and Achilles, Achilles' vengeance for the death of Patroclus, Patroclus' funeral, and the ransom by Priam of Hector's corpse from Achilles. None of these elements could be omitted without destroying the coherence of the primary narrative. Alongside the main plot and amplifying it in a number of ways are the para-narratives which are my concern. These could be omitted without disturbing the course of the primary narrative: their function is artistic. Some of these (2.2.1) are related in the poet's own voice, others (2.2.2) are told by his characters,[1] and all exert influence, directly or indirectly, on the audience's reception of the text. I shall argue that the primary reference of any para-narrative in the poem will be to something else within the poem,[2] as, for example, the scenes on the shield of Achilles (discussed at length in Chapter 3) present a coded reference to the embassy of book 9, its rejection, and the fighting which ensues. The use of a motif in a secondary narrative is likely to relate to its occurrences in the primary narrative: for example, the repetition in the main narrative with reference to Achilles

---

[1] These are secondary narratives.

[2] In accordance with the precept attributed to Aristarchus, Ὅμηρον ἐξ Ὁμήρου σαφηνίζειν. This τόπος has its origins in Porphyry, *Qu. Hom.* (Schrader (1880: 297.16)).

of the motif of the ascending scale of affection used in the paradigm of Meleager is well known, but the motif is also used, as Kakridis[3] has shown, with reference to Hector. Phoenix's speech associates the ascending scale of affection with the parable of the Λιταί, whose message about the consequences of rejecting λιταί is reinforced by the story of Meleager, which illustrates the rejection again and again of λιταί from a succession of persons, each of whom is closer in affection to the addressee than the last. The direct association of the parable of the Λιταί is with Achilles' reception of the embassy, but it also casts retrospective light on Agamemnon's much earlier reception of Chryses' pleas for the return of his daughter. I shall argue that Meleager's rejection of requests presented in ascending scale of affection illumines the rejection of requests presented in ascending scale of affection in the main narrative. Since the motif of such a series of requests is restricted in the main narrative to Achilles and Hector, a comparison of the two heroes is invited in terms of their reaction to these requests. But first of all we must look at the wide variety of quotidian para-narrative functions which establish the habit of expectancy upon which such larger effects rely.

I am deliberately using the term 'para-narrative' rather than 'digression' or 'paradigm'. Digressions are defined by Austin[4] and Andersen[5] as a story outside the time of the poem, but mirroring something in the main narrative. Paradigms[6] have much in common with digressions:[7] they illustrate the present in terms of the mythical 'past', which appears to be quarried for mythical examples of the pattern the auditor is expected to see in the present. The story of the mythical Niobe (*Il.* 24. 602–17) is used as a pattern to illustrate the course of action to be taken by Priam in the present: Niobe ate, although her children had been killed and lay unburied. Her example should be followed by Priam, who should eat, although his son, Hector, has been killed and lies unburied. The past from which such patterns are

---

[3] Kakridis (1949: 43–64).   [4] (1978: 73–4; 1st pub. 1966).
[5] (1987: 8).   [6] See 2.3 below and 4.2.
[7] The distinction, if there really is one, seems to be that paradigms use mythical examples to illustrate the pattern which the addressee is expected to recognize in present events, whereas the examples used in digressions are not mythical.

drawn is not always mythical: they can come from the comparatively recent past, one or two generations back, like the
story of Meleager, a hero of the generation before Troy (*Il*. 2.
642). Meleager abandoned his anger only when the gifts offered
as an incentive to abandon it were no longer on offer: his
story is told to Achilles to persuade him to abandon his anger
and accept gifts for doing so while such gifts are still available.
It looks very much as if the examples used in the paradigms
either take stories in circulation and adapt them to produce a
pattern corresponding to the present events with which they
are compared, or else are freely invented to manufacture the
pattern.[8] Lohmann[9] has much to say about 'paradigmatische
Spiegelung', including the probable invention of material from
outside the Trojan cycle for comparison with events within the
poem. However, these paradigms use events from *outside* the
main narrative: I want to consider in addition the many
episodes *inside* the main narrative which function in the same
way as the paradigms, in that they repeat, sometimes with
variations, the pattern of an episode of the main narrative.
Although paradigms are a form of para-narrative, we still need
the new term, para-narrative (unless we broaden the scope of
'paradigm') to cover stories told by the poet *inside* the time of
the poem, repeating in a minor key the elements of major
events *within* the main narrative.[10] In other words, para-narratives include patterns which do not belong to the past. Their
subject matter can be inside or outside the time of the poem.
In themselves they will not advance the progress of the main
narrative, but will be related to it in some way, through similarities of pattern and detail, sometimes displaying significant
differences from the main narrative. Para-narratives use

---

[8] Cf. aetiologies, which are invented ostensibly to explain e.g. an unusual
cult practice, but really owe their existence to that practice. For example,
Callimachus explains the origin of the cry ἰὴ παιῆον, ἰὴ παιῆον as the cry of the
Delphians when Apollo slew the serpent at Delphi, his first feat of archery:
Callimachus, *h. Ap.* 97–104 and Williams (1978: 82 ad loc.).

[9] (1970: 183–212).

[10] A useful list of definitions of digression, paradigm, and related terms is
provided by de Jong (1987*b*: 82–3) and summarized in Appendix A below.
However, none of the categories discussed there is really broad enough to
include all the narratives used alongside the main narrative: this is why the
term para-narrative is required.

different characters and contexts to replay some episode of the
main narrative, or to anticipate an episode of the main narrative. They function rather like a marquetry inlay which echoes
in its pattern the lines of the piece of furniture into which it is
inlaid. The para-narratives are the key to the interpretation of
the main narrative.

Sometimes the main narrative repeats the elements of a
scene, as happens in the Chryses episode and Priam's ransom of
Hector. Chryses comes to ransom his daughter from the Greeks
at the beginning of the poem and Priam comes to ransom the
body of Hector at the end of the poem. The two scenes closely
resemble each other, and have been described as 'symmetrical'.[11] I agree that these scenes are related, but not in the way a
para-narrative is related to the main narrative. Both the
Chryses episode and Priam's ransom of Hector are essential to
the main narrative. I shall not discuss symmetrical scenes of
this type.

The image of the mirror is a helpful metaphor for the relationship between the para-narrative(s) and the episode of the
main narrative to which it/they relate(s), but the image has
already been used in different senses. I do not want to discuss
Schadewaldt's idea that fragments and reflections in the images
and motifs of the *Iliad* should be related to 'originals' in the
Aethiopis.[12] Nor am I thinking of the way a dream or prediction will offer a kind of reflection in advance of subsequent
events [13] or how a character's account of events which have just
been narrated offers a kind of reflection of those events through
the eyes of that character.[14] The image we require is rather that
of the 'correcting' lens. Reinhardt[15] has shown that episodes of

[11] Reinhardt (1961: 63–8); Lohmann (1970: 204–5); Létoublon (1983*b*: 20);
Rabel (1990: 429).

[12] Schadewaldt (1965: 191–6; 1st pub. 1944).

[13] Létoublon (1983*b*: 21–7), who discusses Penelope's dream of the geese
(*Od.* 19. 536–53) and its relationship to the slaughter of the suitors, and
Calypso's prediction of Odysseus' adventures (*Od.* 12. 36–141) related also by
Odysseus to the Phaeacians.

[14] As, for example, when Achilles tells Thetis about his quarrel with
Agamemnon (*Il.* 1. 366–92), a quarrel just narrated by the poet. 'Mirror
stories' of this kind (see de Jong (1985)) are outside the scope of this discussion.

[15] (1961: 79–81).

the main narrative can refer to each other, like the scenes just mentioned of Chryses and Priam ransoming their children. At *Il.* 9. 104–11, Nestor's reproaches of Agamemnon for taking Briseis from Achilles are an elaboration of the advice he offered earlier:

μήτε σὺ τόνδ' ἀγαθός περ ἐὼν ἀποαίρεο κούρην,
ἀλλ' ἔα, ὥς οἱ πρῶτα δόσαν γέρας υἷες Ἀχαιῶν.

and do not you, although you are noble, deprive this man of the
 maiden,
but let her be, since the sons of the Achaeans gave her to him first as a
 portion of honour.

(*Il.* 1. 275–6)

Nestor had urged that Agamemnon should let Achilles keep the girl, since it was to him that the Greeks first gave her. In the later passage the poet makes his character, Nestor, reflect on the earlier passage and underline in more robust terms what he said there:

οὐ γάρ τις νόον ἄλλος ἀμείνονα τοῦδε νοήσει,
οἷον ἐγὼ νοέω, ἠμὲν πάλαι ἠδ' ἔτι καὶ νῦν,   105
ἐξ ἔτι τοῦ ὅτε, διογενές, Βρισηΐδα κούρην
χωομένου Ἀχιλῆος ἔβης κλισίηθεν ἀπούρας
οὔ τι καθ' ἡμέτερόν γε νόον· μάλα γάρ τοι ἔγωγε
πόλλ' ἀπεμυθεόμην· σὺ δὲ σῷ μεγαλήτορι θυμῷ
εἴξας ἄνδρα φέριστον, ὃν ἀθάνατοί περ ἔτεισαν,   110
ἠτίμησας· ἑλὼν γὰρ ἔχεις γέρας . . .

For no one else will think of a better idea than this,
which I think: I thought it formerly and I still think it now,
I have thought it since the time when, god-born king, you went
and took the maiden, Briseis, from the hut of Achilles, for all his
 anger,
not at all in accordance with my advice.
You gave way to your great-hearted passion
and dishonoured the bravest man, whom the very gods
have vindicated: for you took his prize and keep it.

(*Il.* 9. 104–11)

The poet is in fact explaining himself by presenting a second instance of a particular scene, this time with more clues for the listener on how to interpret it. The second scene views the first through a stronger lens. If we had any doubts about the interpretation of the first scene, Nestor sharpens our focus in

the second. These two scenes in which Nestor reproaches
Agamemnon are both episodes within the main narrative, and
essential to it: they are not para-narratives, but their function of
self-interpretation or even self-explication by the poet is shared
by the para-narratives. Whether para-narratives are told by the
poet in his own voice, with reference to a time within the action
of the poem, or told by one of the poet's characters about an
occasion in the past with some bearing on the present situation,
they will not advance the main narrative. Instead, they will
offer an interval of reflection on the events of the main narrative. Such reflection is achieved through the provision of
material comparable with the events of the main narrative.
This material is used by the poet to direct his audience to a
particular interpretation of the main narrative by means of the
comparisons he invites them to make.

2.2. SIGNPOSTS TO THE AUDIENCE

2.2.1. *Para-narratives by the poet: analogous or parallel situations within the primary narrative*

The poet's account of the games at the funeral of Patroclus, for
instance, is a good example of a para-narrative by the poet. The
funeral games constitute a separate and clearly defined episode
subsidiary to the main plot and narrated at some length and in
detail. A first impression might see little point in the intricate
detail of the account of the funeral games, since it does nothing
for the progress of the primary narrative. At the games we find
played out in miniature within the action of the poem the
elements presented on a larger scale in the main elements of the
primary narrative. But the minor incidents of the games do not
merely fill out the extended narrative of the *Iliad*. On closer
reading[16] we discover that the details of the games are related to
important events of the primary narrative. For example,
Athene, whose support contributed greatly to Diomede's military successes in books 5 and 6, supports her favourite again in
the chariot race in the funeral games. In this race, Apollo
strikes Diomede's whip from his hand (*Il.* 23. 383–4) but

---

[16] For details, see 4.5.

Athene returns it to him (*Il.* 23. 390) and breaks the yoke of the chariot of the main contender, Eumelus (*Il.* 23. 392). Athene's support for Diomede in the early part of the poem is repeated in her behaviour towards him in the funeral games: she positively hampers Ajax (son of Oileus) in the footrace, causing him to slip in the dirt (*Il.* 23. 773–7), so that she can fulfil the prayer for victory of her favourite, Odysseus (*Il.* 23. 770). The apparently arbitrary success or lack of it experienced by the participants in the funeral games turns out to be part of a consistent picture, serving to reinforce the identities of the competitors as they are presented in the primary narrative. The presentation of the fortunes of Odysseus and Diomede in the games corresponds to their fortunes as portrayed in the earlier part of the poem: in this microcosm of the funeral games, the audience is confirmed in its opinion of their respective personalities, and the attitude of the gods towards each is confirmed: Diomede and Odysseus enjoy, and the lesser Ajax does not enjoy, that special quality of success represented as divine assistance.[17]

Of course, it is not particularly startling if in minor episodes the poet maintains the consistency of character established in the primary narrative, or even if he uses minor episodes to confirm expectations in the matter of character already established by the main narrative. But we also find within the action of the poem whole episodes, apparently subsidiary to the main narrative, but displaying repetition of, or correspondence to, whole sequences of events from the primary narrative. Again the funeral games will furnish us with an example, this time in the quarrel of Antilochus and Menelaus (discussed in detail in 4.5 below), which rehearses the elements of the more important central quarrel between Achilles and Agamemnon,[18] and

---

[17] Willcock (1973: 1–4) describes the behaviour of Ajax and Diomede at the Games as 'thematic', reflecting their behaviour elsewhere in the poem and in the tradition. Ajax, son of Oileus does not enjoy divine assistance: his attempt to rape Cassandra provoked the wrath of Athene against the Greeks (cf. *Od.* 1. 325–7). He is killed by Poseidon for boasting that he would escape the perils of the sea without divine aid (*Od.* 4. 502–11). It is worth remembering that Achilles too is behaving in character when he advocates accepting ransom for Chryseis (*Il.* 1. 127), for he had himself accepted ransom for Andromache's mother, captured (*Il.* 6. 425–7), like Chryseis (*Il.* 1. 366), in the sack of Thebe.

[18] The quarrel of Thersites and Agamemnon repeats with a different cast, as

adjusts the audience's retrospective view of it. The quarrel at the funeral games begins when the second prize for the chariot race has already been allocated to Antilochus, but Menelaus argues that the prize rightfully belongs to himself, since Antilochus obtained the prize by cheating. This claim by one of the Atreidae to a prize already allocated to another, less kingly man (in this case, Antilochus), exactly repeats the elements of Achilles' quarrel with Agamemnon. Menelaus and Antilochus resolve their quarrel through mutual concessions: Antilochus yields his prize to Menelaus, without admitting that he cheated in the race, and Menelaus is so charmed by Antilochus' deference that he permits him to keep the prize, while still insisting that it belongs by right to himself. Their concessions remind us of those proposed by Nestor at the beginning of the poem, to resolve the quarrel between Achilles and Agamemnon, when he invited Agamemnon to allow Achilles to retain Briseis, since it was to Achilles that the Greeks first gave her (*Il.* 1. 274–5). At the same time, Nestor urged Achilles not to quarrel with Agamemnon, his social superior (*Il.* 1. 278–81). Neither the quarrel between Achilles and Agamemnon, nor that between Antilochus and Menelaus, makes any overt reference to the other, but the similar issues involved resonate together, and invite comparison. By presenting at the end of the poem the fortunate results achieved when a quarrel is resolved by mutual concessions on the part of the disputants, the poet conveys his approval of Nestor's original advice in book 1 that Achilles should concede Agamemnon's superior status, and that Agamemnon should respect the allocation of Briseis to Achilles by the Greeks. Achilles and Agamemnon are both wrong because they refuse to settle their dispute. Menelaus and Antilochus are both right because they settle theirs. The finely balanced issues at stake in the quarrel between Antilochus and Menelaus remain undecided.[19] The poet indicates no

if in a distorting mirror, some of the elements of the quarrel of Agamemnon and Achilles. This 'mirroring' is discussed by Lohmann (1970: 174–8). Rabel (1990: 432–40) discusses 'parallels' between two episodes of reconciliation, Agamemnon's embassy to Apollo in book 1, and Priam's embassy to Achilles in book 24.

[19] Similarly the issue of compensation on the Shield of Achilles remains undecided: see 3.3.1 below. The correct reaction to an incident like

preference for the case of either, concentrating instead on their mutual concession and reconciliation. The quarrel and reconciliation of Antilochus and Menelaus counterpoints the similar quarrel between Achilles and Agamemnon, and contrasts with their disastrous failure to seek early reconciliation.

2.2.2. *Para-narratives related by the poet's characters*

The secondary narratives (also called digressions)[20] related by the poet's characters tend to display the same uncanny relationship to the main narrative as the ostensibly minor episodes we have just observed to be analogous with, or parallel to, the main plot within the primary narrative. For example, Phoenix (*Il.* 9. 447–57) tells Achilles how he quarrelled with his father, and was cursed with sterility. The story invites Achilles to identify with Phoenix, for both have quarrelled with a superior about a woman. It also hints at unpleasant consequences if Achilles persists in his quarrel with Agamemnon. The poet's characters appear to derive virtually all their secondary narratives from the past, whether from the comparatively recent past,[21] or the remotely mythical past. Many of the secondary narratives related by characters within the poem are either found nowhere else, or vary in significant details from other versions. Willcock[22] argues that the poet displays a fairly flexible attitude towards the past, which he is constantly reinventing in the light of the present, and according to the requirements of the present. For example, Aphrodite, wounded by Diomede, is invited to consider the examples of three divinities who had to endure the suffering inflicted on them by mortals (*Il.* 5. 385–402) although these particular divine sufferings are mentioned

---

Antilochus' questionable victory in the funeral games is illustrated by Nestor's story of his own behaviour in the funeral games at Bouprasion, 4.5 below.

[20] Austin (1978: 74; 1st pub. 1966) defines digressions as 'anecdotes which describe action outside the time of the poem'. For earlier discussions see Oehler (1925) (includes very brief treatment of seventeen 'mythological examples' from the *Iliad*); Gaisser (1969*a*) (again very brief treatment of twenty-four digressions); Hebel (1970) (fuller treatment and discussion of narrative functions of *Wiedererzählungen*: stories put into the mouth of a character in the poem).

[21] 'Reference to the past . . . is prompted by the impulse to find paradigm in the past': Austin (1978: 76; 1st pub. 1966).

[22] (1964; 1977); Braswell (1971); Andersen (1990).

nowhere else, suggesting that all three incidents are invented to provide parallels with the wound of Aphrodite.[23] The habit of inventing the past to suit the requirements of the present can lead to inconsistencies between the poet and his characters with regard to the details of past events. For example, Lycaon indicates to Achilles that he should take him prisoner again and not kill him, because last time he took Lycaon prisoner, Achilles obtained a hundred oxen for him when he sold him: Lycaon has just been ransomed from Lemnos for three times that amount (*Il.* 21. 76–80), and a similar price might be obtainable for him as prisoner again. However, the poet, when he needs to mention a prize for the footrace, tells us of a silver bowl received by Patroclus in exchange for Lycaon (*Il.* 23. 740–8).[24] In other words, Lycaon's ransom was whatever the context now requires it to be. 'Facts' in the Homeric presentation of the past are more fluid than we might think them.[25] Similarly, the same piece of information can be used to support two completely different arguments: Athene and Agamemnon present Tydeus as a hero when they want Diomede to emulate his bravery at Thebes, but for Sthenelus, defending[26] Diomede's honour in war (and his own), Tydeus was a fool for disregarding the portents of the gods. Emphasis and context are crucial to the effect conveyed by any piece of information. The 'digressions' related by the poet's characters have received much more attention than the analogous situations of book 1, and this attention has been focused mainly on whether they have been

[23] Willcock (1964: 145).

[24] For discussion, see Andersen (1990: 36–7). The bowl is associated with Patroclus, in whose honour it is being given away. This kind of association of an object with its past is found also in the paradigmatic association of the boars' tusk helmet (*Il.* 10. 257–70) with treachery in the past: the helmet is used for the treacherous night raid of book 10 on the Trojans' allies: Austin (1978: 83; 1st pub. 1966). The lyre on which Achilles plays (*Il.* 9. 186–9) was captured from Eëtion's city. It reminds us of Achilles' treatment of its defeated community: he accepted ransom for Andromache's mother (*Il.* 6. 425–7), in contrast with Agamemnon's refusal to accept ransom for Chryseis (*Il.* 1. 24–31). It was this refusal by Agamemnon to accept ransom which led Achilles to retire from the battle and console himself with songs and the lyre.

[25] Cf. Willcock (1977: 46–7) for diverging accounts of conversations between Peleus and Achilles in Phthia before the war.

[26] Sthenelus' story of Tydeus, which presents him in an unfavourable light, is described as 'an apologetic paradigm', Austin (1978: 74; 1st pub. 1966).

invented or adapted to suit the occasion of their telling.[27] A frequent reason for such adaptation appears to be to provide a parallel or paradigm for a present situation.

2.3. PARADIGMS

The most frequent type of para-narrative told by the poet's characters is the paradigm. 'Paradigm' means 'example': to illustrate ἐκ παραδείγματος is to illustrate 'from example', and the term is also used to describe the model made by an artist as a pattern for the work planned. The verb παραδείκνυμι means 'exhibit side by side'. Aristotle explains the logic of a paradigm as a kind of induction: it communicates a fact from the past which seems compatible with the present, and by doing so, it explains why people act as they do, or why they must act in a certain way.[28] A narrative paradigm is a λόγος ἀρχαῖος,[29] a story from the past. It is told to explain or illustrate an argument, or to influence the listener to act or not to act in a way resembling the events described in the story.

ὅποι᾽ ἀνὴρ
ἔννους τὰ καινὰ τοῖς πάλαι τεκμαίρεται

the man of sense judges new things by old[30]

says Jocasta, when she has attempted to discredit the value of prophecy in general, and in particular, Tiresias' revelation that Oedipus is the murderer of Laius by describing how her son, destined, according to the oracle, to murder his father, was exposed shortly after birth. She implies that, since the old oracle (that Laius would be killed by his son) did not come true,

---

[27] The paradigm of Meleager has been the main focus of attention: for bibliography, see Ch. 7, nn. 144, 148 below. See also Pedrick (1983) on Nestor.

[28] Aristotle, *Rh.* 1356ᵇ2 f., discussed by van Groningen (1953: 31).

[29] Used at Pindar, *N.* 1. 34 of the account of the infant Heracles strangling the snakes sent by Hera to destroy the twin babies of her rival Alcmene, in illustration of the poet's point that natural gifts and talents must be used for good, 31–4. Chromios, for whom the ode was composed makes good use of his wealth and power to entertain his guests (19–23), and Pindar must make good use of his poetical talents to praise his host, 7, as Heracles made good use of his strength to rescue himself and Iphicles.

[30] Sophocles, *OT* 915–16, discussed by van Groningen (1953: 31 n. 5).

the new prophecy (that Oedipus is the murderer of Laius) will
not come true either.

   Something that happened in the past may well happen again.
For example, the fall of Troy to the Greek expedition is to
some extent anticipated by the repeated references by the poet
and his characters to the sack of Troy by Heracles in the
previous generation. We learn from Tlepolemos (*Il.* 5. 638–42)
that his father, Heracles, sacked Troy[31] because Laomedon did
not fulfil his promise to give Heracles the horses for which he
had come so far. The horses were promised to Heracles for
rescuing Troy from a sea-monster sent by Poseidon: at *Il.* 20.
145–8 the poet mentions a high earthwork fortress built by the
Trojans and Athene as a refuge for Heracles when he was
chased by the sea-monster from the shore to the plain.
Poseidon sent the sea-monster to punish an earlier failure by
Laomedon to honour the terms on which Poseidon and Apollo
served Laomedon for a year. Poseidon built the walls of Troy,
while Apollo herded Laomedon's flocks (*Il.* 21. 443–52)[32] but
when they requested their wages, they were sent away by
Laomedon with threats of mutilation and slavery (*Il.* 21. 453–
7).[33] Although the information concerning Heracles' sack of
Troy is let out in a piecemeal fashion by the poet and his
characters, the cumulative effect of the snippets is to build up
an impression of the Trojans as habitual cheats and deceivers.
The city which defended a bad cause and fell to Heracles in
the previous generation could fall again to the Greeks in the
present generation.[34]

---

[31] Heracles visited Troy on his way back from obtaining the girdle of the
Amazonian queen, Hippolyta (Apollodorus, 2. 5. 9). This was the ninth of his
labours for Eurystheus of Tiryns. Zeus ordered Athene to help Heracles in the
performance of these labours (*Il.* 8. 360), an order she complains Zeus has
forgotten ever since Thetis supplicated him to honour Achilles by letting the
Trojans win (*Il.* 8. 360–72). Athene's support for the Trojans' old adversary,
Heracles, helps to explain her support for their present adversaries, the
Greeks. For discussion see Lang (1983: 147–53), who does not regard these
stories as inventions to provide a precedent, and 2.4. below.

[32] *Il.* 7. 452–3 says Poseidon and Apollo built the walls jointly.

[33] The gods served as labourers to test Laomedon: Hellanicus, *FGrH* 4.26a.
The *Iliad* does not mention Apollo's revenge, but later accounts say that he
sent a plague: Apollodorus, 2. 5. 9.

[34] As the references to Achilles' sack of Thebe, the city of Eëtion, prefigure
the fall of Troy: see Zarker (1965); Austin (1978: 77–8; 1st pub. 1966).

Past experience, whether one's own or other people's, is frequently used as an indicator for the likely future. An example of a pattern which occurred in the past and seems likely to be repeated is found in Glaucus' account to Diomede of the experiences of his ancestor, Bellerophon, whose meteoric career under divine patronage was suddenly cut short. A detailed explanation of the significance of this account, which is still debated, is offered in 5.6 below, where it is argued that attention should be concentrated on the correspondences between the achievements of Bellerophon under divine patronage and the spectacular achievements, under the patronage of Athene, performed by Diomede in the early part of the *Iliad*. Glaucus, it is proposed, is hinting that divine favour is fickle and may be withdrawn at any time, and for no apparent reason, as it was withdrawn, apparently arbitrarily, from Diomede's ancestor Bellerophon. The logic is that since something has happened in the past, it is possible, and might happen again to someone in similar circumstances.

τὰ μὲν οὖν μὴ γενόμενα οὔπω πιστεύομεν εἶναι δυνατά, τὰ δὲ γενόμενα φανερὸν ὅτι δυνατά· οὐ γὰρ ἂν ἐγένετο εἰ ἦν ἀδύνατα.

While we are not yet confident that things which have not happened are possible, it is obvious that what has happened is possible, for it would not have happened if it were impossible.[35]

If something undesirable could not be avoided in the past, it most probably cannot be avoided in the future. This may be observed in Achilles' response to his mother's warning of his own imminent death once he has killed Hector. Achilles argues that even Heracles (and he was a son of Zeus) died. Since even Heracles was subject to death, there is no point in Achilles trying to avoid his own death:

κῆρα δ' ἐγὼ τότε δέξομαι, ὁππότε κεν δὴ 115
Ζεὺς ἐθέλῃ τελέσαι ἠδ' ἀθάνατοι θεοὶ ἄλλοι.
οὐδὲ γὰρ οὐδὲ βίη Ἡρακλῆος φύγε κῆρα,
ὅς περ φίλτατος ἔσκε Διὶ Κρονίωνι ἄνακτι·
ἀλλά ἑ μοῖρ' ἐδάμασσε καὶ ἀργαλέος χόλος Ἥρης.
ὣς καὶ ἐγών, εἰ δή μοι ὁμοίη μοῖρα τέτυκται,
κείσομ' ἐπεί κε θάνω. 120

[35] Aristotle, *Po.* 9. 6. 1451ᵇ16–19.

then I shall accept my fate, whenever   115
Zeus wishes to accomplish it and the other gods.
For not even the might of Heracles escaped fate,
although he was always dearest to lord Zeus, the son of Cronos.
But destiny tamed him, and the troublesome anger of Hera.
So I too, if a like destiny has been fashioned for me,   120
Shall lie when I die.

                                           (*Il.* 18. 115–21)

2.3.1. *The paradigms of personal experience*

The fact that one has oneself done, or experienced, something
in the past is regularly used as an argument for the likelihood
that such an action or experience will be repeated. The greater
immediacy of one's own past experience may carry more con-
viction in argument than accounts of the past experiences of
figures unconnected with the speakers. For example, Nestor,
who has seen three generations perish, and is now ruling over a
fourth, is able to use his own personal experience as a source of
paradigm. At *Il.* 11. 671–762, discussed in detail at 4.3. below,
Nestor uses his own exploits in the Pylian Wars as a pattern for
Patroclus to imitate. The passage is described as a paradigm by
the scholiast[36] to *Il.* 11. 717–18a: τεχνικῶς τῷ παραδείγματι τὸν
Πάτροκλον διδάσκει, εἰ καὶ Ἀχιλλεὺς αὐτὸν εἴργει, λαθόντα
προελθεῖν εἰς τὴν μάχην: 'he skilfully instructs Patroclus through
the paradigm, even if Achilles keeps him back, to go out to the
battle without Achilles noticing.' Nestor offers Patroclus the
pattern of his own personal example, when he fought although
his father wished to prevent him. Nestor's success on this
occasion brought him great personal glory, and made him the
saviour of his people. So Patroclus, even if Achilles disapproves
of his intention to fight in the battle, might win great personal
glory and become the saviour of his people.

2.3.2. *Paradigms from the experience of others*

The main requirement of a persuasive paradigm told to
influence the listener to act in a certain way is that the example
should illustrate a situation remarkably similar to that of the
addressee.[37] 'In these circumstances', it is argued, 'so-and-so

---

[36] Sch. bT ad *Il.* 11. 717–18a 9 (= Erbse (1969–88: iii. 267), 717–18a).
[37] Van Groningen (1953: 86).

did x (or I did x), and therefore you, in a situation just like his (or mine), will/should also do x.' The story of Niobe is a good example of a positive paradigm. In his well-known discussion of the story of Niobe, Willcock indicates how the poet is prepared to add details to the stories used as paradigms to make them correspond more closely to the circumstances of the addressee.[38] When the corpse of Hector has been washed and laid in Priam's mule-cart ready for him to take back to Troy, Achilles wishes to share a meal with Priam before allowing him to depart with the body (*Il.* 24. 601). Priam has eaten nothing since Hector was killed by Achilles (*Il.* 24. 641–2), and might well be unwilling to eat until Hector is buried. To persuade Priam to eat even in such circumstances, Achilles tells the story of Niobe (*Il.* 24. 602–17), whose six sons and six daughters[39] were all killed in one fell swoop by Apollo and Artemis. Niobe had boasted that she was more fortunate in her children than Leto, who had only two.[40] Niobe forgot that her children, although more numerous than Leto's, were not divine like Leto's offspring, Apollo and Artemis.[41] The poet is not relating the myth for its own sake, but to present a situation comparable to that in which Priam presently finds himself. Niobe is the type of the sorrowing mother: her story was told about a rock on Mount Sipylos, north-east of Smyrna. The water flowing down the rock was explained as the tears of the sorrowing mother, still weeping for her children although she had been

[38] Willcock (1964: 141–2).

[39] *Il.* 24. 604 gives the number of Niobe's children as twelve (six sons and six daughters). Aelian, *VH* 12. 36 ἐοίκασιν οἱ ἀρχαῖοι ὑπὲρ τοῦ ἀριθμοῦ τῶν τῆς Νιόβης παίδων μὴ συνᾴδειν ἀλλήλοις. Ὅμηρος (Ω 604) μὲν ἒξ λέγει καὶ τοσαύτας κόρας, Λᾶσος (*PMG* 706) δὲ δὶς ἑπτὰ λέγει, Ἡσίοδος (*fr.* 183 M–W) δὲ ἐννέα καὶ δέκα, εἰ μὴ ἄρα οὐκ εἰσὶν Ἡσιόδου τὰ ἔπη, ἀλλ᾽ ὡς πολλὰ καὶ ἄλλα κατέψευσται αὐτοῦ. Ἀλκμὰν (*fr.* 75 P) δὲ δέκα φησί, Μίμνερμος (*fr.* 19 West) εἴκοσι, καὶ Πίνδαρος (*fr.* 52m(e) Sn.) τοσούτους. (Cf. Aulus Gellius, *NA* 20. 7.) Barrett (1974: 234–5 n. 157) takes Aelian's Ἡσίοδος δὲ ἐννέα καὶ δέκα to be a conflation of Σαπφὼ δὲ δὶς ἐννέα Ἡσίοδος δὲ δὶς δέκα. Bacchylides, *fr.* 20 D 4–6, gives twenty; Sch. A ad *Il.* 24. 604 (from Aristonicus) (= Erbse (1969–88: v. 620), 604a) gives fourteen or twenty; Eustathius, *Il.* 1367. 25–6 gives other numbers (seven, according to Euripides, others fourteen, others twenty). The exact number of Niobe's children does not really affect the force of Achilles' argument.

[40] *Il.* 24. 607–9; Ovid, *Met.* 6. 146–312. For the detail that Niobe and Leto were once friends, see Sappho, 142 (LP).   [41] Apollodorus, 3. 6.

turned to stone.[42] Achilles introduces into his account of Niobe
two details not found in other versions of the story. First,
because he wants Priam to eat, Achilles says that even Niobe
ate (*Il.* 24. 613).[43] We may infer that Niobe's situation is to be
regarded as even worse than Priam's because she lost all her
children on a single occasion, but nevertheless, she ate. Niobe
ate although for nine days her children lay in their blood,
unburied because Zeus had turned all the potential buriers to
stone. This second detail of Niobe's children lying unburied
for nine days is introduced because Priam's son, Hector,
remains unburied for nine days while the gods quarrel among
themselves about the burial of Hector (*Il.* 24. 107–8).[44] Achilles
uses the story of Niobe, whose situation was very like Priam's,
as a precedent for Priam to follow when he finds himself in
circumstances similar to those of Niobe. The story has the
desired effect on its addressee, for he shares the meal prepared
by Achilles (*Il.* 24. 627), and appears glad of some sustenance
other than grief (*Il.* 24. 637–41). Although she eats, Niobe does
not abandon her grief, even when she has been turned to stone:
ἔνθα λίθος περ ἐοῦσα θεῶν ἐκ κήδεα πέσσει, 'there, although a
stone, she broods over her sorrows from the gods' (*Il.* 24. 617).
In the same way, Priam eats without abandoning his grief, and
verbal echoes mark the comparison: ἀλλ᾽ αἰεὶ στενάχω καὶ κήδεα
μυρία πέσσω, 'but ever I grieve and brood over my countless
sorrows' (*Il.* 24. 639). The resonances of the story for the
audience have a wider range, but the main point is surely that
Niobe remembered to eat although her twelve children lay
unburied for nine days: therefore Priam must eat, although his

---

[42] Pherecydes, *FGrH* 3 F 38; Sophocles, *Ant.* 823–33; *El.* 150–2; Callimachus, *h. Ap.* 22–4, and Williams (1978: 32–4 ad loc.); Quintus Smyrnaeus,
1. 294–306; Pausanias, 8. 38. 10; Eustathius, *Il.* 1368. 10. Niobe is associated
with Asia Minor and Mount Sipylos in one of the groups of variants distinguished by Pötscher (1985–6). The other, in which Niobe's boast is punished
by turning her and all her people to stone, he associates with Thebes (cf.
Eustathius, *Il.* 1367. 20).

[43] On the addition of this detail, see Kakridis (1949: 96–105); Willcock
(1964); Macleod (1982: 139).

[44] On the repetition of the motif of lying unburied for nine days, see
Andersen (1987: 5). Macleod (1982: 139) associates the burial of Niobe's
children by the gods with the divine concern in the main narrative that Hector
should be buried.

son, Hector, still lies unburied after nine days. The paradigm of Niobe told by Achilles to persuade Priam to eat invites reflection also on the last occasion when the issue of food and mourning arose. When the corpse of Patroclus was lying unavenged and unburied, Achilles persisted in his resolve to eat nothing, although his friends implored him to eat, and the gods nourished him with ambrosia to keep him from fainting (*Il.* 19. 352–4). Just before Priam's arrival, Achilles eats voluntarily for the first time since Patroclus' death (*Il.* 24. 475). The audience may well infer that Achilles' grief for Patroclus has been more intense than either Priam's grief for Hector, or Niobe's grief for her twelve children.

2.3.3. *Negative paradigms*

The story of Meleager told by Phoenix to Achilles in book 9 is a good example of a negative paradigm, a pattern not to follow. The story is discussed in detail below: it will be sufficient here to show how it is used as a negative or dissuasive paradigm.[45] Phoenix is attempting to persuade Achilles to accept Agamemnon's offer of gifts if only Achilles will abandon his anger and return to the fighting. To illustrate his point that men of old were influenced by gifts and persuasion (*Il.* 9. 524–6), he tells Achilles the story of Meleager. Phoenix describes how, when Meleager's mother cursed him, Meleager withdrew from fighting in defence of his city. A whole string of visitors[46] approached Meleager in turn, to persuade him to give up his anger: the earliest of these visitors promised gifts if Meleager would lay aside his anger. But Meleager was *not* influenced by their persuasion, and delayed too long: when eventually he returned to fight, the question of the gifts was no longer an issue, and he received nothing.[47] Achilles, Phoenix advises, should avoid this pattern by coming back immediately so that he can receive the gifts while they still mean something.[48]

[45] Austin (1978: 74; 1st pub. 1966).

[46] The mother's curse, the withdrawal from the fighting, and the string of visitors all appear to have been invented by the poet to achieve a closer correspondence between the situations of Meleager and Achilles.

[47] Meleager's behaviour in refusing gifts and conciliation until they are no longer relevant prefigures Achilles' behaviour in the *Iliad*.

[48] The story is certainly *not* an illustration of the allegory of the Λιταί, as

2.3.4. Paradigms: αἶνος

The paradigms discussed so far have all been para-narratives told with a view to encouraging the addressee to follow, or not to follow, the course of action taken in the story. But there is another kind of paradigm, this time with a veiled meaning on a deeper level. In this group the deepest meaning of the story is not openly expressed, and will not be intelligible to an unqualified audience. This kind of paradigm is called the αἶνος.[49] The fables of Aesop fall into this category, as do Solon's stories to Croesus about Tellus the Athenian, and Cleobis and Biton.[50] Croesus wants Solon to tell him he is the most fortunate of men, but instead Solon answers him with stories of the lives and deaths of Tellus, and of Cleobis and Biton, whose good fortune endured until the moment of death. Croesus completely misses the point of Solon's stories, and fails to understand that he is being gently reminded that it is still too soon to assess whether his career has been fortunate, because it is not yet over. Croesus understands the stories he is told in the same way as children understand the fables of Aesop. In the fable of the frogs who demand a more vigorous king than the log with which Zeus has issued them,[51] children comprehend only the literal meaning of the story. It continues with Zeus becoming exasperated, and sending the frogs a stork to be their king. The stork gobbles them up. The relevance of the fable to grown-up human political affairs is lost on a childish audience, which fails to grasp the message underlying the surface of the story.[52] I shall devote more space to the αἶνοι than to the other para-narratives in this preliminary discussion, as they have received

Reinhardt (1960*b*: 38) suggests. If it were, Meleager would not only have to reject λιταί (as he does), but he would also have to suffer affliction by Ἄτη, and Phoenix offers no suggestion that Meleager suffers affliction by Ἄτη.

[49] Schadewaldt (1966: 83; 1st pub. 1938).

[50] Herodotus, 1. 30–1.

[51] Aesop, 44 (Hausrath, rev. Hunger (1970: i. fasc. 1, 60–2)).

[52] Bergk (1872: 363) explains αἶνος: 'the folk wisdom of antiquity did not go straight to the point, but was accustomed to imply lessons with imagery and comparison rather than to express them. This elegant and ingenious manner of instruction lies deep in the being of the Greek people. Such a story or speech of comparison was called αἶνος.' The importance of using fables to communicate indirectly with persons of importance is discussed by Meuli (1975: 747–9; 1st pub. 1954).

little attention in the past. Αἶνοι which do not fall into the groups discussed in Chapters 3 and 4 are discussed here in detail.

The term αἶνος occurs four times in Homer: *Il.* 23. 652, 795; *Od.* 14. 508, 21. 109. The predominant meaning distinguished by Hofmann is 'praise':[53] at *Il.* 23. 795 αἶνος is used by Achilles of Antilochus' speech (*Il.* 23. 787–92) in praise of Achilles' fleetness of foot (and that of Ajax and Odysseus, who have both beaten Antilochus in the footrace at the funeral games). Hofmann focuses on the complimentary nature of Antilochus' speech, but it is important to recognize that by his praise of Achilles Antilochus gains something for himself (an extra half-talent of gold (*Il.* 23. 795–6) in addition to the half-talent Achilles has just given him for coming last in the footrace (*Il.* 23. 751, 785)). Achilles says that he will not allow Antilochus to utter his αἶνος in vain (*Il.* 23. 795), suggesting that he regards the compliment as a veiled invitation to even greater generosity than he has already displayed. At *Od.* 21. 109, Telemachus says τί με χρὴ μητέρος αἴνου 'why should I praise my mother?' in the context of inviting the suitors to compete in the archery competition for the hand of Penelope, whom he has already described as a peerless woman (*Od.* 21. 106–9). However, at *Od.* 14. 508, Eumaeus uses αἶνος in the sense of 'cunning story'[54] to refer to the tale just told by Odysseus (*Od.* 14. 462–506). Odysseus' 'cunning story' of how by a trick he obtained the cloak of another man to sleep in at Troy, is a veiled hint to Eumaeus that Odysseus would like to be provided with another cloak now (*Od.* 14. 504).

[53] Hofmann (1922: 49–52). Hofmann (1922: 61–2) associates the verb αἰνεῖν with ἐπαινεῖν: αἰνεῖν is used of praising at *Il.* 23. 552 (ἵνα σ' αἰνήσωσιν Ἀχαιοί, 'so that the Greeks may praise you'), and as the opposite of νεικεῖν at *Il.* 10. 249 (Τυδεΐδη, μήτ' ἄρ' με μάλ' αἴνεε μήτε τι νείκει, 'Son of Tydeus, do not either praise me or reproach me'). See also Chantraine (1968: ii. 35, s.v. αἶνος: αἰνέω: affirmer, approuver, louer); Frisk (1954–70) (αἶνος= Rede, Lobrede; αἰνίσσομαι = in Rätseln sprechen); *LfrGrE* (αἶνος= Ausspruch, eigentlich Gemeintes symbolisch andeutender Ausspruch; lobender Ausspruch); Schadewaldt (1966: 83 n. 2; 1st pub. 1938); Oehler (1925: 24 n. 3 on *Il.* 23. 652); van der Valk (1963: i. 502), who does not accept the explanation of αἶνος given by Sch. bT ad *Il.* 23. 652 (= Erbse (1969–88: v. 467), 652b) as ἀπόκρυφος καὶ ἐσχηματισμένος λόγος. His argument is based on the meaning of αἶνος in Hesiod, *Op.* 202 and Archilochus, *frr.* 81 and 89, where it means a tale with a symbolical meaning.   [54] Hofmann (1922: 52).

Αἶνος at the funeral games

It is this sense of αἶνος as a parable or veiled hint which is most relevant to the discussion of para-narratives. Αἶνος is used at *Il.* 23. 652[55] of Nestor's account of his exploits in the funeral games for Amarynceus at Bouprasion, exploits which Hofmann explains as part of Nestor's praise of, or thanks to, Achilles for his generosity in giving Nestor a prize in the games for Patroclus, even though he is prevented by his age from competing. However, the bT scholiast on *Il.* 23. 652[56] explains αἶνος here as τὸν ἀπόκρυφον καὶ ἐσχηματισμένον λόγον, 'the cryptic and diagrammatic story', suggesting that an αἶνος is a kind of diagram in narrative of the elements of the situation to which it corresponds. It looks very much as if the meaning 'veiled hint' which αἶνος conveys at *Od.* 14. 508 and *Il.* 23. 795 is also appropriate to αἶνος as used at *Il.* 23. 652. Nestor's story of the games at Bouprasion is discussed in detail at 4.5 below: it will suffice here to show how it functions as an αἶνος. The story is told immediately after the resolution of the quarrel between Antilochus and Menelaus over the second prize in the chariot race in the funeral games for Patroclus. It invites consideration of an alternative resolution of the elements of the race and prize-giving common to the accounts of Patroclus' funeral games and those for Amarynceus at Bouprasion. In the games for Patroclus, Menelaus lost the second place in the chariot race to the unfair tactics of Antilochus. Menelaus went on to make an issue of the unfair tactics, demanding arbitration. Antilochus made the first concession, which led to the speedy resolution of the dispute. Nestor's story describes how in the chariot race at Bouprasion, he lost the first place to the Molione, who had some kind of unfair advantage. The nature of their advantage is not clear, but it may have arisen from the fact that the Molione were twins. Unlike Menelaus, Nestor did not make an issue of the unfair tactics by which he was

---

[55] Meuli (1975: 752; 1st pub. 1954) rightly indicates that while the αἶνοι of Nestor and Antilochus in *Il.* 23. 652 and 795 entail praise, this is no more the main meaning of the word in these contexts than it is at *Od.* 14. 491. However, I do not agree with Meuli that the αἶνοι of Nestor and Antilochus have no other purpose than to demonstrate the courtly manners of Nestor and Antilochus, and support their right to prizes.

[56] (= Erbse (1969–88: v. 467), 652b).

defeated: he simply took no notice of the whole thing. Nestor is hinting to Menelaus that his querulous reaction to defeat is inappropriate. If the meaning of Nestor's αἶνος in its context after the quarrel between Antilochus and Menelaus must be spelled out, it is that complete avoidance of a quarrel is even better than its speedy resolution. This αἶνος of Nestor's refers in the first instance to the quarrel between Menelaus and Antilochus but, since that quarrel resembles the central quarrel between Achilles and Agamemnon, Nestor's αἶνος also constitutes a verdict on the wisdom of allowing the quarrel between Achilles and Agamemnon to develop in the first place.[57] Bouprasion is part of Nestor's world: the Molione had a near escape from him when he pursued the Eleian cattle raiders as far as Bouprasion in book 11.[58] Amarynceus is the father of Diores, who is killed at *Il.* 4. 517–26.[59] Nestor might be inventing certain details of his story, but in its broad outline, it appears to have some status within the tradition.

The αἶνος of Zeus' jars

Achilles tells Priam an αἶνος or parable about two[60] jars containing good and evil. From these jars, Zeus is imagined as dispensing to each man either unmixed evil, or a mixture of good and

---

[57] The secondary narratives offer five instances of the quarrel motif: Phoenix quarrelled with his father, and was cursed with sterility; Meleager persists in his quarrel with his mother, and is not rewarded when he returns to battle; the shield of Achilles offers an example of a dispute submitted to the elders for judgement; Antilochus and Menelaus resolve their quarrel at the funeral games through mutual concessions; finally, Nestor tells how he simply would not quarrel at all at the funeral games at Bouprasion. There might be a case for adding Thersites' quarrel with Agamemnon to this list.

[58] The Molione: *Il.* ll. 750; Bouprasion: *Il.* 11. 756, 760. See Kirk (1985–90: i. 219 ad *Il.* 2. 618–19) for topographical information on Bouprasion.

[59] For Amarynceus, see Richardson (1993: 237 ad *Il.* 23. 630–1), and Pausanias, 5. 1. 5 and 5. 3. 4.

[60] The reference of Pindar, *P.* 3. 81–2: ἐν παρ' ἐσλὸν σύνδυο δαίονται βροτοῖς | ἀθάνατοι, 'the deathless gods dole out to mortals two pains for every good' has sometimes been taken to mean that there are three jars, two of evil and one of good (Sch. A ad *Il.* 24. 527–8 (from Aristonicus) (= Erbse (1969–88: v. 607), 527–8a)). However, δοιοί does not mean three, and Plato, *R.* 379d (ὁ μὲν ἐσθλῶν, αὐτὰρ ὁ δειλῶν) and Plutarch, *Mor.* 24a both take it that there are only two jars, one of good and one of evil. Lendle (1957: 110–11 and n. 51) argues that the Homeric jar of evil might well have led to the Hesiodic idea of the jar opened by Pandora (Hesiod, *Op.* 90–9).

Para-Narratives: Introduction

evil, in such a way that no one ever escapes without receiving some share of evil:

δοιοὶ γάρ τε πίθοι κατακείαται ἐν Διὸς οὔδει
δώρων οἷα δίδωσι, κακῶν, ἕτερος δὲ ἑάων·
ᾧ μέν κ' ἀμμείξας δώῃ Ζεὺς τερπικέραυνος,
ἄλλοτε μέν τε κακῷ ὅ γε κύρεται, ἄλλοτε δ' ἐσθλῷ·   530
ᾧ δέ κε τῶν λυγρῶν δώῃ, λωβητὸν ἔθηκε,
καί ἑ κακὴ βούβρωστις ἐπὶ χθόνα δῖαν ἐλαύνει,
φοιτᾷ δ' οὔτε θεοῖσι τετιμένος οὔτε βροτοῖσιν.
ὣς μὲν καὶ Πηλῆϊ θεοὶ δόσαν ἀγλαὰ δῶρα
ἐκ γενετῆς· πάντας γὰρ ἐπ' ἀνθρώπους ἐκέκαστο   535
ὄλβῳ τε πλούτῳ τε, ἄνασσε δὲ Μυρμιδόνεσσι,
καί οἱ θνητῷ ἐόντι θεὰν ποίησαν ἄκοιτιν.
ἀλλ' ἐπὶ καὶ τῷ θῆκε θεὸς κακόν, ὅττι οἱ οὔ τι
παίδων ἐν μεγάροισι γονὴ γένετο κρειόντων,
ἀλλ' ἕνα παῖδα τέκεν παναώριον· οὐδέ νυ τόν γε   540
γηράσκοντα κομίζω, ἐπεὶ μάλα τηλόθι πάτρης
ἧμαι ἐνὶ Τροίῃ, σέ τε κήδων ἠδὲ σὰ τέκνα.
καὶ σέ, γέρον, τὸ πρὶν μὲν ἀκούομεν ὄλβιον εἶναι·
ὅσσον Λέσβος ἄνω, Μάκαρος ἕδος, ἐντὸς ἐέργει
καὶ Φρυγίη καθύπερθε καὶ Ἑλλήσποντος ἀπείρων,   545
τῶν σε, γέρον, πλούτῳ τε καὶ υἱάσι φασὶ κεκάσθαι.
αὐτὰρ ἐπεί τοι πῆμα τόδ' ἤγαγον Οὐρανίωνες,
αἰεί τοι περὶ ἄστυ μάχαι τ' ἀνδροκτασίαι τε.

For a pair of jars lies on the threshold of Zeus
of the gifts which he gives, the one of evils, the other of good things:
to whomsoever Zeus, who delights in thunder, gives a mixture,
that man meets with evil at one moment and at another with good:
but to whomsoever he gives of the baneful things, that man does he
    treat despitefully   531
and dreadful ravening hunger drives him over the holy earth,
and he is held in honour in his dealings with neither gods nor men.
And thus to Peleus the gods gave noble gifts
from the time of his birth: for he surpassed all men   535
in happiness and in wealth, and he was lord over the Myrmidons,
and they made a goddess his wife although he was a mortal.
But God allocated trouble even to him, since not at all
did he have a family of royal children,
but he begot one child, doomed to an untimely end: nor   540
do I tend him in his old age, since far away from my homeland
I sit in Troy, as a grief to you and your children.
You too, old man, we hear, were happy in former times.

As much as Lesbos, the seat of Makar, out to sea contains,
and Phrygia further inland, and the boundless Hellespont,   545
of these lands, old man, they say you were possessed, with wealth
   and sons.
But since the heavenly gods brought this trouble,
battles and slaughterings of men are constant around your city.

                                       (*Il.* 24. 527–48)

Achilles uses this image as an explanation to Priam of the
reason for his sufferings in old age. In a world where it is
impossible to avoid some portion of evil, Priam and Peleus
suffer in old age because they did not suffer in their youth, but
enjoyed great prosperity.[61] Perhaps, in view of their earlier
good fortune, Peleus and Priam might be considered more
fortunate than those to whom Zeus has allocated no share at all
of good, but only unmixed evil.[62] The relevance of the image of
Zeus doling out evil or a mixture of good and evil to mankind is
clearly explained to Priam, for whose benefit Achilles is telling
this αἶνος of the jars.

    Other αἶνοι which use similar imagery to explain the forces at
work in the world are accompanied by no such clear exposition.
Phoenix's αἶνος of the rejected Λιταί as a warning to Achilles of
the risk attendant on rejection of the embassy is discussed in
detail at 7.1.6 below. Phoenix does not provide Achilles with a
direct explanation of the memorable image he presents of the
limping, squinting Λιταί (Prayers) of *Il.* 9. 502–12, toiling after
their headstrong and athletic sister Ἄτη (Delusion). Achilles is
left to infer how the request to Zeus by the rejected Λιταί that
Ἄτη confound the wits of the one who has spurned them
implies that Ἄτη will confound his own wits if he rejects the
embassy. The αἶνοι of Zeus' jars and of the limping Λιταί
are related as figurative images of the forces affecting men,
forces whose application is wider than their immediate context

---

[61] The picture of the starving man who wanders as a vagrant, receiving no
honour from either gods or men has sometimes been taken as an illustration of
one to whom Zeus has allocated only evil. Macleod (1982: 131 ad *Il.* 24.
518–51) certainly considers Priam and Peleus more fortunate than the starving
vagrant, whose physical deprivations neither has experienced.

[62] Pindar, *P.* 3. 87–92, 100–3 uses Peleus' extraordinary good fortune in
marrying Thetis and his deep sorrow at the death of Achilles as a consolation
for the extraordinarily fortunate Hiero of Syracuse, whose prosperity was
tempered with the evil of ill health.

in the poem. At the time of their narration, at any rate, such forces are presented as universal truths, always valid in every context. Their application is universal, and not restricted to the immediate circumstances of the addressee. Occasionally, however, the behaviour on one specific occasion of the forces represented by such images may be offered as an explanation for the recurrence of a similar sequence of events in the primary world.

This is what happens in the case of the images used in Agamemnon's apology to Achilles.[63] Agamemnon explains how Ἄτη managed to affect the wits even of Zeus, so that he was not aware of Hera's deception when she first urged him to swear that the child born that day to a mortal woman should become lord of all his neighbours. Then she sent Eileithyia to hold back the birth of Heracles (Zeus' son, to whom he intended his oath to refer) and advance the birth of Eurystheus. Zeus, Agamemnon says, was so enraged when he realized that Ἄτη had addled his wits, that he swore a great oath that Ἄτη would never come back to Olympus and heaven again. Thereupon he seized her by the hair and flung her out of heaven. She arrived among mankind and became a nuisance to them. Every time Zeus saw his son, Heracles, performing labours for Eurystheus, he lamented the occasion when he had allowed himself to be deceived by Ἄτη.[64] When Agamemnon has completed his account of Zeus' deception by Ἄτη, he explains its relevance to himself: like Zeus, Agamemnon was the victim of Ἄτη. He was unable to free himself of Ἄτη on the day when Hector was killing Greeks by the ships:

> ὡς καὶ ἐγών, ὅτε δὴ αὖτε μέγας κορυθαίολος Ἕκτωρ
> Ἀργείους ὀλέκεσκεν ἐπὶ πρύμνῃσι νέεσσιν   135
> οὐ δυνάμην λελαθέσθ᾽ Ἄτης, ᾗ πρῶτον ἀάσθην.

So I too, when again great Hector of the dancing plume
was killing Greeks by the prows of the ships   135
I was not able to escape the notice of Ἄτη, through whom I first erred.

(*Il.* 19. 134–6)

---

[63] The parallels drawn by Agamemnon between his own experiences in the action of the *Iliad* and Zeus' tribulations on Olympus are analysed by Lohmann (1970: 77).

[64] Davidson (1980: 200) points out that Agamemnon is blithely unaware of the ironic parallel between Heracles in thrall to his inferior, Eurystheus, and Achilles' subordination to the inferior Agamemnon.

The occasion in the past when Ἄτη affected the wits of Zeus is offered as a precedent for Agamemnon's affliction by Ἄτη, which caused him to slight Achilles and persist in slighting him. The fact of something having happened in the past means that it is undeniably possible, and what is possible might happen again. Since in the past Ἄτη afflicted the mind even of Zeus, causing him to err, it is entirely understandable, in Agamemnon's self-exculpatory view, that Ἄτη should have acted against Agamemnon, causing him to err. Of course, the poet has fun at Agamemnon's expense in making him compare himself with Zeus,[65] whose career no modest man would use as a precedent for his own case, but the main point of the image is the precedent offered by Zeus as a victim of Ἄτη.

2.3.5. Paradigms: νεῖκος

Straightforward paradigms use a story from the past to provide a pattern for the addressee, who is to imitate or avoid the course of action illustrated in the paradigm. A paradigm can also be used in support of a νεῖκος, a hostile speech of disapproval.[66] An example of a νεῖκος supported by a paradigm may be found at *Il.* 7. 132–60, where Nestor tells the Greeks how he immediately

[65] However, Rabel (1991: 114–16) argues that Agamemnon makes the comparison between himself and Zeus to justify his control over the army at Troy. Rabel also considers that Agamemnon's account in book 19 of Hera's interference in the plans of Zeus repeats the theme of meddling by a subordinate: Hera attempts to meddle in the plans of Zeus, causing a quarrel and eventual reconciliation between herself and Zeus. Hera's insubordination towards Zeus corresponds to Achilles' insubordination towards Agamemnon. Agamemnon's long speech of 'apology' re-establishes Agamemnon's superiority, which Achilles had upset by interrupting him (*Il.* 1. 292). However, see Taplin (1990: 75–82) for the view that, for historical and political reasons, Agamemnon has been treated with undue deference by scholars.

[66] The νεῖκος may rebuke, insult, command, or threaten, as explained by Adkins (1969: 7–10, 14, 20–1). See Fenik (1968: 205–6, 213), who gives the pattern of a rebuke as (1) criticism, (2) description of a bad situation, (3) call to action; see also Martin (1989: 68–9, 71–6, 83–4, 94, 113–18) and for older bibliography see Latacz (1975: 410–13) on Spott- and Scheltreden. Νεῖκος can also be used of a quarrel, including that which led to the Trojan War (*Il.* 3. 86), or of the quarrel between the Pylians and Epeians in Nestor's stories (*Il.* 11. 671, 737). A νεῖκος may be unsupported by a paradigm, as when Thersites μακρὰ βοῶν Ἀγαμέμνονα νείκεε μύθῳ, 'uttered a speech of reproach against Agamemnon at the top of his voice' (*Il.* 2. 224). (Cf. also νείκεσσεν with no supporting example at *Il.* 4. 336 and νείκεσεν at *Il.* 5. 471 and 21. 480.)

responded to the challenge of Ereuthalion, and made short
work of the champion. The story is part of the introduction to
the direct rebuke which follows: the Greeks are not showing
much enthusiasm to meet Hector's challenge to single combat.
The sequence of thought in Nestor's speech is:

1. Peleus would be extremely disappointed if he knew how
   you all disappoint the promise of your parentage.
2. Would that I were as young as when I met the challenge
   of Ereuthalion and killed him. (This is the paradigm.)
3. If I were as young as I was then, Hector would soon have
   an opponent.
4. None of you is showing much sign of responding to his
   challenge.

The end of the speech is punctuated with ὥς νείκεσσ᾽ ὁ γέρων,
'so the old man reproached them' (Il. 7. 161). The paradigm is
not in itself the νεῖκος: it presents the example (Nestor's
example), which the present generation of Greeks is failing to
equal. The νεῖκος is the reproach that they do not live up to this
pattern.

  Agamemnon (Il. 4. 370–99) and Athene (Il. 5. 800–13) both
present Diomede with the pattern of his father's example: they
use this as the basis of a νεῖκος to the effect that Diomede falls
far short of his father's achievement. As a spur to induce the
addressee to fight, the νεῖκος supported by the paradigm of
someone else's exploit or career is always highly successful.

2.4. PAST PATTERNS NOT REPEATED

2.4.1. More personal experience: precedent among the gods

The tendency of the past to repeat itself is exploited again and
again to provide support for arguments. For example, when
Achilles wants Thetis to ask Zeus to ensure a Trojan victory so
that the Greeks will feel the absence of Achilles, he tells his
mother to remind Zeus of a previous occasion when the
other gods wanted to bind Zeus, but she brought the hundred-
handed giant, Briareus, to assist him simply by sitting beside
him to deter the attempt (Il. 1. 396–406). The story provides a
reason why Zeus should oblige Thetis on this occasion: he owes

her a service for her kindness in the past.[67] Briareus and his
siblings were themselves bound by their father, Ouranos,
and released by Zeus.[68] Willcock[69] regards this story of how
Thetis thwarted the other gods in their attempt to bind Zeus as
an example of ad hoc invention of detail by the poet for his
immediate purposes. According to Willcock,[70] the phrase ὁ γὰρ
αὖτε βίην οὗ πατρὸς ἀμείνων, 'for he is greater in strength than
his father' (*Il.* 1. 404) as used of the giant Briareus/Aegaeon
'simply betrays the carefree composition of Homer'. However,
Hooker[71] argues that the episode of the binding of Zeus to
which Achilles refers at *Il.* 1. 396–406 is not an invention by the
poet, but a fragment of a poetical tradition represented elsewhere in the *Iliad*. The tradition is far richer than we might
suppose, as is demonstrated by Lang,[72] who argues for a complex form of innovation in the details of paradigms, involving
influence by the paradigm upon the main narrative as well as
influence by the main narrative upon the paradigm. In her
view, this two-way influence of narrative and paradigm upon
each other arises from their closeness and from the desire to
strengthen the parallels. She refers to *Il.* 1. 396–404, where
Thetis freed Zeus when the other gods, with specific mention
of Hera, Poseidon, and Athene, tried to bind him, which she
takes to be consistent with *Il.* 21. 441–9, where Poseidon and
Apollo are punished for an unspecified crime (binding Zeus?)
by being made to serve Laomedon for a year. She then argues
that these allusions are not likely to have been invented inde-
pendently to parallel details of the plot of the *Iliad*, but
borrowed from material already existing.[73]

[67] Austin (1978: 74; 1st pub. 1966) classifies this story as a 'hortatory' paradigm. Braswell (1971: 18–19), followed by de Jong (1985: 10–11), explains it as
the '*do ut des*' principle: Achilles forestalls the possible reply 'I would help you
but it won't work', by offering Thetis an argument that she is likely to
persuade Zeus, since he is indebted to her. For other 'facts' about the past
invented to provide parallels to the situations of the main narrative, see
Willcock (1964: 141–54; 1977: 43–9). On the motif of binding as the ultimate
penalty in the divine realm, where there is no death, see Slatkin (1991: 66–9).

[68] Hesiod, *Th.* 501–2.

[69] (1964: 143–4; 1977: 44 n. 15).

[70] (1964: 147).

[71] (1980: 188 n. 4) with further bibliography.

[72] (1983).

[73] Slatkin (1991: 61–2 n. 6) is not quite fair to suggest that Lang (1983)

Zeus uses precedent to reduce Hera to apparent subservience
after she has gone to considerable trouble to seduce him, and
had Hypnos put him to sleep to prevent him from inducing a
Trojan victory (*Il.* 14. 159–351). When Zeus wakes up and
realizes that his wife has tricked him, he furiously reminds her
of an earlier occasion when he went to sleep and she thwarted
his plans by driving Heracles off course to Cos (*Il.* 15. 24–8).
On that occasion Heracles had been on his way home after
sacking Troy (*Il.* 14. 250–4): Zeus undid the effect of Hera's
intervention and brought the hero safe to Argos (*Il.* 15. 29–30).
He punished his wife by suspending her between heaven and
earth, hanging anvils on her feet, and binding her hands with
an unbreakable golden chain.[74] The other gods were unable to
help her, although they wanted to, for Zeus seized any who
made the attempt, and hurled them down to earth (*Il.* 15. 18–
24). Although the point of his story is fairly obvious, Zeus
underlines his meaning:

> τῶν σ' αὖτις μνήσω ἵν' ἀπολλήξῃς ἀπατάων
> ὄφρα ἴδῃ ἤν τοι χραίσμῃ φιλότης τε καὶ εὐνή,
> ἣν ἐμίγης ἐλθοῦσα θεῶν ἄπο καί μ' ἀπάτησας.

I shall remind you again of these things, so that you leave off your
deceits,
so that you see whether lovemaking and bed are any help to you,
in which you came and mingled, apart from the other gods, and led
me astray.

(*Il.* 15. 31–3)

Hera is frightened (*Il.* 15. 34): Zeus has punished her before
and may well do so again. To avoid suffering a second punishment,[75] she swears a solemn oath that she is not acting in
concert with the other gods[76] and that she will attempt to bend
them to Zeus' will (*Il.* 15. 34–46).

'answers' Willcock's demonstrations of 'invention' on the part of the poet.
Willcock argues for invention of detail, not total fabrication, and his arguments are not incompatible with Lang's.

[74] For the golden chain, cf. *Il.* 8. 19–26, where Zeus imagines all the gods
pulling against him on a golden chain, while he, Zeus, pulls it up with all the
gods and the earth and sea attached, and winds it round a crag of Mount
Olympus.

[75] For discussion of Hera as a submissive wife terrorized by her husband's
threats, see Synodinou (1987).

[76] Hera has seen Poseidon fighting on the side of the Greeks (*Il.* 14. 154–6)

Hephaestus and Hypnos both want to avoid repetition of their unpleasant experiences with Zeus in the past. They both say that they suffered for assisting Hera when she was driving Heracles off course on his way home from Troy. Anyway, their attempts to help her did not work, and rebounded on them:[77] Hephaestus claims he was thrown out of heaven by Zeus; he landed in Lemnos, where the Sintians cared for him (*Il.* 1. 590–4). Another ejection of Hephaestus from Olympus may be found at *Il.* 18. 395–405: this time he is thrown out by Hera, who wanted to conceal him because he was lame. Hephaestus remembers that Thetis and Eurynome rescued him, and he worked as their jeweller for nine years.[78] Hypnos, on the other hand, was never in fact thrown out, although Zeus was furiously angry with him and wanted to hurl him out of heaven and into the sea, but was prevented because he could not find him (*Il.* 14. 249–61). Both Hephaestus and Hypnos use Zeus' rough treatment of them on that occasion as an explanation for their unwillingness to help Hera on subsequent occasions.[79] For example, Hera offers Hypnos a golden throne and footstool made by Hephaestus[80] if he will put Zeus to sleep as soon as Zeus and Hera have made love (*Il.* 14. 236–41):[81] Hypnos at

but this time she is not responsible for sending him to fight on the Greek side. She had earlier tried unsuccessfully to persuade Poseidon to help the Greeks (*Il.* 8. 201–7).

[77] Paradigmatic logic: 'I could not help you in the past, so do not expect me to be able to help you now': Austin (1978: 77; 1st pub. 1966).

[78] Willcock (1977: 44 n. 16) takes *Il.* 1. 590–4 as a traditional account of the ejection of Hephaestus and *Il.* 18. 395–405 as a reflection of it.

[79] Braswell (1971: 22) suggests that the assistance Hypnos gave to Hera when Zeus punished her is invented to provide a reason for his unwillingness to help her now. There is certainly some flexibility in the matter of who was thrown out of heaven and by whom. At *Il.* 18. 394–407, Hephaestus uses his rescue by Thetis and Eurynome when he was thrown out of heaven at the wish of Hera to explain his readiness to perform any favour Thetis might require. Braswell (1971: 20–1) treats this story as an ex tempore innovation by the poet, suggesting that Thetis' rescue of Hephaestus is a variant of her rescue of the baby Dionysus, frightened by Lycurgus.

[80] A lost Homeric Hymn to Dionysus mentioned a throne on which Hephaestus made Hera stick fast until she gave him Aphrodite as his wife: *P. Oxy.* 670; Merkelbach (1973: 212–15): cf. Alcaeus, *fr.* 349; Pindar, *fr.* 283; Plato, *R.* 2. 378d; *LIMC* iv. 1. 692–5; Carpenter (1986: 13–29).

[81] For the idea that divine assistance in the past may be considered the basis of entitlement to divine assistance on future occasions see Braswell (1971: 23

first professes himself unwilling to meddle with Zeus (any other god would be less of a problem: *Il.* 14. 244–6), since the last time he sent Zeus to sleep for Hera, she drove Heracles off course in the incident mentioned at *Il.* 15. 24–30. Hera overcomes Hypnos' objections to her request by promising him one of the Graces, Pasithea, to marry (*Il.* 14. 275–6).[82] Hephaestus uses the punishment he suffered on that occasion to argue that Hera should now ingratiate herself with Zeus in case he attacks her if she fails to be amenable (*Il.* 1. 586–9). If she is attacked again, Hephaestus will remember his earlier punishment for helping his mother and will be afraid to come to her assistance.[83] In the cases of Hephaestus, Hypnos, and Hera the precedent of punishment in the past is used to discourage any repetition of the actions for which it was incurred. In the matter of earlier attempts to interfere with the plans of Zeus, all three regard the pattern of the past as an example to be avoided, an *exemplum negativum*.

n. 5). He uses the example of Hera's argument that she brought up Thetis, so out of respect for Hera the gods should show favour to Thetis and her son Achilles (*Il.* 24. 56–63). This is the reverse of the *do ut des* principle of the return of favours discussed by Braswell (1971: 17–20).

[82] The promise of Χαρίτων μίαν ὁπλοτεράων (*Il.* 14. 267) develops εἰδέω χάριν ἤματα πάντα in Hera's initial offer (*Il.* 14. 235). See Janko (1992: 188) ad *Il.* 14. 133–41.

[83] Common elements exist between four instances of favours to Hera by Hypnos or Hephaestus, suggesting some cross-fertilization between the stories: (*a*) Hypnos puts Zeus to sleep and is almost thrown out of heaven as a result (*Il.* 14. 249–61); (*b*) Hypnos is asked to put Zeus to sleep and promised one of the Graces to marry as a reward (*Il.* 14. 275–6); (*c*) for wanting to help Hera when she is suspended from heaven with anvils on her feet, Hephaestus is thrown out of heaven by Zeus (*Il.* 15. 22–4); (*d*) for releasing Hera from a golden throne on which he has trapped her, Hephaestus is given Aphrodite to marry as a reward (see n. 80 above). The golden throne of (*d*) from which Hera cannot move (cf. her immobility in (*c*)) resembles the bed on which Hephaestus traps Ares and Aphrodite (*Od.* 8. 278–81, 296–8) so that they cannot move. Zeus and Hera often find it necessary to escape each other's notice when one of them wants to do something important: another example may be found in *h. Hom.* 1. 7: for new Geneva papyrus, see Hurst (1994). In other accounts it was Hera who threw Hephaestus into the sea because he was lame: see *h. Ap.* 318–20; *Il.* 18. 395–9; Janko (1992: 199 ad *Il.* 14. 295–6).

2.4.2. *Absence of precedent*

The past provides precedents for much of the action of the *Iliad*, reflecting the view that what happens is likely to resemble what has already happened.[84] Therefore, to say that something is happening now as it has never happened before is to draw particular attention to its significance. Paris uses this device to convey the intensity of the sudden passion for Helen which overwhelms him when Aphrodite spirits him away from his duel with Menelaus and deposits him in his bedchamber to face the reproaches (*Il.* 3. 428–38) of Helen. As a result of Menelaus' victory in the duel, Paris might be expected to honour the terms on which it was fought by surrendering Helen and all that came with her (*Il.* 3. 92–3). He is not doing so, and through breaking his agreement to return Helen if he lost the duel, and by making love once more with Menelaus' wife, Paris will turn the tables on his adversary and defeat Menelaus once more:

νῦν μὲν γὰρ Μενέλαος ἐνίκησεν σὺν Ἀθήνῃ
κεῖνον δ' αὖτις ἐγώ· παρὰ γὰρ θεοί εἰσι καὶ ἡμῖν.   440

For now Menelaus is victorious with Athene,
But I shall beat him in turn, for there are gods on our side, too.   440
                                                                       (*Il.* 3. 439–40)

Menelaus may have triumphed on the field, but Paris will now trounce him once more in the bedroom with Helen.[85] Paris is

[84] Cf. Thucydides, 1. 22. 4.

[85] This interpretation is not orthodox. Autenrieth gives 'another time, in future' for αὖτις at *Il.* 3. 440. Leaf (1900–2: i. 151) ad *Il.* 3. 440 (followed by Hooker (1979: 69) and Kirk (1985–90: i. 151) ad *Il.* 3. 440) gives 'some day *sc.* νικήσω', suggesting Paris' projected victory will be on the battlefield. Paris certainly attributes Menelaus' recent victory to assistance received from Athene (*Il.* 3. 439) and looks forward to his own victory with divine assistance. But Paris' divine patron is Aphrodite, who removed him from a difficult situation in the duel (*Il.* 3. 380–2) and went on to force Helen to join her husband in the bedroom (*Il.* 3. 390–420). Paris' rejection of his wife's reproaches is immediately followed by an invitation to make love (*Il.* 3. 441) and a reference to how he abducted her from Sparta. The honour of a husband is dependent on the sexual purity of his wife (Pitt-Rivers 1977: 23): the honour stripped from a husband through the adultery of his wife is acquired by the adulterer (Pitt-Rivers 1977: 92–3). Nestor refers to this when he counsels the Greeks not to be eager to return home until they have slept with the wife of a Trojan (*Il.* 2. 354–6) to avenge the groans of Helen. The injured husband can regain his honour by fighting to recover his wife and avenge himself, as Menelaus has

confident that his passion for Helen is even more intense than it was at the beginning of the affair, when first he humiliated Menelaus by abducting his wife and making love to her on the island of Cranae on the way from Sparta to Troy (*Il.* 3. 442–6).

2.4.3. More paradigms from personal experience: absence of precedent among the gods

Hera engineers an ironically similar episode between herself and her husband, Zeus (*Il.* 14. 159–360). She beautifies herself with all the resources at her disposal,[86] borrows from Aphrodite an irresistible aid to seduction, the κεστὸς ἱμάς (*Il.* 14. 214),[87] on the pretext that she must reconcile Oceanus and Tethys (14. 200–10), and enlists the help of Hypnos as discussed above, to put Zeus to sleep immediately he has succumbed to her charms (*Il.* 14. 236–7). The point of her project is to distract Zeus from his plan to help the Trojans while Poseidon is trying to rally the Greeks.[88] The poet describes how Hera, *en grande tenue*, presents herself to her husband and

> . . . ἴδε δὲ νεφεληγερέτα Ζεύς.
> ὡς δ' ἴδεν, ὥς μιν ἔρως πυκινὰς φρένας ἀμφεκάλυψεν,

successfully fought in his duel with Paris (Jamison 1994: 15–16). Paris' invitation to Helen to make love is thus an invitation to cuckold Menelaus once more. αὖτις can mean 'again', and it seems to me that Paris is inviting Helen to re-establish the situation which existed before the duel.

[86] *Il.* 14. 170–86. 'Die Rüstung ist ihre Toilette': Reinhardt (1961: 291). Hera's toilette is strongly reminiscent of the recurrent arming-scenes (*Il.* 3. 328–38; 11. 16–46; 16. 130–44; 20. 364–91) in which heroes put on their armour according to a set pattern. The interest of the arming scenes is in the decoration and provenance of each item as it is put on, and the descriptive passages are varied according to the interest felt in each individual hero. For discussion of the arming scenes, see Arend (1933: 92–7 and pl. 6, schema 10).

[87] For Kestos as a household name from 1927 on, see Ewing (1971: 95; 1978: 131–2); Carter (1992: 89) (with good illustration, front and back); Keane (1988: 67). During the 1939–45 war Kestos brassières, along with most luxury clothing, were virtually unobtainable, but the manufacturers continued to advertise them to retain the public's interest. One slogan used at this time was 'Woman has no surer ally' (McDowell (1997: 64)): Hera would surely endorse this.

[88] Poseidon tries to rally the Greeks at the beginning of book 13 (*Il.* 13. 38–135, 206–39) and again at *Il.* 14. 135–52. Hera is pleased to see him on this last occasion (*Il.* 14. 154–8). As soon as Zeus is asleep, Hypnos tells Poseidon that there will be an interval for him to help the Greeks (*Il.* 14. 356–60).

οἷον ὅτε πρῶτόν περ ἐμισγέσθην φιλότητι, 295
εἰς εὐνὴν φοιτῶντε, φίλους λήθοντε τοκῆας.

Zeus the cloud-gatherer saw her.
And, as soon as he saw her, desire overwhelmed his shrewd wits,
just as when first they mingled in love-making 295
going to bed without the knowledge of their dear parents.

(*Il.* 14. 293–6)

The motif used by Paris, that the desire he feels now exceeds that which he felt in the early stages of the relationship, is here used by the poet himself. To avoid repetition of information already given by the poet on the subject of Zeus' erotic seizure at the sight of Hera, Zeus must be made to vary the motif to convey to Hera the urgency of the passion which now trans-ports him. Accordingly, after his invitation:

Ἥρη, κεῖσε μὲν ἔστι καὶ ὕστερον ὁρμηθῆναι,
νῶϊ δ' ἄγ' ἐν φιλότητι τραπείομεν εὐνηθέντε,

Hera, you could go thither[89] later on,
but come now, let the two of us be bedded and turn to lovemaking,

(*Il.* 14. 313–14)

Zeus embarks on a catalogue of his amours, in none of which did he experience such transports of desire as he now feels for Hera:[90]

οὐ γάρ πώ ποτέ μ' ὧδε θεᾶς ἔρος οὐδὲ γυναικὸς 315
θυμὸν ἐνὶ στήθεσσι περιπροχυθεὶς ἐδάμασσεν,
οὐδ' ὁπότ' ἠρασάμην Ἰξιονίης ἀλόχοιο,
ἣ τέκε Πειρίθοον, θεόφιν μήστωρ' ἀτάλαντον·
οὐδ' ὅτε περ Δανάης καλλισφύρου Ἀκρισιώνης,
ἣ τέκε Περσῆα, πάντων ἀριδείκετον ἀνδρῶν. 320
οὐδ' ὅτε Φοίνικος κούρης τηλεκλειτοῖο,
ἣ τέκε μοι Μίνων τε καὶ ἀντίθεον Ῥαδάμανθυν·
οὐδ' ὅτε περ Σεμέλης οὐδ' Ἀλκμήνης ἐνὶ Θήβῃ,
ἥ ῥ' Ἡρακλῆα κρατερόφρονα γείνατο παῖδα·
ἡ δὲ Διώνυσον Σεμέλη τέκε, χάρμα βροτοῖσιν· 325
οὐδ' ὅτε Δήμητρος καλλιπλοκάμοιο ἀνάσσης,
οὐδ' ὁπότε Λητοῦς ἐρικυδέος, οὐδὲ σεῦ αὐτῆς,
ὡς σέο νῦν ἔραμαι καί με γλυκὺς ἵμερος αἱρεῖ.

[89] Sc. to reconcile Oceanus and Tethys.
[90] The catalogue takes the form of a priamel: after a preparatory cumulative build-up, a *pointe* (in this case unintentionally comic, at least as far as the speaker is concerned) forms the final line.

For never yet did the love of either goddess or woman   315
rush in a flood like this around the heart in my breast and
   overwhelm it,
not when I loved the wife of Ixion,
who bore Peirithoos, a counsellor equal to the gods:
nor when I loved Danaë, the fair-ankled daughter of Acrisius,
who bore Perseus, the most glorious of all men: 320
nor when I loved the daughter of far-famed Phoenix,
who bore Minos and godlike Rhadamanthys:
nor when I loved Semele, nor when I loved Alcmene in Thebe,
who bore the mighty Heracles as her child:
the former bore Dionysos, a joy to mortals: 325
nor when I loved the lady Demeter of the lovely hair,
nor when I loved the very famous Leto, nor you yourself,
as now I am inflamed and sweet desire transports me.'

                                     (*Il.* 14. 315–28)

This inept performance has been much mocked[91] for its miscalculation of the aphrodisiac effect on a wife of having to
listen to an inventory of her husband's peccadilloes. Zeus is
unintentionally entertaining in his effort to convey his unprece-
dented feelings in what for him is a fairly routine situation. It
is impossible not to laugh at this twist on the motif of absence
of precedent used to underline the intensity of Zeus' response
to Hera's charms. Zeus presents himself not as an ardent lover,
but rather as an eminently resistible old philanderer. Zeus'
clumsiness arises from his condition: he cannot wait. He is
so preoccupied with his own predicament that he bungles
all the preliminaries. Instead of flattering his wife as Paris does
(*Il.* 3. 442–6), by declaring how his present transport of desire
far surpasses anything he ever felt before, even in the days
when their passion was new and fresh, he scandalizes her by
the rehearsal of a catalogue of his liaisons with six mortal
women, and details of the resultant offspring. The conquests
to which he refers are exactly those which will evoke old
quarrels with Hera which he hopes she has forgotten.[92] As

[91] e.g. Eustathius, *Il.* 988. 27–34; van Leeuwen (1913 ad *Il.* 14. 317–27, a
passage which he would omit): 'Uxori nomina pelicum enumerare neque
decorum neque aptum ad persuadendum'. Although of the view that no wife
who knew her onions would be impressed by Zeus' approach, van Leeuwen
thought it might have been effective 'ad virginem Iunonem'!

[92] See Janko (1992: 201–3 ad *Il.* 14. 313–28) with further bibliography and
discussion of Zeus' catalogue as both traditional and innovative.

Edwards[93] points out, Hera cannot afford to protest at Zeus' gaucherie, for fear of spoiling her plan. Even if Zeus' tactics as a lover are not to be recommended, he is not made to resort to ad hoc invention: all the conquests to which he refers are well attested in the tradition.[94]

[93] (1987: 249).

[94] eg. Danaë (*Il.* 14. 319–20): cf. Hesiod, *Cat.* 129. 10–15; 135. 1–5; Europa (*Il.* 14. 321–2): cf. Hesiod, *Cat.* 140; 141. 8–14; Semele (*Il.* 14. 323): cf. Hesiod, *Th.* 940–2; Alcmene (*Il.* 14. 323): cf. *Od.* 11. 267–8; Hesiod, *Th.* 943–4; *Cat.* 193. 19–22; *Sc.* 35–6; Leto (*Il.* 14. 327): Hesiod, *Th.* 918–20. A catalogue of maidens seduced by gods appears at *Od.* 11. 235–65: it is followed by Alcmene (*Od.* 11. 266–70), who was seduced by Zeus, and a catalogue of the wives of mortals (*Od.* 11. 271–327).

3
The Shield of Achilles

3.1 INTRODUCTION: THE WORLD AS IT
APPEARS TO HEPHAESTUS

The function of para-narratives as a commentary on the events
of the main plot of the *Iliad* is seen particularly clearly in the
poet's description of the scenes depicted by Hephaestus on the
shield he makes for Achilles at the request of Thetis. The poet
is perfectly free to describe any decoration he wishes his
audience to imagine on the shield. He could have followed the
pattern of some of his other descriptions of armour and
weapons, which concentrate simply on ornament and luxury.
For example, the bands of gold and the dark blue snakes
decorating Agamemnon's breastplate are lovingly described,
and so is his shield emblazoned with Panic and Fear and a
three-headed snake (*Il.* 11. 19–28, 32–40).[1] The scenes depicted
on the shield are quite different: nowhere else does the poet of
the *Iliad* extrapolate into narrative static motifs such as those
represented on the shield.[2] The poet describes the scenes on the
shield in his own voice: they are like complex moving pictures
of situations which develop even as they are described. The
scenes on the shield of Achilles are the earliest example of
large-scale ecphrasis. On the shield are represented: the earth
with sky and sea, the sun, moon and stars; two cities of mortal
men; men ploughing a field; harvesters in a king's estate, and
the banquet prepared for them; a youth singing a Linos song
for youths and girls working on the vintage; herdsmen by a
river, whose cattle are attacked by a pair of lions; a pasture in a

---

[1] Schadewaldt (1965: 370; 1st pub. 1944) suggests that the motifs on
Agamemnon's shield illustrate the terror he inspires.

[2] For discussion of ancient ecphraseis, see Friedländer (1969: 1–23). For
comparison of the scenes on the shield with ecphraseis in modern Greek traditional material, see Kakridis (1971: 108–24).

valley, with sheepfolds, huts, and pens; youths and maidens in a circular dance; the stream of Oceanus[3] around the rim. Most of the scenes on the shield appear to be traditional motifs: Kakridis draws attention to Pherecydes of Syros' account of the veil decorated with the earth and Ocean given by Zeus to Chthonia on the third day of their marriage, and to Euripides' description of the tapestries decorated with the sun, moon, and stars used as a canopy at Xuthus' celebrations for finding his 'son', Ion.[4] Taplin suggests that the scenes of men ploughing, the harvesters, the vintage, and the cattle attacked by lions on their way to the pasture represent the seasons of the agricultural year: the ploughing (*Il.* 18. 541–9) represents spring; the scene of harvesters on a king's estate (*Il.* 18. 550–6) represents summer; the vintage (*Il.* 18. 561–7) represents autumn; the scene of the cattle attacked by hungry lions while the flocks are in sheepfolds and pens (*Il.* 18. 573–7) represents winter.[5] The heavenly bodies and the seasons are not unusual themes for objects decorated with figured scenes.[6] The mortal figures on the shield are always in a plurality, always in constant movement. They are observed as if from afar, and they are all anonymous; only the gods have names.[7] This observation from a distance suggests that the poet is imagining Hephaestus' friendly impression of the mortal world[8] and conveying it from a divine viewpoint: only other gods and personified forces like Ἔρις (Strife) and Κήρ (Death) are personally recognizable to the divine craftsman. Men are numerous, indistinguishable from one another, and permanently busy about their affairs.[9] The

[3] Later in antiquity Oceanus, which embraces all, was seen as analogous to Homer, who encompasses all human knowledge: see Williams (1978: 85–9) on Callimachus, *h.* 2. 105–13 and Williams (1978: 98–9 appendix) for the idea of Homer as Oceanus.

[4] Kakridis (1971: 110–11); Pherecydes of Syros: DK B2; Euripides, *Ion* 1147–54.

[5] Taplin (1980: 8–9).

[6] See Kakridis (1971: 114–16) for a description by a blind water-carrier of a handkerchief embroidered with the heavens and the stars, the sun, the Pleiades, and the moon, made in Zacynthos as a present for Queen Olga.

[7] Marg (1957: 28).

[8] 'Mit wenig Gemählden machte Homer sein Schild zu einem Inbegriffe von allem, was in der Welt vorgehet' (Lessing 1880: 273, XVIII NE; 1st pub. 1766).

[9] Marg (1957: 32).

usual interpretation of the scenes on the shield is that they are
scenes familiar to the poet's audience from everyday life: they
are not thought to represent specific events, but 'paradigms
of ever-continuing human social activities'.[10] Attention is
usually drawn to the irony of providing Achilles with a shield
decorated with scenes from the everyday life he has effectively
renounced in taking the decision to avenge Patroclus.[11] After
all, Thetis has warned Achilles that his decision to avenge
Patroclus will lead very soon to his own death (*Il*. 18. 95–6) and
when she commissions the armour from Hephaestus, the divine
craftsman expresses the wish that he could be as sure of avert-
ing Achilles' death as he is of providing him with splendid
armour (*Il*. 18. 464–7).

3.2. ANCIENT ECPHRASIS

This is not the way ancient ecphrasis works in its most sophisticated form. We should be looking for some quite specific and
pointed relationship between the scenes described and the
whole poem. We are unlikely to find this relationship in the
scenes traditionally used for figured decoration, the heavenly
bodies and the vignettes of the seasons. However, the two cities
on the shield are not traditional motifs, and we might look for a
significant relationship between them and the poem as a whole.
Ancient ecphrasis functions as a kind of analogous repetition or
reflection of the context in which it occurs. How this works
may be observed in, for example, the *Europa* of Moschus. In
his account of how Zeus, in the form of a bull, abducted Europa
and carried her over the sea to Crete, where he resumed his
normal shape and made her the mother of his children,
Moschus describes a basket carried by Europa as she plays on
the beach with her friends. The scene represented on this
basket (*Europa* 44–61) develops and changes as the events
depicted unfold: we see Io, the daughter of Inachus, in a
frenzy, transformed into a cow, running over the sea to Egypt,
where Zeus strokes her and finally turns her back into a woman.

---

[10] Edwards (1991: 208); also Taplin (1980: 12–14), for whom the shield is a
microcosm of the Homeric picture of the good life: it shows us war in relation
to the world of peace.   [11] Edwards (1991: 209).

The relationship of the event depicted on the basket to the event narrated as the primary subject matter of the poem should be clear: common to each is the bovine transformation, the animal running over the sea, the resumption of normal shape on reaching dry land. In showing the fate of one bride of Zeus, Io, the basket is made to illustrate the fate of Europa, another bride of Zeus, this time in the main narrative. The close connection between the verbal narrative and the moving pictures on the basket is experienced only by the audience.[12] Another example of ecphrasis is found in Catullus, *c*. 64, his poem on the marriage of Peleus and Thetis. The poem moves from Peleus' first sight of Thetis from the Argo, to the guests arriving at the luxurious setting of the wedding feast. Then attention is turned to the scenes embroidered on the coverlet of the wedding couch. This coverlet is described at length (Catullus, 64. 50–266): it shows Ariadne abandoned on the beach, watching the departing ship of Theseus, the lover who has just deserted her. Ariadne is given a long lament for the treatment she has received, but hurrying from another part of the quilt is Dionysus, on fire with love for the rejected girl, whom he will make his bride. The arrival of Dionysus 'te quaerens, Ariadne, tuoque incensus amore' (Catullus, 64. 253), is strongly reminiscent of the arrival in the primary narrative of Peleus, on fire with love for Thetis: 'Thetidis Peleus incensus fertur amore' (Catullus, 64. 19). It is worth remembering that, as Ariadne was rejected by a former lover, Theseus, so Thetis was rejected by a former lover, Zeus (when he discovered that her son would be greater than his father).[13] The scene on the quilt is closely connected with Catullus' primary narrative: both show a wedding between a mortal and a god, and both show a rejected bride consoled by an ardent husband.[14]

[12] See Bühler (1960: 85–108). For discussion of the significance of the scenes in ecphrasis on Europa's basket, see Friedländer (1969: 15) and also Campbell (1991: 52–62), with further bibliography. Campbell on *Europa* 43–4 indicates how Moschus' account of Europa's basket contains verbal echoes of the Homeric description of Achilles' shield, and Hesiod's account of Pandora's diadem (Hesiod, *Th.* 581) and the account of Heracles' shield in Hesiod, [*Sc.*] 154.

[13] Pindar, *I.* 8. 26–34. See also Slatkin (1991: 70–6).

[14] For discussion of ecphrasis in Catullus, 64, see Friedländer (1969: 16–17).

Similarly, Ovid[15] shows Arachne and Athene weaving tapestries which refer directly to the context in which they occur: Arachne is so skilled at weaving that she would like Athene to come in person to compete against her. Athene arrives disguised as an old woman and Arachne competes with her, unaware of the true identity of her visitor. Athene's tapestry (Ovid, *Met.* 6. 70–102) depicts her victory in the contest with Poseidon over the land of Attica, and in the corners she includes a series of women punished for challenging goddesses. Arachne's tapestry (Ovid, *Met.* 6. 103–29) shows scenes of divine misconduct, including Zeus' transformation into a bull to carry off Europa. Athene cannot fault Arachne's weaving, but nevertheless punishes the mortal woman who has challenged her by transforming Arachne into a spider. We realize that the scenes in the corners of Athene's tapestry hinted at some such end to the weaving competition. Arachne's tapestry also alludes to her competition against the disguised goddess, by implicitly criticizing the divine tendency to deceive mortals by the use of confusing disguises.[16] Homer presents a miniature, unexpanded, but comparable example of ecphrasis in weaving in Helen's tapestry (*Il.* 3. 125–8). Iris goes to summon Helen

> ἵνα θέσκελα ἔργα ἴδηαι
> Τρώων θ' ἱπποδάμων καὶ Ἀχαιῶν χαλκοχιτώνων

> so that you may see the marvellous deeds
> of the horse-taming Trojans and bronze-shirted Achaeans.

> (*Il.* 3. 130–1)

However, when Iris arrives, Helen is weaving a tapestry:

> πολέας δ' ἐνέπασσεν ἀέθλους
> Τρώων θ' ἱπποδάμων καὶ Ἀχαιῶν χαλκοχιτώνων,
> οὓς ἕθεν εἵνεκ' ἔπασχον ὑπ' Ἄρηος παλαμάων.

> and she was weaving in the many contests
> of the horse-taming Trojans and bronze-shirted Achaeans,
> which they were suffering for her sake at the hands of Ares.

> (*Il.* 3. 126–8)

---

[15] Ovid, *Met.* 6.
[16] F. J. Williams kindly drew my attention to this example of ecphrasis.

The scenes on Helen's tapestry, even if they are not related in detail, are directly relevant to their immediate context, for Iris has come to summon Helen to witness another contest of arms between the Trojans and the Greeks for her sake, namely the duel to be fought between her husbands, Paris and Menelaus. The verbal repetition (*Il.* 3. 127 = *Il.* 3. 131) underlines the connection. This example alone would be grounds for disagreement with Friedländer's view that ecphrasis develops from its function as mere ornament in the ancient and early classical authors to acquire at a later stage a closer connection with the whole, and a reference to its context.[17] In fact the scenes shown on the shield of Achilles function in a manner at least as sophisticated as the examples of ecphrasis quoted above, both in their relationship to the poem as a whole, and in their reference to its content. I shall demonstrate that the accounts of the cities on the shield go further than the later examples of ecphrasis just discussed, in that they not only refer to their context, but offer some assessment of it. Ecphrasis in Homer is fully developed and highly sophisticated.

I would like to begin by drawing attention to the way in which the descriptions of the two cities on the shield are related in some way to what Thetis tells Hephaestus about Achilles when she commissions the divine craftsman to make armour for her son. Thetis prefaces her request to Hephaestus for armour for Achilles with a brief account of how Agamemnon appropriated Achilles' prize, how Achilles refused to accept compensation, how Achilles would not help the Greeks even when they were desperate, but sent Patroclus in his place, and how Patroclus was killed and stripped of Achilles' armour (*Il.* 18. 44–56). I shall argue that the god is working what Thetis has told him about Achilles into corresponding images included in the divine view of the world he represents on the shield.[18] Certainly it is for the audience alone that the scenes are described by the poet as the god fashions them in his forge.

---

[17] 'Bei den Alten und noch im frühen Hellenismus war die Ekphrasis nichts als Schmuck, der späte Hellenismus nahm sie tiefer in den Zusammenhang des Ganzen hinein und gab ihr eine Beziehung zu dessen Inhalt': Friedländer (1969: 20–1).

[18] 'The shield is a microscope to focus more intently on the minutest details of the specific': Austin (1978: 81; 1st pub. 1966).

Achilles will be in no position to appreciate them until his interview with Priam when his anger has cooled.[19] In the account of the shield the divine smith and the poet become inextricable.[20] Hephaestus/the poet present here an unbiased view of the world and its realities. This is the nearest thing in the whole poem to the poet's view of the events he is narrating.

3.3. THE TWO CITIES ON THE SHIELD

Among the scenes on the shield are two cities, one at peace, the other at war. The situation in each of the two cities is in itself quite difficult to understand, but it is absolutely clear that in the first city, the city at peace, we have a dispute about compensation, and in the second, the city at war, we have a dispute about booty. Thus the disputes in the first and second scenes on the shield mirror the disputes between Agamemnon and Achilles in the main narrative of the poem: the dispute about booty in the second city is mirrored in book 1, where Aga-

---

[19] Marg (1957: 24–5).

[20] Marg (1957: 35) sees Hephaestus as a representative of both artist (Künstler) and poet: he also indicates the relationship between Hephaestus' lameness here, and Demodocus' blindness in *Od.* 8. Schadewaldt (1965: 367; 1st pub. 1944), followed by Reinhardt (1961: 401), identifies the singer who plays for the dancers on the shield (*Il. 18.* 604) with Homer. This identification cannot be proved, of course, and is not helped by the consideration that μετὰ δέ σφιν ἐμέλπετο θεῖος ἀοιδὸς | φορμίζων (*Il.* 18. 604–5) is probably interpolated (Van Thiel 1982: 472), probably from *Od.* 4. 17–19, in order to give the dancers on the shield a musician. The words quoted do not appear at 18. 604–5 in any of the manuscripts of the *Iliad*, but were 'restored' by Wolf (1985: 209, ch. 49 n. 49; 1st pub. 1795) on the authority of Athenaeus, 5. 180–1, who complains that Aristarchus inserted lines which did not belong (*Od.* 4. 15–19 or 17–19?) into Menelaus' celebrations in *Od.* 4, and excised the words μετὰ δέ σφιν ἐμέλπετο θεῖος ἀοιδὸς | φορμίζων at *Il.* 18. 604–5. Aristarchus was right to accept the evidence of the manuscripts here and Athenaeus' assertions are completely at variance with everything we know about Aristarchus' critical methods: see Ludwich (1884–5: i. 439, lines 19–440, line 19 and 536, lines 29–537, line 17); Leaf (1900–2: ii. 315–16) ad *Il.* 18. 604–5; and S. West (1967: 134). Apthorp (1980: 160–5) argues persuasively against the 'restoration' from, among other considerations, its absence from an eccentric pre-Aristarchan papyrus (Pap. 51, Pack (1965: 962); Schubart and Wilamowitz (1907: 18–20, inv. 9774)), which adds a different line, again to give the dancers a musician.

memnon and Achilles quarrel over booty when Agamemnon is obliged to return Chryseis to her father and, so that he will not be left without a prize, appropriates the prize of Achilles, Briseis. The dispute about compensation in the first city corresponds to the embassy of book 9, where Agamemnon attempts to offer compensation for his appropriation of Briseis, and Achilles refuses to accept anything, exactly as the kinsman of the murdered man in the scene on the shield refuses to accept anything. Andersen[21] observed the correspondences between the refusal to accept compensation in the scene on the shield and the refusal to accept compensation in the main narrative: as far as I know, no one has yet drawn attention to the repetition of the quarrel over booty in the main narrative in the scene of the second city on the shield or to the other points of correspondence I shall discuss.

3.3.1. *The first city: arbitration and its benefits*

The city at peace will be our immediate concern. The description of the first city presents an idealized world, celebrating a collective wedding.[22]

> νύμφας δ᾽ ἐκ θαλάμων δαΐδων ὕπο λαμπομενάων
> ἠγίνεον ἀνὰ ἄστυ, πολὺς δ᾽ ὑμέναιος ὀρώρει·
> κοῦροι δ᾽ ὀρχηστῆρες ἐδίνεον, ἐν δ᾽ ἄρα τοῖσιν
> αὐλοὶ φόρμιγγές τε βοὴν ἔχον· αἱ δὲ γυναῖκες   495
> ἱστάμεναι θαύμαζον ἐπὶ προθύροισιν ἑκάστη.
> λαοὶ δ᾽ εἰν ἀγορῇ ἔσαν ἀθρόοι· ἔνθα δὲ νεῖκος
> ὠρώρει, δύο δ᾽ ἄνδρες ἐνείκεον εἵνεκα ποινῆς
> ἀνδρὸς ἀποφθιμένου· ὁ μὲν εὔχετο πάντ᾽ ἀποδοῦναι

[21] (1976: 14–17).

[22] In the idealized court of Sparta, Menelaus is celebrating the double wedding of his son and daughter when Telemachus arrives in Sparta (*Od.* 4. 3–19). Menelaus' daughter, Hermione, is being married to Neoptolemus; Menelaus' bastard son, Megapenthes (whose gloomy *nom parlant* reflects Menelaus' grief at Helen's desertion), is marrying the daughter of Alector. This episode provides a contrast with Paris' abduction of his host's wife when he visited Sparta: here a young man comes from afar and does *not* abuse Menelaus' hospitality. Instead of abduction, the marriages go ahead as planned: indeed, as S. West remarks in Heubeck *et al.* (1988–92: i. 193 ad *Od.* 4. 3 ff.), they are soon forgotten when Telemachus and Pisistratus are inside the palace, where Helen and Menelaus seem to have nothing else to do but entertain Telemachus.

δήμῳ πιφαύσκων, ὁ δ' ἀναίνετο μηδὲν ἑλέσθαι.   500
ἄμφω δ' ἱέσθην ἐπὶ ἴστορι πεῖραρ ἑλέσθαι.
λαοὶ δ' ἀμφοτέροισιν ἐπήπυον, ἀμφὶς ἀρωγοί·
κήρυκες δ' ἄρα λαὸν ἐρήτυον· οἱ δὲ γέροντες
ἥατ' ἐπὶ ξεστοῖσι λίθοις ἱερῷ ἐνὶ κύκλῳ,
σκῆπτρα δὲ κηρύκων ἐν χέρσ' ἔχον ἠεροφώνων·   505
τοῖσιν ἔπειτ' ἤϊσσον, ἀμοιβηδὶς δὲ δίκαζον.
κεῖτο δ' ἄρ' ἐν μέσσοισι δύω χρυσοῖο τάλαντα,
τῷ δόμεν ὃς μετὰ τοῖσι δίκην ἰθύντατα εἴποι.

They were leading brides from their chambers through the town
with brilliant torches, and the wedding song was ringing out abroad.
The dancing youths were whirling, and among them
the pipes and lyres were keeping up their din. The women   495
were standing in admiration, each one in her porch.
The people were assembled in the market place: there a dispute
had arisen, and two men were quarrelling over the blood money
of a murdered man: the first was claiming he was making full
     restitution
in a public statement, while the other was refusing to accept
     anything.[23]

---

[23] I follow Leaf (1887: 123). The translation 'the one was claiming to have
paid it in full . . . but the other was denying that he had received anything'
(Sch. bT ad *Il.* 18. 499–500 (= Erbse (1969–88: iv. 536), 499–500a) followed
by Fraenkel (1950: iii. 789–80 on Aeschylus, *Ag.* 1653)) given as an alternative
to the sense of the translation above by Calhoun (1927: 18–19), Wolff (1946:
37), Hommel (1969: 15–16), MacDowell (1978: 19–21) implies that the issue
before the court is whether the blood money for a homicide has been paid or
not. Hommel argues that the language will bear either interpretation.
Andersen (1976: 18 n. 30) points out that if the victim's kinsman were denying
that he had received anything, we should expect a perfect infinitive, not the
aorist infinitive of the text. (Cf. *Il.* 9. 633 and *Il.* 24. 137 where the aorist is
used of the single occasion when compensation is accepted.) I do not accept
that the perfect infinitives δεδωκέναι and εἰληφέναι used by Sch bT ad *Il.* 18.
497–8 (= Erbse (1969–88: iv. 535–6), 497–8) are adequate equivalents for
ἀποδοῦναι and ἑλέσθαι (*Il.* 18. 500); cf. δεδωκέναι in Sch. bT ad *Il.* 18. 499–500
(= Erbse (1969–88: iv. 536), 499–500a). The aorist infinitive does not stand for
the perfect infinitive. The aorist infinitives ἀποδοῦναι and ἑλέσθαι express
aspect: they are used because compensation is offered only once at this one
formally recognized occasion, and must be accepted or rejected once and for
all on the same formally recognized occasion. Moreover, the negative μηδέν
indicates that the second half of *Il.* 18. 500 is no statement of fact: see Leaf
(1900–2: ii. 305 (and 611)) ad *Il.* 18. 500); Hammond (1985: 80). The issue
under consideration is not whether the ransom has been paid or not, but
whether the victim's kinsmen will accept ransom or exercise their right to
reject it and exact revenge, as argued by Westbrook (1992).

The pair of them were eager to obtain a verdict[24] from a judge,   501
and the people were cheering them on, advocates from both sides.
Then the heralds were restraining the people; but the elders
were sitting on polished stones in a sacred circle,
and they were holding in their hands the sceptres of the loud-voiced
    heralds.
Before them they darted, and they (the elders) were giving their
    judgements in turn.
And in the middle there lay two talents of gold   507
to give to the one among them who would deliver the best verdict.[25]

(Il. 18. 492–508*)*

Murder is not excluded from the idealized world of the
first city,[26] but the dispute arising from refusal to accept compensation for the murder is submitted to the elders for their
arbitration. The poet is indicating the course two disputants
would follow in an ideal world: they would settle their
differences through the judgement of an elder respected by
both parties. This is what Agamemnon and Achilles significantly fail to do, first in failing to heed Nestor's proposals to
resolve their quarrel (*Il.* 1. 274–81), and secondly in Achilles'
refusal to accept the arbitration of the ambassadors (referred to
as γέροντες, elders, *Il.* 9. 89: cf. *Il.* 18. 503). It is true that the
'arbitration' of the ambassadors might better be called Agamemnon's attempt to buy Achilles off and control him at the
same time, and it is hardly surprising that Achilles rejects it.
But the scene on the shield does not take us as far as the terms
of the arbitration between the murderer and his victim's kin: it
just presents their readiness to submit to arbitration, which it
associates with the festivities celebrated in the city at peace.
Willingness to submit to arbitration is presented in a favourable light in the first city on the shield, with implicit criticism
of Achilles' rejection of the arbitration of the ambassadors.
This unfavourable view of his rejection of the embassy is
reinforced by the αἶνος of the Λιταί (see 7.1.6 below), which

[24] In the sense of a 'limit' on the revenge to be exacted, whether a limit on
the amount of ransom, if ransom is to be accepted, or a limit on the punishment to be inflicted if ransom is not acceptable: Westbrook (1992: 75–6).

[25] i.e. a verdict which pacifies both parties and best accommodates the
interests of each: Hommel (1969: 25–34).

[26] As indeed, it is not excluded from Morris's idealized society (Morris
1970: 70–1; 1st pub. 1891).

stresses the benefits consequent on a favourable response to λιταί. The ambassadors are unfortunately associated with Agamemnon's arrogant terms for his reconciliation with Achilles. By means of the αἶνος of the Λιταί and the scene of arbitration in the first city on the shield the poet gives the impression that Achilles should have accepted the embassy, and should have allowed his reconciliation with Agamemnon to be effected in book 9, even on the humiliating terms offered. Achilles' rejection of the embassy may be entirely understandable, but it is a mistake.

On the shield the murderer making a public statement that he wants to pay full restitution reminds us of Agamemnon and his offer to restore Briseis to Achilles and provide compensation for slighting him. The murder victim's kinsman who refuses to accept anything reminds us of Achilles, who rejects the compensation offered by Agamemnon through the ambassadors: ten or twenty times as much would not be enough. Achilles wanted recompense for the whole outrage (*Il.* 9. 378–87), but it is hard to see what form this could take if, as he says there, no offer would be sufficient. The correspondence between the shield's depiction of a refusal to accept compensation, and Achilles' refusal to accept the compensation offered by Agamemnon through the ambassadors is reinforced by Ajax's criticism of Achilles for a similar refusal. Ajax argues that a man accepts compensation even for the murder of a brother or a child: the murderer remains in the community, having paid a great deal, and the kinsman of the dead man restrains his indignation and rage when he has received the blood money (*Il.* 9. 632–6).[27] The injury done to Achilles by Agamemnon is less serious than that done by the murderer to his victim's kin. Therefore, if compensation is acceptable even in cases of murder, it should, in Ajax's view, be acceptable to Achilles, whose grievance is not so acute. Achilles even agrees with Ajax on an objective level: πάντα τί μοι κατὰ θυμὸν ἐείσαο μυθήσασθαι, 'everything you have said is after my own mind' (*Il.* 9. 645), but in practice he is overwhelmed by indignation at Agamemnon's behaviour towards him, and cannot act upon his own objective views. Achilles and Agamemnon remain at

---

[27] Andersen (1976: 15); Westbrook (1992: 70).

loggerheads when the offer of compensation has been made and rejected, but on the shield the situation does not remain dead-locked with the rejection of compensation. Instead the two men on the shield are both eager to obtain a verdict on their dispute from a judge, and approach the elders for this purpose.[28] A prize of two talents is offered to the one (of the elders) who offers the best verdict.[29] And that is where the description of the first city stops: we do not learn what the verdict is, or how the dispute is resolved, because the poet is not concerned to determine which of the parties to the dispute is justified. His interest is in their decision to take their dispute to the elders for arbitration: the scene is closed when the arbitration is set up. It is precisely in the early resort to arbitration that the scene on the shield departs significantly from the repetition of the elements of the quarrel between Achilles and Agamemnon. The other elements, (1) the commission of offence, (2) the offer of compensation, and (3) the rejection of the offer are common to both the main narrative[30] and the scene on the shield. The trial scene on the shield presents a way out of the impasse caused by the rejection of compensation in stark contrast to the deadlock of the main narrative. The scenes of rejoicing in the city which has recourse to the judgement of the elders in a case of rejection of compensation contrast strongly with the tragic events of the main narrative, where the elders (Nestor in book 1 and the ambassadors in book 9) urging Achilles to accept com-pensation are disregarded. The audience might well consider the association of ideas: acceptance of the views of the elders is associated with the rejoicing of a communal wedding on the

[28] The γέροντες here are invited to δικάζειν as the ἡγήτορες ἠδὲ μέδοντες are to δικάζειν between Antilochus and Menelaus at *Il.* 23. 573–4.

[29] The shield shows two talents lying *in the middle* (*Il.* 18. 507) of the circle of elders, to be given to the one who offers the best judgement. The gifts given by Agamemnon to Achilles when the two men are finally reconciled are also displayed *in the middle* (*Il.* 19. 249) of the assembly of Greeks before Aga-memnon swears his oath of reconciliation. Agamemnon's gifts are compensa-tion, and as such, do not correspond to the prize to be offered for the best judgement in the case on the shield, but the image of goods exchanged in the context of resolution of a dispute suggests a loose association between the two talents on the shield and Agamemnon's gifts of reconciliation.

[30] (1) Agamemnon's appropriation of Briseis; (2) Agamemnon's offer of compensation through the embassy of book 9; (3) Achilles' rejection of the embassy.

shield, whereas in the main narrative of the *Iliad* Achilles'
failure to accept the views of the elders is associated with the
loss of what is most precious, with mourning and the funeral
of Patroclus. So it is clear that the issue of compensation
presented in the first city on the shield relates to the issue of
compensation in the main narrative as presented in the embassy
of book 9.

*3.3.2. The second city: the besieged inflict carnage on the flocks of
their besiegers*

The second city is a city under siege. Since the city under siege
is depicted in art from the time of the shaft graves at Mycenae,
and examples of the scene are found in the art of the archaic
period,[31] the city under siege may well be a traditional motif. If
so, it appears to have been worked by the poet in such a way
that the events concerning the second city depicted on the
shield correspond in many details to the events of the Trojans'
success in reaching the Greek ships after Achilles' rejection of
the compensation he is urged to accept by the elders of the
community. The ideal world of the first city, where disputes go
to arbitration and festivities are the order of the day is very
different from the nightmare vision of the second city:

> Τὴν δ' ἑτέρην πόλιν ἀμφὶ δύω στρατοὶ ἥατο λαῶν
> τεύχεσι λαμπόμενοι· δίχα δέ σφισιν ἥνδανε βουλή,   510
> ἠὲ διαπραθέειν ἢ ἄνδιχα πάντα δάσασθαι,
> κτῆσιν ὅσην πτολίεθρον ἐπήρατον ἐντὸς ἔεργεν·
> οἱ δ' οὔ πω πείθοντο, λόχῳ δ' ὑπεθωρήσσοντο.
> τεῖχος μέν ῥ' ἄλοχοί τε φίλαι καὶ νήπια τέκνα
> ῥύατ' ἐφεσταότες, μετὰ δ' ἀνέρες οὓς ἔχε γῆρας·   515
> οἱ δ' ἴσαν· ἦρχε δ' ἄρα σφιν Ἄρης καὶ Παλλὰς Ἀθήνη,
> ἄμφω χρυσείω, χρύσεια δὲ εἵματα ἔσθην,
> καλὼ καὶ μεγάλω σὺν τεύχεσιν, ὥς τε θεώ περ
> ἀμφὶς ἀριζήλω· λαοὶ δ' ὑπολίζονες ἦσαν.
> οἱ δ' ὅτε δή ῥ' ἵκανον ὅθι σφίσιν εἶκε λοχῆσαι,   520
> ἐν ποταμῷ, ὅθι τ' ἀρδμὸς ἔην πάντεσσι βοτοῖσιν,
> ἔνθ' ἄρα τοί γ' ἵζοντ' εἰλυμένοι αἴθοπι χαλκῷ.
> τοῖσι δ' ἔπειτ' ἀπάνευθε δύω σκοποὶ ἥατο λαῶν,

---

[31] For the silver siege rhyton of Shaft Grave IV, see Karo (1930–3: i. 106–8,
no. 481 and figs. 35 and 39; ii, pl. 122). For BM 123–53, a Phoenician silver
dish from Amathus showing a city under siege, see Edwards (1991: 205, fig. 2).

δέγμενοι ὁππότε μῆλα ἰδοίατο καὶ ἕλικας βοῦς.
οἱ δὲ τάχα προγένοντο, δύω δ' ἅμ' ἕποντο νομῆες 525
τερπόμενοι σύριγξι· δόλον δ' οὔ τι προνόησαν.
οἱ μὲν τὰ προϊδόντες ἐπέδραμον, ὦκα δ' ἔπειτα
τάμνοντ' ἀμφὶ βοῶν ἀγέλας καὶ πώεα καλὰ
ἀργεννέων οἰῶν, κτεῖνον δ' ἐπὶ μηλοβοτῆρας.
οἱ δ' ὡς οὖν ἐπύθοντο πολὺν κέλαδον παρὰ βουσὶν 530
εἰράων προπάροιθε καθήμενοι, αὐτίκ' ἐφ' ἵππων
βάντες ἀερσιπόδων μετεκίαθον, αἶψα δ' ἵκοντο.
στησάμενοι δ' ἐμάχοντο μάχην ποταμοῖο παρ' ὄχθας,
βάλλον δ' ἀλλήλους χαλκήρεσιν ἐγχείησιν.
ἐν δ' Ἔρις[32] ἐν δὲ Κυδοιμὸς ὁμίλεον, ἐν δ' ὀλοὴ Κήρ, 535
ἄλλον ζωὸν ἔχουσα νεούτατον, ἄλλον ἄουτον,
ἄλλον τεθνηῶτα κατὰ μόθον ἕλκε ποδοῖιν·
εἷμα δ' ἔχ' ἀμφ' ὤμοισι δαφοινεὸν αἵματι φωτῶν.[33]

[32] Ἔρις appears on the aegis worn by Athene (Il. 5. 740).

[33] Il. 18. 535–8 = Hesiod, [Sc.] 156–9. For the view that the Hesiodic passage is interpolated into the Iliad, see Solmsen (1965: 2–6); Lynn-George (1978). Il. 18. 535–8 appear in all the manuscripts, but according to Van Thiel (1982: 470–1) they are certainly an interpolation, and the whole passage in which they occur (Il. 18. 520–40) is likely to be the work of an interpolator. His judgement is based on the plethora of events in a single passage denoted as a unity by the introductory formula, and the proximity of irreconcilable factors. (I am not convinced that his detection of a doublet between the pastoral scenes and the attack on the herds of this passage and the cattle of the sixth scene on the shield contributes to his argument for interpolation.) Solmsen (1965: 3), followed by Willcock (1978–84: ii. 271) ad Il. 18. 535–8, regards 18. 353–8, with their evident taste for the macabre, as a stain which disturbs the noble beauty and serenity of the Iliad. In his view, the lines are at home in the [Scutum], but might have been composed as an expansion to it. Lynn-George (1978: 400) suggests [Sc.] 248–57 may have been the model for [Sc.] 156–9. He rightly indicates that the subject of Il. 18. 539 is not to be found in the lines immediately preceding (the δαίμονες are not compared with mortals in their behaviour on the battlefield) but is resumed from Il. 18. 534. This point might suggest Il. 18. 535–8 were interpolated into the Iliad as well as being a doublet within the [Scutum]. Janko (1986: 39–40), who discusses other doublets of this kind in the [Scutum], explains them as oral variants introduced by rhapsodic performance during the 6th cent. when the poems were transmitted both orally and in written form. However revolting the description of the personified horrors of Il. 18. 535–8, such figures are not alien to the Iliad, as Leaf (1900–2: ii. 308 ad Il. 18. 535) indicates with reference to Il. 4. 440 (Δεῖμος, Φόβος, and Ἔρις) and Il. 11. 3 (Ἔρις again). Certainly there are reverberations between [Sc.] 158, where the Κήρ drags a corpse by the feet, Il. 18. 535–8, where the Κήρ does the same thing, and Il. 17. 277 and 289–90, where Hippothoos fastens a belt round the ankle of Patroclus to drag him away. The image recurs at Il. 22. 396–8, where Achilles fastens

ὡμίλευν δ' ὥς τε ζωοὶ βροτοὶ ἠδ' ἐμάχοντο,
νεκρούς τ' ἀλλήλων ἔρυον κατατεθνηῶτας.   540

Around the other city two armies of troops were sitting
glittering in their armour. And their opinion was divided,   510
whether to sack it utterly or to divide everything in two,
as much property as the lovely citadel contained within it.
But the inhabitants had not yet succumbed, and were arming
   themselves in secret for an ambush.
To the wall their dear wives and infant children
rushed and stood there, and with them the men with old age upon
   them.
And they went: but Ares and Pallas Athene led them,   516
the pair of them gilded, and both clothed in golden raiment,
handsome and grand with their arms, like gods
both conspicuous: and the troops were smaller.
And they,[34] when they reached the place where it seemed good to set
   an ambush,
at the river, where there was a watering place for all the grazing
   beasts,
there they lay in ambush covered with the reddish bronze.   522
And apart from them two lookouts of their troops were stationed,
looking when they would see the flocks and cloven-hoofed cattle.
But these quickly came in sight, and the two shepherds followed
   together with them
delighting in the Pan pipes, and not at all did they anticipate
   treachery.
But they[35] saw them from a great distance and ran up, and quickly
   then
did they cut off on both sides the herds of cattle and the flocks   528
of white sheep, and they killed the shepherds too.
But they,[36] when they perceived a great commotion among the flocks
as they sat in front of the meeting-places, straightway   531
leaping to their high-stepping horses they went after them and
   arrived forthwith.
They took up their positions and were fighting a battle by the banks
   of the river,
and were smiting one another with brazen spears.

thongs through both Hector's ankles before dragging him behind his chariot.
Since the lines appear in all the manuscripts, and personified figures of strife
appear elsewhere in the *Iliad*, I would certainly not delete these lines.

[34] The inhabitants.
[35] The inhabitants who set the ambush for their besiegers.
[36] The besiegers, still debating how to treat the booty in the city.

And Strife and Confusion were mingling with them, and ruinous
  Doom
holding a man newly-wounded alive, another unwounded,   536
a third, a corpse, she was dragging by the feet through the carnage:
about her shoulders she wore a garment tawny with the blood of men.
And they were closing like living men and fighting
and were dragging away from one another the corpses of the dead.

  (*Il.* 18. 509–40)

The picture of the second city shows us two bands of besiegers
unable to agree on how to treat the property inside the city they
are besieging. The first group wants to destroy the place utterly
(διαπραθέειν, *Il.* 18. 511), whereas the second group wants to
divide up the spoils equally between themselves and the inhabitants.[37] Meanwhile the inhabitants of the city set an ambush at
the watering place on the river, and post two lookouts to watch
for sheep and cattle to come on the scene (*Il.* 18. 516–24).
Flocks soon arrive at the watering place, accompanied by two
shepherds occupied with the music of their pipes (*Il.* 18. 525–
6). The rural idyll is very quickly broken up when the inhabitants of the city kill the unsuspecting shepherds (*Il.* 18. 527–9),
leaving the flocks unprotected. Alerted by the din made by the
terrified cattle, the besiegers rise up from the assembly which
was the scene of their dispute over booty, and go out to battle
with the inhabitants (*Il.* 18. 530–3). The battle is particularly
savage, with Ἔρις (Strife), Κυδοιμός (Confusion), and Κήρ
(Doom) all rampaging on the battlefield.

3.3.3. *Images of the second city repeated in the main narrative*

Marg[38] noted the relationship of the pictures on the shield to
the similes of the main narrative, but seems to have meant a
qualitative relationship, whereby the vignettes of the similes
and the scenes on the shield are alike in their distance from the
events of the main narrative. However, the correspondences
between the rejection of compensation in the first city of the
shield and Achilles' rejection of the compensation offered by
Agamemnon invite the audience to look for similar correspon-

---

[37] Leaf (1900–2: ii. 306 ad *Il.* 18. 511) refers to *Il.* 22. 117–20, where Hector
considers proposing a similar division between the Trojans and the Greeks.

[38] Marg (1957: 29), followed by Taplin (1980: 14–15).

dences between the situation described in the account of the second city and the main narrative. As soon as the account of the second city on the shield is read in this way, its similarities with aspects of the main narrative become apparent. The city under siege on the shield corresponds to Troy.[39] The wives and children and old men (*Il.* 18. 514–15) left behind in it recall the Homilia of book 6 and the Teichoscopia of book 3, as Edwards indicates.[40] The besiegers of the second city stand for the besiegers of Troy, the leaders of the Greeks of the main narrative. The cattle and flocks of the besiegers stand for the troops of the besiegers of Troy, i.e. the Greek troops of the main narrative.[41] The image of the shepherd guarding his flocks corresponds to the relationship between a commander and his troops.[42] The dispute between the two factions of the city's besiegers over the question of booty resembles the dispute between Agamemnon and Achilles over the proper allocation of booty.[43] This dispute has separated off Achilles and his Myrmidons from the remainder of the Greek army, dividing the Greek force into two groups of besiegers.[44] So we find an

[39] Reinhardt (1961: 403) considers the second city as the antithesis of Troy. Andersen (1987: 9) regards the besieged city on the shield as too vague ('too unspecifically ambiguous') to correspond to Troy.

[40] Edwards (1991: 219 ad *Il.* 18. 514).

[41] This image of cattle to represent the troops in a military engagement is found also at Aeschylus, *Ag.* 128–30, where the defenders of Troy are described as κτήνη (herds) to be slaughtered (by the Greeks) before the walls of the city. Lloyd-Jones (1990: 305–9; 1st pub. 1960) rightly prefers the normal meaning of κτήνη as cattle to the meaning χρήματα (property, possessions) given by Hesychius, κ 4308. For discussion of depredation of the flocks of men as a metaphor for the Trojan conflict, see Lonsdale (1990: 49–60 and 122).

[42] Lonsdale (1990: 10, 20–1).

[43] Reinhardt (1961: 403–4), followed by Andersen (1976: 9), mistakenly associates the quarrel between the besiegers over the division of booty with a quarrel between the Greeks over the terms (return of booty captured with Helen) of the Trojans at the end of the first day (*Il.* 7. 400). The Trojans' terms are greeted with silence, until Diomede rejects them outright, and the Greeks shout, μῦθον ἀγασσάμενοι Διομήδεος ἱπποδάμοιο, 'angry at/admiring the speech of horse-taming Diomede' (*Il.* 7. 404). Since no one opposes Diomede, and Agamemnon tells the Trojan herald that he has heard the views of the Greeks (when only Diomede has spoken), ἀγασσάμενοι must in this context mean 'admiring'. There is no quarrel between the Greeks over booty in book 7.

[44] Stanley (1993: 11) is not quite accurate in alluding to 'two armies . . . contending over a city and its hapless flock'. There is only the one army, but it is

army of besiegers divided into two groups in both the second city on the shield and in the main narrative of the siege of Troy, suggesting that the events depicted in the account of the second city on the shield are related to the main narrative's account of the battle at the ships after Achilles' rejection of the compensation offered in the embassy. Certainly, like the first group of the second city's besiegers, Agamemnon wants to destroy Troy utterly: he has expressed a desire to kill even the male child in its mother's womb (*Il.* 6. 57–60).

On the shield the tactical situation of the community under siege is reversed: the beleaguered inhabitants become the aggressors when they profit by the division among their besiegers to lead an attack on the cattle and flocks of the latter. The divided besiegers are thus compelled to abandon their idleness and their division to defend their flocks. This reversal of the tactical situation, whereby the besieged turn the tables and become the aggressors, seems to be related to the beleaguered inhabitants of Troy's reversal of the tactical situation in the main narrative after Achilles' rejection of the compensation offered by Agamemnon through the embassy. In book 15, like the inhabitants of the shield's city under siege, the Trojans reverse their tactical situation when Hector carries the battle as far as the Greek ships and the camp of the Greek besiegers, and compels them to defend their camp.[45] Further, as a result of Achilles' rejection of compensation the Greek besiegers, like the besiegers on the shield, are divided into two groups, those who follow Agamemnon and those who follow Achilles.

On the shield, the inhabitants of the city attack their besiegers' cattle and flocks by the river at a watering place for grazing beasts (*Il.* 18. 520–1).[46] The sheep and cattle set up a

divided. The δύω στρατοί of *Il.* 18. 509 seems to refer to one army depicted in two dimensions, so that a group of besiegers appears on either side of the city: see Sch. A ad *Il.* 18. 509 (= Erbse (1969–88: iv. 541), 509b) and Edwards (1991: 207 and 218–19 ad *Il.* 18. 509). Sch. bT ad *Il.* 18. 509 (= Erbse (1969–88: iv. 541), 509a) thinks the two armies are the besieged and the besiegers.

[45] For discussion of the Trojans' reversal of their tactical situation in books 12 and 15, and for the wall protecting the ships as a kind of enceinte wall, see Lonsdale (1990: 60–70 and 122).

[46] Reinhardt (1961: 404) is surely right to connect the attack by the city's inhabitants on their besiegers with Hector's hope (*Il.* 8. 522) that the Trojans will drive off their besiegers in their ships.

fearful bellowing when their shepherds are killed, and it is in
response to this din that the besiegers rush from the scene
of their dispute, mount their chariots and drive to the river
to defend their flocks and herds (*Il.* 18. 530–4). Similarly,
Patroclus, sitting in the tent of Eurypylus, hears the shout and
panic of the Greeks when the Trojans cross the wall which
protects the ships (*Il.* 15. 392–6) and leaves immediately,
announcing his intention to persuade Achilles to fight (*Il.* 15.
399–404). Patroclus' decision, once the Trojans are over the
wall protecting the ships, to intervene by entreating Achilles to
enter the battle himself or to allow Patroclus to do so, is
followed at *Il.* 15. 630–6 by a simile of a lion attacking a herd
grazing by a river: the shepherd of the herd is inexperienced,
and does not quite know how to repel a ravening wild animal.
The placement of this simile contributes to the impression that
Patroclus will be unequal to his task when he takes upon himself the defence of the Greeks. An earlier simile in the account
of Hector's attack on the ships describes how Hector and
Apollo stampede the Greeks as two wild beasts stampede flocks
of cows and sheep σημάντορος οὐ παρεόντος, when no herdsman
is around (*Il.* 15. 325), and this is taken by Lonsdale[47] as a
reference to the absence of Achilles at this point. It is perhaps
no accident, then, that Achilles is described as ποιμένι λαῶν,
shepherd of the people (*Il.* 16. 2) when Patroclus puts to him
the need to defend the Greeks whose leaders are all wounded.
The epithet is traditional, but surely at this point, a significant
description by the poet to the audience of Achilles (the
shepherd) who is needed to defend the troops (flocks). However, in the event it is not Achilles who returns to fight, but
Patroclus and his Myrmidons who come to the rescue of the
unprotected and terrified Greeks, rather as the besiegers on the
shield come to the rescue of the unprotected and terrified sheep
when their shepherds are killed.

The correspondences between the second city on the shield
and the main narrative do not end here. Marg[48] argued that the
battle between the besiegers and the inhabitants with which the
account of the second city closes is a battle over corpses: νεκρούς
τ᾽ ἀλλήλων ἔρυον κατατεθνηῶτας, 'and they were dragging away

[47] (1990: 68).
[48] (1957: 33), followed by Andersen (1976: 11); Stanley (1993: 4 and 9).

from one another the corpses of the dead' (*Il*. 18. 540), and that it corresponds to the battle over the dead Patroclus. Marg did not illustrate his view (which is surely correct) with a demonstration of further points of contact between the accounts of the battle outside the second city on the shield and the main narrative's account of the battle over Patroclus, although at least two of these are quite startling. First, on the shield, Ares and Athene lead out the troops of the city's inhabitants to ambush the flocks of their besiegers by the river (*Il*. 18. 516). By the river they are joined by Ἔρις, Κυδοιμός, and Κήρ⁴⁹ when the besiegers enter the fight to save their flocks (*Il*. 18. 535). In the main narrative, when Achilles enters the battle to avenge Patroclus, Ares and Athene appear on the battlefield in company with Ἔρις between the city of Troy and the river Simois (*Il*. 20. 48–53) in a situation topographically similar to that depicted on the shield. Secondly, on the shield, the figure of Κήρ is seen dragging a corpse by its foot through the mêlée (*Il*. 18. 537).⁵⁰ This corresponds to the Trojan attempts to drag away the dead Patroclus (*Il*. 17. 277) and in particular to Hippothoon's attempt to drag off the corpse of Patroclus by a sword belt which he attaches to his ankle (*Il*. 17. 289–90).⁵¹ The correspondences between the battle over the panic-stricken flocks of the besiegers outside the second city on the shield, and the panic-stricken Greeks of the main narrative, whom Patroclus enters the battle to defend, are no accident: the shield carried by Achilles when he goes into battle to avenge Patroclus bears a scene with all the elements of the circumstances of Patroclus' death and the battle over his corpse.

3.4. THE SIXTH SCENE ON THE SHIELD

Sheppard notes how the second city's image of a surprise attack on animals grazing by a river appears again in the sixth scene on

---

[49] All three figures appear in earlier contexts too, so their appearance in the battle over Patroclus' corpse is not necessarily to be associated with their appearances on the shield.

[50] Both ambushers and besiegers drag off each other's corpses at *Il*. 18. 540.

[51] Cf. *Il*. 13. 383–4, where Idomeneus drags the dead Othryoneus through the carnage by his foot, and *Il*. 22. 396–8, where Achilles prepares to drag Hector by the feet behind his chariot.

68 The Shield of Achilles

the shield.[52] This time the attack is not made by human assailants, but by two lions which seize a bull as it walks beside a river with the herd on its way from the farmyard to the pasture, accompanied by herdsmen and dogs:

Ἐν δ' ἀγέλην ποίησε βοῶν ὀρθοκραιράων·
αἱ δὲ βόες χρυσοῖο τετεύχατο κασσιτέρου τε,
μυκηθμῷ δ' ἀπὸ κόπρου ἐπεσσεύοντο νομόνδε   575
πὰρ ποταμὸν κελάδοντα, παρὰ ῥοδανὸν δονακῆα.
χρύσειοι δὲ νομῆες ἅμ' ἐστιχόωντο βόεσσι
τέσσαρες, ἐννέα δέ σφι κύνες πόδας ἀργοὶ ἕποντο.
σμερδαλέω δὲ λέοντε δύ' ἐν πρώτῃσι βόεσσι
ταῦρον ἐρύγμηλον ἐχέτην· ὁ δὲ μακρὰ μεμυκὼς   580
ἕλκετο· τὸν δὲ κύνες μετεκίαθον ἠδ' αἰζηοί.
τὼ μὲν ἀναρρήξαντε βοὸς μεγάλοιο βοείην
ἔγκατα καὶ μέλαν αἷμα λαφύσσετον· οἱ δὲ νομῆες
αὔτως ἐνδίεσαν ταχέας κύνας ὀτρύνοντες.
οἱ δ' ἤτοι δακέειν μὲν ἀπετρωπῶντο λεόντων,   585
ἱστάμενοι δὲ μάλ' ἐγγὺς ὑλάκτεον ἔκ τ' ἀλέοντο.

And on it he made a herd of cattle with upright horns:
and the cows were made of gold and tin,
and with lowing they were hurrying from the farmyard to the pasture
beside a burbling river, beside waving reed-beds,   576
and four golden shepherds were marching with the cattle,
and nine dogs with twinkling paws followed them.
But two formidable lions had hold of a loud-bellowing bull
at the head of the cattle, and he with far-carrying lowings   580
was being dragged away: and the dogs and men went after him.
But the two lions broke open the hide of the mighty bull
and gulped the innards and the dark blood: but the shepherds
chased them, rousing up the swift dogs.
But they were deterred from biting the lions,   585
but standing up very near, they were barking and keeping clear.

(Il. 18. 573–86)

Lines 573–8 of this passage recall Il. 18. 525–9, the idyllic image of the cattle of the second city's besiegers arriving at the watering place with their shepherds.[53] Lonsdale considers Il. 18. 573–86 a rephrasing in animal metaphor of the scene of the ambush of the cattle at Il. 18. 525–9. I think the reverse is more likely to be the case: the animal image of the sixth scene is

[52] Sheppard (1922: 7).   [53] Lonsdale (1990: 121–2).

traditional, and is likely to form the basis for a reworking of the
traditional motif to make the attackers of the flocks of the
second city's besiegers human. Lines 579–86 of the passage
from the sixth scene on the shield, where the lions make their
appearance and consume the blood and entrails of the bull
despite the powerless clamour of herdsmen and dogs, recall
another passage, a simile used to describe Menelaus' killing of
Euphorbus:

Ὡς δ' ὅτε τίς τε λέων ὀρεσίτροφος, ἀλκὶ πεποιθώς,
βοσκομένης ἀγέλης βοῦν ἁρπάσῃ ἥ τις ἀρίστη·
τῆς δ' ἐξ αὐχέν' ἔαξε λαβὼν κρατεροῖσιν ὀδοῦσι
πρῶτον, ἔπειτα δέ θ' αἷμα καὶ ἔγκατα πάντα λαφύσσει
δῃῶν· ἀμφὶ δὲ τόν γε κύνες τ' ἄνδρες τε νομῆες   65
πολλὰ μάλ' ἰύζουσιν ἀπόπροθεν οὐδ' ἐθέλουσιν
ἀντίον ἐλθέμεναι· μάλα γὰρ χλωρὸν δέος αἱρεῖ.

As when a mountain-bred lion, trusting in his strength,
snatches the best cow of a grazing herd:
and seizing its neck with his strong teeth he breaks it
first, then he gulps the blood and all the innards
ravaging it, and around him the dogs and the shepherd-men   65
make a great noise from afar, nor are they willing
to go against him, for cold fear seizes them.

(*Il.* 17. 61–7)

Like the lion in this simile, the Trojan Euphorbus was eager to
strip the corpse of Patroclus, but instead Menelaus thrusts a
spear through his neck and starts to strip his armour (*Il.* 17.
45–60) as the lion of the simile breaks the neck of the best cow
of the herd and ravages it. Edwards[54] points not only to the
verbal parallels between *Il.* 17. 61–7 and the shield's image of
two lions ravaging a bull at *Il.* 18. 579–86, which might be
expected in descriptions of a similar action, but also to the links
between the simile and the shield scene in terms of shared
content and sequence of ideas. Lloyd[55] indicates how the correspondences between form and content of the main narrative
and the simile have been carefully worked out, although the
phrase referring to the lion killing a bull is a stock one: *Il.* 17.

[54] Edwards (1991: 69 ad *Il.* 17. 61–9) notes the recurrence of this image at
Il. 18. 579–86 (see Edwards (1991: 227 ad *Il.* 18. 579–86)), but does not
discuss the relationship between the two passages.
[55] (1966: 191–2).

63–4 = *Il.* 11. 175–6.[56] The motif of lions attacking a bull is traditional: the *Iliad* contains 27 similes showing a lion attacking domestic cattle, and 19 of these also mention the efforts of herdsmen and dogs to repel the lion, as we find at *Il.* 18. 583–6 and 17. 65–7.[57] The motif of the lion who wishes to leap over the walls of the steading to plunder the cattle within corresponds to the basic situation of the Greeks at Troy: the Greeks want to penetrate the walls of the city to plunder what is within. But when the tactical situation is reversed and the Trojans attack the Greek wall and ships in books 12 and 15, the lion imagery gravitates to the Trojans.[58] So we find the Trojans compared directly to lions as they rush against the ships (*Il.* 15. 592–3), and there is also an oblique animal metaphor at *Il.* 15. 605–10, where Hector lashes himself to fury like a lion.[59] I have argued in 3.3.3 above that the human attackers of the flocks of the besiegers of the second city on the shield correspond to the Trojans, who have reversed their tactical situation so that they become the aggressors when they turn the battle against the ships of the Greeks in book 15. The lion which attacks the bull and breaks its neck at *Il.* 17. 61–7 evidently corresponds to Menelaus, who wounds Euphorbus with a spear through the neck. The lion image is not therefore applied exclusively to either the Greeks or the Trojans: it is applied rather to the group which happens to be the aggressor at the time. What then, should we make of the hungry lions which attack the bull in the sixth scene on the shield?

The vignette of the sixth scene on the shield is part of a group of four representing the traditional motif of the seasons (see 3.1 above). The cattle are on their way from the yard to the pasture: they would not be left out in the pasture during winter, and the lions might well be hungry during winter. In relation to the other vignettes which can be placed fairly securely in the agricultural calendar (ploughing would be done in the spring, the harvest indicates summer, and the vintage would come in

[56] On wounds to the neck as the lion's method of attack, see Lonsdale (1990: 53–4); see also Moulton (1977: 74 n. 41) for the simile at *Il.* 17. 53–69 as the means by which the main narrative is carried forward at this point.

[57] Lonsdale (1990: 27 and 106). For full discussion of the marauding lion in similes, see Lonsdale (1990: 39–70).

[58] Lonsdale (1990: 122).

[59] For discussion, see Lonsdale (1990: 68–9).

the autumn), the scene of the cattle attacked by a river on their way to the pasture seems to do duty for winter. The seasons of the year have always been a traditional motif, and the poet will employ traditional motifs which are expected by his audience, although he may sometimes develop them in an innovative way. The lions attacking the cattle in the sixth scene on the shield appear as part of a series of four traditional images, and do not correspond to any group within the main narrative in the same way that the ploughmen, harvesters, and vintners of the other seasonal vignettes do not correspond to any particular group within the main narrative. These vignettes simply convey the traditional motif of the seasons in a traditional way. The sun, moon, and stars which appear on the shield are also a traditional motif presented in a traditional way: the motif is not developed, and does not correspond to anything within the main narrative of the poem. Likewise the stream of Ocean is there because it is expected and usual around the rim of figured objects of a circular shape.[60] The city under siege is likely to be another traditional motif. However, the account of the second city on the shield appears to begin from the motif of the city under siege and to develop it by combining it in an innovative way with another traditional image of carnage among docile or timid creatures attacked by a predator at a watering place. Apart from their appearance on the shield, these images occur exclusively in books 15 and 16, where the Trojans have turned the battle against the Greek ships, so that the Greeks are driven back to the sea. So at *Il.* 15. 690–4, Hector attacks the Greeks like an eagle attacks geese, cranes, or swans feeding by a river; at *Il.* 15. 630–6, Hector falls on the Greeks like a lion attacks a cow from a herd grazing by a river; at *Il.* 16. 823–6 Hector kills Patroclus as a lion kills a boar by a spring from which both wish to drink.[61] The predators in the sixth scene on the shield and in the simile at *Il.* 17. 61–5 (where the detail of water is absent) are lions,[62] the predators of traditional imagery. In the second city

[60] See, for example, the silver dish from Praeneste (Villa Giulia, Rome, inv. no. 61565 ill. Edwards (1991: 206, fig. 3)), where the serpent with its tail in its mouth, signifying the stream of Ocean, is clearly visible.

[61] For discussion of these passages, see Moulton (1977: 70, 82 and n. 54, 105); Lonsdale (1990: 68, 114).

[62] For lions, hawks (*Il.* 17. 775–9), and eagles (*Il.* 15. 690–4) as the predators of traditional imagery, see Lonsdale (1990: 26).

on the shield, the detail of the traditional image of carnage among docile creatures at a watering place is altered: the attack on the docile animals comes not from the lions of traditional imagery, but from the ambush set by the inhabitants of the city under siege, to produce a correspondence to the leaderless Greeks panicked by the assault of the inhabitants of the city under siege, the assault of the Trojans on their ships.

3.5. CONCLUSION

Interleaved with the scenes of everyday life on the shield are scenes whose coded significance is directly related to what Thetis told Hephaestus about Achilles. The shield shows the representation of a dispute about compensation corresponding to Achilles' dispute with Agamemnon about compensation for Agamemnon's appropriation of Briseis, with the significant difference that the dispute on the shield is resolved through recourse to the judgement of the elders of the community. The recourse to arbitration on the shield is associated with scenes of rejoicing over weddings. Achilles' rejection of arbitration in the main narrative is implicitly criticized by its contrast with the association of arbitration and rejoicing in the main narrative. The consequences of Achilles' failure to accept the arbitration of Nestor and the ambassadors in his dispute with Agamemnon are represented in the fate of the flocks of the besiegers of the second city on the shield. These flocks are unprotected and vulnerable as a result of a dispute between the besiegers: this dispute corresponds to Achilles' dispute with Agamemnon in the main narrative, which leaves the Greek troops without the protection of Achilles. The besiegers' flocks are caused to panic when the inhabitants of the city attack them. The attack on the flocks of the besiegers by the inhabitants of the second city corresponds to the attack on the troops of the besiegers of Troy by its inhabitants, who drive them back to the ships in book 15. The second city's battle over corpses represents the fighting over the dead Patroclus. The images of the two cities on the shield seem to be decipherable as paradigmatic allusions to the events of the main narrative. Even if at first the significance of the two cities on the shield eludes us, we should entertain the possibility that they may make some internal reference to the events of the main narrative, just as we should try to understand the narratives told alongside the main narrative of the *Iliad* in the same way as we understand the similes: as an illumination of the main narrative. In other words, we should follow the precept attributed to Aristarchus: Ὅμηρον ἐξ Ὁμήρου σαφηνίζειν (make Homer clear from Homer).[63] And this is what I attempt to do in what follows.

[63] See Ch. 2, n. 2 above.

4
Nestor: Paradigms from Personal Experience

4.1 NESTOR'S REPUTATION

The poet signals his approval of Nestor with a highly unusual introduction:

> τοῖσι δὲ Νέστωρ
> ἡδυεπὴς ἀνόρουσε, λιγὺς Πυλίων ἀγορητής,
> τοῦ καὶ ἀπὸ γλώσσης μέλιτος γλυκίων ῥέεν αὐδή·
> τῷ δ' ἤδη δύο μὲν γενεαὶ μερόπων ἀνθρώπων   250
> ἐφθίαθ', οἳ οἱ πρόσθεν ἅμα τράφεν ἠδ' ἐγένοντο
> ἐν Πύλῳ ἠγαθέῃ, μετὰ δὲ τριτάτοισιν ἄνασσεν.

> among them
> sweet-voiced Nestor leaped up, the shrill-voiced orator of the Pylians,
> whose voice flowed sweeter than honey from his tongue:
> already in his time two generations of broad-faced men   250
> had perished, those who formerly were brought up with him, and
>   those they had begotten
> in holy Pylos, and he was ruling over the third generation.
>
> (*Il.* 1. 247–52)

This introduction draws the attention of the audience both to the sweetness of Nestor's rhetoric and to his authority, which derives from his longevity: he has seen two generations of men perish and is now ruling over the third. Nestor occupies a unique position among the Greek heroes at Troy, for he has personally associated with the heroes of the past and has a personal record of achievement in the heroic past. In the course of the *Iliad*, Nestor relates four of his major exploits,[1] which all

---

[1] His advice to the Lapiths when they fought against the Centaurs (*Il.* 1. 262–73); his response to the challenge of Ereuthalion (*Il.* 7. 132–56); his part in the Pylian Wars (*Il.* 11. 605–803); his participation in the funeral games at Bouprasion (*Il.* 23. 630–42).

function as paradigms and help to justify his claim to offer
advice in the present, now that his youth and strength have
gone, and he can be only a speaker of words.[2] Nestor's speeches
of advice to the Greeks are so long that his name used to be
associated with garrulity and irrelevant digressions of unnecessary length,[3] but Austin[4] was able to demonstrate the point of
Nestor's speeches, and interpreted Nestor's accounts of his
past exploits as hortatory paradigms. Once the paradigmatic
function of Nestor's speeches is appreciated, their relevance to
their context is much easier to understand. Although Nestor's
stories might seem to derive from traditional material dealing
with wars in Pylos,[5] or mythological events like the Lapith
wedding feast, their details correspond so closely to the details
of the situation on the occasion of their telling, that they have
often been regarded as αὐτοσχεδιάσματα, improvisations
deliberately invented by the poet to correspond to their
contexts.[6] Nestor is able to use his own record of heroic

---

[2] Eustathius, 100. 29–39.

[3] Leaf (1892: 214); Bowra (1930: 85–6).

[4] Austin (1978: 75–80; 1st pub. 1966).

[5] From the close fit between the topographical detail of the Pylian raid of
Eleian cattle described in *Il.* 11. 670–762, and the district around Pylos
(Kakovatos), Bölte (1934: 319–47) argues that the basis of Nestor's cattle raid
is a piece of late Mycenaean epic originating in Triphylia, and adapted by the
addition of the opponents of the Pylians. The importance of Kakovatos in the
early stages of LH does not appear to have continued into LH IIIC and the
Dark Ages (see Hope-Simpson (1979: 76, 101–2)) and Messenia and southern
Triphylia suffered a catastrophic disaster at the end of LH IIIB (Hope-
Simpson (1979: 127)). There is evidence of a long break in the record of habi-
tation at Nichoria after LH IIIB2 (see McDonald (1992: 767–8; 1983: 322)).
Certainly the accounts of the hostility between Pylians and Arcadians (*Il.* 4.
319; 7. 133–56) and between Pylians and Eleians (*Il.* 11. 670–762; 23. 630–42)
display consistency of the kind also found in the references to Heracles' sack of
Troy (see Ch. 6, n. 14 below), suggesting they had a place in tradition.

[6] Mülder (1910: 47) argued that Nestor's part in the battle of the Lapiths
and Centaurs (see n. 1 above) was invented by the poet for the occasion: cf.
also Cantieni (1942: 70); Von der Mühll (1952: 24 n. 29); and Willcock (1964:
144–5), who argues that Nestor's part was introduced by the poet into a legend
already in existence. Against the view that Nestor's role in this battle is an
invention by the poet, Robert (1920: 6 and 10) argues for a migration which
took stories of the centaurs southwards from Pelion to Aetolia, Elis, and
Arcadia. (Hesiod mentions an Arcadian Lapith, Peirithous: [*Sc.*] 179, *fr.* 166,
and *fr.* 280. 28 M–W. Peirithous is often found in company with Theseus: see
Huxley (1969: 117–20). Pausanias, 5. 5. 8 mentions an Arcadian mountain,

achievement in the past as a pattern for imitation by heroes of
the present generation: when someone must be found to
respond to the challenge issued by Hector (*Il.* 7. 73–91), Nestor
describes an occasion in the past when he himself responded to
such a challenge (*Il.* 7. 132–57). The basis of his νεῖκος (*Il.* 7.
161)[7] is his own business-like response to the challenge of
Ereuthalion, which he contrasts with the dilatory response of
the Greeks to the challenge of Hector. Nestor performed many
notable exploits in his youth, but now that he is old, his
purpose in life is to manage the other Greeks:

> ἀλλὰ καὶ ὧς ἱππεῦσι μετέσσομαι ἠδὲ κελεύσω
> βουλῇ καὶ μύθοισι· τὸ γὰρ γέρας ἐστὶ γερόντων.

But even so, I shall be with the horsemen and command
them with advice and stories: for that is the portion of the elders.

(*Il.* 4. 322–3)

At every turning point in the action of the poem, Nestor offers
advice,[8] frequently supported by a story.[9]

4.2. NESTOR'S ADVICE TO THE LAPITHS
(*IL.* 1. 259–73)[10]

Even before he grew old, Nestor seems to have been offering
successful advice, and when he wants to persuade Agamemnon

Lapithos, and there is a Lapithaion on Taygetos, Pausanias, 3. 20. 7.) West
(1988: 160) argues for the northward migration of the tradition of the legend
about the Pylian Wars to Thessaly, where it merged with late Mycenaean
Thessalian epic: the association of the two traditions is expressed by making
the Pylian Neleus and Pelias of Iolkos twin brothers. On the impossibility of
determining the 'original' version of such stories, see Lang (1983: 142).

[7] Nestor has past achievements of his own to use as the basis of a νεῖκος (a
hostile speech of disapproval: see 2.3.5), whereas Agamemnon's νεῖκος to
Diomede (*Il.* 4. 370–400) refers to the achievements of the previous generation, using the example of Diomede's father, Tydeus (see 5.3.1. below).

[8] In addition to the speeches discussed in this chapter, see *Il.* 2. 337–68; 9.
53–78, 96–113; 10. 169–76. Nestor also explains that his arrangement of the
troops, the horsemen at the front, the infantry behind, and the common
soldiers in the middle (*Il.* 4. 294–307), has succeeded in the past (*Il.* 4. 308–9).

[9] For Nestor's major exploits, the subject matter of his stories, see this
chapter, n. 1 above.

[10] For earlier discussion, see Oehler (1925: 24); Hebel (1970: 8–14); Austin
(1978: 73, 75; 1st pub. 1966).

and Achilles to take his advice (*Il.* 1. 273–4), he describes an occasion in the past when the Lapiths profited by his advice in their battle against the Centaurs. The Lapiths who allowed him to advise them on that occasion were better men than Agamemnon and Achilles, who ought now to follow the precedent set by their betters, and allow Nestor to advise them on the present occasion:[11]

ἀλλὰ πίθεσθ'· ἄμφω δὲ νεωτέρω ἐστὸν ἐμεῖο·
ἤδη γάρ ποτ' ἐγὼ καὶ ἀρείοσιν ἠέ περ ὑμῖν   260
ἀνδράσιν ὡμίλησα, καὶ οὔ ποτέ μ' οἵ γ' ἀθέριζον.
οὐ γάρ πω τοίους ἴδον ἀνέρας οὐδὲ ἴδωμαι,
οἷον Πειρίθοόν τε Δρύαντά τε, ποιμένα λαῶν,
Καινέα τ' Ἐξάδιόν τε καὶ ἀντίθεον Πολύφημον,
Θησέα τ' Αἰγεΐδην, ἐπιείκελον ἀθανάτοισιν·   265
κάρτιστοι δὴ κεῖνοι ἐπιχθονίων τράφεν ἀνδρῶν·
κάρτιστοι μὲν ἔσαν καὶ καρτίστοις ἐμάχοντο,
φηρσὶν ὀρεσκῴοισι, καὶ ἐκπάγλως ἀπόλεσσαν.
καὶ μὲν τοῖσιν ἐγὼ μεθομίλεον ἐκ Πύλου ἐλθών,
τηλόθεν ἐξ ἀπίης γαίης· καλέσαντο γὰρ αὐτοί·   270
καὶ μαχόμην κατ' ἔμ' αὐτὸν ἐγώ· κείνοισι δ' ἂν οὔ τις
τῶν οἳ νῦν βροτοί εἰσιν ἐπιχθόνιοι μαχέοιτο·
καὶ μέν μευ βουλέων ξύνιεν πείθοντό τε μύθῳ·

But obey: you are both younger than I.
for already I have conversed with better men   260
even than you, nor did they ever slight me,
for not yet did I see such men, nor may I see them,
such as Peirithous and Dryas, shepherds of the people,
and Caineus and Exadius, and godlike Polyphemus,
and Theseus, son of Aegeus, like to the immortals.   265
They were the mightiest of men on earth:
they were the mightiest and they fought with the mightiest,
with the mountain-dwelling Centaurs, and terribly they destroyed them.
And with them I associated when I came from Pylos,
from far away, from a distant land, since they sent for me.   270
And I fought on my own: with them no one
of those who are now men on earth would fight.
And they took notice of my advice and obeyed my utterance.

(*Il.* 1. 259–73)

---

[11] For discussion of this passage, see Cantieni (1942: 70); Hebel (1970); Austin (1978: 75; 1st pub. 1966).

This is the first of Nestor's stories, and he tells it in support of his attempt to persuade Agamemnon and Achilles to abandon their quarrel in book 1,[12] to prepare Achilles and Agamemnon for the direct advice which follows:

> μήτε σὺ τόνδ', ἀγαθός περ ἐὼν ἀποαίρεο κούρην   275
> ἀλλ' ἔα, ὥς οἱ πρῶτα δόσαν γέρας υἷες Ἀχαιῶν·
> μήτε σύ, Πηλεΐδη, ἔθελ' ἐριζέμεναι βασιλῆϊ
> ἀντιβίην

and do not you, although you are noble, deprive this man of the
    maiden,
but let her be, since the sons of the Achaeans gave her to him first as a
    portion of honour:
and do not you, son of Peleus, wrangle with the king   277
openly.

(*Il.* 1. 275–8)

Nestor did not need to elaborate this direct advice with the paradigm of the battle of Lapiths and Centaurs: he could simply have indicated that satisfactory results had been obtained from taking his advice in the past.[13] On the simplest level, the story of the Lapiths and Centaurs adds weight to the advice Nestor is about to offer.[14] Through the suspension of time it creates,[15] it focuses attention on the moment when Achilles and Agamemnon decide whether to continue their quarrel or abandon it.

The battle against the Centaurs[16] is mentioned primarily to

[12] For comparison of Nestor's speeches (*Il.* 1. 254–84 and 9. 55–78), see Lohmann (1970: 224–5 and n. 18).

[13] For anecdote as an amplification of persuasion, see Austin (1978: 78; 1st pub. 1966).

[14] Six Lapiths are named as beneficiaries of Nestor's advice (*Il.* 1. 263–5) in contrast to the two men, Agamemnon and Achilles, who stand to profit by it (*Il.* 1. 254–84). This type of inflation is discussed by Lohmann (1970: 78 n. 135).

[15] For the leisurely narration of Homeric digressions, which eclipse the present of the main narrative, driving it from the audience's mind, see Auerbach (1953: 3–7; 1st pub. 1946). Zielinski (1901: 432, 441) includes the narration of past events in his category of simultaneous actions narrated as consecutive events. For later bibliography, see S. Richardson (1990: 225 n. 5). For the digression as a means of arresting the passage of time in narrative, see Austin (1978: 83–4; 1st pub. 1966).

[16] *LIMC* viii. 1 suppl. 671–727, esp. 671–2; ix, nos. 154–234; Gantz (1993: 277–82).

offer a precedent for the value of Nestor's advice. Nestor's part in his story of the Lapiths and Centaurs corresponds exactly to his perception of his role: to manage the Greeks with advice and stories. Nestor does not elaborate on how in his youth he fought valiantly against the Centaurs (*Il.* 1. 271): his point is simply the effectiveness of his advice in the battle against them. The occasion of the Lapiths' battle against the Centaurs is not specified, but it was almost certainly the wedding feast of king Peirithous and Hippodameia,[17] since this is, in later accounts of the Centaurs, *the* conflict in which the Centaurs were defeated by the Lapiths. In the *Odyssey*, the Lapith wedding feast is probably the backdrop for Antinous' example of the Centaur, Eurytion, who addled his wits with wine, and, in a frenzy, did wicked deeds in the house of Peirithous. Eurytion was mutilated by his host to punish him, and banished from the feast: this was the start of the quarrel between men and Centaurs (*Od.* 21. 295–304). Antinous tells the story of Eurytion in the context of suggesting that Odysseus would never have asked to string the bow if he had not been drunk, and that he should be quiet now (and not ask to string the bow and compete to carry off the bride) if he wants to avoid a fate like Eurytion's. Antinous says that Eurytion suffered because he did wicked deeds, but does not specify what they were. However, other versions of Antinous' story[18] explain the battle as the consequence of the centaurs getting drunk at the wedding feast and attempting to rape the bride and the other women. This is not particularly edifying information, and the poet generally avoids gratuitous allusion to sexual misbehaviour. In any case, he has no cause to explain the reason for a battle if it is mentioned only for the effect of Nestor's advice on its outcome. In Nestor's account, he happened to be visiting the Lapiths at the time of their fight with the Centaurs, and his hosts owed their victory

[17] Sch. bT ad *Il.* 1. 262 (= Erbse (1969–88: i. 83), 262a) indicates that the strife of Lapiths and Centaurs was also a strife about women.

[18] Hesiod, [*Sc.*] 178–90; Plutarch, *Thes.* 30; Pausanias, 5. 10. 8; Sch. *Od.* 21. 295; Ovid, *Met.* 12. 210–535; Diodorus Siculus, 4. 70. 3–4 (here the Centaurs win); Apollodorus, *Epit.* 1. 21; 2nd Vatican mythographer (Bode 1834: 111, no. 108), who also cites 1st Vatican mythographer (Bode 1834: 51, no. 162) where the battle is started by Mars throwing a thunderbolt among the guests at the feast. Hyginus, *fab.* 33; Servius on Virgil, *Aen.* 7. 304; *LIMC* ii. 1. 553, no. 420 and illustration ii. 2, pl. 417 (s.v. Ares/Mars).

to his wise advice. He makes no mention of any wedding feast, nor attempted rape of the bride. Nestor appears to be using the incident primarily as an illustration of the satisfactory outcome achieved by taking his advice in the past: similarly good results, he implies, could be attained by taking his advice now.

4.2.1 Bride-stealing by barbarians, past and present

However, the choice of the battle of Lapiths and Centaurs as an anecdote to illustrate the good effects of taking Nestor's advice is significant at two deeper levels. The first of these deeper meanings arises from his allusion to bride-stealing by the Centaurs. If we associate Nestor's battle between the Lapiths and Centaurs with the wedding feast of Peirithous and Hippodameia, then the battle is fought to prevent bride-stealing: the Lapiths fight the Centaurs who want to carry off the Lapith women from the wedding feast. The Lapiths of Nestor's story correspond to the Greeks who, in the main narrative of the *Iliad*, are fighting the Trojans to recover a stolen bride:[19] the Greeks are at Troy to restore Helen to her husband. The mythical Centaurs come to be used in literature and art as a type of the barbarian,[20] and in Nestor's story, they correspond at one level to the barbarian Trojans. Nestor offered advice on a previous occasion of (attempted) bride-stealing by stereotypical barbarians, the Centaurs, and his advice worked. Therefore, taking his advice should work now, when the Greeks are trying to recover another bride (Helen) stolen by barbarians (the Trojans).[21] Through this story from the past, Nestor can say that he was not on the side of the Centaurs when they tried out bride-stealing, and his advice on that occasion prevented the crime. The Trojans are bride-stealers, like the Centaurs, and Nestor's advice will help the Greeks defeat them.

None of this is subversive or dangerous for Nestor, but his third and deepest level of meaning can be expressed only in

[19] On the *Iliad* as a poem about bride-stealing, see Jamison (1994): the article contains unusual comparisons with Indic poetry.

[20] Hall (1989: 52–4, 68, 102, 134 n. 91); Boardman (1993: 24 and pl. V, 93, 203).

[21] On the interaction of Nestor's intervention in the battle against the Centaurs and his intervention in the quarrel between Agamemnon and Achilles, see Lang (1983: 141–2).

veiled terms if he is to avoid giving offence to Agamemnon. All the terms used of Nestor's rhetoric convey the approval of the poet: Nestor is ἡδυεπής, sweet-speaking,[22] the λιγὺς Πυλίων ἀγορητής, the shrill-voiced orator of the Pylians, whose speech flowed sweeter than honey from his tongue (*Il*. 1. 248–9). His advice is worth having, for he speaks ἐΰφρονέων, with prudent mind (*Il*. 1. 253). Nestor is too good an orator to indulge in the rhetoric of blame[23] and he tends to leave overt blame to others.[24] This does not mean that Nestor cannot reprimand or rebuke: he is perfectly able to convey disapproval in an elegant way, avoiding open and direct reproach. Nestor indicates his displeasure and his censure by telling stories which feature the action of which he is complaining. Open reproach is inflammatory: for example, Agamemnon complains (*Il*. 1. 291) of the ὀνείδεα (reproaches) uttered by Achilles, and Nestor rebukes Achilles for wrangling with Agamemnon ἀντιβίην (openly) (*Il*. 1. 278). Nestor's own approach is to avoid direct blame, but his story of the Lapiths and Centaurs implicitly criticizes Agamemnon by presenting the king with the classic example of his own behaviour in appropriating a woman belonging to another. Agamemnon has just threatened to compensate himself for the loss of Chryseis by carrying off a woman allocated as a prize to one of the other Greeks (*Il*. 1. 133–9). Through the story of his advice to the Lapiths when they fought the Centaurs, Nestor implies that Agamemnon is like the Centaurs who get drunk and attempt to steal women.[25] It was drink which inflamed the Centaurs to try to carry off the women at the Lapith wedding

---

[22] Pindar uses this epithet of Homer, *N*. 7. 21. On Nestor's rhetoric as the preferred style of speech among the archaic Greeks, see Martin (1989: 101–13).

[23] Martin (1989: 70).

[24] Achilles (*Il*. 1. 225–44); Thersites (*Il*. 2. 225–42); Diomede (*Il*. 9. 32–49). The exception is *Il*. 9. 104–111, where Nestor finds fault with Agamemnon for slighting Achilles, but the rebuke is delivered in the privacy of Agamemnon's tent, in the presence of the other γέροντες: Nestor does not blame Agamemnon openly in the public assembly.

[25] He is perhaps also implying that Agamemnon is not showing much sense: νοῦς οὐ παρὰ Κενταύροις, no sense among the Centaurs, was a proverb (Diogenianus, 6. 84 in Leutsch and Schneidewin (1958: i. 282). Diogenianus explains the Centaurs' lack of sense as ἐπιλησμονή (absent-mindedness) and being πλεονέκτης (greedy): this last is certainly relevant to Agamemnon's appropriation of Achilles' prize.

feast: οἶνος καὶ Κένταυρον . . . (ἄασε), 'wine (addled) the Centaur too' (*Od.* 21. 295).[26] Achilles calls Agamemnon οἰνοβαρές (*Il.* 1. 225), associating Agamemnon's threatened appropriation of his concubine with drunkenness, an idea taken up and developed in Nestor's use of the story of the Lapith victory over the drunken, bride-stealing centaurs. In this reading, Agamemnon corresponds to the drunken Centaur who wishes to steal a woman, and Achilles to the Lapiths, who succeeded in preventing bride-stealing by taking Nestor's advice. The mutual concessions advised by Nestor at the conclusion of his paradigmatic reminiscence are intended to prevent the theft of a woman: Agamemnon is not to deprive Achilles of Briseis, and Achilles is not to wrangle openly with the king (*Il.* 1. 275–9).[27] Nestor opens his speech of reproach by reminding the Greeks how gratified the Trojans would be if they knew of this quarrel. The Greeks have pursued the Trojans as bride-stealers: now, instead of concentrating their efforts against the enemy, they are themselves stealing one another's women. It would be impossible to say this of Agamemnon openly in the public assembly without uttering ὀνείδεα, reproaches, as indeed Agamemnon complains Achilles has done (*Il.* 1. 291).[28] However, the indirect reproach conveyed in Nestor's paradigm is acceptable, because the crime of the Centaurs is not openly attributed to anyone listening. Agamemnon acknowledges the justice of Nestor's reprimand, admitting Nestor has spoken κατὰ μοῖραν, fitly (*Il.* 1. 286). The point of the paradigm is taken, even if the advice offered is rejected.

[26] Antinous is implying that Odysseus is drunk like the Centaurs at the Lapith wedding feast: that is why he wants to string the bow and enter the competition to carry off Penelope (*Od.* 21. 293–310). For the Centaurs' susceptibility to drink, see Pindar, *fr.* 166 (Snell–Maehler): for Centaurs carrying off women from the wedding feast of Peirithous, see Zenobius, 5. 33 in Leutsch and Schneidewin (1958: i. 134).

[27] On Nestor's proposal of mutual concessions from both Agamemnon and Achilles, see White (1984: 36–7).

[28] The only other person to utter ὀνείδεα in an assembly is Thersites (*Il.* 2. 222, 251).

4.3. NESTOR AND EREUTHALION:
PERSONAL EXAMPLE IN SUPPORT OF νεῖκος
(*IL. 7. 132–56*)[29]

The second of Nestor's paradigmatic reminiscences concerns his defeat of the Arcadian champion Ereuthalion. Hector challenges the Greeks to put up a champion to meet him in single combat, and his challenge makes special allusion to the quality of the Greeks:

> ὑμῖν δ' ἐν γὰρ ἔασιν ἀριστῆες Παναχαιῶν·
> τῶν νῦν ὅν τινα θυμὸς ἐμοὶ μαχέσασθαι ἀνώγῃ,
> δεῦρ' ἴτω ἐκ πάντων πρόμος ἔμμεναι Ἕκτορι δίῳ.   75

For among you are the best of all the Achaeans:
let the one whose heart bids him fight with me
come out here in front of all to be a champion against godlike
    Hector.   75
         (*Il.* 7. 73–5)

But even so, no one comes forward to meet his challenge. Menelaus rebukes the cowardice of the dilatory Greeks with a νεῖκος (*Il.* 7. 96–102), calling them Ἀχαιΐδες, οὐκέτ' Ἀχαιοί, 'Achaean women, men no longer' (*Il.* 7. 96): he threatens to meet Hector's challenge himself (*Il.* 7. 101), a course of action which the poet indicates (*Il.* 7. 104–5) would be the end of him. Agamemnon has to dissuade his brother from this rash undertaking (*Il.* 7. 109–16),[30] and Nestor uses a νεῖκος to obtain a better response from the Greeks, taking up Hector's allusion to their quality in his references to their pedigrees, and offering for their imitation the example of his own response to a much more frightening challenge, that of the giant Ereuthalion, the Arcadians' champion in a war with the Pylians.[31] Wearing the

---

[29] For discussions of this passage, see Oehler (1925: 25); Gaisser (1969a: 8); Hebel (1970: 87–8).

[30] Agamemnon argues that even Achilles would think twice before tackling Hector. On this exaggeration of Hector's achievements, see Willcock (1977: 52).

[31] Nestor's story of his response to the Arcadian challenger has sometimes been thought to come from a body of traditional material on the subject of the wars between the Pylians and the Arcadians. The allusion to Ereuthalion at *Il.* 4. 319 is consistent with Nestor's account of him in book 7. However, chronological improbabilities in the details of book 7 suggest either adaptation of traditional material to provide correspondences with Hector's challenge in

armour given by Ares to Areïthous, the maceman whom
Lycurgus[32] killed, Ereuthalion προκαλίζετο πάντας ἀρίστους,
'challenged all the best of the Pylians'[33] but they all quaked
with fright (*Il.* 7. 150–1). The only one who dared respond to
the challenge was Nestor: although he was the youngest, he
made short work of the champion:[34]

ὢ πόποι, ἦ μέγα πένθος Ἀχαιΐδα γαῖαν ἱκάνει.
ἦ κε μέγ᾽ οἰμώξειε γέρων ἱππηλάτα Πηλεύς,   125
ἐσθλὸς Μυρμιδόνων βουληφόρος ἠδ᾽ ἀγορητής,
ὅς ποτέ μ᾽ εἰρόμενος μέγ᾽ ἐγήθεεν ᾧ ἐνὶ οἴκῳ,
πάντων Ἀργείων ἐρέων γενεήν τε τόκον τε.
τοὺς νῦν εἰ πτώσσοντας ὑφ᾽ Ἕκτορι πάντας ἀκοῦσαι,
πολλά κεν ἀθανάτοισι φίλας ἀνὰ χεῖρας ἀείραι,   130
θυμὸν ἀπὸ μελέων δῦναι δόμον Ἄϊδος εἴσω.
αἲ γάρ, Ζεῦ τε πάτερ καὶ Ἀθηναίη καὶ Ἄπολλον,

book 7, or invention by the poet specifically for the context. In either case
there is no particular concern for very small details. The chronological
difficulties are as follows: Nestor, whose life has extended over three generations (*Il.* 1. 250–3) killed Ereuthalion and stripped him of his armour long ago,
in his youth, perhaps over fifty years back. Ereuthalion had received his
armour from Lycurgus, the killer of the original owner, Areïthous, when
Lycurgus was old. Areïthous must therefore have been killed even more than
fifty years before the 'present', and his son, Menesthius of Arne, would have
to be over 50 when he is killed by Paris (*Il.* 7. 8–10). It is not impossible
that Menesthius is to be imagined in his fifties when he is killed at Troy, but
it seems more likely that the poet has concentrated on establishing the
provenance of the armour, and overlooked the minor point that verisimilitude
would require a grandson of Areïthous rather than a son to be killed by Paris
(Sch. T ad *Il.* 7. 9 (= Erbse (1969–88): ii. 230), 9c). Sch. bT ad *Il.* 7. 9 (= Erbse
(1969–88): ii. 229–30), 9b) introduces a second Areïthous to fill the gap. The
Arcadians altered the details of the story to present themselves in a more
heroic light: while Ereuthalion was still breathing, they attacked the Pylians
and defeated them. In the Arcadian version, the true victor in the single
combat was Ereuthalion, since Nestor disqualified himself by leaping for joy
as he delivered the death-blow. The leap brought Nestor down outside the
area designated for the duel: see Sch. bT ad *Il.* 4. 319 (= Erbse (1969–88): i.
504), 319b); Robert (1920: 193).

[32] Son of Aleus of Tegea: Apollodorus, 3. 9. 1–2; Pausanias, 8. 4. 8.

[33] Cf. ὑμῖν δ᾽ ἐν γὰρ ἔασιν ἀριστῆες Παναχαιῶν, 'for among you are the best of
all the Greeks' (*Il.* 7. 73).

[34] *Il.* 7. 151–3: Hebel (1970: 87–8) indicates the barb aimed at the Greek
leaders (who have so far failed to respond to the challenge of Hector) in Nestor
being the youngest of all his companions when he was the only one who
responded to the challenge of Ereuthalion.

ἤβωμ' ὡς ὅτ' ἐπ' ὠκυρόῳ Κελάδοντι μάχοντο
ἀγρόμενοι Πύλιοί τε καὶ Ἀρκάδες ἐγχεσίμωροι,
Φειᾶς πὰρ τείχεσσιν, Ἰαρδάνου ἀμφὶ ῥέεθρα.   135
τοῖσι δ' Ἐρευθαλίων πρόμος ἵστατο, ἰσόθεος φώς,
τεύχε' ἔχων ὤμοισιν Ἀρηϊθόοιο ἄνακτος,
δίου Ἀρηϊθόου, τὸν ἐπίκλησιν κορυνήτην
ἄνδρες κίκλησκον καλλίζωνοί τε γυναῖκες,
οὕνεκ' ἄρ' οὐ τόξοισι μαχέσκετο δουρί τε μακρῷ   140
ἀλλὰ σιδηρείῃ κορύνῃ ῥήγνυσκε φάλαγγας.
τὸν Λυκόοργος ἔπεφνε δόλῳ, οὔ τι κράτεΐ γε,
στεινωπῷ ἐν ὁδῷ, ὅθ' ἄρ' οὐ κορύνη οἱ ὄλεθρον
χραῖσμε σιδηρείη· πρὶν γὰρ Λυκόοργος ὑποφθὰς
δουρὶ μέσον περόνησεν, ὁ δ' ὕπτιος οὔδει ἐρείσθη·   145
τεύχεα δ' ἐξενάριξε, τά οἱ πόρε χάλκεος Ἄρης.
καὶ τὰ μὲν αὐτὸς ἔπειτα φόρει μετὰ μῶλον Ἄρηος·
αὐτὰρ ἐπεὶ Λυκόοργος ἐνὶ μεγάροισιν ἐγήρα,
δῶκε δ' Ἐρευθαλίωνι φίλῳ θεράποντι φορῆναι·
τοῦ ὅ γε τεύχε' ἔχων προκαλίζετο πάντας ἀρίστους.   150
οἱ δὲ μάλ' ἐτρόμεον καὶ ἐδείδισαν, οὐδέ τις ἔτλη·
ἀλλ' ἐμὲ θυμὸς ἀνῆκε πολυτλήμων πολεμίζειν
θάρσεϊ ᾧ· γενεῇ δὲ νεώτατος ἔσκον ἁπάντων·
καὶ μαχόμην οἱ ἐγώ, δῶκεν δέ μοι εὖχος Ἀθήνη.
τὸν δὴ μήκιστον καὶ κάρτιστον κτάνον ἄνδρα·   155
πολλὸς γάρ τις ἔκειτο παρήορος ἔνθα καὶ ἔνθα.

O alas, to be sure a great grief is coming to the land of Greece.
How the old man, the horseman, Peleus would lament bitterly,   125
the noble counsellor and orator of the Myrmidons,
who, on one occasion in his house, took great pleasure when he asked
    me
and I told him the family and birth of all the Argives.
If he heard that they were all now cowering at the sight of Hector,
he would fervently raise his arms to the gods,   130
that his spirit should enter the house of Hades.
If only, father Zeus, and Athene, and Apollo,
I were young, as when, by the swift-flowing Celadon,
the country-dwelling Pylians and the spear-fighting Arcadians fought,
beside the walls of Pheia, around the streams of Iardanus.   135
And Ereuthalion, a mortal equal to a god, set himself up as their
    champion,
bearing on his shoulders the gear of lord Areïthous,
godlike Areïthous, whom men and fair-girdled women
called by the nickname 'maceman',
because he habitually fought, not with bows and with a long spear,

but he always shattered the ranks with an iron mace.   141
Lycurgus killed him, by treachery and not by might,
in a narrow place on the road, where the mace did not ward off
destruction from him: for before that, Lycurgus anticipated him
and skewered him through the middle with a spear, and he was
    stretched out on his back on the ground:
and he stripped off the gear which brazen Ares provided him.   146
And then he bore the arms in the turmoil of Ares:
but when Lycurgus grew old in the halls,
he gave them to his own companion in arms, Ereuthalion, to wear.
And he, bearing his arms, was challenging all the best.   150
But they trembled very much and were afraid, nor had anyone the
    courage,
but my all-enduring heart with my hardy spirit set me up to combat:
and I was the youngest of all.
And I fought with him, and Pallas Athene gave me the victory.
he was certainly the tallest and the strongest man I killed: 155
for a mighty man he lay there, sprawling this way and that.

                                                    (*Il.* 7. 124–56)

Nestor is comparing the alacrity of his own response to the
challenge of the Arcadian champion long ago with the present
dilatory reaction of the Greeks to the challenge issued by
Hector (*Il.* 7. 38–43). The story of Nestor's exploit is arranged
in the middle of his speech between two passages of invective
against the cowardice of the Greeks.[35] In the first passage (*Il.* 7.
124–31) Nestor conveys his own poor opinion of the Greeks
and their failure to respond to the challenge by attributing
his views on this subject to Peleus: Peleus might once have
delighted in hearing Nestor relate the birth and lineage of
all the Greeks, but now they fall short of the promise of their
pedigrees. If Peleus were to hear how they cower at the sight
of Hector, he would throw up his hands and pray for death
immediately (*Il.* 7. 125–31). This reproach is supported by the
hortatory paradigm, describing in detail an incident to which
Nestor has already alluded in passing (*Il.* 4. 319): his victory
over the Arcadian champion Ereuthalion, who challenged the
Pylians and perished in combat with Nestor. Nestor's speech
concludes with more invective (*Il.* 7. 157–60), this time a direct
reproach to drive home the message of his story about
Ereuthalion: if he had his youth and strength, Hector would

---

[35] For the arrangement of the speech, see Lohmann (1970: 27–8).

soon find he had an opponent, but the ἀριστῆες Παναχαιῶν, 'the best of the Greeks' today, do not measure up to Nestor's pugnacity in his long-lost youth (*Il.* 7. 157–60).

Nestor directs the focus of attention on Ereuthalion to his armour, and we hear much more about Ereuthalion's armour than we hear about him. Ereuthalion comes from nowhere, and Nestor dispatches him in a single line:

καὶ μαχόμην οἱ ἐγώ, δῶκεν δέ μοι εὖχος Ἀθήνη

and I fought with him and Athene gave me the victory   (*Il.* 7. 154)

but no less than fourteen lines are dedicated to the provenance of his armour (*Il.* 7. 137–59).[36] Nestor establishes that the Greeks have pedigrees, even if they do not live up to them, since he described them to Peleus (*Il.* 7. 127–8), but the only pedigree associated with Ereuthalion is that of his armour. We are not told even his father's name,[37] either in book 7 or at *Il.* 4. 319. Ereuthalion's armour was originally the gift of Ares to the maceman Areïthous,[38] who fell victim δόλῳ οὔ τι κράτεΐ γε, 'to guile, not might' (*Il.* 7. 142). Lycurgus[39] cornered him in a narrow place where he could not swing his mace, and ran him through with a spear before he could strike.[40] Lycurgus stripped the armour from the body of Areïthous, and when he grew old, he gave it to his θεράπων, comrade (of inferior status), Ereuthalion (*Il.* 7. 148–9). In this way Nestor conveys that Ereuthalion, for all his size and strength, is not the real thing at all: he is a θεράπων, wearing armour stripped from a corpse he did not kill. Ereuthalion makes a frightening impression, but he is a hollow man, merely the wearer of a suit of armour. Ereuthalion, the challenger of Nestor's story, corresponds, of course, to the present challenger, Hector. Nestor made short

---

[36] The nearest equivalent provenance is that of the boars' tusk helmet, which has passed through the hands of five previous owners before Odysseus wears it (*Il.* 10. 266–71). Autolycus, who stole it, has associations with cunning and guile appropriate to the context of the Doloneia (see Austin (1978: 83; 1st pub. 1966)).

[37] The absence of a patronymic indicates a man lacking in status, who has no identity (see van Groningen (1953: 53–4)). Thersites is introduced without a patronymic (*Il.* 2. 212).

[38] Areïthous appears as a maceman in Pherecydes, *FGrH* 3. 138.

[39] No relation to the Lycurgus of *Il.* 6. 130–40.

[40] Nestor is hinting that δόλος is the way to deal with a terrifying adversary.

work of Ereuthalion, in spite of the terrifying impression
created by the armour-plated champion: he is implying that
whoever responds to Hector's challenge will make short work
of him too, for all the terror he inspires.[41] Nestor's image of
Ereuthalion and his distinguished armour echoes the emphasis
in Hector's challenge on the prospect of stripping armour from
a vanquished enemy. Nestor's description of Areïthous
stretched out dead on the ground, ὁ δ' ὕπτιος οὔδει ἐρείσθη, 'he
was laid out on his back upon the ground' (*Il.* 7. 145), will be
echoed in the description of Hector stretched out on the ground
by the Greek champion, Ajax: ὁ δ' ὕπτιος ἐξετανύσθη, 'he was
stretched out at full length on his back' (*Il.* 7. 271). Nestor is
not entirely fair to dismiss Hector as a negligible adversary by
comparing him to Ereuthalion, who was so easily dealt with.
Even Achilles would be afraid to confront Hector, according to
Agamemnon (*Il.* 7. 113–14). (Significantly, Agamemnon has
not himself taken the opportunity to volunteer.) Nevertheless,
the story of Nestor's response to the challenge of Ereuthalion is
successful as a method of inciting the Greeks to take up
Hector's challenge: at the conclusion of his speech, nine of the
Greek leaders offer to meet Hector (*Il.* 7. 161–8), and the final
choice, Ajax, has to be decided by drawing lots (*Il.* 7. 171).

4.4. NESTOR AND PATROCLUS (*IL.* 11. 605–803): THE CATTLE RAID AGAINST THE ELEIANS[42]

The longest secondary narrative of the *Iliad*, and the third of
Nestor's stories of his heroic past, is that told by Nestor to
Patroclus in book 11. Patroclus is sent by Achilles to Nestor to
find out the name of the casualty Nestor carried off the field (*Il.*
11. 517–18) from the battle in which Agamemnon, Diomede,
and Odysseus are also wounded. As soon as he arrives in
Nestor's tent, Patroclus recognizes the wounded man Achilles

---

[41] See Lohmann (1970: 78 n. 135) for an interpretation which sees the point
of the story as the contrast between Ereuthalion and Hector: Nestor was not
afraid of a giant like Ereuthalion, but the Greeks are afraid of a nonentity like
Hector.

[42] For discussions of this passage see Oehler (1925: 24); Bölte (1934);
Schadewaldt (1966: 82–94; 1st pub. 1938); Gaisser (1969*a*: 5–6, 9–13); Hebel
(1970: 33–6); Austin (1978: 75–6).

saw carried from the battlefield (*Il.* 11. 598–9) as Machaon (*Il.* 11. 651). However, Nestor's long speech prevents Patroclus from returning immediately to convey the name of the wounded man to Achilles. Nestor begins his speech with irony: feigning amazement, he wonders why Achilles is grieving over the sufferings of the Greeks.[43] Then Nestor gives a catalogue of Greeks who have been wounded (*Il.* 11. 659–62), which Patroclus repeats exactly to Achilles (*Il.* 16. 24–7): nowhere is there any reference to Machaon. Achilles is told the names of the Greeks Nestor wishes him to know are wounded, and not the name he tried to discover by sending Patroclus to find it out.[44] Nestor criticizes Achilles for doing nothing but watch the sufferings of the other Greeks, and for refusing to return to battle until the ships are fired (*Il.* 11. 664–7). Then he goes on to describe his own role in a skirmish between the Pylians and the Eleians in his youth:

εἴθ' ὡς ἡβώοιμι βίη δέ μοι ἔμπεδος εἴη,   670
ὡς ὁπότ' Ἠλείοισι καὶ ἡμῖν νεῖκος ἐτύχθη
ἀμφὶ βοηλασίῃ, ὅτ' ἐγὼ κτάνον Ἰτυμονῆα,
ἐσθλὸν Ὑπειροχίδην, ὃς ἐν Ἤλιδι ναιετάασκε,
ῥύσι' ἐλαυνόμενος· ὁ δ' ἀμύνων ᾗσι βόεσσιν
ἔβλητ' ἐν πρώτοισιν ἐμῆς ἀπὸ χειρὸς ἄκοντι,   675
κὰδ' δ' ἔπεσεν, λαοὶ δὲ περίτρεσαν ἀγροιῶται.
ληΐδα δ' ἐκ πεδίου συνελάσσαμεν ἤλιθα πολλήν,
πεντήκοντα βοῶν ἀγέλας, τόσα πώεα οἰῶν,
τόσσα συῶν συβόσια, τόσ' αἰπόλια πλατέ' αἰγῶν,
ἵππους δὲ ξανθὰς ἑκατὸν καὶ πεντήκοντα,   680
πάσας θηλείας, πολλῇσι δὲ πῶλοι ὑπῆσαν.
καὶ τὰ μὲν ἠλασάμεσθα Πύλον Νηλήϊον εἴσω
ἐννύχιοι προτὶ ἄστυ· γεγήθει δὲ φρένα Νηλεύς,
οὕνεκά μοι τύχε πολλὰ νέῳ πόλεμόνδε κιόντι.
κήρυκες δ' ἐλίγαινον ἅμ' ἠοῖ φαινομένηφι   685
τοὺς ἴμεν οἷσι χρεῖος ὀφείλετ' ἐν Ἤλιδι δίῃ·
οἱ δὲ συναγρόμενοι Πυλίων ἡγήτορες ἄνδρες
δαίτρευον· πολέσιν γὰρ Ἐπειοὶ χρεῖος ὄφειλον,
ὡς ἡμεῖς παῦροι κεκακωμένοι ἐν Πύλῳ ἦμεν·

---

[43] Achilles himself will echo this question when he enquires why Patroclus is weeping like a little girl: could it be that Patroclus pities the Greeks (*Il.* 16. 7–8; 17–19)?

[44] For discussion of Nestor's transformation of Patroclus from the agent of Achilles' enquiry to the agent of Nestor's will, see Reinhardt (1961: 258–64).

ἐλθὼν γάρ ῥ᾽ ἐκάκωσε βίη Ἡρακληείη   690
τῶν προτέρων ἐτέων, κατὰ δ᾽ ἔκταθεν ὅσσοι ἄριστοι·
δώδεκα γὰρ Νηλῆος ἀμύμονος υἱέες ἦμεν·
τῶν οἶος λιπόμην, οἱ δ᾽ ἄλλοι πάντες ὄλοντο.
ταῦθ᾽ ὑπερηφανέοντες Ἐπειοὶ χαλκοχίτωνες,
ἡμέας ὑβρίζοντες, ἀτάσθαλα μηχανόωντο.   695
ἐκ δ᾽ ὁ γέρων ἀγέλην τε βοῶν καὶ πῶϋ μέγ᾽ οἰῶν
εἵλετο, κρινάμενος τριηκόσι᾽ ἠδὲ νομῆας.
καὶ γὰρ τῷ χρεῖος μέγ᾽ ὀφείλετ᾽ ἐν Ἤλιδι δίῃ
τέσσαρες ἀθλοφόροι ἵπποι αὐτοῖσιν ὄχεσφιν,
ἐλθόντες μετ᾽ ἄεθλα· περὶ τρίποδος γὰρ ἔμελλον   700
θεύσεσθαι· τοὺς δ᾽ αὖθι ἄναξ ἀνδρῶν Αὐγείας
κάσχεθε, τὸν δ᾽ ἐλατῆρ᾽ ἀφίει ἀκαχήμενον ἵππων.
τῶν ὁ γέρων ἐπέων κεχολωμένος ἠδὲ καὶ ἔργων
ἐξέλετ᾽ ἄσπετα πολλά· τὰ δ᾽ ἄλλ᾽ ἐς δῆμον ἔδωκε
δαιτρεύειν, μή τίς οἱ ἀτεμβόμενος κίοι ἴσης.   705
ἡμεῖς μὲν τὰ ἔκαστα διείπομεν, ἀμφί τε ἄστυ
ἔρδομεν ἱρὰ θεοῖς· οἱ δὲ τρίτῳ ἤματι[45] πάντες
ἦλθον ὁμῶς αὐτοί τε πολεῖς καὶ μώνυχες ἵπποι
πανσυδίῃ· μετὰ δέ σφι Μολίονε θωρήσσοντο
παῖδ᾽ ἔτ᾽ ἐόντ᾽, οὔ πω μάλα εἰδότε θούριδος ἀλκῆς.   710
ἔστι δέ τις Θρυόεσσα πόλις, αἰπεῖα κολώνη,
τηλοῦ ἐπ᾽ Ἀλφειῷ, νεάτη Πύλου ἠμαθόεντος·
τὴν ἀμφεστρατόωντο διαρραῖσαι μεμαῶτες.
ἀλλ᾽ ὅτε πᾶν πεδίον μετεκίαθον, ἄμμι δ᾽ Ἀθήνη
ἄγγελος ἦλθε θέουσ᾽ ἀπ᾽ Ὀλύμπου θωρήσσεσθαι   715
ἔννυχος, οὐδ᾽ ἀέκοντα Πύλον κάτα λαὸν ἄγειρεν,
ἀλλὰ μάλ᾽ ἐσσυμένους πολεμίζειν. οὐδέ με Νηλεὺς
εἴα θωρήσσεσθαι, ἀπέκρυψεν δέ μοι ἵππους·
οὐ γάρ πώ τί μ᾽ ἔφη ἴδμεν πολεμήϊα ἔργα.
ἀλλὰ καὶ ὣς ἱππεῦσι μετέπρεπον ἡμετέροισι   720
καὶ πεζός περ ἐών, ἐπεὶ ὣς ἄγε νεῖκος Ἀθήνη.
ἔστι δέ τις ποταμὸς Μινυήϊος εἰς ἅλα βάλλων
ἐγγύθεν Ἀρήνης, ὅθι μείναμεν Ἠῶ δῖαν
ἱππῆες Πυλίων, τὰ δ᾽ ἐπέρρεον ἔθνεα πεζῶν.
ἔνθεν πανσυδίῃ σὺν τεύχεσι θωρηχθέντες   725
ἔνδιοι ἱκόμεσθ᾽ ἱερὸν ῥόον Ἀλφειοῖο.
ἔνθα Διὶ ῥέξαντες ὑπερμενεῖ ἱερὰ καλά,

[45] The detail that the Epeians attacked on the third day after the Pylians' division of the spoil indicates the relevance of the story to the present situation of the Greeks: the action of the poem is now at the third day after the quarrel over spoil between Achilles and Agamemnon (day 1 ends at *Il.* 1. 605; day 2 at *Il.* 8. 485–8), and the Trojans are attacking the Greek ships.

ταῦρον δ' Ἀλφειῷ, ταῦρον δὲ Ποσειδάωνι,
αὐτὰρ Ἀθηναίῃ γλαυκώπιδι βοῦν ἀγελαίην,
δόρπον ἔπειθ' ἑλόμεσθα κατὰ στρατὸν ἐν τελέεσσι,   730
καὶ κατεκοιμήθημεν ἐν ἔντεσιν οἷσιν ἕκαστος
ἀμφὶ ῥοὰς ποταμοῖο. ἀτὰρ μεγάθυμοι Ἐπειοὶ
ἀμφίσταντο δὴ ἄστυ διαρραῖσαι μεμαῶτες·
ἀλλά σφι προπάροιθε φάνη μέγα ἔργον Ἄρηος·
εὖτε γὰρ ἠέλιος φαέθων ὑπερέσχεθε γαίης,   735
συμφερόμεσθα μάχῃ, Διί τ' εὐχόμενοι καὶ Ἀθήνῃ.
ἀλλ' ὅτε δὴ Πυλίων καὶ Ἐπειῶν ἔπλετο νεῖκος,
πρῶτος ἐγὼν ἕλον ἄνδρα, κόμισσα δὲ μώνυχας ἵππους,
Μούλιον αἰχμητήν· γαμβρὸς δ' ἦν Αὐγείαο,
πρεσβυτάτην δὲ θύγατρ' εἶχε ξανθὴν Ἀγαμήδην,   740
ἣ τόσα φάρμακα ᾔδη ὅσα τρέφει εὐρεῖα χθών.
τὸν μὲν ἐγὼ προσιόντα βάλον χαλκήρεϊ δουρί,
ἤριπε δ' ἐν κονίῃσιν· ἐγὼ δ' ἐς δίφρον ὀρούσας
στῆν ῥα μετὰ προμάχοισιν· ἀτὰρ μεγάθυμοι Ἐπειοὶ
ἔτρεσαν ἄλλυδις ἄλλος, ἐπεὶ ἴδον ἄνδρα πεσόντα   745
ἡγεμόν' ἱππήων, ὃς ἀριστεύεσκε μάχεσθαι.
αὐτὰρ ἐγὼν ἐπόρουσα κελαινῇ λαίλαπι ἶσος,
πεντήκοντα δ' ἕλον δίφρους, δύο δ' ἀμφὶς ἕκαστον
φῶτες ὀδὰξ ἕλον οὖδας ἐμῷ ὑπὸ δουρὶ δαμέντες.
καί νύ κεν Ἀκτορίωνε Μολίονε παῖδ' ἀλάπαξα,   750
εἰ μή σφωε πατὴρ εὐρὺ κρείων ἐνοσίχθων
ἐκ πολέμου ἐσάωσε, καλύψας ἠέρι πολλῇ.
ἔνθα Ζεὺς Πυλίοισι μέγα κράτος ἐγγυάλιξε·
τόφρα γὰρ οὖν ἑπόμεσθα διὰ σπιδέος πεδίοιο,
κτείνοντές τ' αὐτούς ἀνά τ' ἔντεα καλὰ λέγοντες,   755
ὄφρ' ἐπὶ Βουπρασίου πολυπύρου βήσαμεν ἵππους
πέτρης τ' Ὠλενίης, καὶ Ἀλησίου ἔνθα κολώνη
κέκληται· ὅθεν αὖτις ἀπέτραπε λαὸν Ἀθήνη.
ἔνθ' ἄνδρα κτείνας πύματον λίπον· αὐτὰρ Ἀχαιοὶ
ἂψ ἀπὸ Βουπρασίοιο Πύλονδ' ἔχον ὠκέας ἵππους,   760
πάντες δ' εὐχετόωντο θεῶν Διὶ Νέστορί τ' ἀνδρῶν.
ὡς ἔον, εἴ ποτ' ἔον γε, μετ' ἀνδράσιν.

If only I were young and my strength were unfailing   670
as when a quarrel broke out between us and the Eleians
about cattle-rustling, when I killed Itymoneus,
the noble son of Hypeirochos, who used to live in Elis.
I was driving off his cattle in reprisal, but he, defending his cattle,
was struck among the front-fighters by a javelin from my hand,   675
and he fell, and the rustic war host fled on every side.
Then we rounded up booty from the plain, a very great deal,

fifty herds of cattle, as many flocks of sheep,
as many herds of swine, as many wide-grazing herds of goats,
and a hundred and fifty chestnut horses,   680
all mares, and there were foals under many of them.
And these we drove into Neleian Pylos
in the night-time to the city: and Neleus rejoiced in his heart,
because of such success for me going into battle as a young man.
And the heralds cried out with clear voice as soon as the dawn
    appeared,
for all to come to whom a debt was owed in holy Elis.   686
And the leading men of the Pylians gathered together
and made the distribution: for the Epeians owed a debt to many,
as we were few in Pylos, and weakened:
for the mighty Heracles came and weakened us   690
in former years, and all the best he killed,
for we had been twelve sons of the blameless Neleus:
of whom only I was left, and all the others had perished.
The bronze-shirted Epeians grew contemptuous at these things
and treated us with arrogance, and devised wicked deeds.   695
And the old man selected a herd of cattle and a large flock of sheep
picking out three hundred, with shepherds as well.
For a great debt was owed to him too in holy Elis,
four prize-winning horses, chariot and all,
which had gone after prizes: for they were about to race   700
for a tripod: but lord of men Augeias kept them there,
but their driver he sent away grieving for the horses.
The old man, angered at these things, Augeias' words and deeds,
chose a vast quantity for himself: the rest he gave to the people
to divide, so that none of his people should go deprived of his fair
    share.
And so we were settling each score, and around the city   706
we were making sacrifices to the gods; but on the third day the
    Epeians all came,
and there were many of them and many single-hooved horses
and they came with all haste: and with them the Molione were up in
    arms
although they were still boys, not yet experienced in impetuous might.
And there is a city, Thryoessa, a steep hill,   711
far off on the Alpheios, on the border of sandy Pylos:
they encamped around it, eager to destroy it utterly.
But when they were swarming over the whole plain, Athene
came to us in the night, rushing from Olympus, a messenger that we
    must arm,

and throughout Pylos she raised an army not at all unwilling,   716
but very eager to fight. And Neleus did not permit me
to arm myself, and he concealed my horses:
for he said I did not yet know the works of war.
But even so I took a distinguished place among our horsemen   720
although I was an infantryman, since Athene conducted the quarrel so.
There is a river Minyeïos emptying into the sea
near Arene, where we awaited the holy dawn,
we, the Pylian horsemen, while the troops of infantry streamed in.
Then with all haste we were armed with our gear   725
and at midday we came to the holy stream of the Alpheios.
There we made fair sacrifices to mighty Zeus,
and a bull for Alpheios and a bull for Poseidon,
but for grey-eyed Athene, a cow from the herd,
and then we took our dinner throughout the camp in our divisions,
and we went to sleep, every man in his gear   731
by the streams of the river. But the great-hearted Epeians
were surrounding the town, eager to destroy it completely:
but a great work of Ares unfolded before them:
for as the steed of the sun rose above the earth,   735
we met them for battle, with prayers to Zeus and to Athene.
But when indeed the strife of the Pylians and Epeians occurred,
I was the first to kill a man, and carry off his single-hooved horses.
He was Moulios, the spearman: he was the son-in-law of Augeias,
and he was married to the eldest daughter, the fair Agamede,   740
who knew every drug the broad earth produces.
As he approached I struck him with a bronze-tipped spear,
and he fell in the dust: and I rushing into the chariot
took my place with the front-fighters: but the great-hearted Epeians
fled this way and that, when they saw the man fall,   745
the leader of their horsemen, who was always the best at fighting.
But I rushed headlong after them, like the dark whirlwind,
and I captured fifty chariots, and about each one
two men bit the ground with their teeth, tamed under my spear.
And now I would have slain the two sons of Actor, the Molione, two
    boys,
had not their father, the wide-ruling Earthshaker   751
rescued them from the battle, concealing them with heavy mist.
Then Zeus granted great might to the Pylians,
for we chased them as I have described over the broad plain,
killing them, and picking up their fine gear,   755
and we brought our horses to Bouprasion, rich in wheat,
and the Olenian rock, and the place of the hill called Alesion

whence Athene turned the war host back again.
There I killed my last man and left him: but the Greeks
turned their swift horses back from Bouprasion to Pylos,   760
and all glorified Zeus among the gods and Nestor among men.
Thus was I, if ever I was, among men.

(*Il.* 11. 670–762)

In the first half of his story, Nestor describes his central role in
a retaliatory cattle raid on Eleian territory and the subsequent
division of the resulting spoil. Neleus compensates himself
handsomely from the booty for the theft of a chariot and prize-
winning horses (*Il.* 11. 699–702) and the people divide the
remainder of the spoil among themselves. In the second part of
the story, when the Eleians invade Pylian territory to seek
vengeance for the raid, Neleus refuses to give Nestor horses
and equipment to fight against the invaders, arguing (rather
illogically)[46] that his son is inexperienced in warfare. Neleus'
anxiety is understandable: Nestor is all he has left since his
other sons were killed by Heracles (*Il.* 11. 692–3). Despite his
father's prohibition, Nestor fights anyway,[47] on foot at first (*Il.*
11. 721), but then he captures Moulios' chariot (*Il.* 11. 730–9)
and fifty others, and would have killed even the Molione
(who were twins, possibly Siamese twins)[48] if they had not been
rescued by Poseidon (*Il.* 11. 750–2). The Pylians drive their
enemies from their territory, stripping corpses as they go (*Il.*
11. 755), and the hero of the day is Nestor: the Pylians pray to
him as to a god (*Il.* 11. 761).

Bölte[49] regarded this tale as a piece of Late Helladic epic, and
paid much attention to its accurate knowledge of the topo-
graphy of the Pylos region. Hainsworth[50] displays similar
interest in the topographical information, and shares Bölte's

[46] As indicated by Lohmann (1970: 75 n. 131). Hebel (1970: 33–4)
associates Neleus' attempt to prevent Nestor from fighting with the motif of
father or mother attempting to prevent a son from fighting. But the point is
surely that Neleus tries to prevent Nestor from fighting because we need an
example of fighting in the face of opposition: Achilles may try to prevent
Patroclus from fighting, but Patroclus must fight anyway.

[47] For analysis of the fighting, see Fenik (1968: 113–14).

[48] See below, n. 69. It is worth noting that the twins are called the sons of
Actor, but their real father is Poseidon (Sch. A ad *Il.* 11. 750, citing Hesiod, *fr.*
176 M–W) (from Aristonicus) (= Erbse (1969–88: iii. 272), 750).

[49] (1934: 345).

[50] Hainsworth (1993: 296–8 ad *Il.* 11. 670–762).

view that Nestor's story is a fragment of genuinely traditional material, rather than an invention for the occasion as argued by Willcock.[51] The purpose of Nestor's tale, according to Hainsworth, is twofold: Nestor is using an incident from his heroic youth 'firstly to insist upon his credentials and the value of his words . . . and secondly to admonish or exhort. The crucial lines therefore are *Il.* 11. 716–21, where we hear of the eagerness of the Pylians to fight and Nestor's insistence, in spite of his father's opposition, on being their leader; they imply that Patroclus should overcome Akhilleus' opposition and insist on leading the eager Myrmidons to war.'[52] I would agree broadly with Hainsworth as far as he goes, at least on the second purpose of Nestor's story, but he does not draw sufficient attention to the extraordinarily close match between the events described by Nestor and the career of Patroclus in the *Iliad.* Hainsworth ignores Nestor's purpose, with its sinister implications for Patroclus, in retailing all this information to him in their interview.

Certain details of Nestor's story correspond to the situation of the Greeks when the story is told. Agamemnon, Diomede, Odysseus (and Eurypylus) are wounded and out of action (*Il.* 11. 658–64) just as, when Nestor led the cattle raid in the first part of his story, his brothers were out of action because Heracles had killed them (*Il.* 11. 690–3). Other details are more difficult to interpret. We are told how, in spite of Nestor's success in the cattle raid of the first part of the story, his father, Neleus, tried to prevent him from driving back the retaliatory attack by the Epeians three days later, on the grounds that Nestor was too inexperienced in fighting. Nestor fought anyway, and pursued the raiders back into their territory. But how does this information relate to the personal and psychological relationships among the Greeks at the time of its telling: who among the Greeks is holding back whom from the fighting? Which of the Greeks fights anyway, and pursues the raiders into their territory?

The person expected to follow the example of Nestor's energetic heroism is generally taken to be Achilles,[53] doubtless

---

[51] (1977: 44).

[52] Hainsworth (1993: 296).

[53] Oehler (1925: 24): Nestor sets his own exploits against Achilles'

because of Nestor's many references to him. Nestor enquires why Achilles is grieving over the Greeks (*Il.* 11. 656). He criticizes his lack of compassion (*Il.* 11. 664–8): Achilles will be the only one to benefit from his heroism (*Il.* 11. 762–3). Is Achilles going to wait until all the Greeks are dead? If so, he will regret it (*Il.* 11. 763–5). Achilles' father commanded him always to be the best, and to surpass the others (*Il.* 11. 784). Nestor's reference to the paternal advice of Peleus and Menoetius is to 'remind' Patroclus of Menoetius' injunction to give good advice to Achilles (*Il.* 11. 786–9). Patroclus should see if he can persuade Achilles to fight (*Il.* 11. 790–1). The advice attributed to Menoetius is really Nestor's advice to Patroclus. The most perfunctory paternal instruction is ascribed to Peleus to balance the advice of Menoetius to Patroclus.[54] Certainly it is to Achilles that Nestor himself refers as soon as he has related the exploits of his youth:

αὐτὰρ Ἀχιλλεὺς
οἶος τῆς ἀρετῆς ἀπονήσεται· ἦ τέ μιν οἴω
πολλὰ μετακλαύσεσθαι, ἐπεί κ' ἀπὸ λαὸς ὄληται.

> but Achilles
> alone will have the enjoyment of his courage: in truth
> I think he will weep bitterly later on, when the army has perished.
>
> (*Il.* 11. 762–4)

Nestor contrasts the rapturous reception the Pylians gave to his heroism with the isolation of Achilles' alienated position:[55] no one is going to have much benefit from Achilles' ἀρετή if he remains inactive, and a day will come when he regrets his inactivity. Patroclus is intended to retail Nestor's indirect encouragement to Achilles to re-enter the battle: this is the

inactivity; see also Schadewaldt (1966: 82–9; 1st pub. 1938), who argues that the story of Nestor's youthful exploit is developed from a pre-existing source to provide a pattern for Achilles to imitate. Schadewaldt infers the existence of a 'source' from the consistency of the names associated with Nestor here and in his other exploits (Schadewaldt (1966: 85 n. 2); Hebel (1970: 35); Lohmann (1970: 74–5); Austin (1978: 75–6; 1st pub. 1966); Pedrick (1983: esp. 57–9); Martin (1989: 80–1). For the view that *Il.* 11. 671–762 express Nestor's wish to recover the lost strength of youth (as also at *Il.* 23. 629–31) see Bowra (1930: 86); Cantieni (1942: 21–2).

[54] On the reasons for the inconsistency of Peleus' advice in *Il.* 11. 784 with his advice at *Il.* 9. 254–8, see Willcock (1977: 46–7).

[55] Wilamowitz (1920: 203); Schadewaldt (1966: 85; 1st pub. 1938).

usual interpretation of the advice Nestor says Menoetius gave
his son before the expedition left for Troy:

τέκνον ἐμόν, γενεῇ μὲν ὑπέρτερός ἐστιν Ἀχιλλεύς,
πρεσβύτερος δὲ σύ ἐσσι· βίῃ δ' ὅ γε πολλὸν ἀμείνων.
ἀλλ' εὖ οἱ φάσθαι πυκινὸν ἔπος ἠδ' ὑποθέσθαι
καί οἱ σημαίνειν· ὁ δὲ πείσεται εἰς ἀγαθόν περ.

My child, Achilles is the nobler by birth,
but you are the elder: in might he is far better,
but you might well speak a wise word to him, and instruct
and advise him: and he will obey for his own good.

(*Il.* 11. 786–9)

So Schadewaldt argues that Nestor's speech is aimed primarily
at Achilles: only from *Il.* 11. 764, where the advice of Peleus
and Menoetius to their departing sons is mentioned in support
of the two aims set for Patroclus at the end, does the speech
refer in the first instance to Patroclus as Achilles' adviser.[56]
Pedrick even argues that Nestor is telling his story to the wrong
addressee: it is meant, not for Patroclus, but for Achilles.[57]
However, Nestor is the supreme orator of the Greeks: he is not
a bungler who cannot tailor his arguments to their addressee.
In this case Nestor's addressee is Patroclus, and we should try
to see how Nestor's speech relates to him. The suggestion that
Nestor's speech is really meant for Achilles pays too little attention to three parts of it: (1) the significant information that
Nestor fought against his father's wishes; (2) Nestor pursued
the raiders into their own territory; (3) Patroclus is given two
alternative goals: (*a*) to persuade Achilles to fight, or (*b*) if
Achilles has some reason for not fighting, Patroclus must ask to
be allowed himself to return to the fighting in the armour of
Achilles, so that the Trojans think he is Achilles and hold off
from battle:

ἀλλ' ἔτι καὶ νῦν   790
ταῦτ' εἴποις Ἀχιλῆϊ δαΐφρονι, αἴ κε πίθηται.
τίς δ' οἶδ' εἴ κέν οἱ σὺν δαίμονι θυμὸν ὀρίναις
παρειπών; ἀγαθὴ δὲ παραίφασίς ἐστιν ἑταίρου.
εἰ δέ τινα φρεσὶν ᾗσι θεοπροπίην ἀλεείνει
καί τινά οἱ πὰρ Ζηνὸς ἐπέφραδε πότνια μήτηρ,   795

---

[56] Schadewaldt (1966: 87; 1st pub. 1938), followed by Hebel (1970: 59–61).
[57] Pedrick (1983: 59–61), followed by Martin (1989: 80–1).

ἀλλὰ σέ περ προέτω, ἅμα δ' ἄλλος λαὸς ἐπέσθω
Μυρμιδόνων, αἴ κέν τι φόως Δαναοῖσι γένηαι·
καί τοι τεύχεα καλὰ δότω πόλεμόνδε φέρεσθαι,
αἴ κέ σε τῷ εἴσκοντες ἀπόσχωνται πολέμοιο
Τρῶες, ἀναπνεύσωσι δ' ἀρήϊοι υἷες Ἀχαιῶν   800
τειρόμενοι· ὀλίγη δέ τ' ἀνάπνευσις πολέμοιο.
ῥεῖα δέ κ' ἀκμῆτες κεκμηότας ἄνδρας ἀϋτῇ
ὤσαισθε προτὶ ἄστυ νεῶν ἄπο καὶ κλισιάων.

But even now
you might say these things to warlike Achilles, he might be persuaded.
Who knows whether, with God's help, you might move his heart
with your persuasions? The advice of a comrade is an excellent thing.
And if in his heart he is avoiding some prophecy
and his lady mother has given him some message from Zeus,   795
then let him send you, at least, and let the rest of the army of the
     Myrmidons
go with you, and you might become the salvation of the Greeks.
And let him give his fine gear to you to wear into war,
in case the Trojans liken you to him, and desist from the war,
and the warlike sons of the Achaeans have a breathing-space   800
when they are weary. There is little breathing-space in war.
Easily would unwearied men force men exhausted by the battle
back to the city, away from the ships and tents.

(*Il.* 11. 790–803)

It is not difficult to see where my argument is going: Nestor
was the salvation of the Pylians: Patroclus could be the salva-
tion of the Greeks. Nestor is presenting his own example for
Patroclus to imitate, and there is nothing indirect about it.
Nestor fought against his father's wishes and won the day: if
Patroclus cannot persuade Achilles either to fight in person or
to allow him, Patroclus, to fight wearing Achilles' armour,
Patroclus may have to fight anyway, against Achilles' wishes.[58]

[58] Lohmann (1970: 75) thinks the point is in the contrast between Achilles
and Nestor: Nestor fought although he was forbidden, whereas Achilles will
not fight, although he is entreated. Lohmann (1970: 263–71) regards the
Meleager story as a negative paradigm for Achilles, and the Nestor story as a
positive paradigm for Achilles. I agree that Nestor would like Achilles to
follow the example of his exploits: *Il.* 11. 790–1 support this. But the three
points of Nestor's speech mentioned in this section above mean that Nestor's
youthful exploits are a pattern for Patroclus too, and their relevance to him
should not be missed. Sch. bT ad *Il.* 11. 717–18 (= Erbse (1969–88: iii. 267),
717–18a) saw that Nestor is using the story as a paradigm to show Patroclus

The example of Nestor's success in spite of opposition from his father encourages Patroclus to believe that even if he has to fight against Achilles' wishes, he will win the day, like Nestor.

Patroclus sets off with the avowed intention of persuading Achilles to return in person to the fighting, that is, with the intention of achieving the first of the aims set for him by Nestor:

αὐτὰρ ἔγωγε
σπεύσομαι εἰς Ἀχιλῆα, ἵν' ὀτρύνω πολεμίζειν.
τίς δ' οἶδ' εἴ κέν οἱ σὺν δαίμονι θυμὸν ὀρίνω
παρειπών; ἀγαθὴ δὲ παραίφασίς ἐστιν ἑταίρου.

but I shall
hasten to Achilles, to rouse him up to war.
Who knows whether, with God's help, I might move his heart
with my persuasions? The advice of a comrade is an excellent thing.

(*Il.* 15. 401–4)[59]

However, Achilles, by his contemptuous attitude towards his companions in arms, forestalls any attempt by Patroclus to arouse his compassion for their plight and persuade him to help them by fighting in person:

ἦε σύ γ' Ἀργείων ὀλοφύρεαι, ὡς ὀλέσκονται
νηυσὶν ἔπι γλαφυρῇσιν ὑπερβασίης[60] ἕνεκα σφῆς;

or do you feel pity for the Greeks, how they are perishing
by their hollow ships on account of their transgression?

(*Il.* 16. 17–18)

Patroclus criticizes Achilles for this hardened attitude to the sufferings of the Greeks, and without allusion to the possibility of Achilles fighting in person, falls back on the second of the alternative goals proposed by Nestor:

εἰ δέ τινα φρεσὶ σῇσι θεοπροπίην ἀλεείνεις
καί τινά τοι πὰρ Ζηνὸς ἐπέφραδε πότνια μήτηρ,
ἀλλ' ἐμέ περ πρόες ὦχ', ἅμα δ' ἄλλον λαὸν ὄπασσον

that even if Achilles tries to prevent him from fighting, he could and should fight anyway.

[59] *Il.* 11. 792–3 = *Il.* 15. 403–4.
[60] At *Il.* 11. 203 Achilles complained of the ὕβρις (arrogance) of Agamemnon. Now he makes all the Greeks bear responsibility for the ὑπερβασίη (transgression) of which he complains.

Μυρμιδόνων, ἤν πού τι φόως Δαναοῖσιν γένωμαι.
δὸς δέ μοι ὤμοιιν τὰ σὰ τεύχεα θωρηχθῆναι,   40
αἴ κ' ἐμὲ σοὶ ἴσκοντες ἀπόσχωνται πολέμοιο
Τρῶες, ἀναπνεύσωσι δ' ἀρήϊοι υἷες Ἀχαιῶν
τειρόμενοι· ὀλίγη δέ τ' ἀνάπνευσις πολέμοιο.
ῥεῖα δέ κ' ἀκμῆτες κεκμηότας ἄνδρας αὐτῇ
ὤσαιμεν προτὶ ἄστυ νεῶν ἄπο καὶ κλισιάων.   45

But if in your heart you are avoiding some prophecy
and your lady mother has given you some message from Zeus,
then send me, at least, and let the rest of the army of the Myrmidons
go with me, and perhaps I might become the salvation of the Greeks.
And give me your armour to wear on my shoulders,   40
in case the Trojans liken me to you, and desist from the war,
and the warlike sons of the Achaeans have a breathing-space
when they are weary. There is little breathing-space in war.
Easily would unwearied men force men exhausted by the battle
back to the city, away from the ships and tents.   45

(*Il.* 16. 36–45)[61]

This proposal meets with no opposition: Achilles invites
Patroclus to fight in his armour and lead the Myrmidons out to
fight (*Il.* 16. 64–5). Once he has agreed, Achilles positively
urges Patroclus to arm and make haste (*Il.* 16. 126–9). Since
Achilles agrees that Patroclus should fight, there is no question
of his fighting against Achilles' wishes: Nestor's example of
how he fought against his father's wishes addressed an
eventuality which did not in fact arise.

Nestor describes how he and the Pylians drove off the Eleian
raiders and pursued them into their own territory[62] until
Athene stopped the pursuit (*Il.* 11. 754–8). This aspect of
Nestor's story is related to Achilles' later stipulation that
Patroclus should restrict himself to driving the Trojans off
from the ships (*Il.* 16. 80–2): he is not to pursue them to Troy,
in case a god intervenes. The glory of defeating the Trojans is
to be left to Achilles, and Patroclus must not detract from it:

---

[61] Cf. *Il.* 11. 794–803. This repetition conveys Nestor's influence over
Patroclus: see Whitman (1958: 196).

[62] The Eleians are pursued to Bouprasion, the Olenian rock, and the hill of
Alesion (*Il.* 11. 756–7). The Epeians bury Amarynceus at Bouprasion (*Il.* 23.
630–1), suggesting it is in their territory.

μὴ σύ γ' ἄνευθεν ἐμεῖο λιλαίεσθαι πολεμίζειν
Τρωσὶ φιλοπτολέμοισιν· ἀτιμότερον δέ με θήσεις·   90
μηδ' ἐπαγαλλόμενος πολέμῳ καὶ δηϊοτῆτι,
Τρῶας ἐναιρόμενος, προτὶ Ἴλιον ἡγεμονεύειν,
μή τις ἀπ' Οὐλύμποιο θεῶν αἰειγενετάων
ἐμβήῃ· μάλα τούς γε φιλεῖ ἑκάεργος Ἀπόλλων·[63]
ἀλλὰ πάλιν τρωπᾶσθαι, ἐπὴν φάος ἐν νήεσσι   95
θήῃς, τοὺς δ' ἔτ' ἐᾶν πεδίον κάτα δηριάασθαι.

and do not desire to wage war without me
against the war-loving Trojans: you will make me more dishonoured:
and do not, glorying in war and battle-strife,   91
and killing Trojans, lead the way to Ilion,
lest some one of the gods who live for ever
may intervene: for Apollo, the far-shooter, loves them very much:
but turn about, when you set a beacon among the ships,   95
and leave them to fight it out on the plain.

(*Il.* 16. 89–96)

Patroclus' actions in the event correspond to the pattern set for him by Nestor's example: he disregards Achilles' injunction and pursues the Trojans right up to the walls of Troy (*Il.* 16. 702), where a god does indeed intervene, as Achilles feared, and as Athene stopped Nestor's pursuit of the Eleians.[64] Like Nestor, Patroclus succeeds in driving off the enemy: he pursues the Trojans back to the city walls (*Il.* 16. 702–11), as Nestor pursued the Epeians to Bouprasion (*Il.* 11. 756–9), but unlike Nestor, Patroclus does not survive to enjoy the triumph of his achievement. Nestor's persuasion does no personal good either to Patroclus[65] or to Achilles, but in precipitating Patroclus' return to battle and his death, it brings an end to Achilles' anger which has been so detrimental to Greek success at Troy.

---

[63] These lines are strongly reminiscent of Nestor's pursuit of the Epeians (*Il.* 11. 747–58): common to both are the headlong pursuit of the enemy to its territory, and the killing spree halted by divine intervention.

[64] Apollo intervenes against Patroclus (*Il.* 16. 698–709, 784–805). Achilles anticipates Apollo's intervention if Patroclus pursues the Trojans to Troy (*Il.* 16. 93–4). Athene stops Nestor's pursuit of the Eleians (*Il.* 11. 758).

[65] In a rare authorial comment, the poet remarks of Patroclus' errand to Nestor, κακοῦ δ' ἄρα οἱ πέλεν ἀρχή ('it was the beginning of evil for him': *Il.* 11. 604).

4.5. THE αἶνος OF NESTOR'S DEFEAT AT
BOUPRASION

When the prizes for the chariot race in the funeral games for
Patroclus are distributed, the fourth prize, two talents of gold,
is given to Meriones (*Il.* 23. 614–15). When Achilles wants
Eumelus to have the second prize, in spite of the accident that
meant he came in last (*Il.* 23. 537–8), Antilochus protests and
will not yield the second prize to Eumelus (*Il.* 23. 543–7).
Achilles instead gives Eumelus a cuirass stripped from
Asteropaeus (*Il.* 23. 560). Since the prize given to Eumelus was
not one of the five prizes originally allocated for the contest, the
fifth prize remains, and Achilles gives it to Nestor, whose age
prevents him from winning anything by competing. Nestor
makes a long speech accepting the prize, a two-handled cup,
with pleasure, as a mark of the honour due to him from the
Greeks (*Il.* 23. 649).

εἴθ' ὡς ἡβώοιμι βίη τέ μοι ἔμπεδος εἴη
ὡς ὁπότε κρείοντ' Ἀμαρυγκέα θάπτον Ἐπειοὶ   630
Βουπρασίῳ, παῖδες δ' ἔθεσαν βασιλῆος ἄεθλα·
ἔνθ' οὔ τίς μοι ὁμοῖος ἀνὴρ γένετ', οὔτ' ἄρ' Ἐπειῶν
οὔτ' αὐτῶν Πυλίων οὔτ' Αἰτωλῶν μεγαθύμων.
πὺξ μὲν ἐνίκησα Κλυτομήδεα, Ἤνοπος υἱόν,
Ἀγκαῖον δὲ πάλῃ Πλευρώνιον, ὅς μοι ἀνέστη·   635
Ἴφικλον δὲ πόδεσσι παρέδραμον ἐσθλὸν ἐόντα,
δουρὶ δ' ὑπειρέβαλον Φυλῆά τε καὶ Πολύδωρον.
οἴοισίν μ' ἵπποισι παρήλασαν Ἀκτορίωνε,
πλήθει πρόσθε βαλόντες, ἀγασσάμενοι περὶ νίκης,
οὕνεκα δὴ τὰ μέγιστα παρ' αὐτόθι λείπετ' ἄεθλα.   640
οἱ δ' ἄρ' ἔσαν δίδυμοι· ὁ μὲν ἔμπεδον ἡνιόχευεν,
ἔμπεδον ἡνιόχευ', ὁ δ' ἄρα μάστιγι κέλευεν.
ὣς ποτ' ἔον· νῦν αὖτε νεώτεροι ἀντιοώντων
ἔργων τοιούτων· ἐμὲ δὲ χρὴ γήραϊ λυγρῷ
πείθεσθαι, τότε δ' αὖτε μετέπρεπον ἡρώεσσιν.   645

If only I were young, and my strength were steadfast,
as when the Epeians buried Amarynceus   630
at Bouprasion, and the sons of the king held games:
then no man was like me, neither of the Epeians,
nor of the Pylians themselves, nor of the great-hearted Aetolians.
In the boxing I overcame Clytomedes, the son of Enops,

and in the wrestling Ancaius, the Pleuronian, who competed against
me.
I outran Iphiclus, although he was good, in the footrace,   636
and with the spear I out-threw Phyleus and Polydorus.
Only in the chariot race did the two sons of Actor outstrip me,
forging ahead through superior numbers, jealously eager for the
victory,
since the greatest prizes remained for that contest.   640
You see, they were twins: one of them at leisure held the reins,
at leisure he held them, but the other urged on the horses with the
whip.
Such was I once. But now younger men confront
such efforts. And I must obey baneful old age,
but then, however, I was glorious among heroes.   645
                                                     (*Il.* 23. 629–45)

This speech of thanks is described as an αἶνος by the poet (*Il.*
23. 652). An αἶνος is a story told with a hidden meaning, or to
convey a veiled hint (see 2.3.4 above), but the hidden meaning
of Nestor's account of his participation in the games at
Bouprasion has eluded most of its interpreters.[66] What follows
will attempt to explain the veiled hint conveyed by Nestor's
account of the contests and prize-givings in the games at

---

[66] Eustathius, *Il.* 1322. 3–9 takes αἶνος at *Il.* 23. 652 as a reference to
Nestor's praise of Achilles: Antilochus declares (*Il.* 23. 791–2) that no one
except Achilles could compete with Odysseus at running, and at *Il.* 23. 795
Achilles thanks Antilochus for his praise (αἶνος). Αἶνος is used in the sense of
praise also at *Od.* 21. 110, where Telemachus says he will not praise his
mother to the suitors. However, its most frequent sense in Homer, and the
right sense of αἶνος at *Il.* 23. 652, is a moral tale, a story charged with meaning
below the surface, as argued by Meuli (1975: 752; 1st pub. 1954). (I do not
share Meuli's view that the αἶνοι of Nestor and Antilochus in book 23 are told
to support their right to prizes.) Hofmann (1922: 50–1) thought αἶνος in this
context had the sense of *sermo* (discourse), rather than the usual meanings.
This speech of Nestor's has puzzled other interpreters too: Oehler (1925: 24,
no. 16) thinks Nestor relates his athletic triumphs in the past to justify his
acceptance of the prize awarded on an occasion when he can no longer compete, because of his age. Hebel (1970: 134–6) is surprised that Nestor should
refer, when he is offered a prize, to a contest he did not win, and concludes that
since it took two people, the Molione, to beat Nestor in the chariot race, the
story is told as an assertion of his worth. Gaisser (1969a: 13) refers to Nestor's
skill as an athlete in his lost youth, and his pleasure in receiving the prize, but
offers no explanation of the story. Austin (1978: 76; 1st pub. 1966) explains the
meaning of the speech as 'I have proved myself in funeral contests: now it is
for you to compete'.

Bouprasion. Nestor describes a time when he certainly did compete in exactly the contests from which Achilles says he is now debarred by age: boxing, wrestling, throwing the javelin, and the footrace.[67] All these Nestor won without difficulty, but in the chariot race he lost to the twin sons of Actor:

> οἴοισίν μ᾽ ἵπποισι παρήλασαν Ἀκτορίωνε,
> πλήθει πρόσθε βαλόντες, ἀγασσάμενοι περὶ νίκης,
> οὕνεκα δὴ τὰ μέγιστα παρ᾽ αὐτόθι λείπετ᾽ ἄεθλα.   640

only in the chariot race did the two sons of Actor outstrip me,
forging ahead through superior numbers, jealously eager for the
  victory,
since the greatest prizes remained for that contest.   640
                                                        (*Il*. 23. 638–40)

Nestor seems to think he should have won the chariot race too, and lost it only because the sons of Actor[68] exploited some kind of unfair advantage, but he does not make clear what this was. The possibilities suggested are (1) they entered more chariots and used them to impede their fellow-competitors; (2) a conspiracy by the other competitors allowed them an unfair advantage at the start; (3) because their bodies were joined (if they were Siamese twins)[69] they had to compete in a single chariot, which gave them an unfair advantage.[70] The exact nature of the tactics complained of by Nestor does not matter very much: the main point of the methods employed by the Molione in the funeral games for Amarynceus at Bouprasion is their correspondence to the methods employed by Antilochus in the chariot race in the present context of Patroclus' funeral games.[71] Nestor's son, Antilochus, competes in the chariot race

---

[67] Cf. *Il*. 23. 621–2 and 634–5.

[68] The Molione of *Il*. 11. 749.

[69] Ibycus, *fr*. 4, *PMG* 285; Hesiod, *fr*. 18 M–W; Pherecydes, *FGrH* 3. 79b (where their extraordinary advantages are fully described); Sch. A ad *Il*. 11. 751 (from Aristonicus) (= Erbse (1969–88: iii. 273)). Cf. Sch. T ad *Il*. 23. 641 (= Erbse (1969–88: v. 465), 641a).

[70] Sch. A ad *Il*. 23. 638–42 (from Aristonicus) (= Erbse (1969–88: v. 643–5), 638–42).

[71] Common to both episodes are the extreme youth of the victors (we know from *Il*. 10. 710 that in his youth Nestor regarded the Molione as little more than children), and the overwhelming craving for the prizes. The best prizes are allocated to the chariot race (*Il*. 23. 640). Nestor advises Antilochus not to allow the prizes to escape his grasp (*Il*. 23. 314), and he is

at the games for Patroclus,[72] and before the race he is advised
by his father to resort to rather questionable methods:[73] otherwise he has no chance of winning, because his horses are the
slowest:

Ἀντίλοχ᾽, ἤτοι μέν σε νέον περ ἐόντ᾽ ἐφίλησαν
Ζεύς τε Ποσειδάων τε, καὶ ἱπποσύνας ἐδίδαξαν
παντοίας· τῶ καί σε διδασκέμεν οὔ τι μάλα χρεώ·
οἶσθα γὰρ εὖ περὶ τέρμαθ᾽ ἑλισσέμεν· ἀλλά τοι ἵπποι
βάρδιστοι θείειν· τῶ τ᾽ οἴω λοίγι᾽ ἔσεσθαι.   310
τῶν δ᾽ ἵπποι μὲν ἔασιν ἀφάρτεροι, οὐδὲ μὲν αὐτοὶ
πλείονα ἴσασιν σέθεν αὐτοῦ μητίσασθαι.
ἀλλ᾽ ἄγε δὴ σύ, φίλος, μῆτιν ἐμβάλλεο θυμῷ
παντοίην, ἵνα μή σε παρεκπροφύγῃσιν ἄεθλα.
μήτι τοι δρυτόμος μέγ᾽ ἀμείνων ἠὲ βίηφι·   315
μήτι δ᾽ αὖτε κυβερνήτης ἐνὶ οἴνοπι πόντῳ
νῆα θοὴν ἰθύνει ἐρεχθομένην ἀνέμοισι·
μήτι δ᾽ ἡνίοχος περιγίγνεται ἡνιόχοιο.
ἀλλ᾽ ὃς μέν θ᾽ ἵπποισι καὶ ἅρμασιν οἷσι πεποιθὼς
ἀφραδέως ἐπὶ πολλὸν ἑλίσσεται ἔνθα καὶ ἔνθα,   320
ἵπποι δὲ πλανόωνται ἀνὰ δρόμον, οὐδὲ κατίσχει·
ὃς δέ κε κέρδεα εἰδῇ ἐλαύνων ἥσσονας ἵππους,
αἰεὶ τέρμ᾽ ὁρόων στρέφει ἐγγύθεν, οὐδέ ἑ λήθει
ὅππως τὸ πρῶτον τανύσῃ βοέοισιν ἱμᾶσιν,
ἀλλ᾽ ἔχει ἀσφαλέως καὶ τὸν προὔχοντα δοκεύει.   325
σῆμα δέ τοι ἐρέω μάλ᾽ ἀριφραδές, οὐδέ σε λήσει.
ἕστηκε ξύλον αὖον ὅσον τ᾽ ὄργυι᾽ ὑπὲρ αἴης,
ἢ δρυὸς ἢ πεύκης· τὸ μὲν οὐ καταπύθεται ὄμβρῳ·
λᾶε δὲ τοῦ ἑκάτερθεν ἐρηρέδαται δύο λευκὼ
ἐν ξυνοχῇσιν ὁδοῦ, λεῖος δ᾽ ἱππόδρομος ἀμφίς·   330
ἤ τευ σῆμα βροτοῖο πάλαι κατατεθνηῶτος,
ἢ τό γε νύσσα τέτυκτο ἐπὶ προτέρων ἀνθρώπων,
καὶ νῦν τέρματ᾽ ἔθηκε ποδάρκης δῖος Ἀχιλλεύς.

certainly unwilling to relinquish the mare once he has received her (*Il.* 23.
553–4).

   [72] See *LIMC* i. 1. 834, no. 20, s.v. Achilleus 119, no. 494.
   [73] μῆτις (*Il.* 23. 313) and κέρδεα (*Il.* 23. 322). Nestor has advocated the
effectiveness of μῆτις in the past, when he proposed burying the dead and
building a wall round the camp as a means of restoring morale (*Il.* 7. 324), and
again when he proposed sending the embassy to Achilles (*Il.* 9. 93). In his
νεῖκος to the Greeks on the subject of his victory over Ereuthalion, Nestor
mentioned how Lycurgus killed Areïthous δόλῳ, οὔ τι κράτεΐ γε, 'by trickery,
not by might' (*Il.* 7. 142), an idea not dissimilar to the image (*Il.* 23. 315) of the
woodcutter who excels by μῆτις.

τῷ σὺ μάλ' ἐγχρίμψας ἐλάαν σχεδὸν ἅρμα καὶ ἵππους,
αὐτὸς δὲ κλινθῆναι ἐϋπλέκτῳ ἐνὶ δίφρῳ   335
ἧκ' ἐπ' ἀριστερὰ τοῖιν· ἀτὰρ τὸν δεξιὸν ἵππον
κένσαι ὁμοκλήσας, εἶξαί τέ οἱ ἡνία χερσίν.
ἐν νύσσῃ δέ τοι ἵππος ἀριστερὸς ἐγχριμφθήτω,
ὡς ἄν τοι πλήμνη γε δοάσσεται ἄκρον ἱκέσθαι
κύκλου ποιητοῖο· λίθου δ' ἀλέασθαι ἐπαυρεῖν,   340
μή πως ἵππους τε τρώσῃς κατά θ' ἅρματα ἄξῃς·
χάρμα δὲ τοῖς ἄλλοισιν, ἐλεγχείη δὲ σοὶ αὐτῷ
ἔσσεται· ἀλλά, φίλος, φρονέων πεφυλαγμένος εἶναι.
εἰ γάρ κ' ἐν νύσσῃ γε παρεξελάσῃσθα διώκων,
οὐκ ἔσθ' ὅς κέ σ' ἕλῃσι μετάλμενος οὐδὲ παρέλθῃ,   345
οὐδ' εἴ κεν μετόπισθεν Ἀρίονα δῖον ἐλαύνοι,
Ἀδρήστου ταχὺν ἵππον, ὃς ἐκ θεόφιν γένος ἦεν,
ἢ τοὺς Λαομέδοντος, οἳ ἐνθάδε γ' ἔτραφεν ἐσθλοί.

Antilochus, in truth although you are young
Zeus and Poseidon love you, and taught you every aspect
of horsemanship: so I do not really need to instruct you at all,
for you know very well how to negotiate the doubling-post. But your
   horses
are the slowest at running, and so I think there will be trouble.   310
The horses of these men are more fleet, but they themselves do not
know better than you how to deploy guile.
But come then, my friend, cast into your heart guile
of every description, so that the prizes may not escape your clutches.
A woodcutter is far better for guile than for strength: 316
by guile does a helmsman on the wine-dark sea
set straight his swift ship buffeted by the winds:
by guile does charioteer surpass charioteer.
There is the man who, trusting in his horses and his chariot
takes the turn in a wide circle, senselessly, this way or that,   320
and his horses wander on the course, and he does not check them:
but there is also the man who knows cunning arts when driving
   inferior horses;
he keeps his eye on the turning post, and negotiates it keeping close,
   nor does he overlook
how he may first urge the horses to a gallop by means of the oxhide
   reins,
but he controls his team securely and watches the man in front.   325
I will tell you the mark: it is very easy to recognize, and it will not
   escape you.
A pole stands at the height of about six feet above the ground,
of oak or pine: it is not rotted by the rain

and two white stones rest on the ground on either side of it
at the turn of the course, and the race-course is smooth on both sides:
either it is the memorial of some man long dead,   331
or it was a turning post in the time of former men,
and now godlike swift-footed Achilles has made it the turning post.
You drive the chariot and horses so close as to almost touch it,
and lean over in the well-plaited chariot   335
a little to the left of the horses: but goad the horse on the right
urging him, and slacken his reins in your hands.
At the turning post let the left horse almost touch the post
so that the hub of the fashioned wheel may seem to reach the edge.
But avoid hitting the stone,   340
lest you injure the horses and smash the chariot:
that will be a delight to the others and a disgrace to you:
but my friend, be wise and be on your guard.
For if at the turning post you put a spurt on and drive past,
there is no one who could close the distance and catch you, and he
    could not overtake,
not even if he were driving godlike Arion behind you   346
the swift horse of Adrastus, who was from divine stock
or the horses of Laomedon, which the nobility here bred up.

(Il. 23. 306–48)

Nestor's most detailed instructions to Antilochus concern the
negotiation of the turning post. This is the most crucial part of
the race: once the turning post is successfully passed, even a
faster team would not be able to overtake (*Il*. 23. 344–8). All
this might be a ruse to lead the contestants to expect some
trickery at the turn. In the event, the turning post is successfully negotiated by all contestants, but on the return stretch (*Il*.
23. 373–5)[74] Eumelus crashes, his chariot yoke broken by
Athene (*Il*. 23. 392). Diomede is the undisputed victor[75] and
Antilochus has no desire to vie with him (*Il*. 23. 404–6), but he
uses dubious tactics to deprive Menelaus of the second place:
Antilochus drives off the track at a point where it has been
narrowed by rainwater breaking part of it away, and then forces
his way back on to the track when he is level with Menelaus,
causing the latter to fall back to avoid a collision (*Il*. 23.

[74] Gagarin (1983: 38) is wrong to think Idomeneus says Eumelus must have
come to grief while he was rounding the turn. οὐκ ἐτύχησεν ἐλίξας (*Il*. 23. 466)
means 'he did not succeed, he had no luck, *when he had rounded* the turn'.

[75] On Athene's role in Diomede's victory, see Willcock (1973: 3–4).

434–7).[76] At first Menelaus thinks Antilochus is driving like a madman (ἀφραδέως: *Il.* 23. 426),[77] but when he realizes the purpose of Antilochus' manoeuvre, he warns him that he will not be allowed to carry off the second prize without swearing an oath that it was fairly obtained (*Il.* 23. 441). After the race, Achilles wants to give the mare which is the second prize to Eumelus, who comes in last, dragging his broken chariot and driving his horses before him, but Antilochus claims the mare for himself (*Il.* 23. 543–54),[78] proposing that Eumelus should receive an alternative prize. To prevent Antilochus from receiving the prize obtained by cheating, Menelaus intervenes to demand that he should take an oath that he did not use δόλος[79] (trickery) to foul Menelaus' chariot (*Il.* 23. 583–5). Antilochus significantly avoids the oath, because it would brand him as a perjuror.[80] Instead, he decries the hastiness of youth, λεπτὴ δέ τε μῆτις, 'and its slender wisdom'[81] (*Il.* 23. 590), and without any admission of guilt, he yields to Menelaus,[82]

---

[76] Gagarin (1983) suggests Antilochus passes Menelaus at the turn, and wins the race by (legitimate) κέρδεσσιν (cunning) (*Il.* 23. 515), in accordance with his father's advice (ὃς δέ κε κέρδεα εἰδῇ ἐλαύνων ἥσσονας ἵππους . . ., 'but the man who understands cunning when he is driving inferior horses . . .' (*Il.* 23. 322). However, Gagarin ignores *Il.* 23. 374–5, which indicate that all the drama of the race is in the return stretch.

[77] Nestor uses ἀφραδέως to describe the driving of a charioteer who does not know how to control his horses (*Il.* 23. 320).

[78] His language is reminiscent of Achilles' quarrel with Agamemnon, as Eustathius indicated, *Il.* 1315. 29 ff., 53–4, 65 ff. Cf. τὴν δ' ἐγὼ οὐ δώσω (*Il.* 23. 553) and τὴν δ' ἐγὼ οὐ λύσω (*Il.* 1. 29); χείρεσσι μάχεσθαι (*Il.* 23. 554) and χερσὶ μὲν οὔ τοι ἔγωγε μαχήσομαι (*Il.* 1. 298); περὶ δ' αὐτῆς πειρηθήτω (*Il.* 23. 554) and εἰ δ' ἄγε μὴν πείρησαι (*Il.* 1. 302). See also Martin (1989: 188–9). On the characterization of Antilochus, see Willcock (1983).

[79] Odysseus uses δόλος in the wrestling against Ajax (*Il.* 23. 725) and nobody complains, so the use of δόλος does not lead automatically to disqualification.

[80] See Parker (1983: 187 n. 242). The oath proposed would accompany a settlement like that in *Il.* 19. 140–4, where Agamemnon swears (*Il.* 19. 258–65) he has never been to bed with Briseis: see Macleod (1982: 30).

[81] Impossible to translate μῆτις as 'guile' here, but Antilochus uses the word ironically, to refer back to Nestor's advice to employ μῆτις (*Il.* 23. 313–18). Μῆτις may be deprecated or approved, and Antilochus is exploiting its ambiguous nature. Antilochus is dissimulating, and has known perfectly well what he is doing throughout the affair: for discussion, see Vernant and Détienne (1967: 81–3).

[82] Primmer (1970: 9–10) indicates how the poet characterizes Antilochus as πεπνυμένος (discreet) at (*Il.* 23. 586), picking up Menelaus' address to his

giving him the horse he won, and inviting him to take anything else of his he might want in addition (i.e. he offers damages). Menelaus is so disarmed by Antilochus' grace that he allows him to retain the prize and accepts the third prize for himself (*Il.* 23. 613). The elements of Nestor's defeat by an unfair advantage enjoyed by the Molione in the funeral games for Amarynceus at Bouprasion repeat the elements of Antilochus' defeat of Menelaus by dubious tactics in the chariot race in the games for Patroclus. Nestor's story of the contests at Bouprasion and Menelaus' quarrel with Antilochus over the distribution of prizes each repeat on a smaller scale Agamemnon's quarrel with Achilles in book 1 about a prize.[83]

Nestor won all the other contests at Bouprasion, and he implies that he would have won the chariot race too, but for the unfair advantage taken by the sons of Actor, who somehow deprived the favourite, Nestor, of his victory. Nestor advises Antilochus to cheat like the sons of Actor, to employ μῆτις and κέρδος to compensate for his inferior horses, advice Antilochus follows to good effect. The methods advised by Nestor resemble those by which he was himself defeated by the Molione at Bouprasion. So in the chariot race at Patroclus' funeral Antilochus corresponds to the sons of Actor in the chariot race in the funeral games at Bouprasion. Nestor, who was outdone in the chariot race at Bouprasion, is comparing himself with Menelaus, outdone by Antilochus in the games for Patroclus. At these games, Menelaus disputed the award of the second prize to Antilochus, but Nestor describes no dispute with the sons of Actor about the allocation of prizes at the games at Bouprasion. Significantly, his story stops with their victory, and there is nothing in his behaviour after his defeat to correspond to Menelaus' dispute with Antilochus over the prize for second place. This crucial difference is the point of the αἶνος related by Nestor: he did not complain of the unfair tactics by which he was deprived of the first place (never mind the second place, about which Menelaus is making such a fuss).

adversary as Ἀντίλοχε πρόσθεν πεπνυμένε, 'Antilochus, formerly discreet' at *Il.* 23. 570 where Menelaus is demanding Antilochus should take an oath that he never cheated.

[83] See Macleod (1982: 30).

Richardson[84] points out the paradigmatic aspects of Nestor's reminiscence: first, the quarrel over the second prize develops in a way which echoes the main theme of the poem in that Menelaus, like both Agamemnon and Achilles in book 1, feels that he is being unjustly deprived of his due and refuses to accept this; secondly, the defeat of Nestor by the sons of Actor at Bouprasion echoes Antilochus' defeat of Menelaus in the suggestion that it was achieved by tactics or an advantage that were/was not quite fair. But Richardson misses the contrast implied in Nestor's speech between his own tact at Bouprasion, where he made no attempt to initiate a quarrel over the unfair advantage enjoyed by the Molione, and the present rather unedifying quarrel between Menelaus and Antilochus over the second prize. Nestor's self-restraint at Bouprasion so long ago is rewarded by the prize he now receives, but he is telling the story to contrast his own dignified acceptance of defeat with Menelaus' insistent claims (to the less than prestigious second place) on the present occasion. The story is not an expression of regret for the lost athletic ability of Nestor's youth;[85] it is an αἶνος which conveys a veiled hint on both its immediate context, the quarrel between Antilochus and Menelaus, and the quarrel at the centre of the poem, that between Achilles and Agamemnon. When Nestor received provocation which might have been grounds for a quarrel, he simply ignored it—as Antilochus and Menelaus might have done, and, indeed, as Achilles and Agamemnon might have done too.

4.5.1. Nestor's effectiveness

Nestor's first surreptitious rebuke to Agamemnon through the story of the Lapiths and Centaurs reaches its target, but Agamemnon refuses to allow his behaviour to be altered by it, and persists in his quarrel with Achilles. This is the only time Nestor's authority fails. In spite of the initial failure of his first story to alter the course of events, the influence he exerts through his later stories can hardly be overestimated. The paradigm of his personal example in the Pylian Wars turns out to have a stronger effect on Patroclus than the advice of

---

[84] (1993: 224–5).
[85] As might be inferred from the surface meaning of *Il.* 23. 629.

Achilles, since Patroclus does not turn back after repelling the Trojan attack, as Achilles instructed him, but follows the example of Nestor's pursuit of the Eleians by pursuing the Trojans back to the walls of Troy. Patroclus meets his death while imitating the example of Nestor in the Pylian Wars. This is instrumental in putting an end to the μῆνις, anger of Achilles, since only the need to avenge Patroclus can cause Achilles to abandon his anger and re-enter the battle. Therefore Nestor's influence over Patroclus is an indirect cause of Achilles' return to the battle. Nestor has both the first and the last word on quarrels, first on that between Agamemnon and Achilles and finally on that between Menelaus and Antilochus (with implicit reference to the first quarrel). Nestor's final story, the αἶνος of how he accepted defeat at Bouprasion, elegantly conveys his disapproval of Menelaus for bothering to wrangle with Antilochus over the prize for the second place. It also effectively conveys Nestor's unfavourable opinion of Agamemnon's dispute with Achilles over a prize allocated in a similar public distribution.

Nestor's speeches, and the examples he offers from experience gained in his youth, are always relevant to their context, always illustrating situations analogous to those prevailing at the time of their narration, and always offering discreet advice on the best way of proceeding in the circumstances. It is through the paradigms presented in the anecdotes of his past experience that Nestor fulfils what he himself explains as his function: to command the Greeks with βουλῇ καὶ μύθοισι (advice and stories) (*Il.* 4. 322–3). As soon as we decide to regard Nestor's anecdotes and stories from his youth as the advice to the Greeks he says they are, it is not difficult to appreciate their relevance to their contexts in the poems, and their role in directing and commenting on its events.

5
Diomede: Debate in Para-Narrative

5.1 THE DESIRABILITY OF DIVINE FAVOUR

Many of those fighting at Troy are the sons of heroes who took part in the famous exploits of the previous generation, such as the Argonautica or the Calydonian boar hunt, or fought in its wars, such as the expedition of the Seven against Thebes or Heracles' sack of Troy. Diomede's father, Tydeus, fought and died in the expedition against Thebes, and his successes there are held up to Diomede as an example to follow. An exploit of Tydeus' while fighting against the Thebans introduces a whole series of para-narratives clustered round the figure of Diomede. In these para-narratives the issue of divine patronage is a recurrent theme, and it would not be an exaggeration to say that they present an argument or debate on the merits of divine patronage. Only the audience is aware of all the stages of this debate. Agamemnon and Athene, who have their own reasons for wanting Diomede to fight, urge him to imitate his father's triumphs, achieved with the help of Athene. They imply that Diomede should be confident of the goddess's help, and count on her assistance. Once Achilles has withdrawn from the battle, Agamemnon must have a fighter to replace him, and Diomede fulfils that function in the first part of the *Iliad*: he must uphold the cause of Agamemnon and Menelaus against the Trojans. Athene encourages Diomede to regard himself as a divine favourite while she uses him as her instrument to settle scores of her own against her personal enemies, Ares and Aphrodite. The other side of the argument is presented through Sthenelus and Glaucus, who have no ulterior motives for manoeuvring Diomede into fighting. They present divine favour as something fickle and unreliable, using the examples of Tydeus and

Bellerophon, both of whom achieved glittering successes while they enjoyed divine patronage, but both suffered when that patronage was suddenly withdrawn.

5.2. THE STAGES OF THE ARGUMENT

The stages of the argument in para-narratives are as follows:

Diomede and the example of Tydeus:

1. Agamemnon urges Diomede to fight like his father, Tydeus, who achieved great things against the Thebans with the help of Athene.
2. The counter-argument from Sthenelus: the Seven were not as great as their sons, who conquered Thebes when their fathers had failed. Their fathers perished through their own folly.
3. Athene reproaches Diomede: his father fought even when she forbade it, but Diomede will not fight when she tells him to. With Athene's help, Diomede could fight even Aphrodite and Ares.

The argument resumed:

4. Dione hints at dire consequences for mortals who fight with gods.
5. Diomede tells of Lycurgus, a real fighter against gods, who suffered terribly for his actions.
6. Glaucus alludes to the transience of mortal affairs: look at Bellerophon. The gods favoured him and he achieved much: he was no θεομάχος, but they suddenly hated even him, and he suffered terribly.

This debate deliberates on the merits and demerits of success achieved through divine assistance, the very issue with which Diomede is confronted. In the event, Diomede chooses to fight with divine assistance, but his fighting career comes to an abrupt end when such assistance is not forthcoming and he is wounded. Diomede has often been observed to function as a replacement for Achilles in the first part of the *Iliad*,[1] and the

---

[1] Schadewaldt (1966: 60–1, 155; 1st pub. 1938); Pestalozzi (1945: 17); Erbse (1961: 173–6); Lohmann (1970: 221); Kullmann (1984: 314); Redfield (1975: 3).

debate on the advantages or otherwise of divine patronage is perhaps relevant also to Achilles, who enlists divine help to ensure that the Greeks feel the effects of his absence, and who is certainly disenchanted with the result. Thetis reminds him that Zeus has accomplished everything he requested: the Greeks have suffered terribly in his absence and have been driven back to the ships (*Il.* 18. 74–7). Achilles agrees that Zeus has omitted nothing of what he asked, only now it gives him no pleasure, since Patroclus, whom he loved as his own life, is dead (*Il.* 18. 79–82). In other words, divine assistance is ultimately of dubious value to the mortals who enjoy it, since it is either withdrawn without warning, as in the case of Diomede, or brings unlooked-for and tragic developments, as in the case of Achilles. But we must begin with the debate as it unfolds around Diomede.

5.3. DIOMEDE AND THE EXAMPLE OF TYDEUS

The burden of living up to the expectations created by his father's achievements is willingly borne by Diomede, who is himself anxious not to fall short of his family reputation. It might help to consider the broader picture of Tydeus' career and that of his family as they appear in later stories. Tydeus, an Aetolian by birth, was exiled from his native land for the murder of a kinsman.[2] He settled in Argos, where he married Deïpyle, the daughter of king Adrastus of Argos. Tydeus was one of the Seven against Thebes,[3] in which campaign he enjoyed great success under the patronage of Athene. In the fighting at Thebes, Tydeus killed Melanippus, and was himself wounded by his victim. As he lay on the field, Athene approached to tend him with a remedy from Zeus, which was to make Tydeus immortal. The intention of the goddess was

---

[2] Either his brother: Pherecydes, *FGrH* 3 F 122; Hyginus, *fab.* 69; Eustathius, *Il.* 14. 122, 971. 5–10; Sophocles, *TrGF* iv. 799 (Radt); Statius, *Theb.* 1. 401; Lactantius Placidus on Statius, *Theb.* 1. 401–2 = Jahnke (1898: 47–8, no. 401); or his paternal uncle: Sch. T ad *Il.* 14. 114 (= Erbse (1969–88: iii. 584), 114b); Apollodorus, 1. 8. 5.

[3] For lists of the Seven, see Aeschylus, *Th.* 375–641; Sophocles, *OC* 1303–25; Euripides, *Ph.* 1104–34; *Supp.* 857–928; Diodorus Siculus, 4. 65. 7; Hyginus, *fab.* 70; Statius, *Theb.* 5. 661–71.

frustrated, however, by Amphiaraus, the brother-in-law of Adrastus, who, although he fought against the Thebans as one of the Seven, on the same side as Tydeus and Adrastus, was nevertheless personally hostile to Tydeus. Amphiaraus cut off the head of Melanippus, and gave it to Tydeus, who, in the frenzy of the battlefield, devoured the brain of his enemy, to the disgust of Athene as she approached him. In the circumstances, Athene did not apply Zeus' remedy, and left Tydeus to his fate.[4] His grave at Thebes,[5] Diomede says (*Il*. 14. 114), is marked with a tumulus, indicating that he received a hero's burial.

Like his father before him, Diomede also fought at Thebes. The sons of the Seven, the Epigonoi, returned to Thebes ten years after their fathers had died there: after a battle in which the Theban leader, Laodamas, perished, the inhabitants of Thebes were persuaded by the seer, Tiresias, to quit the city of Thebes, taking their families with them. The Epigonoi took possession of the city and burned it to the ground.[6] As a result of his own and his father's inclusion in the events of the Theban cycle, Diomede has two reputations to contend with: that of his father, in the generation before the Trojan War, and his own, as one of the victors over Thebes. The example of his father, Tydeus, in an exploit performed with the help of Athene, is held up to Diomede on two occasions, by Agamemnon (*Il*. 4. 370–400) and by Athene (*Il*. 5. 800–13).

---

[4] Sch. AbT ad *Il*. 5. 126, citing Pherecydes *FGrH* 3 F 97 (= Erbse (1969–88: ii. 22)); Sch. Pindar, *N*. 10. 12; Tzetzes ad Lyc. 1066; Apollodorus, 3. 6. 8 (Amphiaraus killed and beheaded Melanippus); Pausanias, 9. 18. 1 (Melanippus killed by Amphiaraus); Statius, *Theb*. 8. 716–66 (Capaneus who killed and beheaded Melanippus); *LIMC* ii. 953–4, s.v. Athanasia, no. 1 for illustration of a lost red-figure bell-crater with good illustration of Melanippus with coiffure undisturbed by the operation. For discussion of the monstrous nature of the Seven in the *Thebaid*, see Reinhardt (1960*a*: 14–15). The *Iliad* avoids mention of such savagery as that displayed by Tydeus towards Melanippus: see Griffin (1977: 46–7).

[5] According to Pausanias, 1. 39. 2, he was buried at Eleusis: for the Bronze Age cemetery below the Geometric cemetery at Eleusis, see Mylonas (1953: 81–7 and fig. 10).

[6] Sch. bT ad *Il*. 4. 406 (= Erbse (1969–88: i. 517), 406a); Herodotus, 5. 61; Apollodorus, 3. 7. 3–4; Hyginus, *fab*. 71; Diodorus Siculus, 4. 66.

5.3.1. Stage 1. Agamemnon's νεῖκος to Diomede (Il. 4. 370–400)

When the truce for the duel between Paris and Menelaus has
been broken by Pandarus' shot wounding Menelaus (*Il.* 4. 116–
40), Agamemnon is obliged to urge the Greeks to fight again.
He begins with collective encouragement (*Il.* 4. 236–9) then
makes individual friendly approaches[7] before changing his
method to the νεῖκος.[8] When Odysseus refutes (*Il.* 4. 350–5)
Agamemon's νεῖκος (*Il.* 4. 338–48) to Peteos and himself, Agamemnon turns his attention to Diomede.[9] He accuses him of
showing little enthusiasm for the fighting and compares him
unfavourably with his father, Tydeus:

> ὦ μοι, Τυδέος υἱὲ δαΐφρονος ἱπποδάμοιο,   370
> τί πτώσσεις, τί δ' ὀπιπεύεις πολέμοιο γεφύρας;
> οὐ μὲν Τυδέϊ γ' ὧδε φίλον πτωσκαζέμεν ἦεν,
> ἀλλὰ πολὺ πρὸ φίλων ἑτάρων δηΐοισι μάχεσθαι,
> ὡς φάσαν οἵ μιν ἴδοντο πονεύμενον· οὐ γὰρ ἔγωγε
> ἤντησ' οὐδὲ ἴδον· περὶ δ' ἄλλων φασὶ γενέσθαι.   375
> ἤτοι μὲν γὰρ ἄτερ πολέμου εἰσῆλθε Μυκήνας
> ξεῖνος ἅμ' ἀντιθέῳ Πολυνείκεϊ, λαὸν ἀγείρων·
> οἱ δὲ τότ' ἐστρατόωνθ' ἱερὰ πρὸς τείχεα Θήβης,
> καί ῥα μάλα λίσσοντο δόμεν κλειτοὺς ἐπικούρους·
> οἱ δ' ἔθελον δόμεναι καὶ ἐπήνεον ὡς ἐκέλευον·   380
> ἀλλὰ Ζεὺς ἔτρεψε παραίσια σήματα φαίνων.
> οἱ δ' ἐπεὶ οὖν ᾤχοντο ἰδὲ πρὸ ὁδοῦ ἐγένοντο,
> Ἀσωπὸν δ' ἵκοντο βαθύσχοινον λεχεποίην,
> ἔνθ' αὖτ' ἀγγελίην ἐπὶ Τυδῆ στεῖλαν Ἀχαιοί.
> αὐτὰρ ὁ βῆ, πολέας δὲ κιχήσατο Καδμεΐωνας   385
> δαινυμένους κατὰ δῶμα βίης Ἐτεοκληείης.
> ἔνθ' οὐδὲ ξεῖνός περ ἐὼν ἱππηλάτα Τυδεὺς
> τάρβει, μοῦνος ἐὼν πολέσιν μετὰ Καδμείοισιν,
> ἀλλ' ὅ γ' ἀεθλεύειν προκαλίζετο, πάντα δ' ἐνίκα
> ῥηϊδίως· τοίη οἱ ἐπίρροθος ἦεν Ἀθήνη.   390
> οἱ δὲ χολωσάμενοι Καδμεῖοι, κέντορες ἵππων,
> ἂψ ἄρ' ἀνερχομένῳ πυκινὸν λόχον εἷσαν ἄγοντες,

[7] To Idomeneus (*Il.* 4. 257–64); to the Ajaxes (*Il.* 4. 287–91); and to Nestor
(*Il.* 4. 313–16).

[8] Νεῖκος means a reproachful or taunting speech, or a quarrel: see 2.3.5
above. In this case, Agamemnon's taunts are intended to spur the addressee to
greater efforts. The verb νείκεσσεν (*Il.* 4. 336, 368) indicates the nature of his
speech.

[9] On the responses of Odysseus and Diomede to the νείκεα of Agamemnon,
see Martin (1989: 70–2).

κούρους πεντήκοντα· δύω δ' ἡγήτορες ἦσαν,
Μαίων Αἱμονίδης, ἐπιείκελος ἀθανάτοισιν,
υἱός τ' Αὐτοφόνοιο, μενεπτόλεμος Πολυφόντης.   395
Τυδεὺς μὲν καὶ τοῖσιν ἀεικέα πότμον ἐφῆκε·
πάντας ἔπεφν', ἕνα δ' οἶον ἵει οἰκόνδε νέεσθαι·
Μαίον' ἄρα προέηκε, θεῶν τεράεσσι πιθήσας.
τοῖος ἔην Τυδεὺς Αἰτώλιος· ἀλλὰ τὸν υἱὸν
γείνατο εἷο χέρεια μάχῃ, ἀγορῇ δέ τ' ἀμείνω.   400

O alas, son of Tydeus, the skilful tamer of horses,   370
why are you skulking, why are you gazing at the ranks of war?
To Tydeus it was not pleasant to skulk thus in fear,
but to fight with the enemy far in front of his comrades.
So they said, who saw him at work, for I did not
meet him, nor did I even see him, but they say he was superior to the
    rest.
For certainly he came without hostility to Mycenae   376
a guest-friend with god-like Polynices, recruiting an army.
At the time they were assaulting the holy walls of Thebes,
and they were entreating us to give them glorious allies.
And the people were willing to grant them, and they approved what
    they commanded,
but Zeus dissuaded them by revealing ill-omened signs.   381
But they, when they were gone, and were a distance on their road,
they came to the meadowy Asopus, deep-grown with rushes,
and there the Greeks appointed Tydeus to be their ambassador,
and he went, and met with many Cadmeians   385
feasting in the halls of the mighty Eteocles.
And there, although he was a stranger, the horseman Tydeus was not
    afraid,
although he was alone among many Cadmeians,
but he challenged them to athletic contests and won them all
with ease: such a helper was Athene to him.   390
But the Cadmeians were angry, the goaders of horses,
And they went and set an ambush for him on his way back:
fifty young men, and there were two leaders,
Maeon, the son of Haemon, like to the immortals,
and the son of Autophonus, the steadfast Polyphontes.   395
Tydeus unleashed an ignominious fate on these too:
he killed all of them, and he sent one to return home all alone.
He sent back Maeon, trusting in the portents of the gods.
Such was Tydeus, the Aetolian. But he begot a son
worse than himself in battle, but better at talking.   400

                                               (*Il.* 4. 370–400)

Tydeus, Agamemnon says, always fought in the forefront of
the battle: he did not hang back, merely gazing at the ranks of
war. He goes on to relate an anecdote about Tydeus arriving at
Mycenae with the Theban pretender, Polynices, to raise forces
for the expedition against Thebes: the Mycenaeans approved
the project and would have given allies, but they were prevented from doing so by the unfavourable signs sent by Zeus
(*Il.* 4. 376–81). Agamemnon is arguing that the earlier readiness of his people to support the cause of Diomede's father
means that now Diomede, in his turn, should support the cause
of Agamemnon and his brother.[10] The anecdote continues, with
Tydeus sent on ahead of Polynices, to take a message to the
Thebans. Although he is among enemies, Tydeus challenges
the Thebans to athletic contests,[11] all of which he wins easily,
with the help of Athene. The angry Thebans set an ambush of
fifty men to intercept Tydeus on his return journey, but, θεῶν
τεράεσσι πιθήσας, trusting in the portents of the gods (*Il.* 4. 398),
he kills them all, except one.[12] The pertinent qualities of
Tydeus conveyed by this anecdote of Agamemnon's are (1) his
complete lack of fear, (2) his enjoyment of the patronage of
Athene (*Il.* 4. 390), (3) his piety displayed in careful attention
to and trust in, signs from the gods.[13] Diomede is not like his
father, Agamemnon says: he is worse in battle, and better at
speaking in the assembly. This last is not a compliment to
Diomede's rhetorical powers: Agamemnon is implying he is
not much good for anything.

---

[10] Andersen (1978: 35). Agamemnon seems unaware of the obvious flaw in
his argument: in the event no help was given to Polynices and Tydeus.

[11] The parallel with Odysseus' challenge to the Phaeacians (*Od.* 8. 202–33)
is made by Kirk (1985–90: i. 369–70 ad *Il.* 4. 385).

[12] The exploits of Tydeus mentioned as an example to Diomede at *Il.* 4.
370–400 and 5. 800–13 might originate in the *Thebaid*: see Robert (1920: 932).
If they do, they bear the hallmarks of exaggeration and adjustment for the
present context: Polyphontes, son of Autophonus, the second murderer in
the ambush for Tydeus, sounds like a *nom parlant* akin to Polyidus, the seer
(*Il.* 13. 663), and Harmonides, the carpenter (*Il.* 5. 59): see Willcock (1964:
144–5).

[13] On these qualities, see Andersen (1978: 38–9).

5.3.2. Stage 2. The counter-argument from Sthenelus

Tydeus is known only by his reputation, and not personally by anyone fighting at Troy (*Il.* 4. 374–5), not even his son (*Il.* 6. 222–3), since he left for the war against Thebes before Diomede was old enough to remember him. As a rather shadowy figure from the past, his exploits should provide the poet's characters with ideal examples with which to support their arguments, permitting the use of selective anecdotes without the danger of being reminded of inconvenient or contradictory material by someone familiar with the whole story.

Agamemnon is caught out in this assumption, since some very inconvenient material on the subject of Tydeus is mentioned by Sthenelus, who is not the primary addressee of Agamemnon's νεῖκος, but who is unable to contain himself at Agamemnon's misrepresentation:

> Ἀτρεΐδη, μὴ ψεύδε᾽ ἐπιστάμενος σάφα εἰπεῖν·
> ἡμεῖς τοι πατέρων μέγ᾽ ἀμείνονες εὐχόμεθ᾽ εἶναι·
> ἡμεῖς καὶ Θήβης ἕδος εἵλομεν ἑπταπύλοιο,   405
> παυρότερον λαὸν ἀγαγόνθ᾽ ὑπὸ τεῖχος ἄρειον,
> πειθόμενοι τεράεσσι θεῶν καὶ Ζηνὸς ἀρωγῇ·
> κεῖνοι δὲ σφετέρῃσιν ἀτασθαλίῃσιν ὄλοντο·
> τῶ μή μοι πατέρας ποθ᾽ ὁμοίῃ ἔνθεο τιμῇ.   410

Son of Atreus, do not tell blatant lies when you know how to speak truly.
We claim to be far better than our fathers.   405
We even captured the seat of seven-gated Thebes
leading a smaller army under the strengthened walls,
trusting in the portents of the gods and the help of Zeus.
But the Seven perished as a result of their recklessness.   409
Therefore do not, please, place our fathers in equal honour with us.

(*Il.* 4. 404–10)

Sthenelus complains about Agamemnon's suppression of pertinent facts: Ἀτρεΐδη, μὴ ψεύδε᾽ <u>ἐπιστάμενος</u> σάφα εἰπεῖν, 'Son of Atreus, do not tell blatant untruths *when you know* how to speak truly' (*Il.* 4. 404),[14] as if Agamemnon had deliberately omitted information detrimental to the impression he desired to create. Sthenelus points to the end of the first expedition against

---

[14] On other public corrections of Agamemnon's misleading representations, see Lohmann (1970: 44 n. 72).

Thebes: the Seven perished σφετέρῃσιν ἀτασθαλίῃσιν, through their own recklessness (*Il.* 4. 409), whereas their sons had smaller forces but were not thereby prevented from avenging their fathers and destroying Thebes.[15] It is not remotely convenient to Agamemnon's purposes to be reminded that all the daring risks taken by Tydeus culminated in ἀτασθαλία, or that the expedition of the Seven ended disastrously, even if he let out a hint at all this himself, by his reference to the παραίσια σήματα, the ill-omened signs sent by Zeus when the envoys came to Mycenae to raise troops. Sthenelus echoes Agamemnon's words in derision: πειθόμενοι τεράεσσι θεῶν καὶ Ζηνὸς ἀρωγῇ, 'trusting in the portents of the gods and the help of Zeus' (*Il.* 4. 408) caps Agamemnon's remark (*Il.* 4. 398) that Tydeus dealt with the Cadmeian ambush θεῶν τεράεσσι πιθήσας, 'trusting in the portents of the gods'. Tydeus simply put his confidence (πιθήσας) in the portents of the gods, whereas the sons of the Seven were obedient (πειθόμενοι) to the portents of the gods, and that explains their success. They were receptive to Zeus' ἀρωγῇ (succour) too: they were not taking any chances. By contrast, Tydeus ignored the παραίσια σήματα (the ill-omened signs) sent by Zeus, when he was raising troops for the expedition against Thebes (*Il.* 4. 381). Fortunately for Agamemnon, the disastrous conclusion of the first Theban expedition is instantly hushed up, for Diomede is not disposed to hear a word against the reputation of his father: he silences Sthenelus immediately, accepting Agamemnon's right to use the νεῖκος as a means of urging men to fight, and reminding Sthenelus of the immediate need to concern themselves with the battle.

However, the damage has been done: the poet has used Sthenelus' intrusion to draw the attention of the audience to the ἀτασθαλία, recklessness, of the Seven, which brought about their deaths. In the first instance, Agamemnon's unfavourable comparison of Diomede with his father through relating a specific anecdote about Tydeus works very well as a spur to Diomede's efforts on the battlefield. The same anecdote from the career of Tydeus is used by Athene herself to taunt Diomede to greater efforts.

---

[15] An 'apologetic' paradigm in justification of himself and Diomede: Austin (1978: 74; 1st pub. 1966).

5.3.3. *Stage 3. Athene's reproach to Diomede (Il. 5. 800–13)*

Pandarus wounds Diomede (*Il.* 5. 98–100) and Diomede prays
to Athene to be able to kill Pandarus (*Il.* 5. 115–20). Athene
restores his strength (*Il.* 5. 122–3)[16] and gives him the ability to
distinguish gods from men on the battlefield: she forbids him to
fight with gods, except for Aphrodite (*Il.* 5. 127–32). Diomede
does indeed kill Pandarus (*Il.* 5. 290–6) and he wounds
Aphrodite and drives her from the field (*Il.* 5. 336–40, 352).
When the wound Pandarus gave him begins to be troublesome
(*Il.* 5. 795–8), Athene expands the anecdote already told by
Agamemnon (of Tydeus' visit to Thebes as a messenger) again
to compare Diomede unfavourably with his father:[17]

ἦ ὀλίγον οἷ παῖδα ἐοικότα γείνατο Τυδεύς.   800
Τυδεύς τοι μικρὸς μὲν ἔην δέμας, ἀλλὰ μαχητής·
καί ῥ' ὅτε πέρ μιν ἐγὼ πολεμίζειν οὐκ εἴασκον
οὐδ' ἐκπαιφάσσειν, ὅτε τ' ἤλυθε νόσφιν Ἀχαιῶν
ἄγγελος ἐς Θήβας πολέας μετὰ Καδμείωνας
δαίνυσθαί μιν ἄνωγον ἐνὶ μεγάροισιν ἔκηλον·   805
αὐτὰρ ὁ θυμὸν ἔχων ὃν καρτερόν, ὡς τὸ πάρος περ,
κούρους Καδμείων προκαλίζετο, πάντα δ' ἐνίκα
ῥηϊδίως· τοίη οἱ ἐγὼν ἐπιτάρροθος ἦα.
σοὶ δ' ἤτοι μὲν ἐγὼ παρά θ' ἵσταμαι ἠδὲ φυλάσσω,
καί σε προφρονέως κέλομαι Τρώεσσι μάχεσθαι·   810
ἀλλά σευ ἢ κάματος πολυάϊξ γυῖα δέδυκεν,
ἤ νύ σέ που δέος ἴσχει ἀκήριον· οὐ σύ γ' ἔπειτα
Τυδέος ἔκγονός ἐσσι δαΐφρονος Οἰνεΐδαο.

Tydeus got a son who little resembles him.   800
Tydeus was certainly small in stature, but he was a fighter.
Even when I did not permit him to fight
or rush madly into the fray, when he came without the Achaeans
as a messenger to Thebes, among many Cadmeians,
I bade him feast in the halls in peace: 805
but he, keeping up his spirits as before,
was challenging the youths of the Cadmeians, and every contest he
    won
with ease, such a helper was I to him.

[16] The comparison of Diomede to a wounded lion (*Il.* 5. 136–42) indicates
that Athene does not heal the wound, as is required on the occasion of
Athene's νεῖκος to Diomede: see Erbse (1961: 172).
[17] For the opposition of Diomede to the pattern of Tydeus in Athene's
speech, see Lohmann (1970: 14–15).

And yet beside you I stand and watch over you,
and I bid you to fight with a will against the Trojans,   810
but either weariness caused by impetuosity in battle has overcome
    your limbs
or perhaps, of course, cowardly fear holds you back. Then you are not
the offspring of Tydeus, the wise son of Oeneus.

                                                        (*Il.* 5. 800–13)

In other words, Tydeus displayed aggression even when
Athene told him not to: his son, on the other hand, will not
fight even with Athene's encouragement. This time Diomede
rises to the bait of the νεῖκος:[18] it is not fear which makes him
hold back, but Athene's own command not to fight with the
gods, except for Aphrodite. He is not fighting now, because he
can see Ares on the battlefield. Athene and Agamemnon use the
past exploit of Tydeus under divine patronage to urge Diomede
to excel now under divine patronage.

5.4. DIOMEDE'S CHOICE: SUCCESS NO. I
WITH DIVINE FAVOUR

This same anecdote of Tydeus' visit to the enemy territory of
Thebes is used by Diomede as the basis of two prayers to
Athene. These are outside the argument begun with the use of
the anecdote, but since they request divine assistance, they
indicate Diomede's choice of the policy advocated by Agamemnon and Athene. When Diomede makes his first prayer to
Athene to be able to kill Pandarus, who wounded him, he
requests that as surely as Athene stood beside his father Tydeus
in the fighting, he may be able now to kill Pandarus:

κλῦθί μευ, αἰγιόχοιο Διὸς τέκος, Ἀτρυτώνη,   115
εἴ ποτέ μοι καὶ πατρὶ φίλα φρονέουσα παρέστης
δηΐῳ ἐν πολέμῳ, νῦν αὖτ' ἐμὲ φῖλαι, Ἀθήνη·
δὸς δέ τέ μ' ἄνδρα ἐλεῖν καὶ ἐς ὁρμὴν ἔγχεος ἐλθεῖν,
ὅς μ' ἔβαλε φθάμενος καὶ ἐπεύχεται, οὐδέ μέ φησι
δηρὸν ἔτ' ὄψεσθαι λαμπρὸν φάος ἠελίοιο.   120

Hear me, child of aegis-bearing Zeus, Atrytone,   115
if ever you stood beside my father with kindly intent
in hot combat, now show affection to me too, Athene.

---

[18] *Il.* 5. 815–24, see Lohmann (1970: 19).

Grant that I may slay this man and come within a spear's cast of him,
who struck me before I saw him, and boasts about it, saying
I will not look much longer on the brightness of the light of the sun.

(Il. 5. 115–20)

In the confrontation with Pandarus, Athene guides Diomede's
spear to kill him *(Il.* 5. 290). She does not, however, literally
stand beside Diomede until it suits her: after mentioning how
she assisted Tydeus even when he disobeyed her command to
be peaceable, she adds that now she is standing beside Diomede
and watching over him *(Il.* 5. 808–9) (since she now requires
him to disobey her earlier instructions not to fight with gods).
Then she pushes Sthenelus out of the chariot and climbs in
herself, so that she is literally standing beside Diomede *(Il.* 5.
837). She deflects Ares' spear from herself and her companion
(Il. 5. 853–4) and leans on Diomede's to wound Ares *(Il.* 5.
856).[19] Her object achieved, she returns to the hall of Zeus *(Il.*
5. 907–9). Her patronage is not disinterested: Diomede serves
as her instrument against Ares and Aphrodite.[20] The second of
Diomede's two prayers to Athene follows much debate in para-
narrative: it is discussed below.

5.5. THE ARGUMENT RESUMED

5.5.1. Stage 4. The fate of the θεομάχος: Dione's catalogue (Il. 5.
382–415)

The support of one god does not necessarily save its recipient
from punishment by another,[21] and the argument begun with
Agamemnon's and Athene's taunts that Diomede falls short of
the example of his father is continued through the catalogue of
Dione. Diomede is, of course, unaware of this paradigmatic
story told by Dione to console the wounded Aphrodite, who
approaches her mother for comfort when she is wounded by
Diomede and flees from the battlefield. After a short list of
other gods injured by mortals, Dione ends her speech with a

---

[19] Aeneas complains about similar divine assistance to Achilles *(Il.* 20.
98–100).

[20] For Diomede as Athene's instrument, see Erbse (1961: 161–4): Diomede
makes Athene's hatred of Aphrodite his own (Erbse 1961: 167).

[21] Kirk (1985–90: ii. 103 ad *Il.* 5. 406–9).

complex threat against Diomede: fighting the gods is gross impiety, and Diomede should look out in case someone stronger than Aphrodite should fight with him and leave Aigialea grieving for her husband. In fact Aphrodite will have her revenge on Diomede, in the short term through her champion, Paris, who wounds Diomede in the foot, and in the long term through the infidelity of Aigialea. Dione's speech is worth examination:

τέτλαθι, τέκνον ἐμόν, καὶ ἀνάσχεο κηδομένη περ·
πολλοὶ γὰρ δὴ τλῆμεν Ὀλύμπια δώματ' ἔχοντες
ἐξ ἀνδρῶν, χαλέπ' ἄλγε' ἐπ' ἀλλήλοισι τιθέντες.
τλῆ μὲν Ἄρης, ὅτε μιν Ὦτος κρατερός τ' Ἐφιάλτης,   385
παῖδες Ἀλωῆος, δῆσαν κρατερῷ ἐνὶ δεσμῷ·
χαλκέῳ δ' ἐν κεράμῳ δέδετο τρισκαίδεκα μῆνας·
καί νύ κεν ἔνθ' ἀπόλοιτο Ἄρης ἆτος πολέμοιο,
εἰ μὴ μητρυιή, περικαλλὴς Ἠερίβοια,
Ἑρμέᾳ ἐξήγγειλεν· ὁ δ' ἐξέκλεψεν Ἄρηα   390
ἤδη τειρόμενον, χαλεπὸς δέ ἑ δεσμὸς ἐδάμνα.
τλῆ δ' Ἥρη, ὅτε μιν κρατερὸς πάϊς Ἀμφιτρύωνος
δεξιτερὸν κατὰ μαζὸν ὀϊστῷ τριγλώχινι
βεβλήκει· τότε καί μιν ἀνήκεστον λάβεν ἄλγος.
τλῆ δ' Ἀΐδης ἐν τοῖσι πελώριος ὠκὺν ὀϊστόν,   395
εὖτέ μιν ωὑτὸς ἀνήρ, υἱὸς Διὸς αἰγιόχοιο,
ἐν Πύλῳ ἐν νεκύεσσι βαλὼν ὀδύνῃσιν ἔδωκεν·
αὐτὰρ ὁ βῆ πρὸς δῶμα Διὸς καὶ μακρὸν Ὄλυμπον
κῆρ ἀχέων, ὀδύνῃσι πεπαρμένος· αὐτὰρ ὀϊστὸς
ὤμῳ ἔνι στιβαρῷ ἠλήλατο, κῆδε δὲ θυμόν.   400
τῷ δ' ἐπὶ Παιήων ὀδυνήφατα φάρμακα πάσσων
ἠκέσατ'· οὐ μὲν γάρ τι καταθνητός γ' ἐτέτυκτο.
σχέτλιος, ὀβριμοεργός, ὃς οὐκ ὄθετ' αἴσυλα ῥέζων,
ὃς τόξοισιν ἔκηδε θεούς, οἳ Ὄλυμπον ἔχουσι.
σοὶ δ' ἐπὶ τοῦτον ἀνῆκε θεὰ γλαυκῶπις Ἀθήνη·   405
νήπιος, οὐδὲ τὸ οἶδε κατὰ φρένα Τυδέος υἱός,
ὅττι μάλ' οὐ δηναιὸς ὃς ἀθανάτοισι μάχηται,
οὐδέ τί μιν παῖδες ποτὶ γούνασι παππάζουσιν
ἐλθόντ' ἐκ πολέμοιο καὶ αἰνῆς δηϊοτῆτος.
τῷ νῦν Τυδεΐδης, εἰ καὶ μάλα καρτερός ἐστι,   410
φραζέσθω μή τίς οἱ ἀμείνων σεῖο μάχηται,
μὴ δὴν Αἰγιάλεια, περίφρων Ἀδρηστίνη,
ἐξ ὕπνου γοόωσα φίλους οἰκῆας ἐγείρῃ,
κουρίδιον ποθέουσα πόσιν, τὸν ἄριστον Ἀχαιῶν,
ἰφθίμη ἄλοχος Διομήδεος ἱπποδάμοιο.   415

Endure it, my child, and bear up although you are distressed:
For many who have Olympian halls endured
at the hands of men, inflicting troublesome pains on one another.
Ares endured when Otus and mighty Ephialtes,   385
the sons of Aloëus bound him in a mighty chain.
He was imprisoned in a brazen jar for thirteen months,
and doubtless Ares, insatiate of war, would have perished
had not their stepmother, the very beautiful Eeriboea,
told Hermes about it. And he stole Ares out of it,   390
Already wasting away, and the troublesome chain was wearing him
     out.
Hera endured when the mighty son of Amphitryon
shot her in the right breast with a triple-barbed arrow.
Then an incurable pain seized her too.
Hades, the monster, endured with these a swift arrow   395
when the same man, the son of aegis-bearing Zeus
striking him in Pylos among the corpses, gave him up to pain.
And he went to the hall of Zeus and lofty Olympus,
Grieving at heart, transfixed with pain: but the arrow
had been driven through his burly shoulder, and he was sore at
     heart.
Paeon sprinkled pain-assuaging drugs on it and cured it.   401
For not at all was he a mortal.
Savage agent of violent deeds, who paid no heed to the impiety of his
     action,
who, with his bow, distressed the gods who dwell on Olympus.
The grey-eyed goddess Athene urged this man on against you: 405
the ninny, nor does the son of Tydeus know in his heart
that he does not live long who fights with immortals,
nor do his children call him 'papa' at his knees
when he comes from the war and the terrible din of battle.
So now let the son of Tydeus, even if he is very strong,   410
look out in case someone stronger than you may fight with him,
lest Aigialea, the wise daughter of Adrastus,
the strong wife of horse-taming Diomede,
may rouse her servants from sleep with long lament,
longing for her wedded husband, the best of the Achaeans.   415
                              (*Il.* 5. 382–415)

While Dione's story has a bearing on Aphrodite's immediate
situation, it also makes direct reference to Diomede. Aphrodite
has a slight graze from Diomede's spear, and she is making a
terrible fuss about it: very well, Dione says, but three other

gods had to endure far worse pain inflicted by mortals.[22]
Ares endured it when Otus and Ephialtes bound him and
imprisoned him for thirteen months in a jar. He was rescued by
his stepmother, Eeriboea, who persuaded Hermes to release
him (*Il.* 5. 385–91). Hera endured when Heracles shot her with
an arrow in the breast (*Il.* 5. 392–4). Hades too was shot by
Heracles with an arrow in the shoulder, and had to be treated
by Paeon, who applied pain-killing drugs (*Il.* 5. 395–402).
Aphrodite too, by implication, must endure her wound. However, Dione's story not only offers an example to Aphrodite,
Diomede's victim, but also hints at disaster for the θεομάχος,
Diomede. The paradigmatic catalogue of gods who endured
suffering inflicted by mortals is rounded off with some
generalizing remarks about θεομάχοι, first in condemnation of
the wickedness of Heracles, who fought with gods:

> σχέτλιος, ὀβριμοεργός, ὃς οὐκ ὄθετ' αἴσυλα ῥέζων,
> ὃς τόξοισιν ἔκηδε θεούς, οἳ Ὄλυμπον ἔχουσι

savage agent of violent deeds, who paid no heed to the impiety of his
     action,
who with his bow distressed the gods who dwell on Olympus

(*Il.* 5. 403–4)

and secondly of the folly of Diomede:

> σοὶ δ' ἐπὶ τοῦτον ἀνῆκε θεὰ γλαυκῶπις Ἀθήνη·
> νήπιος, οὐδὲ τὸ οἶδε κατὰ φρένα Τυδέος υἱός,
> ὅττι μάλ' οὐ δηναιὸς ὃς ἀθανάτοισι μάχηται,
> οὐδέ τί μιν παῖδες ποτὶ γούνασι παππάζουσιν
> ἐλθόντ' ἐκ πολέμοιο καὶ αἰνῆς δηϊοτῆτος.

---

[22] For analysis of the structure of Dione's catalogue, see Lohmann (1970: 53
n. 93). On the story as inherited material used to construct a paradigm, see
Andersen (1978: 61–8); Lang (1983: 153–7). On the story as a consolatory
paradigm see Austin (1978: 74; 1st pub. 1966). For comparison with the 'consolation' of the wounded Ares (*Il.* 5. 889–901) and the wounded Artemis (*Il.*
21. 505–13), see Fenik (1968: 41). Ares is wounded also in Hesiod, [*Sc.*]
359–67: for discussion, see Huxley (1969: 185–6). For the argument that Ares'
wounding by Heracles at Pylos (Hesiod, [*Sc.*] 359–67) was inspired by his
wound in *Iliad*, book 5, see Janko (1986: 45 and 59). For comparison with a
fragment of Panyassis (Matthews (1974: 91–5 fr. 16K)) listing gods who
endured suffering inflicted by mortals, see Beye (1964: 365).

the grey-eyed goddess Athene urged this man on against you: 405
the ninny, nor does the son of Tydeus know in his heart
that he does not live long who fights with immortals,
nor do his children call him 'papa' at his knees
when he comes from the war and the terrible din of battle.

(*Il.* 5. 405–9)

Diomede should look out, Dione says, in case someone better
than Aphrodite should fight him,[23] and leave Aigialea and her
children grieving for (the fallen) Diomede (*Il.* 5. 411–15).[24]

Athene, as Dione tells Aphrodite (*Il.* 5. 405–6), uses
Diomede and his ἀριστεία for her own purposes, to settle scores
against her fellow gods. In the course of fighting amongst
themselves, gods do get hurt by mortals (*Il.* 5. 383–4).
Diomede explains (*Il.* 5. 818) that he has been holding back and
not fighting because of Athene's orders not to fight with gods.
However, it does not follow that he will be immune from any
adverse consequences of fighting with gods when, on Athene's
instructions, he fights first Aphrodite (*Il.* 5. 131–2), and then
Ares (*Il.* 5. 829–31). Athene's instructions offer no guarantee of
immunity from the consequences of fighting gods.[25] The

---

[23] It will be a long time before someone better at fighting than Aphrodite
engages with Diomede, and that someone will be her favourite, Paris.

[24] It would be a mistake to take τις ἀμείνων σεῖο, 'someone better than you',
as a reference to Apollo, whom Diomede pursues as the god is retrieving the
wounded Aeneas, since Apollo does not even take Diomede seriously as an
opponent: he merely brushes him aside three times, and then frightens him by
shouting at him (*Il.* 5. 437–9). In any case, the object of Diomede's three
rushes is not Apollo, but Aeneas, whom Apollo is carrying from the battlefield. For comparison of this scene with Achilles' three rushes after Hector,
who is snatched away by Apollo, see Fenik (1968: 46–7; 212–13). The scene is
also comparable with Patroclus' three rushes up the batter of the walls of
Troy, only to be forced to give ground by Apollo (*Il.* 16. 702–9), see Bannert
(1988: 42–4), but Apollo is not rescuing anyone in book 16.

[25] Failure to comply with Athene's command to attack Ares would doubtless have had adverse consequences too. The instructions of the gods are not
always for the benefit of the recipient, who often finds himself in a double
bind: he is guilty if he disobeys a divine command, but must himself bear the
responsibility for whatever he does in obedience to it. Orestes must obey the
command of Apollo to avenge his father (Aeschylus, *Ch.* 1029–32), but in the
process he commits the crime of matricide. (Clytemnestra's fate is approved
by the Dioscuri in Euripides' play, but the matricide committed by Orestes is
not: Euripides, *El.* 1244.) I do not agree with Andersen (1978: 61–2) that
Diomede is exonerated by the precedents in Dione's catalogue. Athene

goddess is simply exploiting for her own ends Diomede's heroic desire to measure up to the glorious reputation of his father. Athene urges him on to even greater exploits than those he achieves in response to taunts of the same nature from Agamemnon. Agamemnon's νεῖκος results in Diomede winning great glory by his victories over mortal opponents, but Athene taunts him so that he fights and is victorious, even against gods.

5.5.2. Stage 5. The fate of another θεομάχος: *Diomede's story of Lycurgus (Il. 6. 130–43)*

However, it remains an unwise policy to fight with gods, and Diomede himself tells a story which illustrates this in his battlefield encounter with Glaucus in book 6, the next step in the debate conducted by means of the para-narratives clustered around Diomede. There is no regular pattern for the verbal exchanges between warriors before engaging in battle:[26] generally the effect of preliminary taunts is to spur the addressee to fight, but there are instances where he thinks better of it, and this battlefield exchange between Diomede and Glaucus ends with the challenger retreating from his initial challenge. Diomede begins by demanding to know Glaucus' identity: if he is a god, Diomede will not fight with him.[27] He proceeds to his account of Lycurgus, who did fight with a god, even if only a small one, and who came to no good as a result:[28]

τίς δὲ σύ ἐσσι, φέριστε, καταθνητῶν ἀνθρώπων;
οὐ μὲν γάρ ποτ' ὄπωπα μάχῃ ἔνι κυδιανείρῃ
τὸ πρίν· ἀτὰρ μὲν νῦν γε πολὺ προβέβηκας ἁπάντων   125
σῷ θάρσει, ὅ τ' ἐμὸν δολιχόσκιον ἔγχος ἔμεινας·

nowhere assumes responsibility for Diomede's actions in obedience to her commands, as Andersen suggests (1978: 85).

[26] See Fenik (1968: 101), and the following passages discussed by Fenik (1968: 66): *Il.* 6. 125–7; 17. 16–17, 30–2; 20. 178–98; 21. 150–1.

[27] Diomede's failure to recognize Glaucus after ten years at Troy was recognized as a problem in antiquity, see Maftei (1976: 13). Avery (1994: 499–501) offers two reasons why Glaucus might be mistaken for a god: (1) the combatants are not aware that the gods left the battle at *Il.* 5. 907–9, and (2) the golden armour worn by Glaucus is more appropriate to a god than to a man.

[28] For analysis of the structure of Diomede's speech (ring composition), see Lohmann (1970: 12).

δυστήνων δέ τε παῖδες ἐμῷ μένει ἀντιόωσιν.
εἰ δέ τις ἀθανάτων γε κατ᾽ οὐρανοῦ εἰλήλουθας,
οὐκ ἂν ἔγωγε θεοῖσιν ἐπουρανίοισι μαχοίμην·
οὐδὲ γὰρ οὐδὲ Δρύαντος υἱός, κρατερὸς Λυκόοργος,
δὴν ἦν, ὅς ῥα θεοῖσιν ἐπουρανίοισιν ἔριζεν.
ὅς ποτε μαινομένοιο Διωνύσοιο τιθήνας
σεῦε κατ᾽ ἠγάθεον Νυσήϊον· αἱ δ᾽ ἅμα πᾶσαι
θύσθλα χαμαὶ κατέχευαν, ὑπ᾽ ἀνδροφόνοιο Λυκούργου
θεινόμεναι βουπλῆγι· Διώνυσος δὲ φοβηθεὶς   135
δύσεθ᾽ ἁλὸς κατὰ κῦμα, Θέτις δ᾽ ὑπεδέξατο κόλπῳ
δειδιότα· κρατερὸς γὰρ ἔχε τρόμος ἀνδρὸς ὁμοκλῇ.
τῷ μὲν ἔπειτ᾽ ὀδύσαντο θεοὶ ῥεῖα ζώοντες,
καί μιν τυφλὸν ἔθηκε Κρόνου πάϊς· οὐδ᾽ ἄρ᾽ ἔτι δὴν
ἦν, ἐπεὶ ἀθανάτοισιν ἀπήχθετο πᾶσι θεοῖσιν·   140
οὐδ᾽ ἂν ἐγὼ μακάρεσσι θεοῖς ἐθέλοιμι μάχεσθαι.
εἰ δέ τίς ἐσσι βροτῶν, οἳ ἀρούρης καρπὸν ἔδουσιν,
ἆσσον ἴθ᾽ ὥς κεν θᾶσσον ὀλέθρου πείραθ᾽ ἵκηαι.

Who are you, my friend, of mortal men?
For I have never seen you before in the battle which brings glory to
    men.
But now you have come a long way in front of all   125
in your hardihood, in that you waited for my long-shadowing spear.
Unhappy are the parents whose sons come to meet with my might.
But if you are in fact one of the immortals and you have come down
    from heaven
I, at any rate, would not fight with the heavenly gods.
For even the son of Dryas, strong Lycurgus,   130
was not long-lived, who strove against the heavenly gods.
He chased the nurses of wild Dionysus
down holy Nysa, and they all at once
dropped their wands on the ground, struck by the murderous
    Lycurgus
with a pole-axe. And Dionysus, terrified,   135
dived under the wave of the sea, and Thetis received him in her bosom
frightened and in a fit of trembling at the man's shouting.
The gods who live easy were angry with him,
And the son of Cronus made him blind. Still he did not last long,
since he was hated by all the gods.   140
Nor would I wish to fight with the blessed gods.
But if you are one of mortals, who eat the fruit of the ploughland,
come nearer, so that you may come quickly to the end of death.

(*Il.* 6. 123–43)

Lycurgus, in Diomede's account, chased the nurses of Dionysus, attacking them with an ox-goad, or with a sacrificial axe: the nurses dropped all the ritual objects they were using, and Dionysus himself, terrified at the man's shouting, leapt into the sea, where Thetis comforted him.[29] Lycurgus, the θεομάχος, was blinded by Zeus: he became an object of hatred to all the gods, and he did not last long, Diomede relates.[30] As if he were himself the very embodiment of caution in such matters, Diomede goes on to say that he would not care, in view of the example he has just quoted, to fight with gods. These are not the words of a man with much self-awareness: although he has just been fighting with Aphrodite and Ares, he describes the fate of one who fought with a god without appearing to anticipate any connection between the behaviour he describes and his own recent activities. He seems unaware that he could be telling this story against himself.[31]

The story of Lycurgus, the θεομάχος who fought against gods and came to grief, is counterpointed by the story of

---

[29] We have been here before. The burdens dropped, the instantaneous flight of the divinity, the armed man in pursuit of a god, are elements encountered in Diomede's attacks on Aphrodite and Ares in book 5. Aphrodite is wounded by Diomede as she carries her son, Aeneas, also wounded by Diomede, off the field (*Il.* 5. 348–51). She drops Aeneas with a shriek (*Il.* 5. 343) and flees from the battlefield (*Il.* 5. 352) to be comforted by Dione (*Il.* 5. 382–415). Ares, wounded by Diomede and Athene, flees from the field with a roar (*Il.* 5. 858–68) and goes to Zeus, who, despite some disparaging remarks, arranges for treatment from Paeon (*Il.* 5. 899).

[30] Martin (1989: 127–8) mistakenly regards this story as a wish-fulfilment fantasy, identifying Diomede with Lycurgus (the aggressor) and Glaucus with Dionysus and the nurses (who run away).

[31] Kirk (1985–90: ii. 172 ad *Il.* 6. 128–43) accepts Diomede on his own terms, taking his tone to be complacent or sarcastic when he says he would not fight against a god. Kirk offers no explanation of why 'the singer makes him avoid all reference to recent exploits against gods in book 5, where he was given special sanction by Athene, but rather adduce, in accord with the lighter and more reminiscent tone of this encounter as a whole, the unfamiliar *exemplum* of Lukorgos and Dionusos'. The importance of the *exemplum* of Lycurgus is not its unfamiliarity, but that Lycurgus fought against a god and he *did not escape consequences*. The whole point about behaving arrogantly is that you don't see yourself clearly and with an outsider's eye while you're doing it: your own actions are always exempt from the rules, even when you know the rules very well. This is Diomede's trouble: he forgets that the rules apply to him too, and that he has already contravened them.

Diomede: Debate in Para-Narrative 131

Bellerophon in Glaucus' genealogy: Bellerophon was not a θεομάχος, but came to grief anyway.

5.5.3. Stage 6. Loss of divine favour without fighting gods: the genealogy of Glaucus and the exploits of Bellerophon (Il. 6. 145–211)

Glaucus explains his identity by relating his genealogy:

Τυδεΐδη μεγάθυμε, τίη γενεὴν ἐρεείνεις;   145
οἵη περ φύλλων γενεή, τοίη δὲ καὶ ἀνδρῶν.
φύλλα τὰ μέν τ' ἄνεμος χαμάδις χέει, ἄλλα δέ θ' ὕλη
τηλεθόωσα φύει, ἔαρος δ' ἐπιγίγνεται ὥρη·
ὣς ἀνδρῶν γενεὴ ἡ μὲν φύει ἡ δ' ἀπολήγει.

εἰ δ' ἐθέλεις καὶ ταῦτα δαήμεναι, ὄφρ' ἐῢ εἰδῆς   150
ἡμετέρην γενεήν, πολλοὶ δέ μιν ἄνδρες ἴσασιν·
ἔστι πόλις Ἐφύρη μυχῷ Ἄργεος ἱπποβότοιο,
ἔνθα δὲ Σίσυφος ἔσκεν, ὃ κέρδιστος γένετ' ἀνδρῶν,
Σίσυφος Αἰολίδης· ὁ δ' ἄρα Γλαῦκον τέκεθ' υἱόν,
αὐτὰρ Γλαῦκος τίκτεν ἀμύμονα Βελλεροφόντην·   155
τῷ δὲ θεοὶ κάλλος τε καὶ ἠνορέην ἐρατεινὴν
ὤπασαν· αὐτάρ οἱ Προῖτος κακὰ μήσατο θυμῷ,
ὅς ῥ' ἐκ δήμου ἔλασσεν, ἐπεὶ πολὺ φέρτερος ἦεν,
Ἀργείων· Ζεὺς γάρ οἱ ὑπὸ σκήπτρῳ ἐδάμασσε.

τῷ δὲ γυνὴ Προίτου ἐπεμήνατο, δῖ' Ἄντεια,   160
κρυπταδίη φιλότητι μιγήμεναι· ἀλλὰ τὸν οὔ τι
πεῖθ' ἀγαθὰ φρονέοντα, δαΐφρονα Βελλεροφόντην.
ἡ δὲ ψευσαμένη Προῖτον βασιλῆα προσηύδα·
"τεθναίης, ὦ Προῖτ', ἢ κάκτανε Βελλεροφόντην,
ὅς μ' ἔθελεν φιλότητι μιγήμεναι οὐκ ἐθελούσῃ."   165
ὣς φάτο, τὸν δὲ ἄνακτα χόλος λάβεν οἷον ἄκουσε·
κτεῖναι μέν ῥ' ἀλέεινε, σεβάσσατο γὰρ τό γε θυμῷ,
πέμπε δέ μιν Λυκίηνδε, πόρεν δ' ὅ γε σήματα λυγρά,
γράψας ἐν πίνακι πτυκτῷ θυμοφθόρα πολλά,
δεῖξαι δ' ἠνώγειν ᾧ πενθερῷ, ὄφρ' ἀπόλοιτο.   170
αὐτὰρ ὁ βῆ Λυκίηνδε θεῶν ὑπ' ἀμύμονι πομπῇ.
ἀλλ' ὅτε δὴ Λυκίην ἷξε Ξάνθον τε ῥέοντα,
προφρονέως μιν τῖεν ἄναξ Λυκίης εὐρείης·
ἐννῆμαρ ξείνισσε καὶ ἐννέα βοῦς ἱέρευσεν.
ἀλλ' ὅτε δὴ δεκάτη ἐφάνη ῥοδοδάκτυλος Ἠώς,   175
καὶ τότε μιν ἐρέεινε καὶ ἤτεε σῆμα ἰδέσθαι,
ὅττι ῥά οἱ γαμβροῖο πάρα Προίτοιο φέροιτο.
αὐτὰρ ἐπεὶ δὴ σῆμα κακὸν παρεδέξατο γαμβροῦ,
πρῶτον μέν ῥα Χίμαιραν ἀμαιμακέτην ἐκέλευσε

πεφνέμεν· ἡ δ' ἄρ' ἔην θεῖον γένος, οὐδ' ἀνθρώπων,   180
πρόσθε λέων, ὄπιθεν δὲ δράκων, μέσση δὲ χίμαιρα,
δεινὸν ἀποπνείουσα πυρὸς μένος αἰθομένοιο,
καὶ τὴν μὲν κατέπεφνε θεῶν τεράεσσι πιθήσας·
δεύτερον αὖ Σολύμοισι μαχέσσατο κυδαλίμοισι·
καρτίστην δὴ τήν γε μάχην φάτο δύμεναι ἀνδρῶν.   185
τὸ τρίτον αὖ κατέπεφνεν Ἀμαζόνας ἀντιανείρας.
τῷ δ' ἄρ' ἀνερχομένῳ πυκινὸν δόλον ἄλλον ὕφαινε·
κρίνας ἐκ Λυκίης εὐρείης φῶτας ἀρίστους
εἷσε λόχον· τοὶ δ' οὔ τι πάλιν οἶκόνδε νέοντο·
πάντας γὰρ κατέπεφνεν ἀμύμων Βελλεροφόντης.   190
ἀλλ' ὅτε δὴ γίγνωσκε θεοῦ γόνον ἠὺν ἐόντα,
αὐτοῦ μιν κατέρυκε, δίδου δ' ὅ γε θυγατέρα ἥν,
δῶκε δέ οἱ τιμῆς βασιληΐδος ἥμισυ πάσης·
καὶ μέν οἱ Λύκιοι τέμενος τάμον ἔξοχον ἄλλων,
καλὸν φυταλιῆς καὶ ἀρούρης, ὄφρα νέμοιτο.   195
ἡ δ' ἔτεκε τρία τέκνα δαΐφρονι Βελλεροφόντῃ,
Ἴσανδρόν τε καὶ Ἱππόλοχον καὶ Λαοδάμειαν.
Λαοδαμείῃ μὲν παρελέξατο μητίετα Ζεύς,
ἡ δ' ἔτεκ' ἀντίθεον Σαρπηδόνα χαλκοκορυστήν.
ἀλλ' ὅτε δὴ καὶ κεῖνος ἀπήχθετο πᾶσι θεοῖσιν,   200
ἤτοι ὁ κὰπ πεδίον τὸ Ἀλήϊον οἶος ἀλᾶτο,
ὃν θυμὸν κατέδων, πάτον ἀνθρώπων ἀλεείνων·
Ἴσανδρον δέ οἱ υἱὸν Ἄρης ἆτος πολέμοιο
μαρνάμενον Σολύμοισι κατέκτανε κυδαλίμοισι·
τὴν δὲ χολωσαμένη χρυσήνιος Ἄρτεμις ἔκτα.   205
Ἱππόλοχος δ' ἔμ' ἔτικτε, καὶ ἐκ τοῦ φημι γενέσθαι·
πέμπε δέ μ' ἐς Τροίην, καί μοι μάλα πόλλ' ἐπέτελλεν,
αἰὲν ἀριστεύειν καὶ ὑπείροχον ἔμμεναι ἄλλων,
μηδὲ γένος πατέρων αἰσχυνέμεν, οἳ μέγ' ἄριστοι
ἔν τ' Ἐφύρῃ ἐγένοντο καὶ ἐν Λυκίῃ εὐρείῃ.   210
ταύτης τοι γενεῆς τε καὶ αἵματος εὔχομαι εἶναι.

Great-hearted son of Tydeus, why do you ask my descent?   145
As is the generation of leaves, so is the generation of men.
Some leaves the wind scatters on the ground, but others
the flourishing wood produces as the season of spring comes on.
So one generation of men flourishes, and another withers away.
But if you want to learn this too, so that you may know well   150
our descent, it is something that many men know.
There is a city, Ephyra, in a corner of horse-pasturing Argos;
there Sisyphus used to live, who was the craftiest of men,
Sisyphus, the son of Aeolus. And he begot a son, Glaucus,
And Glaucus begot the blameless Bellerophontes: 155

on him the gods bestowed beauty and comely manliness.
But Proetus plotted evil against him in his heart,
and drove him out of the society of the Argives, since he was very
    much the better.
For Zeus subdued the Argives under Proetus' sceptre.
The wife of Proetus, the godlike Anteia,   160
was frantic to unite with Bellerophon in secret love, but by no means
could she persuade him, for he was noble-hearted, the wise
    Bellerophon.
And she lied when she spoke to her husband:
'May you lie dead, Proetus, if you do not kill Bellerophon,
who wanted to unite with me in love-making against my will.'   165
So she spoke, and anger seized the king at what he heard.
He avoided killing him, for his soul shrank from it in awe,
but he sent him to Lycia, and he furnished baleful signs,
having scratched on a folded tablet many things that should work his
    destruction,
and he bade him to show it to Anteia's father, so that he would perish.
But he went to Lycia under the blameless escort of the gods.   171
But when he came to Lycia and reached the streams of Xanthus,
Eagerly did the lord of broad Lycia honour him:
he entertained him for nine days and sacrificed nine oxen.
But when the tenth rosy-fingered dawn appeared,   175
Then he questioned him, and asked to see the signs
which he brought from his son-in-law, Proetus.
But when he received the evil sign from his son-in-law,
first he commanded him to kill the raging Chimaera:
this was of divine race, not of men: 180
in front she was a lion, behind a snake, and in the middle a goat,
breathing terribly the might of raging fire,
and her he killed, trusting in the portents of the gods.
Secondly he fought with the glorious Solymoi:
that, he said, was the mightiest battle of warriors he had entered.
Thirdly he killed the Amazons, peers of men.   186
And he devised another hidden trick for him on the way back:
picking the best men from broad Lycia
he set an ambush, but they did not go home again,
for the blameless Bellerophon killed every one.   190
But when the king began to realize that he was the goodly offspring of
    a god,
he kept him there, and gave him his daughter,
and he gave him half the honour of his kingdom.
Yes, and the Lycians allocated to him an estate far above the others,

fair with vineyards and arable land, for his enjoyment.   195
And the king's daughter bore three children to the wise Bellerophon,
Isander and Hippolochus, and Laodameia.
And wile-weaving Zeus lay beside Laodameia,
and she bore the godlike Sarpedon of the brazen armour.
But when even he was hated by all the gods,   200
Then he wandered alone on the plain of wandering,
eating out his heart, avoiding the paths of men,
And Ares, insatiate of war, killed his son Isander
as he struggled against the glorious Solymoi.
And Artemis of the golden reins killed his daughter in anger.   205
And Hippolochus begot me, and I claim to be his son.
And he sent me to Troy and gave me many very urgent instructions,
always to be the best, and to be superior to the others,
and not to disgrace the race of my fathers, who were
very much the best both in Ephyra and in broad Lycia.   210
This, you see, is the family and blood from which I claim descent.

        (*Il.* 6. 145–211)

The genealogy is introduced with the famous lines on the transience of human life, in which the generations of men are compared to the generations of leaves, with their unabating cycle of
withering in the autumn to be replaced with new growth in the
spring. Men are not much, in other words: they all perish and
all are replaced. Then, in the context of his genealogy, Glaucus
emphasizes the story of his ancestor, Bellerophon, as a paradigm,[32] with the object of persuading Diomede to take the long-
term view, to look at the end result of heroic exploits performed
with divine assistance. The story of Bellerophon is justly
famous, but I summarize it here to show how it is related to the
examples of Lycurgus and Tydeus. Glaucus' grandfather,
Bellerophon, came from Ephyra, near Corinth, but he was sent
to Lycia by king Proetus, when the queen, Anteia, after her
advances to Bellerophon had been rebuffed, falsely accused him
to the king of making such advances to *her*.[33] Proetus packed
Bellerophon off to his father-in-law in Lycia with σήματα λυγρά,

---

[32] I disagree with Austin (1978: 74; 1st pub. 1966), who classes it as an
'apologetic' paradigm. For analysis of the structure of Glaucus' speech, see
Lohmann (1970: 89–91).

[33] Bellerophon is a kind of 'virtuous-Joseph' figure: see Gen. 39: 7–20. For
other virtuous Josephs, see Otten (1953: 125–48); Pritchard (1969: 23–5; 1st
pub. 1950); West (1997: 365).

baleful signs in a folded tablet (a letter?)[34] (*Il.* 6. 168), indicating that Bellerophon should be put to death.[35] Bellerophon
was lavishly entertained for nine days by the Lycian king,
during which time he made so favourable an impression on the
king, that on the tenth day when the latter saw the signs with
their deadly import, he was loath to kill his guest in accordance
with Proetus' request. He attempted to resolve his difficulty by
sending Bellerophon to perform certain impossible tasks, from
which he did not expect his visitor to return, but Bellerophon
proved indestructible by these means. The first ἀδύνατον, or
impossible task, was to kill the Chimaera, the second to fight
the Solymoi, the third to fight the Amazons. When even they
failed to destroy him, the king set an ambush of warriors to
waylay Bellerophon as he returned, and he killed them all (*Il.* 6.
190). At this point the king gave up trying to destroy his guest,
but kept him with him, recognizing his divine descent,[36] and
married his daughter to him, giving him half his kingdom. The
royal marriage produced three children: Isander, Hippolochus,
and Laodameia. Laodameia actually became a bride of Zeus,
and the mother of Sarpedon. For no reason at all in Glaucus'
account, Bellerophon's happiness turns to ashes, and he
suddenly becomes an object of hatred to all the gods (*Il.* 6. 200).
He wanders on the barren plain,[37] eating out his heart, and
avoiding the paths of other men. His earlier victory over the
Solymoi did not destroy them, and his son perishes in an
engagement with them. The brilliant career of his daughter,
Laodameia, who lay with Zeus and became the mother of
Sarpedon, is suddenly cut short when she is killed by a wrathful

[34] On writing see Morris and Powell (1997: 3–32; for this passage, 27). On
the use in the Late Bronze Age of hinged folding wooden tablets recessed to
accommodate wax for writing on, see Payton (1991); Mylonas-Shear (1998:
187–9).
[35] Cf. Uriah the Hittite (2 Sam. 11). On this and other eastern motifs in the
Bellerophon story, see Burkert (1983); West (1997: 364–7).
[36] Sch. T ad *Il.* 6. 191 (= Erbse (1969–88: ii. 165), 191b[1]) makes him son of
Poseidon and Mestra.
[37] 'Plain of wandering': Robert (1920: 184 n. 2) favours a play on words
between Ἀλήϊον and ἀλᾶσθαι: see also Radermacher (1943: 107–8); Kirk (1985–
90: ii. 187 ad *Il.* 6. 201–2); West (1997: 367). Alternatively, 'horse-plain':
Malten (1925: 128) suggests an association between Ἀλήϊον and the Lycian
word for 'horse'.

Artemis, apparently quite at random. Hippolochus, Glaucus'
father, is the only one of Bellerophon's children to survive.

What is the point of all this sudden misery? Why do the gods
suddenly become so hostile? Gaisser explains the Homeric
account of Bellerophon simply as an illustration of the famous
line

οἵη περ φύλλων γενεή, τοίη δὲ καὶ ἀνδρῶν

As is the generation of leaves, so is the generation of men.

(*Il.* 6. 146)[38]

But the reference to the leaves and the story of Bellerophon will
not be simply decorative. The story of Bellerophon and the
reversal of his circumstances will be relevant to their context in
the poem. In Willcock's view Glaucus is driven to speak of his
ancestor at such length because he is nervous of the coming
engagement with Diomede: he is 'maundering . . . in an attempt
to postpone the inevitable'.[39] Whatever Glaucus is doing, he is
not 'maundering'. His speech is marked by the coherence,
lucidity, and prolixity to be found in epic speeches in moments
of crisis. It is well structured,[40] interesting, and long. If it is
paradigmatic, we would do well to remember that 'in paradigmatic digressions the length of the anecdote is in direct proportion to the necessity for persuasion at the moment'.[41] De
Jong[42] argues that Glaucus refers to the former prestige of his
family and how he came to be its last representative because the
duty of restoring its former splendours has devolved upon him.
This may partly explain the long account of Bellerophon and
his troubles, but Diomede is hardly likely to be deterred from
his intention of fighting with Glaucus by learning from
Glaucus' battlefield speech that the warrior confronting him is
the last representative of a noble line, intent on restoring its
ancient prestige.[43] Andersen rightly connects the career of

[38] On Glaucus' genealogy as an illustration of the sentiments of this line, see
Gaisser (1969*b*: 167–74); Redfield (1975: 102).

[39] Willcock (1992: 70–1). Cf. Craig (1967: 243–5).

[40] On the structure, see Lohmann (1970: 89–91).

[41] Austin (1978: 79; 1st pub. 1966): for his discussion of amplification see
Austin (1978: 78 and n. 20). For examples of amplification in other writers, see
Kennedy (1963: 56, 63, 102, 201, 217, 270, 277–8, 284, 317).

[42] (1987*b*: 162–8).

[43] Martin (1989: 128–9) argues unconvincingly that Glaucus' prestige is

Tydeus with that of Bellerophon, since both were victorious θεῶν τεράεσσι πιθήσας, trusting in the portents of the gods (*Il.* 4. 398, 6. 183). He also associates the story of Bellerophon with the story of Lycurgus, a connection established by a phrase found in both stories, ἀπήχθετο πᾶσι θεοῖσιν, 'he became an object of hatred to all the gods' (*Il.* 6. 140, 200). At *Il.* 6. 200, where the phrase is used of Bellerophon, who did nothing to provoke divine hostility, it is prefaced by καὶ κεῖνος ἀπήχθετο πᾶσι θεοῖσιν, *even he* became an object of hatred to all the gods, in a reference back to *Il.* 6. 140, where Lycurgus incurred the hatred of all the gods when he fought against Dionysus. It is not surprising that Lycurgus should have become the object of divine hatred, but it is astonishing that Bellerophon should have incurred such hatred, since nothing is said about how it was provoked. The effect of the two stories together is to suggest that divine favour is capricious, and that it is essential to look at the end of a career touched by it.[44] All this is certainly an excellent way of understanding the use of these examples, but it is important to look at what is behind a story too, because the connections between Tydeus, Bellerophon, and Diomede are even deeper than Andersen suggests.

5.6. BELLEROPHON AS A COUNTER-EXAMPLE TO THE EXAMPLE OF TYDEUS

Included in Diomede's challenge to Glaucus is the paradigm of Lycurgus, the θεομάχος who came to grief. The paradigm is counterpointed by the paradigm in Glaucus' genealogy of Bellerophon, who was not a θεομάχος, but came to grief anyway. Not only does the paradigm of Bellerophon counterpoint the paradigm of the θεομάχος, Lycurgus: it also functions as a counter-example to the example of Tydeus which Diomede has been urged to follow. In many respects Bellerophon is like Tydeus: it becomes clear that despite the spectacular privileges he enjoyed as a result of divine favour, no one would wish to suffer his misfortunes. We are not told that Bellerophon, like

enhanced by the contrast between Bellerophon's miseries, and his own relatively prosperous circumstances.

[44] Andersen (1978: 101–7).

Tydeus, is exiled for murder. Glaucus does not allude to the murder of Bellerus which caused Bellerophon to change his name from Leophontes to Bellerophontes, and to flee to Proetus for purification,[45] just as later Diomede will not mention the reason why Tydeus left Aetolia.[46] Secondly, Bellerophon defeated the Chimaera for the king of Lycia θεῶν τεράεσσι πιθήσας, 'trusting in the portents of the gods' (*Il.* 6. 183). We might have expected to hear of Pegasus here,[47] but instead we find another parallel with Tydeus, who defeated the ambush of the Thebans θεῶν τεράεσσι πιθήσας (*Il.* 4. 398). His assistance on this occasion came more precisely from Athene (*Il.* 4. 390). Thirdly, Bellerophon's annihilation of the ambush of warriors set for him as he returned from fighting the Amazons (*Il.* 6. 188–90), has a counterpart in Tydeus' defeat of the ambush of fifty men set by the Thebans on his way home from defeating them in athletic contests (*Il.* 4. 392–8). Fourthly, Bellerophon marries a daughter of the king of Lycia (*Il.* 6. 192), just as Tydeus marries a daughter of Adrastus, the king of Argos (*Il.* 14. 121). The half of the kingdom Bellerophon receives from his father-in-law (*Il.* 6. 193) corresponds to the lands and wealth received by Tydeus from his father-in-law (*Il.* 14. 121–4). All this is in agreement with Andersen's observations. However, mythology offers a reason for Bellerophon's fall from grace, although Glaucus omits to mention it, just as there was a reason why Athene did not confer immortality on Tydeus, although the poet allows no one to mention that either. The absence in both cases of any explanation of the reasons why divine favour was suddenly withdrawn makes its withdrawal seem quite arbitrary.

Hesiod refers to Pegasus and how Bellerophon rode him when he killed the Chimaera.[48] The motif of the winged horse is used by vase painters and others as a decorative motif from the early seventh century, and becomes a popular subject. The winged horse is shown alone, or with the Chimaera.[49] It is

[45] Apollodorus, 2. 3; Tzetzes ad Lyc. 17; id. *H.* 7. 810–15; Sch. bT ad *Il.* 6. 155 (= Erbse (1969–88: ii. 158), 155b).

[46] See n. 2 above. For discussion of this and other elements in the Aetolian tradition known to the poet but not used by him, see Andersen (1982: 7–16).

[47] Malten (1944: 3–4).

[48] Hesiod, *Th.* 280–6, 319–25, *fr.* 43a, 70–91 M–W.

[49] Poulsen and Dugas (1911: 382–3 and fig. 47); Malten (1925: 143–54; von

reasonable to suppose the role of Pegasus would have been known to the poet of the *Iliad* and his audience,[50] since the story was circulating over a wide area at an early date. If the poet and his audience knew of Pegasus, they almost certainly knew the end of the story: not only did Bellerophon ride Pegasus when he performed the 'impossible' tasks set for him by the king of Lycia: he went on to misuse his winged steed[51] by attempting to ride on Pegasus to heaven, but the horse was stung by a gadfly sent by Zeus, and threw his rider, so that Bellerophon fell to earth and was lamed.[52] The absence of any reference to Bellerophon's terrible fall from Pegasus does not mean that the details were unknown to the poet, or that he deliberately suppresses fantastical elements:[53] after all, he admits the Chimaera, which is not exactly normal. The poet mentions what it suits him to mention, and, like Pindar,[54] does not mention everything he knows about a story simply because he is committed to telling it. If it contains elements inconvenient to his purpose, he may suppress them,[55] but the audience may still be aware of the reverberations of material omitted.[56]

The overall effect of the story told by Glaucus is to present

Steuben (1968: 11–13); Gantz (1993: 313–16); *LIMC* iii. 1. 255, s.v. Chimaira, nos. 105–7; vii. 1. 214–30, s.v. Pegasus, nos. 1–7, 14–41, 89; with Bellerophon (*IIA*), s.v. Pegasus, nos. 93–114; Bellerophon fighting the Chimaira (*IIC* 2), nos. 145–65.

[50] Robert (1920: 26, 291).

[51] Hesiod, *Th.* 325; Pindar, *O.* 13. 63–92; Apollodorus, 2. 3.

[52] Pindar, *I.* 7. 44–7; Euripides, *Bellerophontes, frr.* 306, 307 (Nauck 1926: 451); Asclepiades of Tragilus, *FGrH* 12 F 13; Hyginus, *fab.* 57; *poet. astr.* 2. 18 (in this version, Bellerophon dies in his fall); pseudo-Eratosthenes, 18 (Robert). The ancient evidence is summarized by Bethe, *RE* iii. 1. 24–51, and discussed by Radermacher (1943: 97–117).

[53] For the well-established view that fantastic elements are suppressed because the poet takes the human as his standard, rather than the divine, see Murray (1960: 175 n. 2; 1st pub. 1907); Malten (1925: 130); Kraus (1948: 13); Kakridis (1949: 14–18, 41; 1971: 163); Kullmann (1956: 22–5 (magic rejected in favour of psychology), 41, 81–2, 147); Petersmann (1981: 54–7).

[54] Pindar draws attention to his silence about the fall of Bellerophon, *O.* 13. 91. For discussion of Homeric omissions from the story of Bellerophon, see Peppermüller (1962).

[55] On negative points glossed over, see Malten (1944: 5); Gaisser (1969b: 172); Hebel (1970: 124–7).

[56] See Lang (1983).

Bellerophon as one who achieved unimaginably great successes while he enjoyed divine favour, but from whom divine favour was suddenly unaccountably withdrawn, plunging him into misery. The story has a bearing, of course, on the addressee, Diomede: he too has been enjoying divine favour, and has achieved astounding success as a result, but divine favour is not to be relied upon, and may be withdrawn without explanation at any time, as happened in the case of Bellerophon. The story of Bellerophon is used to invite consideration of the disadvantages, as well as the advantages, of a career under divine patronage.

It is essential to look at the whole picture when examples are offered. Diomede is offered the positive example of Tydeus as a pattern to be followed and the negative counter-example of Bellerophon as a pattern to be avoided. Both Tydeus and Bellerophon enjoy a brilliant career under divine patronage, but the patronage is suddenly withdrawn. Agamemnon and Athene, who urge Diomede to follow the example of Tydeus do not draw attention to the end of Tydeus' career. Tydeus is being presented to Diomede in an attractive light, as a model to imitate, one who performed remarkable exploits with divine favour. In contradiction of his otherwise glowing report of Tydeus, Agamemnon mentions the παραίσια σήματα, the ill-omened signs from Zeus, which Tydeus ignored when he went to Thebes (*Il*. 4. 381). Further doubt is cast on the example of the Seven as a pattern to be imitated when Sthenelus reveals how the Seven perished at Thebes failed by their own ἀτασθαλία (*Il*. 4. 409).[57] Tydeus died at Thebes through the

---

[57] Sthenelus' outburst is used in exactly the same way as the apparently throwaway remarks (which are in fact directional) of minor characters in later literature. The damage to Tydeus' glowing example is done by Sthenelus' apparently eccentric outburst, and by Agamemnon's indiscreet reference to the παραίσια σήματα, 'ill-omened signs' (*Il*. 4. 381). See Scodel (1992: 81) for the view that because the Seven are said to perish by their own folly, their fate is not the unpredictable decision of an arbitrary deity. She takes Sthenelus' remark as essentially optimistic: if Tydeus had continued to exercise the wisdom he showed in Agamemnon's story, he would not have perished in the attack on Thebes. However, Agamemnon's reference to παραίσια σήματα (*Il*. 4. 381) should not be overlooked, for it suggests that the Theban expedition was not a wise undertaking. However much personal wisdom Tydeus continued to display, nothing could save a man who ignored the signs sent by Zeus.

ἀτασθαλία of the Seven, and divine patronage did not save him:
Il. 14. 114 mentions Tydeus' grave at Thebes.[58]

There is no conclusive evidence to connect the ἀτασθαλία of
the Seven with the later stories telling how Athene did not
confer immortality on Tydeus because of his brutal treatment
of Melanippus, but the poet of the *Iliad* knows many more
stories and more details of stories than he actually relates.[59]
Ἀτασθαλία is used elsewhere of the mistreatment of a corpse
giving rise to divine anger: Achilles is described as ἀτάσθαλος
(*Il*. 22. 418), when he mistreats the corpse of Hector, refusing
to give him up for burial, and thereby provoking the gods to be
angry as Thetis indicates:

> οὐ γάρ μοι δηρὸν βέῃ, ἀλλά τοι ἤδη
> ἄγχι παρέστηκεν θάνατος καὶ μοῖρα κραταιή.
> ἀλλ' ἐμέθεν ξύνες ὦκα, Διὸς δέ τοι ἄγγελός εἰμι·
> σκύζεσθαι σοί φησι θεούς, ἐὲ δ' ἔξοχα πάντων
> ἀθανάτων κεχολῶσθαι, ὅτι φρεσὶ μαινομένῃσιν   135
> Ἕκτορ' ἔχεις παρὰ νηυσὶ κορωνίσιν οὐδ' ἀπέλυσας.

for you will not live long now, believe me, but already
death and strong fate are standing beside you.
But understand from me, I am the messenger of Zeus to you:
he says the gods are angry with you, and he himself far above all

[58] According to Sch. AT[il] ad *Il*. 14. 114 (from Didymus) (= Erbse (1969–88:
iii. 583), 114a), the line Τυδέος, ὃν Θήβῃσι χυτὴ κατὰ γαῖα καλύπτει, 'Tydeus,
whom a sepulchral mound at Thebes conceals' was athetized by Zenodotus,
and did not appear in Aristophanes. Apthorp (1980, following Nauck (1963:
27; 1st pub. 1848); Düntzer (1848: 168); Wecklein (1918: 56–7)) assumes
transposition of the names, and suggests emendation to 'omisit Zen., ath.
Aristoph.' The verse was athetized by Aristarchus, who thought Homer was
an Athenian. According to an Attic tradition first found in Aeschylus,
Eleusinians (Severyns 1928: 223–4), Tydeus was buried at Eleusis, where some
MH cist-graves were enclosed as a heroon, no doubt already dedicated to the
Seven in the Late Geometric period (Coldstream 1979: 351). The *Thebaid*
told of how Tydeus died at Thebes and Athene decided not to immortalize
him because of his brutality towards Melanippus: it might have ended with
the funerals of the Seven outside Thebes (see Sch. AbT ad *Il*. 5. 126 citing
Pherecydes *FGrH* 3 F 97 (= Erbse (1969–88: ii. 22); *Thebais* F5 (Davies
(1988)); Severyns (1928: 219–20, 223–4)); Vermeule (1987: 138–44)).
Aristarchus might well have athetized *Il*. 14. 114 because he preferred the
Athenian tradition on the place of Tydeus' burial. However, Pausanias (9. 18.
2) says Tydeus' burial-place was shown at Thebes, and there is no reason to
prefer the Attic tradition.
[59] See Griffin (1977).

the gods has been angered, because in your mad heart   135
you keep Hector beside the beaked ships, and you did not release him.

(*Il.* 24. 131–6)

The ἀτασθαλία of Tydeus certainly resulted in his death, and
might well have been connected with divine mistreatment of
his enemy's corpse. Achilles is described by Priam as ἀτάσθαλος
(*Il.* 22. 418) in connection with his mistreatment of his enemy's
corpse. This mistreatment is the occasion of divine anger (*Il.*
24. 131–6) heralding Achilles' own death. The events of
Diomede's career foreshadow those of Achilles' career at Troy,
and the abrupt conclusion of his fighting career anticipates the
eventual eclipse of Achilles' star after the closure of the poem.
Like Tydeus, Bellerophon, in spite of his earlier successes
under divine patronage, suffered at the end of his career when
the gods hated him.

5.7. DEBATE IN PARA-NARRATIVE

The argument conducted in the para-narratives told to
Diomede and by him is may be summarized as follows:

A. Diomede should imitate the career of Tydeus under
divine patronage:

1. *pro* Agamemnon;
2. *contra* Sthenelus: Tydeus perished when divine patronage
   was withdrawn;
3. *pro* Athene: under her direction Diomede can fight even
   with gods;

B. Warnings about divine patronage:

4. Dione: the fate of the θεομάχος will not be pleasant;
5. Diomede tells of Lycurgus, a θεομάχος who came to grief;
6. Glaucus: men are ephemeral creatures: the gods favoured
   Bellerophon and he achieved much. He was no θεομάχος,
   but they suddenly hated him, and he suffered terribly.

Divine favour, in other words, is not particularly desirable: it
may be taken away as arbitrarily as it is given. Without paying
much attention to the end of the brilliant careers of Tydeus and
Bellerophon under divine patronage which he has been invited
to consider, Diomede follows their example.

5.8. DIOMEDE'S CHOICE: SUCCESS NO. 2
WITH DIVINE FAVOUR

The second of Diomede's two prayers is found in the Doloneia
of book 10, the account of the night raid on the camp of the
Trojans' Thracian allies. Diomede requests Athene to follow
him as she followed his father on the occasion of Tydeus' visit
to Thebes, and dispatched the ambush of Thebans lying in wait
for him on his return journey (*Il.* 4. 370–400).

> κέκλυθι νῦν καὶ ἐμεῖο, Διὸς τέκος, Ἀτρυτώνη·
> σπεῖό μοι ὡς ὅτε πατρὶ ἅμ᾽ ἕσπεο Τυδέϊ δίῳ   285
> ἐς Θήβας, ὅτε τε πρὸ Ἀχαιῶν ἄγγελος ᾔει.
> τοὺς δ᾽ ἄρ᾽ ἐπ᾽ Ἀσωπῷ λίπε χαλκοχίτωνας Ἀχαιούς,
> αὐτὰρ ὁ μειλίχιον μῦθον φέρε Καδμείοισι
> κεῖσ᾽· ἀτὰρ ἂψ ἀπιὼν μάλα μέρμερα μήσατο ἔργα
> σὺν σοί, δῖα θεά, ὅτε οἱ πρόφρασσα παρέστης.   290
> ὣς νῦν μοι ἐθέλουσα παρίσταο καί με φύλασσε.
> σοὶ δ᾽ αὖ ἐγὼ ῥέξω βοῦν ἦνιν εὐρυμέτωπον
> ἀδμήτην, ἣν οὔ πω ὑπὸ ζυγὸν ἤγαγεν ἀνήρ·
> τήν τοι ἐγὼ ῥέξω χρυσὸν κέρασιν περιχεύας.

Now hear me too, child of Zeus, Atrytone,
follow me as when you followed my father, the godlike Tydeus   285
to Thebes, when he went as a messenger in advance of the Greeks.
He left the bronze-shirted Achaeans at the Asopus,
but he carried a conciliatory message to the Cadmeians
thither. But on the way back he was plotting truly horrible deeds
with your help, divine goddess, when you kindly stood beside him.
So now graciously stand beside me and protect me.   291
And I will sacrifice to you a broad-browed heifer, one year old,
unbroken, which no man yet has led under the yoke.
I will sacrifice her and gild her horns.

(Il. 10. 284–94)

The night raid on the Thracian camp is a trip into enemy territory, like Tydeus' visit to Thebes. Odysseus and Diomede
obtain from the Trojan spy, Dolon, information on the disposi-
tion of the Trojan allies and especially the newly-arrived
Thracians and their king, Rhesus, with his splendid horses.
They kill Dolon, and when they reach the camp of the
Thracians, they kill twelve men and the king, Rhesus. As they
prepare to drive off his horses, Athene does indeed pro-

vide assistance:[60] just before Apollo intervenes by waking Hippocoon, the cousin of the murdered Rhesus, she stands near Diomede (*Il.* 10. 508) and warns him to retreat. Apollo arrives on the scene to witness, to his chagrin, Athene following Diomede back to the Greek camp (*Il.* 10. 515–16) as Diomede said in his prayer she had followed Tydeus.

Since antiquity the Doloneia has been regarded as a separate composition from the *Iliad*, allegedly displaying no connection with the books preceding it and following it. The T scholion to *Il.* 10. 1 expresses the earliest doubts about its authenticity: φασὶ τὴν ῥαψῳδίαν ὑφ᾽ Ὁμήρου ἰδίᾳ τετάχθαι καὶ μὴ εἶναι μέρος τῆς Ἰλιάδος, ὑπὸ δε Πεισιστράτου τετάχθαι εἰς τὴν Ἰλιάδα, 'they say that the song was drawn up by Homer separately, and is not part of the *Iliad*, and was set into the *Iliad* by Pisistratus'.[61] The story of the night raid has long been regarded as an attempt to redress the balance in favour of the Greeks after the Trojan success of book 8 and the unsuccessful embassy to Achilles in book 9.[62] There is some truth in this idea of redressing the balance, but I cannot accept the idea of wholesale, large-scale interpolation to achieve it. The relationship between the usages and motifs of book 10 and book 2[63] argues against the view that the Doloneia is a later insertion into the *Iliad*. The reference to Tydeus' visit to the Thebans (*Il.* 4. 370–400; 5. 800–14) in Diomede's prayer to Athene connects the events of the Doloneia to events described earlier in the *Iliad*, and I think the subject matter of the Doloneia has much in common with the account of Tydeus' visit to the Thebans, as I shall argue below. The Doloneia is best understood as a further example of Diomede's success with divine favour, and Diomede's career with divine patronage offers a pattern of the career of Achilles with the divine interventions obtained by his mother, Thetis.

---

[60] The Thracian king, Rhesus, has a bad dream that Diomede is standing beside him. The dream is realized, διὰ μῆτιν Ἀθήνης, 'through the device of Athene' (*Il.* 10. 497): see Fenik (1964: 45–52) for discussion of how dreams stand by the dreamer's head. In this case the dream turns out to be Diomede.

[61] Sch. T ad *Il.* 10. 1 (= Erbse (1969–88: ii 2), 1b).

[62] For older bibliography on redressing the balance, see Von der Mühll (1952: 183). The contrasts and reversals of the book are discussed by Klingner (1940).

[63] Von der Mühll (1952: 85). Danek (1988: 20–47, esp. 29), finds book 10 to be about 56% formulaic, about the same as the *Iliad* as a whole.

The events leading up to the night raid of book 10 are confused and the purpose of the patrol itself is not clear. The Greeks give a string of different reasons for wanting to hold the meeting which eventually decides to send the patrol: to send a spy against the Trojans (*Il.* 10. 38); to visit the Greek guards in case they fall asleep (10. 97–9); to deliberate whether to remain or flee (10. 146–7); the proximity of the Trojans (10. 160–1); the danger of the situation (10. 172–4). We hear nothing about Rhesus or his horses before the patrol sets off. Nestor intends the raid to find out whether the Trojans intend to spend the night in the plain or withdraw into the city (10. 207–10). Odysseus raises this question in Nestor's very words during the interrogation of Dolon (10. 409–11): Dolon answers all the other questions, but not this one, and he is never pressed to answer it.[64] Dolon directs the patrol to a fresh goal, namely the acquisition of the horses of Rhesus (10. 436–41). Rhesus himself achieves nothing in the Doloneia: he is killed while he sleeps and his horses provide booty for Odysseus and Diomede. The main narrative is not advanced by the Doloneia, so the episode must have some other purpose.

Fenik argues that the Doloneia represents an adaptation of material based on the same general tradition as that used by the pseudo-Euripidean play, the *Rhesus*. In this play the purpose of the raid is to kill Hector (575–6; 580–1; 595–8), but under the guidance of Athene, Diomede and Odysseus kill Rhesus, who will be invincible if he survives the night (600–5). A scholion to *Il.* 10. 435[65] records an oracle which said that Rhesus would be invincible if he drank the water of the river Scamander, and if his horses drank its waters and grazed its pastures. Another scholion[66] refers to an account in Pindar of how Rhesus fought for one day as an ally of the Trojans: Hera feared for the Greeks and sent Athene to destroy him. Athene's instrument was Diomede (or Odysseus and Diomede). Clearly there were

[64] This repetition caused Aristarchus to athetize *Il.* 10. 409–11: see Bolling (1944: 121–2).

[65] Sch. AD ad *Il.* 10. 435 in Dindorf (1875–88: i. 364). Hainsworth is wrong to attribute this scholion to Arn/A. I am indebted to Richard Janko (personal communication) for pointing out this error.

[66] Sch. bT ad *Il.* 10. 435 citing Pindar, *fr.* 262 (= Erbse (1969–88: iii. 93)). Again, Richard Janko kindly indicated that Hainsworth (1993: 151) is mistaken in attributing this scholion to Arn/A.

accounts in which Rhesus played a larger part than his incon-
sequential role in the *Iliad* suggests. These accounts seem to
agree on the motivation of the patrol (to kill Hector) and on the
role of Athene. There seems to be some cross-fertilization
between these clear accounts and the confused account of the
Doloneia. For example, the detail that the night is already two-
thirds gone (*Il*. 10. 251–3) can be related to Athene's concern in
the *Rhesus* that if Rhesus survives the night, he will destroy the
Greek army.[67]

The poet's awareness of the motivation for the night patrol in
the account he is adapting for the Doloneia is perhaps the
explanation for some cross-fertilization between different parts
of the *Iliad*. For example, Nestor's desire to know whether the
Trojans will spend the night in the plain or retire into the city
(*Il*. 10. 207–10) can be related to Polydamas' advice to withdraw into the city rather than spend the night on the plain (*Il*.
18. 254–66).[68] Hector boastfully rejects this advice (*Il*. 18. 306–
8) and warns Polydamas never to repeat it (*Il*. 18. 295). However, just before his fateful encounter with Achilles, Hector
realizes that if he now tries to seek shelter within the walls,
Polydamas will be the first to reproach him and remind him of
how he rejected advice to withdraw inside the walls.[69] He also
realizes that his rejection of Polydamas' advice and his confidence in his own powers will be the cause of his people's
destruction (*Il*. 22. 99–108). In other words, the question raised
by Nestor (*Il*. 10. 207–10) may be associated in the poet's mind
with a threat to Hector's life, and the attempt on Hector's life
which motivated the night patrol in the non-Iliadic accounts
might explain the appearance of the question in book 10.

Details such as the oracle that Rhesus would be invincible if
he drank the water of the Scamander resemble details found in
the Cyclic epic tradition,[70] but it is impossible to prove that
before book 10 of the *Iliad* was composed, the story of Rhesus
existed in the tradition in a form like that of the non-Iliadic
accounts. However, the unsatisfactory motivation of both the

[67] Fenik (1964: 26).

[68] Fenik (1964: 47).

[69] Polydamas, like Andromache (*Il*. 6. 431–9), urges Hector to fight like a
defender.

[70] Fenik (1964: 5–15). See Griffin (1977: 40) for the suppression of the
fantastic, the miraculous, and the romantic in the *Iliad*.

council and the patrol suggests that the poet is abbreviating and condensing material for his own purposes[71] in the same way as he is prepared to introduce changes into the details of other well-known story shapes like those of Niobe and Meleager, to suit his narrative purpose. I prefer this view to that of Danek, whose statistical and stylistic examination of the Doloneia leads him to conclude that it was composed not long after the composition of the *Iliad* by a poet rooted in the same tradition as the poet of the *Iliad*. The epic was circulating, in Danek's view, in the form of performances of individual songs, and the inclusion of a further song was not experienced as a departure from the norm.[72] Whether the material from which the Doloneia is adapted pre-dates or post-dates the composition of the *Iliad*, the important question must surely be what purpose does the adaptation of this material serves in the context of book 10. To decide this, it will help to consider other episodes in the poem which bear some resemblance to the raid in book 10.

Odysseus and Diomede in the Iliadic version of the raid were sent to find out whether the Trojans intended to spend the night in the plain or retire into the city (*Il.* 10. 208–10). They never do find this out, but they do truly horrible things to the Thracians and their king, Rhesus, who are sleeping in their camp on the plain. The raid displays certain similarities with Tydeus' visit to the Cadmeians feasting in the palace of Eteocles (*Il.* 4. 370–400, the passage referred to in 5.3.1. above). This visit by Tydeus to the Thebans appears to be that mentioned by Diomede in his prayer to Athene before the patrol sets out. Diomede prays for protection like that she gave to his father, Tydeus, on the occasion of his visit to the Thebans. Tydeus was sent by the Greeks to deliver a message (*Il.* 4. 384; 5. 804), but we never hear anything about the message.[73] The message does not matter: the story shape of the daring raid by small numbers into hostile territory requires a motivation, but in itself the motivation is unimportant. The point of the story is the terrible carnage inflicted by the daring hero or heroes on the enemy in their own city or camp. We can

---

[71] See Fenik (1964: 40–62).

[72] Danek (1988: 234).

[73] Until *Il.* 10. 288, where we learn that it was conciliatory.

see the same story shape in Helen's account (*Od.* 4. 244–64) of how Odysseus, disguised as a beggar, penetrated the city of Troy for an undisclosed purpose (said in Proclus' summary of Lesches' *Little Iliad*[74] to be a spying mission to plan how to steal the palladium), had a bath from Helen and told her the plans of the Greeks, slaughtered numbers of Trojans, and returned to the Greek camp, having gained much information.[75] The infiltration of enemy territory and the daring slaughter of the enemy in their own quarters is the point. In the Odyssean story just mentioned, Helen appears in the same role as will later be taken by Eurycleia.[76] Odysseus does not make the same mistake with Eurycleia of telling her all his plans as he made with Helen when he told her all the plans of the Greeks. There is a remarkable resemblance between Odysseus' slaughter of the suitors in the territory they have made their own and his slaughter of Trojans before leaving Troy in Helen's account. It has never been noted that Helen's story functions as a paradigm to encourage Telemachus to believe in his father's ability to infiltrate hostile enemy territory in successful disguise and wreak havoc upon his opponents, as he eventually will wreak havoc on the suitors in his own house.

When Diomede sets off with Odysseus on the raid, his prayer to Athene refers to his father's visit to the Thebans in the palace of Eteocles. Only now do we learn that the message Tydeus took to the Thebans was μειλίχιον (conciliatory, *Il.* 10. 288), so that the message is in contrast with the horrible deeds he plotted against the Thebans (*Il.* 10. 289). If, as seems probable, the visit to Thebes by Tydeus referred to at *Il.* 10. 285–9 is that mentioned also at *Il.* 4. 384, then the horrible deeds Diomede says Tydeus was plotting on his way back (*Il.* 10. 289) must refer to the ignominious fate he inflicted on the members of the ambush set by the Thebans (*Il.* 4. 396–7). How can Diomede say Tydeus was plotting the horrible things he was going to do to the Thebans on his way back, when Tydeus had no certain indication that he was going to be ambushed on his way back, or that he would meet Thebans to whom he would be in a position to do horrible things? Did he infer from

---

[74] Proclus, *Il. Parv.* 19–24: Davies (1988: 52).

[75] Fenik (1964: 13) relates this passage to the Doloneia.

[76] For bibliography, see Heubeck *et al.* (1988–92: i. 208–9 ad *Od.* 4. 242 ff.).

the anger of his hosts (*Il.* 4. 391) that he might expect retaliation for defeating them in athletic contests? Or is this incon-
gruity the result of a trick played on the poet by his memory as
he composed?[77] The important point is that the account of the
infiltration of enemy territory by Odysseus and Diomede and
their slaughter of the enemy in their own camp in book 10 can
be satisfactorily explained by the poet's manipulation of a story
shape in his repertoire to provide a characteristic parallel with
the account of the infiltration of enemy territory by Tydeus and
his slaughter of Thebans in their own territory in books 4 and
5. Diomede's prayer for the same protection as his father had
from Athene on his visit to the Thebans is granted to him in the
Doloneia, where for the second time we see that his successes
are achieved with the divine favour of Athene.

5.9. WITHDRAWAL OF DIVINE FAVOUR FROM DIOMEDE: THE LAMING MOTIF

Like Tydeus and Bellerophon, Diomede too will eventually
find himself without the protection of Athene, when he comes
to pay the penalty for fighting Ares and Aphrodite. The end of
his fighting career in the *Iliad* is not dissimilar to Bellerophon's.
Diomede joins the Achaean rout (*Il.* 8. 157–8) after a warning
from Nestor that he is no longer followed by strength from
Zeus (*Il.* 8. 140). Athene continues to help Diomede in the
Doloneia of book 10, the night raid on the Thracian camp.
However, she does not guide Diomede's spear (*Il.* 11. 349)
when he makes a cast at Hector and fails to kill him. Diomede
seems to ascribe his failure to Athene's absence, for he hopes to
have a second chance at killing Hector, εἰ πού τις καὶ ἔμοιγε θεῶν
ἐπιτάρροθός ἐστι, 'if someone of the gods is a helper to me too'
(*Il.* 11. 366).[78] He never has his second attempt at Hector,
because Ares and Aphrodite pay him out for his exploits
against them in book 5. Like Ares (*Il.* 5. 842), Diomede bends

[77] See Janko (1981: 261).
[78] = *Il.* 20. 453 (see Ch. 6, Table A and 6.6 below): cf. τοίη οἱ ἐπίρροθος ἦεν
Ἀθήνη, 'such a helper was Athene to him' (Agamemnon, speaking of Tydeus,
Il. 4. 390); τοίη οἱ ἐγὼν ἐπιτάρροθος ἦα, 'such a helper was I to him' (*Il.* 5. 808;
the speaker is Athene).

to strip the corpse of the man he has just killed, and like Ares (*Il.* 5. 858–67), he is wounded and forced to flee the battlefield (*Il.* 11. 369–400). The wound is made by an arrow fired from a hiding-place by Paris,[79] the favourite of Aphrodite, striking Diomede in the foot (*Il.* 11. 377). Diomede professes hardly to have noticed the wound, but it still necessitates his withdrawal from the field, and it puts an end to his active participation in the fighting. Diomede will appear only in an advisory capacity after receiving this wound, until he competes in the funeral games for Patroclus. The wounding by Paris is associated with a sudden, unexplained absence of the divine assistance on which Diomede has come to rely, and the arrow fired by Paris, Aphrodite's protégé, may be understood to be the sudden, unlooked-for working of divine vengeance in retribution for the attacks of Diomede, the θεομάχος, on Aphrodite and Ares.[80] Diomede should have been alerted by his own story of Lycurgus and his punishment for attacking Dionysus to the eventuality of retribution for his own assaults on gods. What is more, Paris' arrow strikes him in the foot, laming him, as divine chastisement lamed Bellerophon, whose apparently arbitrary loss of divine favour and miserable decline Diomede has recently been invited to consider. No one except Diomede in the *Iliad* is shot in the foot, but Paris' wounding Diomede is echoed in the *Aethiopis*, where Paris shoots Achilles in the heel and kills him.[81] The similarity is almost certainly to be

---

[79] Paris always hits his target. As Eurypylus is stripping a corpse, Paris wounds him in the thigh (*Il.* 11. 581–3). He kills Euchenor (*Il.* 13. 671–2): see Fenik (1968: 95–6, 234–5). For comparison of the two passages in which Diomede is wounded by an archer (Pandarus (*Il.* 5. 95–113) and Paris (*Il.* 11. 369–400)) see Fenik (1968: 20–1); Erbse (1961: 175–6); *LIMC* iii. 396–409, s.v. Diomedes (*V. Q*), nos. 112–14; Gantz (1993: 613).

[80] Scodel (1992), whose work I could not obtain until this chapter was virtually completed, understands the story of Lycurgus as a paradigm of divine anger for Diomede, and the story of Bellerophon as a paradigm of divine caprice. Her view (82) that the paradigms do not quite fit, and that Diomede's actions are never punished in the poem, overlooks the exact correspondence indicated by the (suppressed) laming motif in the careers of Bellerophon and Diomede.

[81] This version of the death of Achilles is given by Apollodorus, *Epit.* 5. 3; Proclus, *EGF* 33–4; Quintus Smyrnaeus, 3. 26–387, esp. 62; Hyginus, *fab.* 107. Achilles' death at the hands of Apollo and Paris is foretold by Hector as he is dying (*Il.* 22. 358–60). For an illustration of a lost Chalcidian amphora

explained in terms of the career of Diomede as a kind of foreshadowing of the career of Achilles, and to some extent, that of
Patroclus. Given the tendency of Homeric poetry to repeat
motifs for artistic reasons, it is not necessary to conclude that
the Iliadic scene of Diomede's wound from Paris is modelled
on the *Aethiopis*.

5.10. DIVINE RETRIBUTION AGAINST DIOMEDE

Dione, as we saw, hinted at the possibility that someone better
than Aphrodite might fight with Diomede, and leave Aigialea
and her children grieving for his loss. As it happens, Diomede
is not killed at Troy and Athene favours him once more,
causing him to win the chariot race in the funeral games for
Patroclus. The Homeric poems reveal nothing of events after
his safe return from Troy, *Od.* 20. 181–2, but later sources tell
of his discovery on returning from Troy that his wife, Aigialea,
had been unfaithful in his absence, and was plotting against
him[82] (Aphrodite's revenge for the wound at *Il.* 5. 336–40). He
took refuge at the altar of Hera, and managed to escape by night
with his companions, eventually reaching Italy, where king
Daunus killed him.[83] The end of Bellerophon's career as related

showing the dead Achilles with an arrow in his heel, see Woodford (1993: 94,
fig. 89) or *LIMC* i. 1. 182–3, s.v. Achilleus (*XXVI*), no. 850, ill. *LIMC* i. 2,
pl. 850. Paris is named and shown with his bow. For an image of the arrow
reaching Achilles through a forest of legs, see Schefold (1966: 46, fig. 14). For
association of Diomede's wound in the heel with that of Achilles, see
Pestalozzi (1945: 15–17); Von der Mühll (1952: 195–6); Erbse (1961: 173–6);
P. Kakridis (1961: 293 n. 1); Fenik (1968: 234–5) (for Fenik, the closest connection is between *Il.* 5. 95–133 and *Il.* 11. 369, rather than between *Il.* 11. 369
and the wound of Achilles in the *Aethiopis*); Heubeck (1974: 46); Kullmann
(1984: 313 n. 14).

[82] Virgil, *Aen.* 11. 277; Sch. bT ad *Il.* 5. 412 (= Erbse (1969–88: ii. 64–5),
412b); Gantz (1993: 619–20).

[83] Mimnermus, *fr.* 22 (West); Timaeus, *FGrH* 566 F 53; Sch. ad Lyc. 615
(Scheer 1958: 207–8; 1st pub. 1881). He visited Calydon to avenge insults
to his grandfather, Oeneus, and reinstated him as king (Euripides, *Oeneus*
(Nauck 1926: 536, no. 558); Hyginus, *fab.* 175), an adventure which comes
before the Trojan expedition in Apollodorus, 1. 8. 6, but after Troy in the
account of Antoninus Liberalis 37, in which Diomede is driven to Italy on his
return journey from Calydon to Argos. In Apulia he is received by Daunus,
who rewards him with a portion of land and the hand of his daughter for his

to Diomede by Glaucus anticipates the unhappy end awaiting
Diomede.

assistance against the Messapians. He founds Agyrippa (Strabo, 6. 284;
Lycophron, 592–609). He dies in old age in Italy or in Argos, or disappears in
the isles of Diomede (where his companions are changed into birds: this transformation occurs on the way to Italy in Virgil, *Aen.* 11. 272–4; Ovid, *Met.* 14.
484–509), or he is murdered by Daunus (Strabo, 6. 284; Pliny, *Nat.* 10. 127;
Polyaenus, *Strateg.* 8. 18).

6

Genealogy as Paradigm

We might find genealogy boring, but it was not thought to be boring in the ancient world. Genealogy was entertainment[1] as we see from an incident when Odysseus and Nestor visited Phthia to invite Achilles and Patroclus to join the expedition against Troy (*Il.* 11. 769–88) and Nestor describes how Peleus 'took pleasure'[2] as he listened to him recounting the τόκος and γενεή of all the Greeks:

ὅς ποτέ μ᾽ εἰρόμενος μέγ᾽ ἐγήθεεν ᾧ ἐνὶ οἴκῳ
πάντων Ἀργείων ἐρέων γενεήν τε τόκον τε

who on one occasion in his house, took great pleasure when he asked me
and I told him the family and birth of all the Argives.

(*Il.* 7. 128–9)

Genealogical material can also send signals to the reader, some-times as one of a series of correspondences which invite com-parison of a pair or group of episodes, sometimes in para-digmatic fashion, where the career of a famous ancestor invites comparison with the career of a character in the poem. When the poet's characters give information on their descent, they

---

[1] Van Groningen (1953: 47), who gives (47–61) a valuable discussion of the importance of ancestors. See also M. L. West (1985: 8–11, 125–7) on Hesiod, *Th.* 44–51, where the poet describes how the Muses entertain Zeus with the genealogies of gods and mortals; Thomas (1989: 174): as far as Polybius was concerned, genealogy was the right kind of history for someone who liked listening (τὸν . . . φιλήκοον, Polybius, 9. 1. 4), and Hippias of Elis found the Spartans enthusiastic about the genealogies of heroes and men, together with other antiquarian knowledge (ἀρχαιολογία), although they were not at all keen on more demanding subjects, like music and mathematics (Plato, *Hp. Ma.* 285d).

[2] Or 'groaned': Zenodotus humorously substituted μέγα δ᾽ ἔστενεν (he groaned loudly) for μέγ᾽ ἐγήθεεν, Sch. A ad *Il.* 7. 127 (from Aristonicus) (= Erbse (1969–88: ii. 250), 127a).

tend to list a succession from father to son,[3] and it tends not to extend back very far.[4] This is typical of family traditions which tend to emphasize both immediate predecessors and the most important ancestors, especially the hero or god regarded as the founder of the family, often at the expense of the intermediate generations, which may even be lost.[5] Homer has nothing, for example, to correspond to Herodotus' account of the succession of three hundred and forty-one kings of Egypt recounted to Hecataeus.[6]

6.1. FATHERS

Very often, all the poet reveals about a man's descent is the name of his father: for example, of thirty-seven men killed in book 5, we are told the names of the fathers of eighteen. The bereaved father is a dominant motif throughout the *Iliad*.[7] We may learn something of the father's occupation, as in the case of Phereclus:

τέκτονος υἱὸν

Ἀρμονίδεω, ὃς χερσὶν ἐπίστατο δαίδαλα πάντα   60
τεύχειν· ἔξοχα γάρ μιν ἐφίλατο Παλλὰς Ἀθήνη·
ὃς καὶ Ἀλεξάνδρῳ τεκτήνατο νῆας ἐΐσας
ἀρχεκάκους, αἳ πᾶσι κακὸν Τρώεσσι γένοντο
οἷ τ' αὐτῷ, ἐπεὶ οὔ τι θεῶν ἐκ θέσφατα ἤδη.

the son of the carpenter,

Joiner,[8] who knew how to fashion every intricate thing   60

---

[3] Suggesting that lateral relationships were of little interest: Thomas (1989: 191 n. 97).

[4] On the brevity of Homeric genealogies, see Thomas (1989: 174 n. 41): the maximum is eight generations (Aeneas) and two generations would be more usual. Orally transmitted genealogies tend to peter out in the third or fourth generation, and this was generally so in the case of aristocratic families of 5th-cent. Athens too, where families tended to organize vaguely remembered forebears into a continuous succession from father to son to enhance family prestige: Thomas (1989: 123–31, 158, 168–9).

[5] Thomas (1989: 158).

[6] Herodotus, 2. 143. On the impression conveyed that this lengthy list of office-bearers constitutes a genealogy, see S. West (1991: esp. 144–54).

[7] See Griffin (1980: 123–7).

[8] Or the son of Τέκτων (Carpenter), the son of Ἀρμονίδης (Joiner): cf. *Od*. 8. 114, Τεκτονίδαο, son of Carpenter. See Beye (1964: 355).

with his hands: for Pallas Athene loved him exceedingly.
For Alexander too, he had built well-proportioned ships
beginning mischief, which became an evil for all the Trojans
and for himself, since he did not know the Fates' decrees from the
gods.

(*Il.* 5. 59–64)

Phereclus was, like his father, a joiner and a smith: despite the favour of Athene, which explains his skill, he did not know the destined use of his work.[9] He brought trouble on himself by building ships for Paris, which were subsequently used for the abduction of Helen: this began the war in which Meriones kills him.

Eurydamas, the father of Polyidus and Abas, was a prophet, who gave no interpretation of his sons' dreams before they left for the war, where they were to be slain by Diomede, who

Ἄβαντα μετῴχετο καὶ Πολύιδον,
υἱέας Εὐρυδάμαντος, ὀνειροπόλοιο γέροντος·
τοῖς οὐκ ἐρχομένοις ὁ γέρων ἐκρίνατ᾽ ὀνείρους,   150
ἀλλά σφεας κρατερὸς Διομήδης ἐξενάριξε·
βῆ δὲ μετὰ Ξάνθον τε Θόωνά τε, Φαίνοπος υἷε,
ἄμφω τηλυγέτω· ὁ δὲ τείρετο γήραϊ λυγρῷ,
υἱὸν δ᾽ οὐ τέκετ᾽ ἄλλον ἐπὶ κτεάτεσσι λιπέσθαι.
ἔνθ᾽ ὅ γε τοὺς ἐνάριζε, φίλον δ᾽ ἐξαίνυτο θυμὸν   155
ἀμφοτέρω, πατέρι δὲ γόον καὶ κήδεα λυγρὰ
λεῖπ᾽, ἐπεὶ οὐ ζώοντε μάχης ἐκ νοστήσαντε
δέξατο· χηρωσταὶ δὲ διὰ κτῆσιν δατέοντο.

went after Abas and Polyidus,
the sons of Eurydamas, the old man, the interpreter of dreams.
The old man did not interpret their dreams for them as they went
forth,   150
but mighty Diomede slew them.
And he went after Xanthus and Thoos, the two sons of Phainops,
both of tender age. Their father was distressed by wretched old age,
nor did he beget another son to leave to inherit his possessions.
There Diomede slew them, and took away the life   155

---

[9] In this he resembles Tydeus, whose exploits at Thebes were performed with the assistance of Athene (*Il.* 4. 390, 5. 808) but without regard for the ill-omened signs sent by Zeus which caused the people of Mycenae to discountenance the expedition against Thebes (*Il.* 4. 381). Tydeus perished at Thebes (*Il.* 4. 409). See 5.3.1 and 2 above.

from both of them, but for their father he left wailing and sorrowful
   griefs,
since not alive did he receive them returning from the battle.
And their relatives divided up the property.

(*Il.* 5. 148–58)

The allusion to the bereaved father of Xanthus and Thoos,
Diomede's next victims, adds to the pathos of their death, as
does mention of details such as the rich possessions divided up
among remoter kin after the slaughter of the sons who should
have inherited them.

6.2. PARENTAL REPUTATION

A man may be referred to as the son of his father by means of
the patronymic rather than by his own name.[10] The sons of distinguished fathers feel it incumbent on them to conform to the
precedent of the paternal reputation. Glaucus was urged by his
father not to disgrace the family:

καί μοι μάλα πόλλ᾿ ἐπέτελλεν,
αἰὲν ἀριστεύειν καὶ ὑπείροχον ἔμμεναι ἄλλων,
μηδὲ γένος πατέρων αἰσχυνέμεν, οἳ μέγ᾿ ἄριστοι
ἔν τ᾿ Ἐφύρῃ ἐγένοντο καὶ ἐν Λυκίῃ εὐρείῃ.   210

   and he gave me many very urgent instructions,
always to be the best, and to be superior to the others,
and not to disgrace the race of my fathers, who were
very much the best both in Ephyra and in broad Lycia.   210

(*Il.* 6. 207–10)

Hector tells Andromache how consciousness of his father's
reputation prevents him from holding back from the war

ἐπεὶ μάθον ἔμμεναι ἐσθλὸς
αἰεὶ καὶ πρώτοισι μετὰ Τρώεσσι μάχεσθαι,   445
ἀρνύμενος πατρός τε μέγα κλέος ἠδ᾿ ἐμὸν αὐτοῦ.

   since I have learned to be noble
always, and to fight among the foremost Trojans,   445
earning my father's great glory, and my own.[11]

(*Il.* 6. 444–6)

---

[10] On the primacy of the father–son relationship, see G. Strasburger (1954:
24–6).
[11] Conversely, Odysseus refers to himself as the father of his son (*Il.* 4. 354)
and prays to live up to his reputation as the father of Telemachus (*Il.* 2. 260).

Many of those fighting at Troy are the sons of heroes who fought in the wars of the previous generation, such as the expedition of the Seven against Thebes or Heracles' sack of Troy. Diomede's father, Tydeus, fought and died in the expedition against Thebes, and his successes there are frequently held up to Diomede as a precedent and an example to follow. The reputation of the father may be used as a means of friendly encouragement to his son, as in Agamemnon's encouragement to Teucer, the bastard son of Telamon:

Τεῦκρε, φίλη κεφαλή, Τελαμώνιε, κοίρανε λαῶν,
βάλλ᾽ οὕτως, αἴ κέν τι φόως Δαναοῖσι γένηαι
πατρί τε σῷ Τελαμῶνι, ὅ σ᾽ ἔτρεφε τυτθὸν ἐόντα,
καί σε νόθον περ ἐόντα κομίσσατο ᾧ ἐνὶ οἴκῳ·
τὸν καὶ τηλόθ᾽ ἐόντα ἐϋκλείης ἐπίβησον.   285

Teucer, dear heart, son of Telamon, commander of war hosts,
go on shooting thus, so you may be a light of deliverance to the
    Greeks,
and to your father, Telamon, who brought you up when you were
    little,
and, bastard though you were, cared for you in his house.
Bring great glory to him now, although he is far away.   285
                                                        (*Il*. 8. 281–5)

The father's reputation may also provide the material of a νεῖκος,[12] a taunting reproach. A hero who is failing to act as the speaker requires may be taunted with being worse than his father, as Diomede is taunted by Agamemnon (*Il*. 4. 370–400). In extreme cases, the speaker may affect to believe that the addressee is not really his father's son, as Athene to Diomede (*Il*. 5. 800–13); Patroclus to Achilles (*Il*. 16. 33–5); Tlepolemus to Sarpedon:

Σαρπῆδον, Λυκίων βουληφόρε, τίς τοι ἀνάγκη
πτώσσειν ἐνθάδ᾽ ἐόντι μάχης ἀδαήμονι φωτί;
ψευδόμενοι δέ σέ φασι Διὸς γόνον αἰγιόχοιο   635
εἶναι, ἐπεὶ πολλὸν κείνων ἐπιδεύεαι ἀνδρῶν
οἳ Διὸς ἐξεγένοντο ἐπὶ προτέρων ἀνθρώπων·
ἀλλ᾽ οἷόν τινά φασι βίην Ἡρακληείην
εἶναι, ἐμὸν πατέρα θρασυμέμνονα θυμολέοντα·

---

[12] See 2.3.5 above. On the νεῖκος (which has a variety of senses), see esp. Adkins (1969); also Nagy (1979: 222–42); Martin (1989: 68–76).

ὅς ποτε δεῦρ' ἐλθὼν ἕνεχ' ἵππων Λαομέδοντος　640
ἐξ οἴης σὺν νηυσὶ καὶ ἀνδράσι παυροτέροισιν
Ἰλίου ἐξαλάπαξε πόλιν, χήρωσε δ' ἀγυιάς.

Sarpedon, counsellor of the Lycians, what necessity have you
to cower here, you who are a man unacquainted with war?
They lie who say that you are a scion of aegis-bearing Zeus,　635
since you fall far short of those men
who were born of Zeus in the days of generations before us.
But such a one they say was the mighty Heracles,
my father, bravely steadfast, lion-hearted.
He once came here on account of the horses of Laomedon,　640
with only six ships, and fewer men
he sacked the city of Ilion, and made desolate its streets.

(*Il.* 5. 633–42)[13]

Tlepolemus' νεῖκος is based on the idea that the present and the
future should be like the past: one has an obligation to live up to
the achievements of one's father. Tlepolemus is living up to his
father's reputation, in his enthusiasm to fight Sarpedon. He
implies that Sarpedon, who is cowering away from the war, is
not living up to the reputation of his father, Zeus, and that
Sarpedon's lack of enthusiasm for the battle belies his pater-
nity. The sack of Troy by Heracles, Tlepolemus' father, was
entirely in keeping with his divine parentage. Heracles sacked
Troy in the previous generation with only six ships and fewer
men than the Greeks have brought to Troy to recover Helen.[14]

This reference to the sack of Troy by Heracles is consistent
with many other references in the *Iliad* and other ancient
authors.[15] It seems that Heracles went to Troy to rescue
Hesione, the daughter of king Laomedon, from the sea
monster[16] sent by Poseidon after Laomedon cheated Apollo and
Poseidon of their wages when they were bound to him for a
year as labourers: Poseidon built the walls of Troy, and Apollo
herded the cattle of Laomedon (*Il.* 21. 443–7). Athene and the
Trojans built Heracles a high earthwork so that he could escape

---

[13] On the pattern of Tlepolemus' speech, see Fenik (1968: 66–7).
[14] For Heracles' sack of Troy see *LIMC* v. 1. 112–13(4), nos. 2792 (east
pediment of Aphaia temple on Aegina); 2793 (west pediment of Athenian
Treasury, Delphi).　　[15] See Janko (1992: 191–2 ad *Il.* 14. 250–61).
[16] For Heracles' rescue of Hesione, see *LIMC* viii. 1. 732, s.v. Ketos (E),
no. 24, ill. *LIMC* viii. 2. 497, pl. 24; *LIMC* i. 624, s.v. Hesione (C), no. 4 (said
to equal 732 Ketos (E), no. 25, but the details appear not to correspond).

from the sea-monster when it chased him from the plain to the seashore (*Il.* 20. 145–8). The earthwork survives to the time of the Trojan War, because it is used by Poseidon and the other gods supporting the Greeks (*Il.* 20. 149–50). As a reward for rescuing his daughter from the monster, Laomedon promised Heracles some of his partly divine horses (*Il.* 5. 265–70),[17] but in the event these were no more forthcoming than the wages of Apollo and Poseidon had been (*Il.* 5. 650–1). Heracles sacked Troy in revenge (*Il.* 5. 640–2). When he set off for home, Hypnos sent Zeus to sleep, enabling Hera to persuade the winds to make a storm which drove Heracles off course to the island of Cos, with the loss of all his friends (*Il.* 14. 250–6; 15. 26–8). Zeus rescued him there and returned him to Argos (*Il.* 15. 29–30).[18] Reinhardt[19] and Erbse[20] conclude that nothing is known of the Coan adventures of Heracles, indicating that the storm on the way home is a motif of the *Nostoi* (*The Returns Home*, a lost poem by Agias known from a summary by Proclus). However, Hesiod[21] tells how Heracles fought the sons of Eurypylus, king of Cos, for a trivial reason, on his way back from Troy, where he had gone to collect the horses of Laomedon. He went on from there to kill the giants at Phlegre. A similar account is found in Plutarch:[22] Heracles wrestled with Antagoras, son of Eurypylus, king of Cos, for a ram: the Meropes came to assist Antagoras and the Greeks came to help Heracles. Heracles became exhausted, fled to the house of a Thracian woman, and disguised himself in women's clothing to escape detection. Kullmann[23] argues convincingly for the existence of a Heracles epic which included these episodes. It looks very much as if the poet is making use when it suits him, of snippets of information derived from other epics in circulation.[24]

[17] See Kirk (1985–90: ii. 123–4 ad *Il.* 5. 640–2).
[18] Agamemnon will be blown off course on his return journey from Troy, and brought back to Argos by Hera and the other gods (*Od.* 4. 512–21).
[19] (1961: 104).
[20] (1986: 21).
[21] Hesiod, *Cat.* 43. 60–5.
[22] Plutarch, *Mor.* 304c–d.
[23] (1956: 25–35).
[24] See Lang (1983: 147–64). Craik (1980: 184–6) argues that Heracles' visit to Troy is an αἴτιον for how the Dorians took Cos.

By his allusion to the sack of Troy by Heracles in the previous generation, Tlepolemus is made to establish a precedent: the city could be sacked again (by the son of Heracles?) in the present generation. The idea that the city which fell before could fall again introduces the possibility that Sarpedon is fighting for a doomed cause. In the event, Sarpedon kills Tlepolemus (*Il.* 5. 557–9) but has the worst of their verbal exchange, for Sarpedon is provoked into revealing (*Il.* 5. 648–54) that Troy fell to Heracles because of the folly of Laomedon, who refused to give up the horses Heracles had come so far to collect. This has the unfortunate effect of introducing another precedent, this time for treachery on the part of the Trojans in the previous generation: Laomedon did not give Heracles the horses he had promised in return for the rescue of his daughter from a sea-monster (*Il.* 20. 145–8).[25] Laomedon answered Heracles εὖ ἔρξαντα, 'who had done him a favour', κακῷ μύθῳ, 'with an evil word', οὐδ᾽ ἀπέδωχ᾽ ἵππους ὧν εἵνεκα τηλόθεν ἦλθε, 'nor did he give *back* the horses for which he had come from afar' (*Il.* 5. 650–1). The notion of giving *back* the horses is impossible, since they were never previously in Heracles' possession. Laomedon had promised horses which belonged to him, not Heracles. The incident is an example of Trojan duplicity in the previous generation: Laomedon had accepted a favour from Heracles, but did not give what he had promised in return. The idea of giving something *back* might well have emerged in the secondary story about Laomedon as a result of the influence of the incident in the primary narrative to which the story of Laomedon is to correspond.[26] For 'horses' in the previous generation, read 'Helen' in the present: Menelaus did the duplicitous Paris a favour by entertaining him in Sparta, and Paris repaid him by making off with his wife. The Greeks came from afar to recover her, but the Trojans did not give her *back*, even when Paris was defeated in his single combat with Menelaus.[27] Sarpedon is made to

[25] For discussion of the pair of paradeigmata (*Il.* 5. 635–42 and 20. 145–8) which together make up the story of Heracles' benefaction and Laomedon's treachery, see Lang (1983: 150–3).

[26] For the two-way traffic between the situations in the *Iliad* and the *exempla*, or secondary narratives, adduced to illustrate it, see Lang (1983: 140) and for her discussion of the story of Laomedon (1983: 159–60).

[27] The Trojan elders are in favour of returning Helen (*Il.* 3. 159–60) and

convey, inadvertently, not that the present generation of Trojans is as good as its fathers, but that it is *no better than its fathers*.[28] The Trojans always were cheats, and they still are: true to form, Laomedon did not honour his promise to Heracles and Priam is not honouring his oath to return Helen when Paris is defeated in the duel. The present generation is living up to the reputation of its predecessors.

6.3. GRANDFATHERS AND EARLIER ANCESTORS

Tlepolemus mentions his father Heracles, who is a son of Zeus: Tlepolemus can trace his ancestry back to his grandfather. On a number of other occasions in the *Iliad* we hear of a grandfather: Laomedon is the famous grandfather of Aesepus and Pedasus (*Il.* 6. 20–4);[29] Evenus is the grandfather of Cleopatra, Meleager's wife (*Il.* 9. 556–62); Cisseus is the maternal grandfather of Iphidamas (*Il.* 11. 231–40).[30] Crethon and Orsilochus, the twin sons of Diocles who fall victim to Aeneas, are in fact great-grandsons of the river Alpheius (*Il.* 5. 544–9). The descendants of rivers frequently serve as hapless victims, and

Priam swears an oath to return her if Menelaus wins the duel against Paris (*Il.* 3. 250–91) but seems unable to carry out his promise (*Il.* 7. 368–78) after Paris' objections (*Il.* 7. 362–4).

[28] Martin (1989: 127) admires Sarpedon's cunning in implying that Heracles won only by default, through the ἀφραδίη, senselessness, of Laomedon, but Sarpedon's reference to Laomedon's treachery surely detracts from his own case.

[29] An undistinguished pair of twins who fall victim to Diomede. Aesepus is the name of a river below Mount Ida (*Il.* 2. 825); Pedasus is a town on the river Satnioeis (*Il.* 6. 34). Their father Boukolion is Laomedon's eldest son (*Il.* 6. 24) but he is illegitimate, and does not appear in the genealogy of Laomedon (*Il.* 20. 237–8).

[30] Cisseus brought up Iphidamas in Thrace and gave him one of his daughters (who would in fact have been one of Iphidamas' aunts) in marriage (*Il.* 11. 222–6). Immediately after the wedding Iphidamas went to Troy, where Agamemnon killed him. The death of a young person who has not yet married (see Kaibel (1878: 372. 26–31); Peek (1955: 68 and 748)) or the death of a newly-married person, epitomized in the simile of the dead bridegroom (*Il.* 23. 222–3), is regarded as particularly tragic (see Griessmair (1966); Lattimore (1962: 112, 118, 184–98); Achilles Tatius, *Leucippe and Kleitophon* 1. 13; Alexiou (1974: 195) for Alexandra Tsipi's lament for a girl widowed five days after her marriage; Holst-Warhaft (1992: 19); Rehm (1994: 27, 31–42)).

this is certainly true in the case of Asteropaeus, the son of
Pelegon of Paeonia, who tells his challenger, Achilles about his
grandfather, the river Axius:

Πηλεΐδη μεγάθυμε, τίη γενεὴν ἐρεείνεις;
εἴμ᾽ ἐκ Παιονίης ἐριβώλου, τηλόθ᾽ ἐούσης,
Παίονας ἄνδρας ἄγων δολιχεγχέας· ἥδε δέ μοι νῦν   155
ἠὼς ἐνδεκάτη, ὅτ᾽ ἐς Ἴλιον εἰλήλουθα.
αὐτὰρ ἐμοὶ γενεὴ ἐξ Ἀξιοῦ εὐρὺ ῥέοντος,
Ἀξιοῦ, ὃς κάλλιστον ὕδωρ ἐπὶ γαῖαν ἵησιν,
ὃς τέκε Πηλεγόνα κλυτὸν ἔγχεϊ· τὸν δ᾽ ἐμέ φασι
γείνασθαι.   160

Great-hearted son of Peleus, why do you ask my descent?
I am from fertile Paeonia, far away,
and I lead the Paeonian men with their long-shadowing spears. And
    this for me   155
is the eleventh dawn since I came to Ilion.
But my descent is from the broad-flowing Axius,
from Axius, which lets flow the fairest water over the earth,
who begot Pelegon, famous with the spear. They say
that Pelegon begot me.   160
                              (*Il.* 21. 153–60)

The relationship of Asteropaeus to the river Axius is the reason
why the river Xanthus supports him against Achilles (*Il.* 21.
145–7). Achilles in reply, traces back his descent one generation
further than Asteropaeus, revealing that he is the son of Peleus,
grandson of Aeacus, and great-grandson of Zeus.

χαλεπόν τοι ἐρισθενέος Κρονίωνος
παισὶν ἐριζέμεναι ποταμοῖό περ ἐκγεγαῶτι.   185
φῆσθα σὺ μὲν ποταμοῦ γένος ἔμμεναι εὐρὺ ῥέοντος,
αὐτὰρ ἐγὼ γενεὴν μεγάλου Διὸς εὔχομαι εἶναι.
τίκτε μ᾽ ἀνὴρ πολλοῖσιν ἀνάσσων Μυρμιδόνεσσι,
Πηλεὺς Αἰακίδης· ὁ δ᾽ ἄρ᾽ Αἰακὸς ἐκ Διὸς ἦεν.
τῶ κρείσσων μὲν Ζεὺς ποταμῶν ἁλιμυρηέντων,   190
κρείσσων αὖτε Διὸς γενεὴ ποταμοῖο τέτυκται.
καὶ γὰρ σοὶ ποταμός γε πάρα μέγας, εἰ δύναταί τι
χραισμεῖν· ἀλλ᾽ οὐκ ἔστι Διὶ Κρονίωνι μάχεσθαι,
τῶ οὐδὲ κρείων Ἀχελώϊος ἰσοφαρίζει,
οὐδὲ βαθυρρείταο μέγα σθένος Ὠκεανοῖο,   195
ἐξ οὗ περ πάντες ποταμοὶ καὶ πᾶσα θάλασσα
καὶ πᾶσαι κρῆναι καὶ φρείατα μακρὰ νάουσιν·

ἀλλὰ καὶ ὃς δείδοικε Διὸς μεγάλοιο κεραυνὸν
δεινήν τε βροντήν, ὅτ᾽ ἀπ᾽ οὐρανόθεν σμαραγήσῃ.

It is difficult for you to strive with the children
of the all-powerful son of Cronos, although you are born of the river.
You were saying you are the son of the broad-flowing river,   186
But I claim that I am a descendant of great Zeus.
A man begot me who is lord of many Myrmidons,
Peleus, the son of Aeacus. But Aeacus was the son of Zeus.
Therefore as Zeus is greater than tidal rivers,   190
So moreover, the descent of Zeus is greater than that of a river.
For here is the great river beside you, if at all
he can help you. But it is not possible to fight with Zeus, son of
     Cronos,
whom not even lord Achelous rivals,
nor the great might of deep-flowing Oceanus,   195
from whom all rivers, and all the sea,
and all springs and deep wells flow.
But even Oceanus fears the thunderbolt of mighty Zeus
and his dreadful thunder, when it roars from heaven.

(*Il.* 21. 184–99)

Achilles offers this information in open competition in the
matter of ancestry with the rivers and their descendants: *Il.*
21. 194–5 indicate that Asteropaeus' fluvial ancestor is fairly
unimportant, as rivers go: all rivers are inferior to Oceanus,[31]
who is no match for Zeus. Just as no river could hope to rival
Zeus, so no descendant of a river could be a match for a descendant of Zeus.[32] Genealogy is used to determine social hierarchy,

[31] Aristonicus says (Sch. A Ge ad *Il.* 21. 195 (= Erbse (1969–88: v. 168),
195a[1])) that Zenodotus omitted this line because Achelous is the source of all
the other rivers. Megacleides did not write it because he thought no stream
greater than that of Achelous. Pausanias, 8. 38. 10 gives Achelous as the origin
of all rivers. Van der Valk (1963–4: ii. 363–5) argues that Zenodotus omitted
lines for subjective reasons, in this case because he knew that in Homer and
the tragedians, Achelous occurs in the meaning 'water' and by omitting *Il.* 21.
195, he could attribute the detail to Homer. Apthorp (1980: 24) emphasizes
the reference by the sources to *omission* rather than *athetesis*. He draws
attention (1980: 80 and 118 n. 34) to the presence at this line of the διπλῆ
περιστιγμένη, the special sign used by Aristarchus to mark verses omitted by
Zenodotus but which Aristarchus regarded as genuine. It may be of interest
to know that the relationship between Oceanus and the rivers was used in
antiquity to express the relationship between Homer and subsequent poets:
see Ch. 3, n. 3 above.

[32] Idomeneus explains his success after killing three men to Deiphobus' one

which tends to serve as a predictor of success on the battlefield. In conflicts between the descendants of mortals, the son of the more important individual is victorious, and when two sons of immortals fight, the victor is the son of the more important god.[33]

6.4. DIOMEDE'S GENEALOGY AS A CLAIM TO STATUS

Descent may also be invoked to support a claim to be taken seriously, as at *Il.* 14. 115–25, when Diomede supports his advice on strategy with an account of his family through four generations to his great-grandfather, Portheus. Diomede offers advice on strategy on two occasions, and on both occasions his advice is juxtaposed to that of Nestor. On the first of these (*Il.* 9. 46–9) he simply dissociates himself from Agamemnon's proposal (*Il.* 9. 27–8)[34] to abandon the war and flee. Nestor explains Diomede's failure to offer any constructive advice on this occasion as the result of his youth and inexperience, and he himself goes on (*Il.* 9. 113, 165–70) to propose sending the embassy to Achilles. When the embassy fails, Diomede dissociates himself from it too (*Il.* 9. 698). The second occasion when Diomede offers advice on strategy comes when the wounded Greek leaders, Agamemnon, Odysseus, and Diomede, meet Nestor to deliberate how best to repel the Trojan attack (*Il.* 14. 27–9). Nestor begins by advising the wounded men not to re-enter the fighting (*Il.* 14. 61–3). Agamemnon again proposes flight (*Il.* 14. 74–81), an idea rejected this time by Odysseus (*Il.* 14. 83–102), so Agamemnon invites a further proposal: whether from a young man or an old one,[35] he will not fail to be pleased with it.

(*Il.* 13. 449–52) by describing his descent from Zeus through his grandfather, Minos, and his father, Deucalion, to justify his own allusion to himself as Ζηνὸς γόνος, the 'son' of Zeus (*Il.* 13. 449).

[33] Létoublon (1983*b*: 34–6). The discussion between Zeus and Hera before Sarpedon (son of Zeus) falls victim to the mortal Patroclus (not Achilles, as Létoublon (1983*b*: n. 23)) justifies this exception to the rule.

[34] His habitual method of obliging others to come up with ideas in a crisis: cf. *Il.* 2. 73–5, 140–1; 9. 27–8. McGlew (1989) argues that the πεῖρα is a means of inviting the Greeks to contemplate the shameful act of flight and reject it.

[35] ἢ νέος ἠὲ παλαιός, 'whether from a young man or from an old man' (*Il.* 14.

The way is thus prepared for Diomede to propose that the wounded leaders return to the battlefield to put fresh heart into those still fighting, while themselves keeping out of range of missiles, to avoid further injuries:

ἐγγὺς ἀνήρ—οὐ δηθὰ ματεύσομεν—, αἴ κ' ἐθέλητε   110
πείθεσθαι, καὶ μή τι κότῳ ἀγάσησθε ἕκαστος,
οὕνεκα δὴ γενεῆφι νεώτατός εἰμι μεθ' ὑμῖν·
πατρὸς δ' ἐξ ἀγαθοῦ καὶ ἐγὼ γένος εὔχομαι εἶναι,
Τυδέος, ὃν Θήβῃσι χυτὴ κατὰ γαῖα καλύπτει.

Πορθεῖ γὰρ τρεῖς παῖδες ἀμύμονες ἐξεγένοντο,   115
ᾤκεον δ' ἐν Πλευρῶνι καὶ αἰπεινῇ Καλυδῶνι,
Ἄγριος ἠδὲ Μέλας, τρίτατος δ' ἦν ἱππότα Οἰνεύς,
πατρὸς ἐμοῖο πατήρ· ἀρετῇ δ' ἦν ἔξοχος αὐτῶν.

ἀλλ' ὃ μὲν αὐτόθι μεῖνε, πατὴρ δ' ἐμὸς Ἄργεϊ νάσθη
πλαγχθείς· ὡς γάρ που Ζεὺς ἤθελε καὶ θεοὶ ἄλλοι.   120
Ἀδρήστοιο δ' ἔγημε θυγατρῶν, ναῖε δὲ δῶμα
ἀφνειὸν βιότοιο, ἅλις δέ οἱ ἦσαν ἄρουραι
πυροφόροι, πολλοὶ δὲ φυτῶν ἔσαν ὄρχατοι ἀμφίς,
πολλὰ δέ οἱ πρόβατ' ἔσκε· κέκαστο δὲ πάντας Ἀχαιοὺς
ἐγχείῃ· τὰ δὲ μέλλετ' ἀκουέμεν, εἰ ἐτεόν περ.   125
τῶ οὐκ ἄν με γένος γε κακὸν καὶ ἀνάλκιδα φάντες
μῦθον ἀτιμήσαιτε πεφασμένον, ὅν κ' ἐὺ εἴπω.
δεῦτ' ἴομεν πόλεμόνδε καὶ οὐτάμενοί περ ἀνάγκῃ.
ἔνθα δ' ἔπειτ' αὐτοὶ μὲν ἐχώμεθα δηϊοτῆτος
ἐκ βελέων, μή πού τις ἐφ' ἕλκεϊ ἕλκος ἄρηται·   130
ἄλλους δ' ὀτρύνοντες ἐνήσομεν, οἳ τὸ πάρος περ
θυμῷ ἦρα φέροντες ἀφεστᾶσ' οὐδὲ μάχονται.

The man is near at hand—we shall not look long—if you are willing
to be persuaded and you are not each resentful with indignation
because by birth I am the youngest of you.   112
I too claim to be son of a noble father,
Tydeus, whom a mound of earth covers in Thebes.
For three sons were born to Portheus,   115
and they lived in Pleuron and sheer Calydon:
Agrios and Melas, and the third was the horseman, Oeneus,
the father of my father. And in quality he was distinguished among
   them.
And he lived there, but my father travelled away

108), surely refers to *Il.* 9. 36, where both young and old are said to know of Agamemnon's νεῖκος to Diomede at *Il.* 4. 370–400. See Janko (1992: 162–3 ad *Il.* 14. 110–32), where the references to *Il.* 4. 370–400 and 9. 34–6 are discussed.

and settled in Argos, for so, perhaps, Zeus wanted it, and the other
    gods.   120
And he married one of the daughters of Adrastus, and lived in a house
rich in substance, and he had wheat-bearing ploughland
in abundance, and many orchards planted all round,
and many flocks were his. And he surpassed all the Argives
with the spear. You will have heard of these things, if it is really true.
Therefore you could not, saying that I was base by birth, and
    cowardly,
reject a proposal made by me, if my proposal is good.   127
Let us go to the war, although we are wounded, since we must.
When there, let us keep ourselves out of the slaughter,
out of range of the missiles, so that no one adds to his wounds.   130
But let us rouse up the others and send them in, those until now
giving way to their feelings, standing aloof from the war, without
    fighting.

                                       (*Il.* 14. 110–32)

Although Diomede's proposal is hardly original, it derives
weight and significance from two factors in the approach leading up to it. In the first place, Diomede is the last of Agamemnon's three advisers to speak: he is preceded by Nestor
and Odysseus, neither of whom has anything particularly appo-
site to say.[36] Secondly, Diomede leads up to the advice he has to
offer with the preface that his youth should not detract from the
value of his proposal,[37] since he is the son of a noble father, and
comes of a good family. He supports his statement with an
account of his genealogy back to his great-grandfather. The

[36] This use of two speeches which say very little as a prelude to a third
putting forward a constructive idea is very similar to the motif of the 'mistaken
questions', where the speaker, in answer to his own question, suggests one or
two possibilities which are not the case, delaying and heightening the
significance of the correct answer when it is given. For this motif, see Kakridis
(1949: 108–20); see also Łanowski (1947: 185–6 and n. 17) on Theocritus, 1.
66–8, 71–6, 80–2: of the three questions, it is always the third which meets
with the affirmative answer.

[37] μῦθον ἀτιμήσαιτε (*Il.* 14. 127) surely echoes μῦθον ἀτιμήσειε (*Il.* 9. 62),
where the speaker is Nestor. At *Il.* 9. 60–2 Nestor asserts his seniority as the
reason why the Greeks will not treat with contempt what he has to say when he
supports Diomede's refusal to flee from Troy. At *Il.* 14. 127 Diomede has just
asserted the prestige of his family as the reason why the Greek leaders will not
treat with contempt what he has to say about strategy. The verbal echo
suggests that Diomede remembers the earlier incident, and recalls how Nestor
gave a reason why his advice should be heeded on that occasion.

mention of Tydeus buried under a tumulus at Thebes indicates that Diomede's father received a hero's burial, the fitting end to an heroic career.[38] All this forms a lengthy preliminary to his actual proposal to encourage those still fighting. The audience has been gradually familiarized with much of the material Diomede here recounts on the subject of his family, but this is the first time Diomede himself has publicly asserted his own ancestry. It is effective: Diomede's advice is put into action without further comment.[39]

6.5. TROJAN GENEALOGIES

6.5.1. The genealogies of Glaucus and Aeneas: Glaucus

Both Diomede and Achilles listen to a long genealogy from an opponent on the battlefield: Diomede listens to that of Glaucus, and Achilles listens to that of Aeneas. We have already seen how for the benefit of Diomede, Glaucus traces his family back through six generations to Aeolus in Corinth (*Il.* 6. 154–5; 196–206), dwelling at considerable length on the career of his grandfather, Bellerophon (*Il.* 6. 156–95). The career of Bellerophon functions as a paradigmatic warning to Diomede as he listens to it: Bellerophon enjoyed extraordinary favour from the gods, but this favour was suddenly withdrawn in an apparently arbitrary fashion, and the same thing might happen to Diomede, who has been achieving remarkable feats under the patronage of Athene just before he hears about Bellerophon. Glaucus is saved by his genealogy from fighting with Diomede, since the genealogy reminds Diomede of an ancestral guest-friendship between his grandfather, Oeneus, and Glaucus' grandfather, Bellerophon. The divine favour which preserved Bellerophon when he was falsely accused by Proetus' wife, and in his exploits against the Chimaera, the Amazons, and the Solymoi provides a precedent for the divine favour shown to Glaucus at the conclusion of his interview with

[38] On the role of burial and the grave monument in ensuring survival after death in memory, see Sourvinou-Inwood (1981: 31–3).

[39] In this sense his genealogy is an 'apologetic paradigm' told 'to establish his right to be heard in a deliberative council': Austin (1978: 74; 1st pub. 1966).

Diomede: Zeus takes away the wits of Glaucus, causing him to consent to the unequal exchange of armour Diomede has proposed. In material terms Glaucus has the worst of the exchange, but his consent to it (when Zeus' intervention has robbed him of his wits) probably buys him his life.

6.5.2. The genealogies of Glaucus and Aeneas: Aeneas

Both Glaucus and Aeneas serve as an adversary for the leading Greek fighter in the absence of Hector. When Diomede meets Glaucus and learns his genealogy, Hector is absent from the battlefield, taking Helenus' message to Troy. Later on, Hector is absent from the battlefield when Achilles, who is eager to fight with Hector, meets Aeneas. Aeneas' genealogy is the most extended genealogy of all (eight generations), and it is related (*Il.* 20. 230–40), like that of Glaucus, to an adversary on the battlefield:

εἰ δ᾽ ἐθέλεις καὶ ταῦτα δαήμεναι, ὄφρ᾽ ἐΰ εἰδῇς
ἡμετέρην γενεήν, πολλοὶ δέ μιν ἄνδρες ἴσασι·
Δάρδανον αὖ πρῶτον τέκετο νεφεληγερέτα Ζεύς,   215
κτίσσε δὲ Δαρδανίην, ἐπεὶ οὔ πω Ἴλιος ἱρὴ
ἐν πεδίῳ πεπόλιστο, πόλις μερόπων ἀνθρώπων,
ἀλλ᾽ ἔθ᾽ ὑπωρείας ᾤκεον πολυπίδακος Ἴδης.
Δάρδανος αὖ τέκεθ᾽ υἱὸν Ἐριχθόνιον βασιλῆα,
ὃς δὴ ἀφνειότατος γένετο θνητῶν ἀνθρώπων·   220
τοῦ τρισχίλιαι ἵπποι ἕλος κάτα βουκολέοντο
θήλειαι, πώλοισιν ἀγαλλόμεναι ἀταλῇσι.
τάων καὶ Βορέης ἠράσσατο βοσκομενάων,
ἵππῳ δ᾽ εἰσάμενος παρελέξατο κυανοχαίτῃ·
αἱ δ᾽ ὑποκυσάμεναι ἔτεκον δυοκαίδεκα πώλους.   225
αἱ δ᾽ ὅτε μὲν σκιρτῷεν ἐπὶ ζείδωρον ἄρουραν,
ἄκρον ἐπ᾽ ἀνθερίκων καρπὸν θέον οὐδὲ κατέκλων·
ἀλλ᾽ ὅτε δὴ σκιρτῷεν ἐπ᾽ εὐρέα νῶτα θαλάσσης,
ἄκρον ἐπὶ ῥηγμῖνος ἁλὸς πολιοῖο θέεσκον.
Τρῶα δ᾽ Ἐριχθόνιος τέκετο Τρώεσσιν ἄνακτα·   230
Τρωὸς δ᾽ αὖ τρεῖς παῖδες ἀμύμονες ἐξεγένοντο,
Ἶλός τ᾽ Ἀσσάρακός τε καὶ ἀντίθεος Γανυμήδης,
ὃς δὴ κάλλιστος γένετο θνητῶν ἀνθρώπων·
τὸν καὶ ἀνηρείψαντο θεοὶ Διὶ οἰνοχοεύειν
κάλλεος εἵνεκα οἷο, ἵν᾽ ἀθανάτοισι μετείη.   235
Ἶλος δ᾽ αὖ τέκεθ᾽ υἱὸν ἀμύμονα Λαομέδοντα·

Λαομέδων δ' ἄρα Τιθωνὸν τέκετο Πρίαμόν τε
Λάμπον τε Κλυτίον θ' Ἱκετάονά τ', ὄζον Ἄρηος·
Ἀσσάρακος δὲ Κάπυν, ὁ δ' ἄρ' Ἀγχίσην τέκε παῖδα·
αὐτὰρ ἔμ' Ἀγχίσης, Πρίαμος δ' ἔτεχ' Ἕκτορα δῖον.   240
ταύτης τοι γενεῆς τε καὶ αἵματος εὔχομαι εἶναι.

But if you want to learn this too, so that you may know well
our descent, it is something that many men know.
Cloud-gathering Zeus first begot Dardanus,   215
and he built Dardania, since the holy city of Ilion
had not yet been built in the plain as a city of mortal men
but they still inhabited the slopes of Ida, rich in springs.
And Dardanus begot a son, king Erichthonios,
who was the very richest of mortal men.   220
His three thousand horses used to graze over the water meadows,
mares, delighting in their tender foals.
Even the North Wind was enamoured of them as they grazed,
and likening himself to a dark-maned stallion, he lay with them,
and they conceived and bore twelve foals.   225
And when they bounded over the grain-giving ploughland,
they ran over the top grains of the ears of wheat, nor did they snap
    them off.
But when they bounded also over the broad back of the sea,
they ran on the breaking wave-crests at the grey sea's edge.
And Erichthonios begot Tros, as a lord for the Trojans,   230
and three blameless sons were born to Tros,
Ilos and Assarakos, and godlike Ganymede,
who was very much the fairest of mortal men.
And the gods bore him away to be a cup-bearer to Zeus
because of his beauty, so that he might be with the immortals.   235
And Ilos begot a son, the blameless Laomedon,
and Laomedon begot Tithonus and Priam,
and Lampus, and Clytius, and Hiketaon, scion of Ares.
And Assarakos begot Capys, who begot a son, Anchises.
But Anchises begot me, and Priam begot godlike Hector.   240
This is the family and blood from which I claim descent.

(Il. 20. 213–41)

These two extended genealogical passages, Glaucus to
Diomede and Aeneas to Achilles, will be considered not only in
their immediate contexts, but also together, because they form
part of the raft of correspondences between the career of
Diomede in the first half of the poem, and the career of Achilles

in the final books.[40] The two genealogical episodes mirror
each other,[41] and each forms part of a mirrored sequence of
encounters. It will be instructive to consider how the mirroring
is achieved, since the two genealogies are quite different in content, and the issues they explore are quite dissimilar. Reinhardt
regards both genealogies as a homage by the poet to a family.[42]
Adkins suggests that Aeneas establishes an ascendancy over
Achilles by his genealogy, which explores the issues of social
status and divine patronage.[43] Willcock, who interprets the

[40] The correspondences between Achilles and Diomede are listed by von
Scheliha (1943: 185): Helenos compares Diomede with Achilles as a fighter
(*Il.* 6. 99–101); both fight with Aeneas, who is rescued by Aphrodite from
Diomede (*Il.* 5. 297–318) and from Achilles by Poseidon (*Il.* 20. 178–348);
both Diomede (*Il.* 11. 345–68) and Achilles (*Il.* 20. 421–51; 22. 214–363)
defeat Hector; both Diomede (*Il.* 6. 127) and Achilles (*Il.* 21. 151) say:
δυστήνων δέ τε παῖδες ἐμῷ μένει ἀντιόωσιν, 'the sons of unhappy men meet with
my strength'; the expression ἐγγὺς ἀνήρ, 'near is the man' is used by Diomede
of himself (*Il.* 14. 110) and by Achilles of the killer of Patroclus (*Il.* 20. 425);
Diomede reproaches Agamemnon (*Il.* 9. 32–49), as does Achilles (*Il.* 1. 122–9,
149–71, 225–44, 293–303); Athene helps Diomede (*Il.* 5. 121–3, 290, 793–859)
and Achilles (*Il.* 20. 448–9; 22. 214–95), and no one else. She gives Diomede
(*Il.* 5. 4–7) and Achilles (*Il.* 18. 203–14) St Elmo's fire from helmet and shield
(and cf. *Il.* 19. 379–83, where fire flashes from the shield and helmet made for
Achilles by Hephaestus when the hero first tries them on; see also *Il.* 22.
317–19, where the gleam of light off Achilles' spear is compared to a star).
Only Achilles and Diomede fight with gods, Achilles with the river god (*Il.* 21.
212–82), and Diomede with Ares (*Il.* 5. 841–59) and Aphrodite (*Il.* 5. 330–54).

[41] Lohmann (1970: 89–90) distinguishes three stages in the structure of the
first part of Glaucus' speech: (1) introduction, (2) three ancestors, (3)
Bellerophon's adventures in Corinth. This order is mirrored in the second
part, where we find (1) Bellerophon's adventures in Lycia, (2) three more
ancestors, and (3) closing remarks. Lohmann (1970: 91–3) detects a similar
structure in Aeneas' speech to Achilles, which also falls into two halves, each
split into three parts. As in the case of Glaucus, whose family tree is centred in
Argos and Lycia, Aeneas' family tree is centred in two places, Ida and Troy,
and three generations are identified in each place. Similarities between the two
genealogies have always been noted: in his discussion Reinhardt (1961:
511–13) points to the use of the same frame for the genealogy of Glaucus and
for that of Aeneas: *Il.* 20. 213–14, 241 = *Il.* 6. 150–1, 211. However, it is worth
noting that unlike Glaucus, Aeneas is not invited to relate his genealogy, and
that he and Achilles, unlike Glaucus and Diomede, are well known to each
other: see Heitsch (1965: 63–6 and 66 n. 1).

[42] Reinhardt (1961: 513): 'eine Huldigung des Dichters an ein Geschlecht'.

[43] Adkins (1975: 241–7). However, it is not at all clear that Aeneas succeeds
in establishing his superiority to Achilles: it is a nice question whether Aeneas'
paternal descent from Zeus over eight generations and his maternal descent

length of Glaucus' account of his lineage and his silent compliance in the unequal exchange of armour as evidence of his
nervousness as the weaker party, interprets the encounter of
Aeneas with Achilles in much the same way: Aeneas, daunted
at the prospect of Achilles as an adversary, relates his genealogy
at such length as a means of delaying the evil moment when he
must fight him.[44] However, Aeneas, whether nervous or not,
makes no such gesture as the exchange of armour, and unlike
Glaucus, invites his adversary to fight him (*Il.* 20. 257–8).
Unlike the family tree of Glaucus, Aeneas' genealogy does not
appear to offer a paradigm about the unreliability of divine
favour to its addressee. The theme of fighting against gods, so
prominent in the encounter of Glaucus and Diomede, is quite
absent from the encounter of Aeneas and Achilles. Achilles'
challenge to Aeneas has nothing resembling Diomede's account
of Lycurgus, who incurred divine hatred by his attack on
Dionysus.

The theme common to both genealogies is that of divine
favour bestowed on ancestors. It functions both as a factor in
human achievement, and as a precedent for divine favour about
to be shown to the descendants of these ancestors. The divine
favour shown to Glaucus' ancestor, Bellerophon, provides a
precedent for divine favour (even if the recipient is made to
look a fool) to Glaucus at the conclusion of his interview
with Diomede. Divine favour features similarly in Aeneas'
interview with Achilles. Aeneas' genealogy includes a number
of ancestors whose enjoyment of divine favour is well known
(even if Aeneas does not explain this favour in detail):
Ganymede, whose beauty caused the gods to take him to
heaven to be their cup-bearer; Tithonus, who was married to
the Dawn; Anchises, who was the husband of Aphrodite.[45]
Aeneas himself is not really equal to the fight against Achilles,
but the favour shown by the gods to his ancestors provides a

from Aphrodite outweigh Achilles' closer relationship with Zeus on his
father's side, and the inferior goddess, Thetis, as his mother. It is Poseidon
who reveals Aeneas' inferiority to Achilles, when he rescues Aeneas and tells
him to avoid Achilles, ὅς σεῦ ἅμα κρείσσων καὶ φίλτερος ἀθανάτοισιν, 'who is at
the same time better than you, and dearer to the gods' (*Il.* 20. 334).

[44] Willcock (1992: 69–70).
[45] *Il.* 20. 232–5, 237, 239–40.

precedent for the divine favour which will be shown to Aeneas
when Poseidon rescues him from Achilles and warns him to
avoid Achilles in future (*Il*. 20. 335–8).

Distinguished ancestry is all very well, as Aeneas makes
clear (*Il*. 20. 242–3), but a man's ability may be enhanced or
diminished according to the whim of Zeus or another of the
gods. This is well illustrated in *Il*. 13. 427–54, where the poet in
his own voice gives details of the family connections of
Alcathoös, the best man in the whole Troad. He was the son
of Aisyetes and son-in-law of Anchises; his wife was
Hippodameia, the eldest daughter of Anchises. Idomeneus has
divine assistance when he kills him: Poseidon deprives
Alcathoös of the power of movement, so that Idomeneus can
hit him with the spear. Alcathoös is one of three Trojans (the
others are Othryoneus (*Il*. 13. 363) and Asius (*Il*. 13. 389–93))
killed by Idomeneus in an incident where his adversary,
Deiphobus, kills only one Greek, Hypsenor (*Il*. 13. 411). The
Trojans are receiving support from Zeus, who is honouring his
promise to Thetis (*Il*. 1. 503–30), and the Greeks are receiving
support from Poseidon, disguised as a man. Idomeneus taunts
Deiphobus with the recent casualty lists: three Trojans killed
by himself as compared to one Greek killed by Deiphobus.
Then he goes on to refer to his own descent from Zeus:
Idomeneus is son of Deucalion, son of Minos, son of Zeus.
Deiphobus avoids single combat with this descendant of
Zeus, and seeks assistance from Aeneas, another descendant of
the gods.

The connection between the extended genealogies of
Glaucus and Aeneas is established by verbal repetitions in the
introduction to, and conclusion of, their genealogies (Table A,
1(*c*)). Both Glaucus and Aeneas are saved from the full consequences of fighting with their opponent by divine intervention at the conclusion of their encounters (Table A, 1(*d*)).
The element obviously common to both the Glaucus/Diomede
encounter and the Aeneas/Achilles encounter, namely the
extended genealogy, draws attention to other correspondences
between the two encounters (Table A, 1). A pattern emerges
from certain events of Diomede's career which anticipates the
pattern of certain events of Achilles' career: both Diomede and
Achilles make an unsuccessful attempt on Hector, who on each

occasion is rescued by Apollo (Table A, 2(*b*)).[46] Both Diomede and Achilles pray for a second chance at killing Hector, and each prays to have divine assistance in the encounter when it comes (Table A, 2(*c*)). Diomede has no second chance at Hector, but Achilles receives the assistance of Athene in his second meeting with Hector, and kills him (Table A, 3). Divine favour appears to be withdrawn from both Diomede and Achilles: Athene's assistance is suddenly absent for Diomede when he is shot in the foot and lamed by an arrow fired by Paris. Although Achilles has the protection of the gods until he kills Hector, thereafter he is to suffer what fate has decreed for him (*Il.* 20. 120–8): the tradition tells us that Achilles will die when he is shot in the foot by an arrow fired by Paris and Apollo at the Scaean gates (*Il.* 22. 359–60).[47]

6.6. MIRRORING IN THE EVENTS OF ACHILLES' CAREER

Table A shows not only how events of Diomede's career correspond to events of the career of Achilles, but also how events from the early stages of Achilles' return to the fighting anticipate and refer to later episodes in his career. Achilles' abortive attempt on Aeneas (Table A, 1) should be associated not only with Diomede's encounter with Glaucus, but also with Achilles' abortive first attempt on Hector (Table A, 2). The opening words of Aeneas' speech to Achilles are exactly repeated by

---

[46] Schoeck (1961: 70, 76) compares Diomede's four rushes at Apollo (*Il.* 5. 436–9) after the god has rescued Aeneas with Achilles' four rushes at Apollo (*Il.* 20. 445–8) after the god has rescued Hector.

[47] Allen (1912: v. 106, lines 7–9) = Davies (1988: 47, lines 20–1). For a Roman representation of the Scaean gates in this context, see *LIMC* i. 1. 183, no. 854. On the death of Achilles, see ibid. 181–5. Schoeck (1961: 76–7) links Achilles' death at the Scaean gates with the prayer of the Trojan women (*Il.* 6. 307), that *Diomede*, whom the Trojans fear more than they ever feared Achilles (*Il.* 6. 99), should fall at the Scaean gates. Schoeck also associates Diomede's arrow in the foot with Achilles' arrow in the foot, and refers to a lost Chalcidian amphora (see Woodford 1993: 94, fig. 89; *LIMC*, s.v. Achilleus, pl. 850) showing two arrows in the body of Achilles, one in the heel and one in the shoulder: he suggests a correspondence with the two arrows involved in (1) Diomede's shoulder wound from Pandarus' arrow (*Il.* 5. 188, 795; and (2) the arrow of Paris in Diomede's foot.

TABLE A. To show how Diomede's meetings with Glaucus and Hector anticipate Achilles' meetings with Aeneas and Hector

Diomede	Achilles
1. (*a*) In the absence of Hector, who has departed for Troy (5. 407–15)	1. (*a*) When looking for single combat with Hector (20. 76)
(*b*) Diomede challenges Glaucus (6. 123–9; 142–3)	(*b*) Achilles challenges Aeneas (20. 178–98)
(*c*) who tells him his genealogy:	(*c*) who tells him his genealogy:

<table>
<tr><td>

εἰ δ' ἐθέλεις καὶ ταῦτα δαήμεναι,
ὄφρ' ἐΰ εἰδῇς
ἡμετέρην γενεήν, πολλοὶ δέ μιν
ἄνδρες ἴσασιν·

. . . . . .

ταύτης τοι γενεῆς τε καὶ αἵματος
εὔχομαι εἶναι

If you wish to learn this too, so
that you may know well
my descent, and many men
know it:

. . . . . .

this is the lineage and blood
I claim to be from.
(6. 150–1; 6. 211)

</td><td>

εἰ δ' ἐθέλεις καὶ ταῦτα δαήμεναι,
ὄφρ' ἐΰ εἰδῇς
ἡμετέρην γενεήν, πολλοὶ δέ μιν
ἄνδρες ἴσασιν·

. . . . . .

ταύτης τοι γενεῆς τε καὶ αἵματος
εὔχομαι εἶναι

If you wish to learn this too, so
that you may know well
my descent, and many men
know it:

. . . . . .

this is the lineage and blood I
claim to be from.
(20. 213–14; 20. 241)

</td></tr>
</table>

(*d*) Abortive conclusion: they do not fight.	(*d*) Abortive conclusion: Poseidon rescues Aeneas.
2. (*a*) Unsuccessful attempt, without divine help, on Hector (11. 349–52).	2. (*a*) Unsuccessful attempt, without divine help, on Hector (20. 441–2).
(*b*) Diomede's spear stopped by the helmet given to Hector by Apollo (11. 352–3, 363).	(*b*) Hector rescued by Apollo (20. 443–4).
(*c*) Prayer for second chance at Hector, with divine assistance:	(*c*) Prayer for second chance at Hector, with divine assistance:

<table>
<tr><td>

ἐξ αὖ νῦν ἔφυγες θάνατον, κύον· ἦ
τέ τοι ἄγχι
ἦλθε κακόν. νῦν αὖτέ σ' ἐρύσατο
Φοῖβος Ἀπόλλων
ᾧ μέλλεις εὔχεσθαι ἰὼν ἐς δοῦπον
ἀκόντων.

</td><td>

ἐξ αὖ νῦν ἔφυγες θάνατον, κύον· ἦ
τέ τοι ἄγχι
ἦλθε κακόν. νῦν αὖτέ σ' ἐρύσατο
Φοῖβος Ἀπόλλων
ᾧ μέλλεις εὔχεσθαι ἰὼν ἐς δοῦπον
ἀκόντων.

</td></tr>
</table>

ἦ θήν σ᾽ ἐξανύω γε καὶ ὕστερον
ἀντιβολήσας
εἴ πού τις καὶ ἔμοιγε θεῶν
ἐπιτάρροθός ἐστι.
νῦν αὖ τοὺς ἄλλους ἐπιείσομαι, ὅν
κε κιχείω.

Now you have escaped death
again, you dog. Mark well,
it was a very near thing. Now
Phoebus Apollo rescued you
once more,
to whom you must pray on
your way to the heavy fall of
javelins.
Anyway, I shall surely finish
you off when I meet you
later,
if some one of the gods is a
helper to me.
Now I shall attack the others,
whomever I may encounter.
(11. 362–7)

ἦ θήν σ᾽ ἐξανύω γε καὶ ὕστερον
ἀντιβολήσας
εἴ πού τις καὶ ἔμοιγε θεῶν
ἐπιτάρροθός ἐστι.
νῦν αὖ τοὺς ἄλλους ἐπιείσομαι, ὅν
κε κιχείω.

Now you have escaped death
again, you dog. Mark well
it was a very near thing. Now
Phoebus Apollo rescued you
once more,
to whom you must pray on
your way to the heavy fall of
javelins.
Anyway, I shall surely finish
you off when I meet you
later,
if some one of the gods is a
helper to me.
Now I shall attack the others,
whomever I may encounter.
(20. 449–54)

3.

4. Diomede's fighting career ended
when he is shot in the foot and
lamed by an arrow fired by Paris
(11. 376–7).

3. Second chance at Hector with
divine assistance from Athene:
Hector killed (22. 214–363).

4. Achilles killed when he is shot in
the foot by an arrow fired by Paris
and Apollo (22. 359–60;
Apollodorus, *Epit.* 5. 5).

Hector[48] when he responds to Achilles' challenge (*Il.* 20. 429).
Poseidon helps Aeneas when he mists Achilles' eyes before
picking up Aeneas and removing him from the battlefield (*Il.*
20. 321–8): Aeneas' rescue by Poseidon anticipates Hector's
rescue by Apollo, who snatches up Hector and conceals him in
mist (*Il.* 20. 443–4).

[48] Πηλεΐδη, μὴ δή μ᾽ ἐπέεσσί γε νηπύτιον ὣς | ἔλπεο δειδίξεσθαι, ἐπεὶ σάφα οἶδα
καὶ αὐτός | ἠμὲν κερτομίας ἠδ᾽ αἴσυλα μυθήσασθαι, 'Son of Peleus, do not expect
to frighten me with words, | like a little child, since I also know very well |
how to speak in the genres of both taunting and unseemliness' (*Il.* 20. 200–2 =
Il. 20. 431–3).

6.7. DIVINE FAVOUR AND THE CONSEQUENCES
OF ITS WITHDRAWAL

The issue of divine favouritism, the feats it makes possible, and
the effects of its withdrawal, as explored in the examples of the
paradigms discussed in Diomede's meeting with Glaucus in
book 6 and realized in his later attempt on Hector in book 11,
when Athene does not help him, and he is lamed, prepare the
way for the more intensely serious developments in the final
books of the *Iliad*, where the inferiority to Achilles of the
Trojan heroes is initially compensated by divine assistance.
This assistance is eventually withdrawn. When Aeneas meets
Achilles, he is aware of his dependence on the gods:

Ζεὺς δ' ἀρετὴν ἄνδρεσσιν ὀφέλλει τε μινύθει τε,
ὅππως κεν ἐθέλῃσιν· ὁ γὰρ κάρτιστος ἁπάντων.

Zeus increases and decreases valour in men,
just as he wishes, for he is the strongest of all.

(*Il.* 20. 242–3)

Shortly afterwards, when Hector meets Achilles for the first
time, he concedes that his own birth is baser than Achilles', but
he is prepared to gamble on receiving divine support:

οἶδα δ' ὅτι σὺ μὲν ἐσθλός, ἐγὼ δὲ σέθεν πολὺ χείρων.
ἀλλ' ἤτοι μὲν ταῦτα θεῶν ἐν γούνασι κεῖται.

I know that you are noble, and I am much baser than you,
but surely these things lie on the knees of the gods.

(*Il.* 20. 434–5)

Hector's confidence in the gods is not misplaced in this first
encounter with Achilles, for Apollo snatches him away from
Athene and Achilles (*Il.* 20. 443–4). However, the examples of
Tydeus, Bellerophon, and Diomede all indicate that divine
favour is eventually withdrawn, and not before it has led its
'beneficiary' into overconfidence, the prelude to ruin. Hector's
early successes are due to the intervention of Zeus[49] in accordance with his promise to Thetis in book 1. Conscious of Zeus'
part in the Trojan success, Hector becomes overconfident, and

---

[49] Menelaus retreats from the body of Patroclus because he is conscious that
Zeus is assisting Hector. Menelaus thinks it pointless to fight against a god (*Il.*
17. 98–9).

is led to boast of the divine favour he enjoys (*Il.* 18. 293–4).[50] He couples his boasting with his rejection of Polydamas' advice (*Il.* 18. 254–83) to take the army back to the city when they learn of Achilles' imminent return to the battle. Too late, Hector recognizes his ἀτασθαλία (*Il.* 22. 104), which will lead to the destruction of his people.[51] His patron, Apollo, makes no attempt to defy Zeus' scales when Hector's κῆρ weighs heavier than Achilles' (*Il.* 22. 212–13): Apollo abandons Hector (*Il.* 22. 213) to Achilles and Athene, who deceives Hector into supposing he has the support of his brother, Deiphobus. Hector recognizes Athene's deception when he asks Athene/ Deiphobus for a second spear, only to find there is no one there (*Il.* 22. 298–9). No example of the sudden, unaccountable end of a run of good luck under the aegis of divine patronage is ever told to Hector, but he acknowledges that his present plight must be the will even of Zeus and Apollo, his former patrons, who were friendly before, but now will do nothing to save him from his fate:

> ἦ γάρ ῥα πάλαι τό γε φίλτερον ἦεν
> Ζηνί τε καὶ Διὸς υἷι ἑκηβόλῳ, οἵ με πάρος γε
> πρόφρονες εἰρύατο· νῦν αὖτέ με μοῖρα κιχάνει.

> for long since this was the choice
> of Zeus and of the far-shooter son of Zeus, who formerly
> shielded me gladly. But now fate is upon me.

> (*Il.* 22. 301–3)

Zeus prophesied the end of Hector's run of good luck and his death at the hands of Achilles (*Il.* 15. 68), although he gives him glory for a short time, to make up for the fact that he will never return to Andromache (*Il.* 17. 206–8).

Similarly, the limit to Achilles' enjoyment of divine favour is already fixed and has been presaged by the corresponding career of Diomede: one of the gods will stand beside Achilles too, and give him strength on the day he kills Hector. At that time he will be conscious that the best of the gods love him, but thereafter he must suffer what fate has decreed for him (*Il.* 20.

---

[50] On divine favour as a prelude to deception, see Deichgräber (1952: 108–9): for his discusssion of divine favour resulting in delusion in Hector's case, see Deichgräber (1952: 117–19).

[51] Cf. *Od.* 10. 437, where Odysseus' ἀτασθαλία in entering the cave of the Cyclops leads to the deaths of many of his crew.

120–8). As Hector lies dying, he warns Achilles that he too will become the victim of the gods when they eventually turn against him:[52]

φράζεο νῦν, μή τοί τι θεῶν μήνιμα γένωμαι
ἤματι τῷ ὅτε κέν σε Πάρις καὶ Φοῖβος Ἀπόλλων
ἐσθλὸν ἐόντ᾽ ὀλέσωσιν ἐνὶ Σκαιῇσι πύλῃσιν.

Consider now, lest I become the occasion of the wrath of the gods against you,
on that day when Paris and Phoebus Apollo
will destroy you, although you are noble, at the Scaean gates.

(*Il.* 22. 358–60)

The gods very quickly become angry with Achilles when Hector's warning does not deter him from mistreating his victim's corpse. This causes Priam to describe him as ἀτάσθαλος (*Il.* 22. 418) and the anger of the gods is aroused against Achilles (*Il.* 24. 113–16, 134–6). Although Achilles does not perish in the *Iliad*, the imminent and inevitable conclusion of his career under divine patronage[53] is indicated to the reader by the warnings he receives from Thetis that if he chooses to fight at Troy (*Il.* 1. 415–18) and avenge Patroclus' death (*Il.* 18. 96), his own death will not be far away. Hector's dying prophecy of Achilles' death reinforces these warnings from the goddess. But the earlier patterns of Tydeus' ἀτασθαλία and loss of divine favour, Bellerophon's enjoyment of divine favour and its precipitate withdrawal, Athene's assistance to Diomede and her absence at the sudden conclusion of his fighting career when he is shot in the foot and lamed, foreshadowing the conclusion of Achilles' career (he will be shot in the foot and killed), all act as precedents which cause the reader to bear in mind the inevitable and tragic outcome of Achilles' choice of a glorious career under divine patronage.

[52] British Museum Catalogue of Vases E468 shows Apollo abandoning Hector, and as he goes away, pointing an arrow at the foot of Achilles.

[53] Achilles differs from other beneficiaries of divine patronage in the moment of his disillusion with it. For Achilles, the worst is not death, which he fully expects, but the loss of Patroclus (*Il.* 18. 79–82).

7
The Paradigm of Meleager:
Application and Implication

The *Iliad*'s version of the story of Meleager presents that hero as the recipient of a number of requests from a succession of persons. Each of these requests is for the same thing: the hero should abandon his wrath and fight in defence of the town. This version of the story displays correspondences with the situation of Achilles: like Meleager, Achilles receives requests from a series of ambassadors, and each of these ambassadors corresponds to a figure in the succession of persons approaching Meleager. The ambassadors, like those who approached Meleager, all ask Achilles to lay aside his anger and fight in their defence. Meleager neglected the early requests put to him, despite the accompanying offer of a handsome present (a wealthy estate): he did not fight until requested to do so by his wife, but by the time of his wife's request, the emergency of his city had escalated to a crisis, the offer of the handsome present was past, and Meleager returned to the fighting empty-handed. The story of Meleager appears to be offered to Achilles as an example of a hero who was angry, but who laid aside his anger, as Achilles is being urged to do. It is presented as a dissuasive pattern, an example to be avoided: Achilles is being asked to return to battle in exchange for the handsome presents offered in the early stages of the sequence of approaches: he is being advised not to delay until he is requested to return to the fighting by someone he cannot refuse. Nothing suggests that the Calydonian elders or the priests they send to offer gifts to Meleager have close ties of affection with Meleager, but they are rapidly followed by members of Meleager's family, his dearest friends, and finally his wife, who persuades him to go out and fight. Kakridis saw in the series of figures who ask Meleager to return to battle an 'ascending scale of affection', a series of persons ever dearer to the hero than the last. In Kakridis' view, the approaches of the ambassadors to Achilles in book 9 and the entreaties of Patroclus in book 16 represent a further instance of the motif of the ascending scale of affection. Kakridis also observed that this motif, the series of requests from persons ever dearer to the recipient than the last, is not restricted to Achilles and Meleager, but occurs in the case of one other character in the poems, namely Hector. Hector is approached in book 6 by the women of Troy, who ask him about their menfolk on the battlefield; by his mother and sister, who offer him wine; by Helen, who invites him to rest; and finally by his wife, who asks him to direct the battle from the tower of Troy. As Kakridis showed, the requests of all these women would, if granted, have the effect of keeping Hector in Troy and restricting the heroism he displays.

In order to understand how the motif, a series of requests in ascending scale of affection, is used by the poet, we need to look at the nature of the relationships of the persons in these three ascending scales to the person they are approaching, and to decide if there is any correspondence between the persons appearing in the three scales. We also need to look at the nature of the requests presented in ascending scale of affection, the terms used to describe them, and what is requested of the addressee. We shall find that the requests to Meleager and those to Achilles may be classed as λιταί (prayers, entreaties), and some, but not all, of the requests put to Hector are so described. The consequences of refusing λιταί, whether or not they are presented by a series of persons in ascending scale of affection, are discussed by Phoenix in the αἶνος of the Λιταί (allegory of the Prayers) which he relates to Achilles in the long speech in which he also tells the story of Meleager. The poet shows Agamemnon, Achilles, Meleager, and Hector refusing λιταί, and we shall see whether they suffer the consequences implied by the αἶνος. To plumb the significance of the requests put to these four heroes, it is important to recognize and understand the distinctions between undifferentiated petitions, λιταί, and supplication (a term which is currently very loosely applied). We shall begin by considering the nature of the approaches made to Achilles, which are significantly different from the approaches he would like to receive.

7.1. THE NATURE OF λιταί (PRAYERS)

7.1.1. Achilles anticipates supplication (Il. 11. 609–10)

Achilles, deprived by Agamemnon of his prize, the concubine Briseis, refuses to fight and threatens to return home, but, instead of leaving Troy, he requests his mother, Thetis, to arrange with Zeus for the Greeks to suffer defeat in his absence and so recognize his worth. In book 9 of the poem the situation is so desperate that an embassy visits Achilles to offer him gifts if he will lay aside his anger and fight. Despite the value of the gifts and the many arguments of the ambassadors in favour of accepting the offer, Achilles refuses it. By book 11 many of the most distinguished Greek warriors are wounded, causing Achilles to anticipate some fresh overture to himself:

νῦν ὀίω περὶ γούνατ᾽ ἐμὰ στήσεσθαι Ἀχαιοὺς
λισσομένους· χρειὼ¹ γὰρ ἱκάνεται οὐκέτ᾽ ἀνεκτός.²

now I think the Greeks will stand around my knees
λισσόμενοι; for necessity which can no longer be borne has come on them.

(Il. 11. 609–10)

The approach Achilles here imagines would amount to supplication, since he hopes to see the Greeks clustered around his *knees*. Such an approach, if it came, would be different from the approach of the embassy, which addresses λιταί³ to Achilles, but makes no supplication.

---

¹ χρειώ is used repeatedly after the rejection of the embassy (*Il.* 10. 118, 142, 172; 11. 609), recalling Achilles' words (*Il.* 1. 340–1): εἴ ποτε δὴ αὖτε | χρειὼ ἐμεῖο γένηται ἀεικέα λοιγὸν ἀμῦναι, 'if ever again | *need* of me should arise to ward off shameful destruction', when he foresees the desperation of the Greeks in his absence.

² This line (with the variation λισσόμενος) is spoken earlier by Nestor at *Il.* 10. 118 with reference to Menelaus, who ought to be toiling round the Greeks in preparation for the council which will send Diomede and Odysseus into the camp of the Trojan allies by night. Further examples of a distinguished hero λισσόμενος his allies and compatriots to fight in an emergency are found at *Il.* 15. 660 (of Nestor) and *Il.* 5. 491 (Sarpedon considers Hector should be λισσόμενος). See Table C.

³ As Phoenix says (*Il.* 9. 520): cf. Diomede (*Il.* 9. 628).

7.1.2. Has he forgotten the embassy?

Il. 11. 609–10 (and *Il.* 16. 72–3, where Achilles tells Patroclus how the ditches would soon fill up with the dead of the routed Trojans εἴ μοι κρείων Ἀγαμέμνων | ἤπια εἰδείη, 'if Agamemnon were to show a friendly attitude towards me') say nothing about the embassy which conveyed Agamemnon's extravagant offer to Achilles in book 9. They must mean either that the fresh approach Achilles has in mind will be quite different from the embassy he has already received, or that the speaker of these lines knows nothing of the embassy, and they belong to a version of the poem in which the embassy did not appear. Achilles' anticipation of the Greeks' at his knees (*Il.* 11. 609–10), as Hainsworth explains

cannot be reconciled with a previous appeal to Akhilleus such as we have in book 9, except by rather forced argument, e.g. that the content of a scene is always relevant only to its immediate context and may ignore what is to come and what has been, or . . . 'might be explicable either as a pardonable oversight by a single poet or even as a deliberate neglect by Achilles of offers which were unaccompanied by any frank admission of Agamemnon's high-handedness' (Kirk, *Songs* 214) . . . The verses therefore remain a strong indication that the Embassy is among the latest of the ideas and episodes built into the *Iliad* whose contribution to the poem is here and in book 16 overridden by an older concept of a vengeful Akhilleus.[4]

The most extreme version of the view that *Il.* 11. 609–10 are inconsistent with the embassy of book 9 must be that of Page, who argues that the whole embassy is a later interpolation:

Now it seems very obvious that these words (*Il.* 11. 609–10) were not spoken by an Achilles about whose knees the Achaeans were in fact standing in supplication on the previous evening . . . The words imply that he had received no embassy at all . . . for that which Achilles anticipates as future, and even yet as contingent, had actually occurred on the previous evening: the Greeks *had* supplicated at his feet—they *had* proclaimed their intolerable need—and he had spurned them . . . The passage is obviously, in effect, a denial that any approach had yet been made to Achilles.[5]

---

[4] Hainsworth (1993: 289–90 ad *Il.* 11. 609).

[5] Page (1959: 305–7). Van Thiel (1982: 87) supports Page's view. However, *LIMC* i. 1. 107–8, s.v. Achilleus (XII), 437 shows a bronze tripod leg of 625–600 BC with three ambassadors led by Phoenix.

Both Hainsworth and Page treat the appeals made to Achilles in the embassy and those to be made in the overture he anticipates (*Il.* 11. 609–10) as equivalent, amounting to the same thing, but Kirk, in the passage[6] quoted by Hainsworth, suggests the absence of any 'frank admission of Agamemnon's high-handedness' is the reason why Achilles seems to ignore the embassy of book 9 when contemplating the pleasurable prospect of the Greeks at his knees, λισσόμενους (entreating). This idea is taken up by Agathe Thornton, for whom the embassy is 'the most extensive supplication sequence in the whole of the *Iliad*'.[7] She finds Agamemnon's attitude in the matter of the embassy unsatisfactory,[8] because he is not truly suppliant: far from abasing himself, he insists on his superior honour,[9] whereas the *supplication*[10] of the ambassadors is duly humble. In her interpretation of *Il.* 11. 609–10, Achilles wants 'to see the Achaeans—Agamemnon or the Achaeans or both, he does not distinguish—abasing themselves in the suppliants' ritual gesture of touching or embracing his knees':[11] in her view the fact that Agamemnon sits down to address the assembly when he is reconciled with Achilles (*Il.* 19. 76) gives him the crouching position expressive of 'the suppliant's self-abasement'.[12] Achilles' requirement (*Il.* 11. 609–10) that the Greeks should make the ritual gesture of touching or embracing his knees, as indicated by Thornton, was long ago understood by Schadewaldt, who saw in *Il.* 11. 609–10 no inconsistency with the events of the embassy: in book 9 the Greeks had not entreated Achilles 'kniefällig' (falling at his knees), that is, at any price, and they had not made the kind of appeal he wanted.[13]

[6] Kirk (1962: 214).

[7] Thornton (1984: 123).

[8] Thornton (1984: 132).

[9] Thornton (1984: 126).

[10] My italics: Thornton (1984: 125) regards the embassy as a supplication.

[11] Thornton (1984: 133).

[12] Thornton (1984: 128–9). It is far more likely to result from the wound in his arm (acquired *Il.* 11. 252–3, and still troublesome, 19. 51–3). The wounds of Odysseus, Diomede, and Agamemnon contrast with Achilles' unscathed condition in book 19.

[13] Schadewaldt (1966: 81; 1st pub. 1938); cf. Eichholz (1953: 137–48, at 142–3). We should not necessarily infer that Achilles, when he rejects the embassy, has already formulated the idea of holding out for what he antici-

However, the careful distinction established by these scholars, between supplications involving ritual gestures or verbal expression[14] of such ritual gestures as clasping the knees, and appeals which are confined to humble entreaties, is robustly (and erroneously) dismissed by Page: 'it is fantastic to suppose that what happened in the Ninth Book was such that a distinction can be drawn between this passage (*Il.* 11. 609–10) and that [the embassy] on the ground that, although the ambassadors earnestly implored Achilles, they were not actually *said* to stand about his knees'.[15]

The one thing that emerges distinctly from all this discussion is that the approach Achilles envisages (*Il.* 11. 609–10) the Greeks will make to him is to be a supplication: they are to cluster at his knees λισσόμενοι, and it is the allusion to knees which identifies their anticipated appeal as a supplication. There is no agreement on whether the embassy to Achilles constituted a supplication or not,[16] and we cannot hope to

pates in *Il.* 11. 609–10. The following all take the allegory of the Λιταί as integral both to book 9 and to the rest of the poem: Scott (1912: 68–77); Bassett (1938: 71, 197–20); Kakridis (1949: 11–16); Segal (1988: 90–105); Ebel (1972: 87–104); Rosner (1976: 314–27).

[14] This is the distinction between 'full supplication' and 'figurative supplication' made by Kopperschmidt (1967: 20–5), and discussed by Gould (1973: 77): 'figurative supplication' he thinks, lacks the full ritual significance of the completed action, and is used when the situation calls for no more than an intensification of the language of diplomatic appeal, or where the completed ritual would be impractical or unwise. See also Lynn-George (1983: 36–113; 1988: 201–5, 287 n. 27), who emphasizes the role of speech in supplication and argues that Chryses should be regarded as a suppliant.

[15] Page (1959: 307). Tsagarakis (1971: 257–77) argues against inconsistency between the embassy and *Il.* 11. 609–10. In his view (1971: 259) Achilles is dissatisfied with the embassy because nobody in it 'offered him any prayers', in the sense of prayers to a god. But this is not the only sense of 'prayers' in English, or the right one here. The Λιταί of the αἶνος function as attempts to persuade: Fränkel (1975: 63; 1st pub. 1951) is right that prayers look askance because they wish to steer the stubborn man away from his unbending path. Griffin (1995: 133) on *Il.* 9. 502–14 translates Λιταί as Prayers, but I think he is mistaken to add 'for forgiveness and harmony'. Harmony perhaps, but not forgiveness: that idea comes from Benveniste (1973: 503; 1st pub. 1969), and is unfounded as I shall show.

[16] Lynn-George (1983: 169–71; and briefly 1988: 167) regards the question whether the embassy constitutes a supplication as 'undecidable', because there is no 'yes/no answer from the supplicated' to which the reader can respond, and because of the difference in how the episode is perceived by the two sides

understand the rejected embassy to Achilles, or its relationship to the story of Meleager until we establish whether the approaches to Achilles in the embassy and the approaches to Meleager in the paradigm are equivalent, and whether either amounts to a supplication, which would have serious consequences if rejected. We shall begin by considering what constitutes supplication.

7.1.3. Supplication, Ἱκετεία

The clearest explanation of ἱκετεία, supplication, is the groundbreaking article by Gould,[17] in which he defined ἱκετεία,[18] explaining it as almost a 'game'[19] which required certain ritual gestures such as clasping the knees, the right hand, touching the beard or chin,[20] or sitting in dejection at the hearth,[21] possibly clasping a child of the person supplicated. The ritual gestures may be performed in fact or metaphorically,[22] by the use of such words as γουνοῦμαι, 'I clasp your knees' (even though the speaker may be some distance away, and make no physical contact at all, as at *Od*. 6. 149). Such physical contact, real or metaphorical, places the person supplicated under a solemn obligation towards the suppliant, who is sacred to Zeus and under his protection. It produces feelings of αἰδώς (respect,

---

involved: Achilles continues (*Il*. 11. 609–10) to expect an Achaean supplication, whereas the Achaeans are said to feel that the embassy constituted a supplication which was rejected and abandoned.

[17] Gould (1973: 74–103).

[18] Lynn-George (1983: 36–113) deconstructs Gould's definition of ἱκετεία and concludes that any definition in terms of significant ritual actions will be over-restrictive, excluding a great deal which fails to qualify as full supplication. His argument risks serious confusion between undifferentiated requests and entreaties and requests in the context of supplication. Supplication places the recipient under a solemn obligation which the gods may be expected to uphold and sanction in the event of rejection. See Lynn-George (1988: 287 n. 27) for a much briefer statement of this view. For the danger of pollution when the rights of suppliants are violated, see Parker (1983: 146). Undifferentiated requests and entreaties do not entail the solemn obligation and divine sanction associated with supplication.

[19] On the serious nature of certain games, see Huizinga (1970: 24; 1st pub. 1944): on play as ritual, Huizinga (1970: 33–46, 78–82).

[20] Gould (1973: 76–7, 96).

[21] *Od*. 7. 153–69; Thucydides, 1. 136. 3; Gould (1973: 78–9, 97).

[22] Gould (1973: 77).

shame) in the recipient, which inhibit his aggression. Burkert interprets the gesture of touching the knees, or more exactly, the hollow of the knee, as an appeasement gesture (an invitation to sit down) intended to disarm aggression in the person supplicated.[23] Rejection of a supplication provokes the anger of Zeus. The ritual of supplication gives a paradoxical strength to the weak and helpless.[24] Even if it resembles a game, the ritual is intensely serious. The game has 'rules', and in cases where physical contact is actually made, rather than metaphorically expressed, the obligations on the recipient of the supplication cease to apply if the physical contact is broken, as happens in the case of Lycaon, who has clasped Achilles' knees (*Il.* 21. 68) but then makes the fatal mistake of letting go and flinging out his arms (*Il.* 21. 115): when the contact is broken, Achilles kills him (*Il.* 21. 116–19).[25]

7.1.4. Ἱκετεία *(supplication) in the* Iliad

Gould lists the examples of ἱκετεία (supplication) in the *Iliad*[26] (see Table B): he gives a total of fifteen, two of which are queried, and a total of twenty-five references to the fifteen cases. The number of examples of ἱκετεία should probably be raised to sixteen,[27] and the total number of references to supplication should be raised to twenty-seven.[28] Of these sixteen supplications, that of Thetis to Zeus is referred to seven times, and Priam's supplication to Achilles six times: the others are mentioned only once. In these twenty-seven references to supplication, we find four references to ἱκέτης (suppliant) or

---

[23] Burkert (1979: 44–5 with 164 n. 42 and 46–7, figs. 3 and 4).

[24] Gould (1973: 100).

[25] Gould (1973: 77, 80–1). Parker (1983: 181–2) argues that Lycaon is a 'spare me' suppliant rather than a 'help me' suppliant, and therefore does not enjoy the protection of Zeus Hikesios, and has no absolute claim to mercy.

[26] Gould (1973: 80 n. 39).

[27] Three of which are queried, because Gould's list conflates two references: Priam and Hecuba to Hector (*Il.* 22. 35–91) is given the reference *Il.* 22. 240. At *Il.* 22. 240, we find Athene disguised as Deiphobus, giving a false account of how Priam and Hecuba entreated him/her γουνούμενοι (by his/her knees) not to go out to join Hector in facing Achilles. Γουνούμενοι indicates verbal supplication.

[28] Because *Il.* 24. 357, where Priam's herald proposes entreating Hermes and touching his knees, was overlooked.

TABLE B. Supplication in the *Iliad*

Additions to Gould's list are marked**.

Doubtful instances listed by Gould appear in parentheses

1. 407   τῶν νῦν μιν μνήσασα παρέζεο καὶ λαβὲ γούνων
         remind him now of these things, and sit by him, and take him by
         the knees

     427   καί μιν γουνάσομαι καί μιν πείσεσθαι ὀΐω
         and I shall supplicate him by his knees and I think I shall per-
         suade him

     500   καί ῥα πάροιθ' αὐτοῖο καθέζετο, καὶ λάβε γούνων
         σκαιῇ, δεξιτερῇ δ' ἄρ' ὑπ' ἀνθερεῶνος ἑλοῦσα
         λισσομένη προσέειπε Δία Κρονίωνα ἄνακτα
         and she sat down before him and took him by the knees
         with her left hand, and with her right she took hold of him under
         the chin
         and entreating him she addressed lord Zeus, the son of Cronos

     512   ... Θέτις δ' ὡς ἥψατο γούνων,
         ὣς ἔχετ' ἐμπεφυυῖα ...
         ... and Thetis, as she was clasping him by the knees,
         so she held fast ...

     557   ἠερίη γὰρ σοί γε παρέζετο καὶ λάβε γούνων
         for at day-break she sat beside you and clasped you by the knees

8. 371   ἥ οἱ γούνατ' ἔκυσσε καὶ ἔλλαβε χειρὶ γενείου
         λισσομένη τιμῆσαι Ἀχιλλῆα πτολίπορθον
         who kissed his knees and took hold of him by the beard with her
         hand
         entreating him to honour Achilles, the sacker of cities

15. 76   ἤματι τῷ ὅτ' ἐμεῖο θεὰ Θέτις ἥψατο γούνων
         λισσομένη τιμῆσαι Ἀχιλλῆα πτολίπορθον
         on that day when the goddess Thetis clasped me by my knees
         entreating me to honour Achilles, the sacker of cities

6. 45   Ἄδρηστος δ' ἄρ' ἔπειτα λαβὼν ἐλλίσσετο γούνων
         But then Adrestus took hold of him by the knees and entreated
         him

9. 451   ... ἥ δ' αἰὲν ἐμὲ λισσέσκετο γούνων
         ... and she was always entreating me by my knees

     581   πολλὰ δέ μιν λιτάνευε γέρων ἱππηλάτα Οἰνεὺς
         οὐδοῦ ἐπεμβεβαὼς ὑψηρεφέος θαλάμοιο
         σείων κολλητὰς σανίδας, γουνούμενος υἱόν
         and the old man, the horseman, Oeneus, entreated him over and
         over
         standing on the threshold of the high-roofed chamber
         shaking the panelled doors, supplicating his son by his knees

10. 454   ἦ, καὶ ὁ μέν μιν ἔμελλε γενείου χειρὶ παχείῃ
         ἁψάμενος λίσσεσθαι ...

He spoke, and he was on the point of touching his beard with his thick hand,
and entreating

11. 130   ... τὼ δ' αὖτ' ἐκ δίφρου γουναζέσθην
    ... and they two, from the chariot, supplicated him by his knees

15. 660   λίσσεσθ' ὑπὲρ τοκέων γουνούμενος ἄνδρα ἕκαστον
He was entreating, supplicating each man in the name of his parents

16. 573   ἀτὰρ τότε γ' ἐσθλὸν ἀνεψιὸν ἐξεναρίξας
ἐς Πηλῆ' ἱκέτευσε καὶ ἐς Θέτιν ἀργυρόπεζαν
          but then he killed his noble cousin
and made supplication to Peleus and to Thetis of the silver feet

18. 457   τοὔνεκα νῦν τὰ σὰ γούναθ' ἱκάνομαι, αἴ κ' ἐθέλησθα
υἱεῖ ἐμῷ ὠκυμόρῳ δόμεν ἀσπίδα
For this reason I am coming now to your knees, if you may be willing
to give my swift-fated son a shield

20. 463   —ὁ μὲν ἀντίος ἤλυθε γούνων
εἴ πώς εὖ πεφίδοιτο λαβὼν καὶ ζωὸν ἀφείη
          —he came before his knees
if somehow he would spare him, taking him prisoner alive, and would let him go

21. 64   ... ὁ δέ οἱ σχεδὸν ἦλθε τεθηπὼς
γούνων ἅψασθαι μεμαώς
    ... but he, astonished, came close to him,
seeking to clasp him by the knees

    68   ... ὁ δ' ὑπέδραμε καὶ λάβε γούνων
    ... but he ran under it, and clasped him by his knees

    71   αὐτὰρ ὁ τῇ ἑτέρῃ μὲν ἑλὼν ἐλλίσσετο γούνων
But he, with one hand, clasped him by his knees and began to entreat him

    74   "γουνοῦμαί σ', Ἀχιλεῦ· σὺ δέ μ' αἴδεο καί μ' ἐλέησον·
ἀντί τοί εἰμ' ἱκέταο, διοτρεφές, αἰδοίοιο"
'I supplicate you by your knees, Achilles: but respect and pity me:
I am as good as a reverend suppliant to you, nurtured by the gods'

    97   ὣς ἄρα μιν Πριάμοιο προσηύδα φαίδιμος υἱὸς
λισσόμενος ἐπέεσσιν
So the shining son of Priam addressed him,
entreating him with words

(115   ἔγχος μέν ῥ' ἀφέηκεν, ὁ δ' ἕζετο χεῖρε πετάσσας
(he let go the spear, and sat, stretching out his hands)

** 22. 74   ἀλλ' ὅτε δὴ πολιόν τε κάρη πολιόν τε γένειον
αἰδῶ τ' αἰσχύνωσι κύνες κταμένοιο γέροντος
τοῦτο δὴ οἴκτιστον πέλεται δειλοῖσι βροτοῖσιν.
But when the dogs defile the grey head, the grey beard,
and the privy parts of a slaughtered elder,

		this indeed is most pitiful to unhappy mortals.
** 80		. . . ἑτέρηφι δὲ μαζὸν ἀνέσχε
		. . . and with the other hand, she held up a breast
240		λίσσονθ᾽ ἑξείης γουνούμενοι, ἀμφὶ δ᾽ ἑταῖροι
		αὖθι μένειν
		they were entreating me, supplicating me one after the other by
		my knees, and my comrades round me, to remain there
338		λίσσομ᾽ ὑπὲρ ψυχῆς καὶ γούνων σῶν τε τοκήων
		I entreat you by your soul, and by your knees, and by your
		parents
(414		πάντας δ᾽ ἐλλιτάνευε κυλινδόμενος κατὰ κόπρον)
		(he was entreating them all, rolling in the dung)
24.	158	ἀλλὰ μάλ᾽ ἐνδυκέως ἱκέτεω πεφιδήσεται ἀνδρός
		but very zealously will he spare a suppliant
	187	ἀλλὰ μάλ᾽ ἐνδυκέως ἱκέτεω πεφιδήσεται ἀνδρός
		but very zealously will he spare a suppliant
	**357	γούνων ἁψάμενοι λιτανεύσομεν, αἴ κ᾽ ἐλεήσῃ
		clasping him by the knees we shall entreat him, if he will pity
	465	τύνη δ᾽ εἰσελθὼν λαβὲ γούνατα Πηλεΐωνος,
		καί μιν ὑπὲρ πατρὸς καὶ μητέρος ἠϋκόμοιο
		λίσσεο καὶ τέκεος . . .
		and you go in and take the knees of the son of Peleus
		and entreat him in the name of his father, and his mother of the
		lovely hair
		and his son . . .
	478	χερσὶν Ἀχιλλῆος λαβὲ γούνατα καὶ κύσε χεῖρας
		in your hands take the knees of the son of Peleus and kiss his
		hands
	570	καὶ ἱκέτην περ ἐόντα, Διὸς δ᾽ ἀλίτωμαι ἐφετμάς
		although you are a suppliant, and I may sin against the
		commands of Zeus

ἱκετεύω (supplicate), nineteen references to knees, actual or metaphorical, three references to beards or chins, two references to parents, and one to the ψυχή.[29] All this information is most easily assimilated from Table B. Gould queries ἐλλιτάνευε κυλινδόμενος κατὰ κόπρον, he was entreating while rolling in the dirt (*Il.* 22. 414), which might possibly be a supplication: Priam is entreating the Trojans to allow him to go and supplicate Achilles for the return of Hector's body, but it really is not clear that rolling in the dirt while entreating constitutes a supplication—I think not, because there is no reference

---

[29] For the significance of ψυχή (*Il.* 22. 338) see Onians (1951: 96–7). For chin, Onians (1951: 132–3); for knees, Onians (1951: 174–86).

to the normal rituals of supplication, and because rolling in the dirt is elsewhere (*Il.* 18. 26–7) a sign of grief, not supplication.[30] Priam and Hecuba (*Il.* 22. 33–91) make a most interesting supplication to Hector: to begin with, they *are* his parents, and one's parents may be cited by suppliants as a basis for their appeal (*Il.* 15. 660; 22. 338). Secondly, their appeal is based firmly on indisputably generative, or life-giving portions of the anatomy. The holiness of the knees, γούνατα, and chin, γένειον, which are frequently mentioned in contexts of supplication, arises from their association with generation: they derive from the γεν/γον root,[31] and are regarded as sexual parts. Hecuba exposes her breasts, as she pleads with Hector τάδε τ' αἴδεο καί μ' ἐλέησον | αὐτήν, 'respect these and pity me' (*Il.* 22. 82–3). Hecuba's gesture reasserts the intimacy between mother and new-born infant which once existed between herself and Hector.[32] She appeals to his pity for herself, and the exposed breasts are calculated to make him turn away in shame.[33] The suppliant is attempting to kindle shame in the supplicated.[34] Priam, who knows Troy will not last long if Hector is killed, seeks to dissuade his son from meeting Achilles in single combat, describing the shame of his own aged body lying dead by the doorway, while the dogs he fed at table now feed on his flesh (*Il.* 22. 66–71). In a comparison which must already be a

---

[30] See Lateiner (1995: 107). The grieving relatives take on pollution in the first part of the death ritual, immediately following the death: Sourvinou-Inwood (1983: 37–9; 1991: 277 n. 85).

[31] Onians (1951: 233, 235–6).

[32] As argued by Loraux (1990: 59–62).

[33] Cairns (1993: 91). Loraux (1986: 90–102; esp. 99–100) considers the distinction made by Hecuba between αἰδώς for the exposed breast and pity for herself *invalidates* Redfield's equation of her formula with that of a captive appealing for mercy on the battlefield: Redfield (1975: 157 and n. 14). It must be said, however, that Lycaon appeals on the battlefield to αἰδώς (shame, respect) and pity (*Il.* 21. 74) (Cairns 1993: 113–17), but both αἰδώς and pity are to be for *him*. Priam asks Achilles to αἰδεῖο θεούς, 'respect the gods' and pity him, making a distinction not unlike Hecuba's. Hecuba's gesture indicates supplication: see Lateiner (1995: 107). For the ultimate in expressive body language, see Tacitus, *Annals* 14. 8. 6 = Dio Cassius, 61. 13. 5; see also [Seneca], *Octavia* 368–72. (Agrippina, aware that her executioners were acting on the orders of Nero, her son, indicated her womb, and told them to strike there.)

[34] Gould (1973: 87–90); Crotty (1994: 19–20, 36–8).

standard motif,[35] he contrasts the beauty of a young man lying dead with the piteous spectacle of an old man whose white head and privy parts (αἰδῶ) are ravaged by the dogs (*Il.* 22. 73–5). Crotty suggests the self-abasement of the suppliant makes clear the value of other goods, such as his life or the life of his child, for the sake of which he is emboldened to confront the supplicated. The recipient of supplication, as he is reminded of his love for his own dependants and his own life, is made to remember his own vulnerability.[36] This suggests that the underlying significance of supplication is an appeal to common humanity, and perhaps we should deduce from the references in supplication to words derived from the γεν/γον root that it is an appeal to life itself.[37] However this may be, the aspect of Gould's list of supplications in the *Iliad* most significant for our present concerns is that it omits all reference to the embassy to Achilles. The only passages from book 9 to appear in Gould's list are Phoenix's mother's appeal to her son and Oeneus' appeal to Meleager: Althaea, λισσέσκετο γούνων, entreated her son by his knees (*Il.* 9. 451) and Oeneus appealed to his son γουνούμενος, by his knees (Il. 9. 583), something the ambassadors in book 9 certainly do not do to Achilles.

7.1.5. Ἱκετεία *and* λιταί *(supplication and prayers)*

When, in the course of his quarrel with Agamemnon, Achilles first announces his intention of returning home (*Il.* 1. 169–70) Agamemnon retorts that he himself will not entreat Achilles to remain on his account: οὐδέ σ᾽ ἔγωγε | λίσσομαι[38] εἵνεκ᾽ ἐμεῖο μένειν, 'nor am I entreating you to remain on my account' (*Il.* 1. 173–4).

[35] Cf. Tyrtaeus, *fr.* 10, 21–30 West. See Griffin (1980: 117). Crotty (1994: 36–7) argues for a contradiction in Priam's appeal; he is seeking to arouse αἰδώς (shame, respect) in Hector, but also ἔλεος (pity), which would cause him to violate αἰδώς. 'Priam's mutilation by his own dogs illustrates the destruction of civilised values by the savagery of war': Segal (1971*b*: 33). On the relationship between Priam's verbal account of the desecration of his person, and Hecuba's gesture, see Loraux (1986: 100). On the heightened emotional effect of the unusual language used by Priam, see Richardson (1987: 178–80).   [36] Crotty (1994: 91–2).

[37] Onians (1951: 97, 132f., 174f., 180f., 233, 235); Gould (1973: 96–7).

[38] Bannert (1981: 77–8 n. 21) rightly emphasizes Achilles' use of λισσομένους (*Il.* 11. 610) as a reference to Agamemnon's categoric refusal to entreat (λίσσεσθαι) at *Il.* 1. 173.

Λίσσομαι,[39] which Agamemnon here says he is not doing, is used in the sense of 'entreat you (in an attempt to change your mind)', a sense carried also in *Il.* 9. 501, where it is preceded by στρεπτοὶ δέ τε καὶ θεοὶ αὐτοί, 'even the gods themselves are flexible':

> στρεπτοὶ δέ τε καὶ θεοὶ αὐτοί,
> τῶν περ καὶ μείζων ἀρετὴ τιμή τε βίη τε.
> καὶ μὲν τοὺς θυέεσσι καὶ εὐχωλῆς ἀγανῆσι
> λοιβῇ τε κνίσῃ τε παρατρωπῶσ᾽ ἄνθρωποι   500
> λισσόμενοι, ὅτε κέν τις ὑπερβήῃ καὶ ἁμάρτῃ.

even the gods themselves are flexible,
whose quality, honour, and force are even greater.
And with sacrifices and kindly prayers, and
with libations and burnt sacrifices men (cause them to) change their
   minds   500
λισσόμενοι when someone oversteps the mark and does wrong.

(Il. 9. 497–501)

So Agamemnon will not entreat Achilles λισσόμενος in an attempt to change his mind, but in the embassy he sends others to effect a change of mind in Achilles. The ambassadors themselves say, in speaking of the embassy, that Agamemnon has sent the best of the Greeks to entreat (λίσσεσθαι) Achilles (*Il.* 9. 520). When the ambassadors return, without success, to Agamemnon, Diomede tells Agamemnon that he should not have entreated (λίσσεσθαι) Achilles (*Il.* 9. 698). One of the ambassadors, Phoenix, tells Achilles the allegory of the Λιταί (Prayers) to illustrate the nature of the approach being made to him. There are eleven occurrences of λιταί and parts of λίσσεσθαι, λιτάνευειν, and λιτέσθαι in book 9.[40] The internal references all regard the approaches of the ambassadors in book 9 as Λιταί and the verb for these approaches as λίσσεσθαι. There are forty-nine instances of λιταί or λίσσεσθαι in the *Iliad*,[41] but

---

[39] For the senses in which λίσσομαι (pray, entreat) is used in the *Iliad*, see Table C.

[40] *Il.* 9. 451, 465, 501, 502, 511, 520, 574, 581, 585, 591, 698.

[41] See Table C. The references to λιταί, λίσσεσθαι, λιτανεύειν are *Il.* 1. 15, 174, 283, 374, 394, 502; 2. 15, 69; 4. 379; 5. 358, 491; 6. 45; 8. 372; 9. 451, 465, 501, 502, 511, 520, 574, 581, 591, 698; 10. 118, 455; 11. 609; 15. 77, 660; 16. 46, 47; 18. 448; 19. 304, 305; 20. 469; 21. 71, 74, 98, 368; 22. 35, 91, 240, 338, 414, 418; 23. 196, 609; 24. 357, 467, 485. (Rosner (1976: n. 18) gives only forty-six references to λίσσεσθαι.)

TABLE C. Summary of the fifty uses of λίσσομαι (pray, entreat), Λιταί (Prayers), λιτάνευω in the *Iliad*

Uses associated with supplication are underlined.

* *denotes appeals to fight.*

1. Appeals from a Leader to Allies and Colleagues to Fight

5. 491 ἀρχοὺς λισσομένῳ τηλεκλειτῶν ἐπικούρων
   entreating the leaders of the far-famed allies (to stand firm unwearying)
   (Sarpedon: Hector should be entreating the allies to fight)

*10. 118 λισσόμενος· χρειὼ γὰρ ἱκάνεται οὐκέτ᾿ ἀνεκτός
   entreating: for necessity which can no longer be borne has come upon him
   (Menelaus should, Nestor says, be entreating the Greeks to help him)

15. 660 <u>λίσσεθ᾿ ὑπὲρ τοκέων γουνούμενος ἄνδρα ἕκαστον</u> (Gould, n. 39, 15. 660)
   he was entreating each man, supplicating in the name of his parents
   (Nestor to the Greeks)

2. To an Angry Hero Refusing to Fight

1. 174 λίσσομαι εἵνεκ᾿ ἐμεῖο μένειν. . .
   I am (not) entreating you to remain on my account
   (Agamemnon refuses to λίσσεσθαι Achilles)

1. 283 λίσσομ᾿ Ἀχιλῆϊ μεθέμεν χόλον. . .
   I entreat Achilles to let go his anger
   (Nestor, speaking to the Greek assembly in 1.)

9. 520 ἄνδρας δὲ λίσσεσθαι ἐπιπροέηκεν ἀρίστους
   he has sent out the best men to entreat you
   (Phoenix to Achilles, of the embassy)

9. 574 πύργων βαλλομένων· τὸν δὲ λίσσοντο γέροντες
   of the fortifications under bombardment: but the elders entreated him
   (Phoenix of the appeals to Meleager to fight)

9. 581 <u>πολλὰ δέ μιν λιτάνευε γέρων ἱππηλάτα Οἰνεὺς</u> (Gould, n. 39, 9. 581 ff.)
   and the old man, the horseman Oineus, entreated him over and over again
   (approaches to Meleager)

9. 585 ἐλλίσσονθ᾿· ὁ δὲ μᾶλλον ἀναίνετο, πολλὰ δ᾿ ἑταῖροι
   they were entreating him: but he refused all the more, and his companions
   . . .
   (Meleager entreated by his mother and sisters)

9. 591 λίσσετ᾿ ὀδυρομένη καί οἱ κατέλεξεν ἅπαντα
   she was entreating him with lamentation, and she enumerated to him. . .
   (Cleopatra to Meleager)

9. 698 μηδ᾿ ὄφελες λίσσεσθαι ἀμύμονα Πηλείωνα
   nor ought you to have entreated the blameless son of Peleus
   (Diomede to Agamemnon after the failure of the embassy)

*11. 610 λισσομένους· χρειὼ γὰρ ἱκάνεται οὐκέτ᾿ ἀνεκτός
   entreating: for necessity which can no longer be borne has come upon them
   (Achilles imagines the Greeks at his knees, entreating him to fight)

18. 448 εἴων ἐξιέναι· τὸν δὲ λίσσοντο γέροντες
and were (not) allowing them to go outside: but the elders entreated him
(Thetis to Hephaestus, relating the course of Achilles' anger)

3. Appeals in the Context of Battlefield Supplications

6. 45 Ἄδρηστος δ᾽ ἄρ᾽ ἔπειτα λαβὼν ἐλλίσσετο γούνων (Gould, n. 39)
and then Adrestus clasped his knees and entreated
(Adrestus to Menelaus)

10. 455 ἁψάμενος λίσσεσθαι (Gould, n. 39, 10. 454 ff.)
(he was about) to entreat him, touching (his beard)
(Dolon to Diomede)

20. 469 ἱέμενος λίσσεσθ᾽. . . (Gould, n. 39, 20. 463 ff.)
desiring to entreat him
(Tros to Achilles)

21. 71 αὐτὰρ ὁ τῇ ἑτέρῃ μὲν ἑλὼν ἐλλίσσετο γούνων
but with one hand he took hold of his knees and entreated him
(Lycaon supplicating Achilles)

21. 73 καί μιν λισσόμενος (φωνήσας) ἔπεα πτερόεντα προσηύδα (Gould, n. 39, 21. 64 ff., 115)

and entreating (addressing) him, he spoke winged words
(Lycaon supplicating Achilles)

21. 98 λισσόμενος ἐπέεσσιν· ἀμείλικτον δ᾽ ὄπ᾽ ἄκουσε
entreating him with words: but he heard an unsoftened voice
(Lycaon supplicating Achilles)

22. 338 λίσσομ᾽ ὑπὲρ ψυχῆς, καὶ γούνων, σῶν τε τοκήων (Gould n. 39, 22. 338 ff.)
I entreat you by your soul, and by your knees, and by your parents
(Hector pleading with Achilles to return his body to his family for burial)

4. To Reverse the Fate of Someone in Enemy Hands

1. 15, 1. 374 χρυσέῳ ἀνὰ σκήπτρῳ, καὶ λίσσετο πάντας Ἀχαιοὺς
on a golden sceptre, and he was entreating all the Achaeans
(Chryses, to recover his daughter)

22. 418 λίσσωμ᾽ ἀνέρα τοῦτον ἀτάσθαλον, ὀβριμοεργόν
I may entreat this presumptuous man of the wicked deeds
(Priam wanting to leave Troy to recover Hector's corpse)

24. 357 γούνων ἁψάμενοι λιτανεύσομεν
touching his knees we shall entreat him
(Priam's herald to Priam on sighting Hermes, as they go to ransom Hector)

24. 467 λίσσεο . . . καὶ τέκεος (Gould, n. 39, 24. 465)
and entreat him (by his father, and his mother of the lovely hair) and by his
child
(Hermes advising Priam on supplicating Achilles)

24. 485 τὸν καὶ λισσόμενος Πρίαμος πρὸς μῦθον ἔειπε (Gould, n. 39, 24. 477 ff.)
and entreating him Priam spoke a word
(Priam supplicating Achilles)

5. Appeals for Intervention by a Third Party against an Adverse Decision

1. 394 ἐλθοῦσ᾽ Οὔλυμπόνδε Δία λίσαι (Gould, n. 39, 1. 407 ff.)

going to Olympus, entreat Zeus
(Achilles requests Thetis to supplicate Zeus)

1. 502 λισσομένη προσέειπε Δία Κρονίωνα ἄνακτα (Gould, n. 39, 1. 427 ff.)
   entreating she addressed lord Zeus, the son of Cronos
   (Thetis, supplicating Zeus to honour Achilles)

8. 372, 15. 77 λισσομένη τιμῆσαι Ἀχιλλῆα πτολίπορθον (Gould, n. 39, 8. 370 ff.,
   15. 76 ff.)
   entreating him to honour Achilles, sacker of cities
   (Athene on Thetis' supplication of Zeus)

9. 511 λίσσονται δ' ἄρα ταί γε Δία Κρονίωνα κιοῦσαι
   and they go to Zeus the son of Cronos, and entreat him
   (Phoenix on Λιταί, requesting punishment of those who rebuff them)

6. Appeals for a Change of Mind

2. 15, 2. 69 Ἥρη λισσομένη·
   Hera, by her entreaties (has brought the gods round to her view)
   (Zeus to the evil Dream sent to Agamemnon)

9. 451 μητέρ' ἐμήν· ἡ δ' αἰὲν ἐμὲ λισσέσκετο γούνων (Gould, n. 39, 9. 451 ff.)
   my mother: and she was always entreating me by my knees
   (Phoenix on his mother's request that he seduce the concubine)

9. 465 αὐτοῦ λισσόμενοι κατερήτυον ἐν μεγάροισι
   entreating me, they kept me there in the halls
   (Phoenix on his kinsmen's entreaties not to leave)

19. 304 λισσόμενοι δειπνῆσαι· ὁ δ' ἠρνεῖτο στεναχίζων
    entreating him to dine: but he, with groans, was refusing
    (of the Greeks entreating Achilles to eat although grieving for Patroclus)

19. 305 λίσσομαι, εἴ τις ἔμοιγε φίλων ἐπιπείθεθ' ἑταίρων
    I entreat you, if any one of my companions will obey me
    (Achilles to the Greeks not to urge him to eat)

22. 35 λισσόμενος φίλον υἱόν· ὁ δὲ προπάροιθε πυλάων (Gould, n. 39, gives wrong
    reference)
    entreating his son, but he, before the gates
    (Priam attempts to persuade Hector not to meet Achilles)

22. 91 πολλὰ λισσομένω· οὐδ' Ἕκτορι θυμὸν ἔπειθον (Gould, n. 39, gives wrong
    reference)
    with many entreaties, but they did not persuade the spirit in Hector
    (Priam and Hecuba attempt to dissuade Hector from meeting Achilles)

22. 240 λίσσονθ' ἑξείης γουνούμενοι (Gould, n. 39, 22. 240)
    they were entreating me one after the other, with supplications
    (Priam and Hecuba to Deiphobus/Athene not to leave the city) (not, as
    Gould, to Hector)

?22. 414 πάντας δ' ἐλλιτάνευε κυλινδόμενος κατὰ κόπρον (Gould, n. 39, 22. 414 ff.)
    he was entreating them, rolling in the dung
    (Priam, attempting to leave Troy for the Greek camp)

23. 609 τῷ τοι λισσομένῳ ἐπιπείσομαι, ἠδὲ καὶ ἵππον
    I shall comply with his entreaties and (I shall give him) the horse
    (Menelaus of Antilochus' concession)

7. Appeals to a Third Party for Assistance

21. 368 πολλὰ λισσόμενος, ἔπεα πτερόεντα προσηύδα
with many entreaties he addressed winged words
(the river Scamander to Hera, for Hephaestus to stop his onslaught)

23. 196 πολλὰ δὲ καὶ σπένδων χρυσέῳ δέπαϊ λιτάνευεν
even as he poured libations from a golden cup, he entreated them
(Achilles to the winds, to come and light Patroclus' pyre)

8. Appeals to Obtain Something

5. 358 πολλὰ λισσομένη, χρυσάμπυκας ἤτεεν ἵππους
with many entreaties she asked for the horses with frontlets of gold
(Athene borrows horses from Ares)

4. 379 καί ῥα μάλα λίσσοντο δόμεν κλειτοὺς ἐπικούρους
and very much they entreated us to give them famous allies
(Tydeus and Polynices request allies at Mycenae)

16. 47 οἷ αὐτῷ θάνατόν τε κακὸν καὶ κῆρα λιτέσθαι
(for he was about) to entreat for evil death and doom for himself
(Patroclus asks Achilles for his armour to wear in battle)

9. Other Appeals

9. 501 λισσόμενοι, ὅτε κέν τις ὑπερβήῃ καὶ ἁμάρτῃ
entreating, whenever someone oversteps the mark and does wrong
(Phoenix: the gods themselves are flexible when men entreat them)

9. 502 καὶ γάρ τε Λιταί εἰσι Διὸς κοῦραι μεγάλοιο
for Prayers are the daughters of great Zeus
(Phoenix on the allegory)

16. 46 ὣς φάτο λισσόμενος, μέγα νήπιος· . . .
so he spoke entreating, the great fool: . . .
(of Patroclus' request to go out in Achilles' armour)

only nineteen of them appear in the contexts of the supplications on Gould's list.[42] Λιταί and λίσσεσθαι are more frequent outside the context of supplication as defined by Gould than they are in it.[43] In reserving the term 'supplication' for those passages which employ reference to the ritual gestures performed in fact, or verbally,[44] Gould excludes certain passages regularly described by many of his predecessors as 'supplications', most notably Chryses' approach to the Greeks in book

[42] *Il.* 1. 394, 502; 6. 45; 8. 372; 9. 451, 581; 10. 455; 15. 77, 660; 20. 469; 21. 71; 22. 35, 91, 240, 338, 414; 24. 357, 467, 485. See Table B.

[43] Λίσσεσθαι occurs, for example, as a verb of exerting pressure in the contexts of ἄνωγα (bid), κελεύω (tell), ἐποτρύνω (rouse up): Corlu (1966: 305–8). See also Gould (1973: n. 12).

[44] To say ἱκάνω τὰ σὰ γούνατα, 'I come to your knees', is equivalent to performing the act of supplication: see Létoublon (1980: 330).

1,[45] the embassy to Achilles in book 9,[46] and the αἶνος of the
Λιταί (allegory of the Prayers).[47]

The restriction introduced by Gould of the term 'supplication' to passages in which clear allusion is made to the ritual
gestures of ἱκετεία (supplication), or to the terms ἱκέτης
(suppliant), ἱκετεύω (supplicate) has been all but obliterated by
later writers on the subject, who certainly do not restrict their
discussion of 'supplication' in the *Iliad* to the examples listed
by Gould in his note 39. For example, Thornton translates
Λιταί as 'Supplications' even while she draws attention to the
absence of the allegory of the Λιταί from Gould's list of supplications.[48] She treats the Chryses episode in book 1 as a supplication,[49] and the embassy to Achilles as the main supplication
sequence of the *Iliad*,[50] although neither appears in Gould's
list. The distinction established by Gould between passages
which refer explicitly to the rituals and gestures of ἱκετεία and
other requests, however urgent, is highly significant: after all,
as we have seen, Lycaon is killed when he lets go of Achilles'
knees, thereby breaking the (literally) vital contact of the ritual.
If the ritual contact of ἱκετεία makes the difference between

[45] Plato, *R.* 3. 393d3 Chryses as ἱκέτης (suppliant). See also Benveniste
(1973: 502; 1st pub. 1969).
[46] Sch. T ad *Il.* 9. 150–2 (= Erbse (1969–88: ii. 430), 150–2); Sch. bT ad *Il.*
9. 300 (= Erbse (1969–88: ii. 459), 300a and b); Sch. bT ad *Il.* 9. 304 (= Erbse
(1969–88: ii. 460), 304a); Sch. bT ad *Il.* 9. 515 (= Erbse (1969–88: ii. 507),
515a); Sch. T ad *Il.* 9. 523 (= Erbse (1969–88: ii. 509), 523a); Sch. bT ad *Il.* 9.
642 (= Erbse 1969–88: ii. 534) treat the embassy as supplication from Agamemnon and from the Greeks. 'The embassy comes with all the appearance of
suppliants': Bowra (1930: 19): cf. Vickers (1973: 487); Ebel (1972: 86–104).
[47] Sch. bT ad *Il.* 9. 503 (= Erbse (1969–88: ii. 505), 503b); Sch. bT ad *Il.* 9.
509 (= Erbse (1969–88: ii. 507), 509b); Heraclitus, *All.* c37; Delatte (1951:
443–4); Corlu (1966: 298–9, 315); Benveniste (1973: 502; 1st pub. 1969).
Whitfield (1967: 65) gives forty-one 'supplications' in the *Iliad*, including the
Chryses episode, the allegory of the Λιταί, and the embassy to Achilles.
[48] Thornton (1984: 116–17 and n. 17). For Crotty (1994: 92), the story of
the Λιταί 'concerns a plea for reconciliation, rather than supplication as such',
although he still thinks the story 'confirms the complexity of supplication's
significance'.
[49] Thornton (1984: 109–10, 113–14, 125). See also Lynn-George (1983:
46–54; 1988: 287 n. 27); Griffin (1980: 26, 55); Pedrick (1982: 131); Cairns
(1993: 115); Crotty (1994: 88); Seaford (1994: 66).
[50] Thornton (1984: 123): see also Whitfield (1967); Rosner (1976: 320);
Yamagata (1991).

living and dying, then we need to be very circumspect about equating λίσσομαι, which occurs so frequently outside the context of ἱκετεία, with the ritual itself. I shall confine the terms ἱκετεία and supplication to the examples found in Gould's n. 39, with the two additional examples[51] discussed above. Λιταί and λίσσεσθαι may occur in the context of ἱκετεία, but they are not identical with it,[52] even if the difference may seem very slight.

[51] *Il.* 22. 35–91; 24. 357.

[52] Welcker (1857: 712), quoted by Autenrieth (1920), gives 'Bitte, reuige Bitte' for λιτή (from λίσσομαι). The personified Λιταί are regarded as Prayers of Repentance. This meaning is followed by Leaf (1900–2: i. 408 on *Il.* 9. 503 and 505); Ebeling (1880–5: i): 'λιτή (λίσσομαι) (1) precatio, preces'. (2) 'Λιταί deae (. . . reuige Bitten) quae Aten sequuntur . . .'. The first indication I have been able to find of the idea of supplication in the meaning of Λιταί is in Cunliffe (1924): 'make entreaty or petition to, entreat, supplicate, beg, entreat, pray to do, to pray to (a divinity)'. He describes the Λιταί as 'prayers of repentance, for forgiveness, addressed by an offender to the person injured'. Delatte (1951: 444 n. 1) regards Λιταί as Supplications (cf. Humbert (1960: 259): 'le requête suppliante'), and considers the Λιταί passage was never well interpreted because it was thought to be about prayers. Thornton (1984: 114 n. 7) suggests the translation 'Prayers' for Λιταί is open to the misunderstanding that they are directed primarily to the gods. Benveniste (1973: 503; 1st pub. 1969) attempted to reconcile λίσσομαι with Latin *litare* (after Hoffmann 1954: 814): *litare* derived from **lita* = Gr. λιτή, to which it was not originally related, but from which it was borrowed. See also Pokorny (1959: 664): λίσσομαι and litare connected on the grounds of **lita* from λιτή, to obtain a favourable omen, appease the divinity: a λιτή had to mean a 'prayer to offer reparation . . . or a prayer to obtain from the god for oneself reparation for an outrage'. The attempt is questioned by Frisk (1954–70): it would never work in the case of λίσσομαι used of the Greeks pressing Achilles to eat, nor in his reponse with a request that they should not urge him (*Il.* 19. 303–6). Corlu (1966: 293) defines λίσσομαι as 'solliciter instamment quelqu'un en faisant appel à sa bien-veillance', but soon introduces confusion by giving ἱκέτης as the *nomen agentis* for the verb λίσσομαι, which lacks its own term for the agent (1966: 315) (cf. Létoublon 1980: 334). He deduces, from a number of instances of γουνοῦμαι or γουνάζομαι joined with λίσσομαι, that λίσσομαι was originally accompanied by taking hold of the knees, but against this is Onians' (1951: 174) argument that clasping the knees is secondary to the reference to them, as in similar appeals by the head (or ψυχή). Chantraine (1968: ii. 643–4) gives λίσσομαι as 'supplier, demander à un dieu', close to ἱκετεύω. Létoublon (1980: 325–6) associates λίσσομαι with Lithuanian *lytësti*, to touch, by analogy with the association between ἱκάνω and Lithuanian *siékiu*, to reach with the hand. The confusion is well discussed by Aubriot (1984), who maintains a clear distinction between λίσσομαι and supplication, arguing that λίσσομαι is frequent outside contexts of supplication (1984: 1 and n. 10). She uses 'Implorations' to translate Λιταί, since 'Implorations' implies neither prayer nor supplication: Aubriot (1984: 2

At *Il.* 11. 609–10, Achilles is anticipating two things which are to happen simultaneously: he is savouring the prospect of λιταί (prayers, entreaties) to fight presented in the context of ἱκετεία (supplication).[53] He wants to see the Greeks at his knees (supplicating), as they attempt to prevail on him to change his mind (λισσομένους, entreating). Although the Greeks have already attempted to change his mind in the embassy, they did not supplicate while they did so, and it is the gratifying combination of λιταί in the ritual of ἱκετεία to which Achilles looks forward at *Il.* 11. 609–10. All his pleasure lies in anticipation, for he never receives λιταί in the envisaged context of ἱκετεία. There is no inconsistency between the λιταί of the embassy and Achilles' anticipation of the supplication of the Greeks clustering at his knees λισσόμενοι (*Il.* 11. 609–10) and no need for any of the special pleading Hainsworth thought would be necessary to reconcile the two. No formal explanation of the workings of ἱκετεία is found in the *Iliad*, and the poet appears to assume an understanding of the ritual in his audience. By contrast, the significance of λιταί and the consequences of rejecting them, something repeatedly explored in the action of the *Iliad*, are explained in detail in abstract terms in the αἶνος of the Λιταί (allegory of the Prayers).

7.1.6. The αἶνος *of the* Λιταί *(the allegory of the Prayers)*

καὶ γάρ τε Λιταί εἰσι Διὸς κοῦραι μεγάλοιο
χωλαί τε ῥυσαί τε παραβλῶπές τ᾽ ὀφθαλμώ,
αἵ ῥά τε καὶ μετόπισθ᾽ Ἄτης ἀλέγουσι κιοῦσαι.
ἡ δ᾽ Ἄτη σθεναρή τε καὶ ἀρτίπος, οὕνεκα πάσας   505
πολλὸν ὑπεκπροθέει, φθάνει δέ τε πᾶσαν ἐπ᾽ αἶαν
βλάπτουσ᾽ ἀνθρώπους· αἱ δ᾽ ἐξακέονται ὀπίσσω.
ὃς μέν τ᾽ αἰδέσεται κούρας Διὸς ἆσσον ἰούσας,
τὸν δὲ μέγ᾽ ὤνησαν καί τ᾽ ἔκλυον εὐχομένοιο·
ὃς δέ κ᾽ ἀνήνηται καί τε στερεῶς ἀποείπῃ   510

n. 1). Supplication attempts to establish an obligation rather than produce a change of mind (Aubriot 1984: 3), as λιταί often attempt to do.

[53] The only emergency where λιταί to fight are ever uttered in a context of ἱκετεία in the main action of the poem is *Il.* 15. 660: Nestor, γουνούμενος, 'supplicating by their knees', addresses λιταί to the Greeks to fight when they have been driven back to their ships. It is possible that *Il.* 9. 581–3 (Oeneus' entreaties and supplication to Meleager to fight) should also be considered λιταί to fight in the context of ἱκετεία.

λίσσονται δ' ἄρα ταί γε Δία Κρονίωνα κιοῦσαι
τῷ Ἄτην ἄμ' ἕπεσθαι, ἵνα βλαφθεὶς ἀποτείσῃ.

For there are Prayers too, the daughters of great Zeus,
lame, and wrinkled, and squint-eyed,
who walk with good heed, even if they are behind Delusion.[54]
But Delusion is strong and straight of limb, on which account   505
she far outruns all the Prayers and arrives first all over the world,
doing harm to mortals: and they (the Prayers) afterwards apply a cure.
The man who reverences the daughters of Zeus as they come near,
him do they greatly bless, and hear him when he prays.
But the man who rejects them and stubbornly refuses   510
they pray Zeus, the son of Cronos, as they go,
For Delusion to follow him, so that he may come to grief and pay the
　penalty.

(*Il.* 9. 502–12)

This passage is an αἶνος,[55] which may, as explained in Section

[54] Ἄτη is difficult to translate. It seems to refer to a temporary absence of
understanding for which the gods are often held responsible: see Dodds (1951:
2–3); Barrett (1964: 206 on Euripides, *Hipp*. 241). From the idea that ἄτη can
be a punishment from the gods, usually for ὕβρις, comes an extension of the
term to the objective disasters resulting from ἄτη, so that ἄτη acquires the
general sense of 'ruin': Dodds (1951: 38). The difficulty in finding one word to
translate it may be understood from Hesiod: Ἄτησιν are personified at Hesiod,
Op. 216; at *Op*. 231 Ἄτη is linked with Hunger; at *Op*. 352 ἄτησιν are explained
by M. L. West (1978: 224–5) as the opposite of κέρδεα (good counsels). I have
translated by 'Delusion' to convey the temporary absence of understanding.

[55] Heraclitus, *All*. 37, takes the Λιταί passage as an allegorical αἶνος, arguing
that the characteristics of penitents are transferred to the prayers so that they
are lame and crooked. It is worth remembering that although the Λιταί follow
behind Ἄτη, they are not penitents for the damage she has done: they are seeking to apply a cure for it afterwards. They should not be considered as penitents in any sense. The allegorical interpretation of Homer as exemplified in
Heraclitus, *All*. 1 and Longinus, 9. 7 should be rejected. Pfeiffer (1968: 5) follows Heraclitus in taking the Λιταί passage as an allegory, arguing that an allegory has no story, and an αἶνος has. An explanation of the development of allegorical interpretations of the Homeric poems may be found in Tate (1929;
1930; 1934). Reinhardt (1960*b*: 37–40) argues that Homeric 'allegories' are a
form of αἶνος resembling Aesopic fables. For αἶνος used of beast fables see Gow
(1950) on Theocritus, 14. 43, where he cites Hesiod, *Op*. 202; Archilochus, *frr*.
174, 185 (M. L. West (1980) = Diehl (1936: i (section 3, on iambics), 40, no.
89; 37, no. 81)): cf. Callimachus, *fr*. 194. 6. An αἶνος conveys its message by
means of a story, whereas a proverb, παροιμία, has no story (Ammonius, *de
diff*. 18). Αἶνος is sometimes used of proverbial sayings without a story:
Callimachus, *fr*. 178. 9; Euripides, *fr*. 508 (Collard *et al*. (1995: i. 264) =

2.3.4. above, be understood at face value, but which in fact conveys a veiled message below the surface meaning. The αἶνος presents the Λιταί as daughters of Zeus.[56] Λιταί may not be despised with impunity: although the αἶνος portrays them as lame and decrepit, their power should not be underestimated, since they are able to confer great blessings, and Zeus himself cannot refuse them. Phoenix uses his αἶνος of the Λιταί diplomatically to reinforce the advice δάμασον θυμὸν μέγαν, 'tame your great passion' (Il. 9. 496), offered directly to Achilles. The Λιταί of the αἶνος should of course be related in the present context to the pleas of the ambassadors. The shift from direct advice to generalization in abstract terms achieves two things. First, Phoenix is afforded a tactful way to convey a warning to a social superior, avoiding too much direct instruction and implicit criticism. Secondly, our interpretation of what has already happened and what is still to come is influenced by its reflection on the events of the poem in the language of personified abstract concepts, Λιταί (Prayers) and Ἄτη (Delusion).[57]

Nauck (1926: 524)); *AP* 9. 17, and this seems to be the nature of *Il.* 9. 508–12, which refer to the powers of Λιταί. The image of them toiling after the strong and vigorous Ἄτη illustrates the αἶνος of *Il.* 9. 508–12 and is easy to understand in the context of the poem. I translate αἶνος as 'allegory' with the sense of fable, parable (2. 3. 4. above) rather than with Heraclitus' sense of metaphor.

[56] Reinhardt (1960b: 37) explains the idea that the Λιταί are daughters of Zeus because Zeus is the ἐπιτιμήτωρ ἱκετάων, the avenger of suppliants (*Od.* 9. 270 cited by Sch. bT ad *Il.* 9. 502 = Erbse (1969–88: ii. 505)) from whom the suppliant requests an audience. Their lowly posture is in keeping with this idea, but it is worth remembering that although the Prayers follow behind Ἄτη, they are in no sense penitents for the damage she has done. Their appearance should be associated rather with the terrifying exigences of deformity: see n. 75 below.

[57] Havers (1910: 227–34) believes the basic meaning of ἄτη to be a blow which paralyses the mind: he distinguishes six types of ἄτη: Ohnmacht, Betaubung (unconsciousness, stupefaction); Wahnsinn (insanity); Betörung, Verblendung (delusion, infatuation); Trug (illusion, deception); Verschuldung, Frevel, Sunde (blame, sacrilege, trespass); Strafe, Ungluck, Schaden (penalty, misfortune, damage): Havers (1910: 239). If ἄτη means a blow, it would follow that damage from some exterior source would lead to Verblendung (mental blindness), for which the individual affected would not be responsible. If, on the other hand, we should view mental blindness as the factor which leads to damage, the individual affected must bear some of the responsibility. Seiler (1954: 409–17) finds no evidence that ἄτη is a blow or wound, and considers the active-passive concept of an agent who causes or sends ἄτη foreign to the original concept of the word: one does not become

The first part of the αἶνος seems to envisage two incidents: in
the first incident (*Il.* 9. 502–7) we find a kind of race:[58] Ἄτη and
Λιταί seem almost to set off simultaneously when their starting
pistol is fired, but because Ἄτη is stronger and faster, she
arrives first, and through her, some mischief is done. The
second incident shows us the Λιταί, who have all this time been
laboriously toiling on their way, arrive when the damage has
already been done, and by their efforts attempt to undo it. This
part of the αἶνος reflects in the first instance on what has already
happened in the *Iliad*, namely Agamemnon's appropriation of
Achilles' prize, and on what is presently happening in the
embassy: the Λιταί arrive after the damage has been done and
attempt to apply a cure, as the ambassadors are now attempting
to cure the damage done by Agamemnon's appropriation of
Briseis from Achilles in book 1. This is the relevance of the first
part of the αἶνος to Achilles' present situation. The second part
of the αἶνος (*Il.* 9. 508–12) is proverbial. It is divided from the
first part by the asyndeton between *Il.* 9. 507 and 508. This
second part looks forward to Achilles' response to the embassy
rather than back to past events, and there is more than a hint of
menace in the warning that, while great blessings lie in store for
one who offers a favourable response to Λιταί (for Achilles if he
gives a favourable response to the λιταί of the ambassadors), in
the event of a stubborn refusal Ἄτη will be dispatched at the

'verblendet' as a result of another's action, one simply is 'verblendet'. In the
case of Eurytion (*Od.* 21. 295 ff.), his ἄτη is his behaviour, but also the damage
he does/suffers. At *Il.* 19. 91 and 129, Zeus ἄασατο and as a virtual equivalent,
Hera ἀπάτησεν (deceived) him. At *Il.* 19. 91 and 129, Ἄτη is the one who ἄαται
everyone. Dawe (1967: 97) finds the evidence does not permit us to decide
between these two alternatives: in book 9 and book 19 the individual must bear
at least some of the responsibility for ἄτη, and the idea seems to bridge the gap
between human and divine responsibility. Dawe distinguishes seven types of
ἄτη: that in the allegories of book 9 and book 19 is a category all to itself.
LfrGrE gives the sense of ἄτη in books 1, 9, 16, and 19 as damage to the mind,
Verhängnis (doom), goddess of mental damage, Verblendung. Edwards (1991:
245–7, with bibliography on ἄτη) ad *Il.* 19. 85–138 points out that it is the
characters themselves, not the poet, who ascribe their actions to the effects of
ἄτη. See also n. 233 below.

[58] See Sidwell (1992: 111–12) for more on Ἄτη's athletic feats against a dis-
abled opponent, not lame, this time, like the Λιταί, but a man held in a
wrestling grip (πάλαισμα, Sophocles, *OT* 880) who οὐ ποδὶ χρησίμῳ χρῆται,
'does not use his useful foot' (Sophocles, *OT* 878–9) to trip his opponent.

request of the Λιταί to pursue the man who has rebuffed them, and arrange for him to come to grief.[59] Achilles has already refused the λιταί of Odysseus: at *Il.* 9. 510 στερεῶς (stubbornly) suggests that if he goes on to refuse Phoenix too, he may expect a visitation from Ἄτη resulting in some unspecified catastrophe.

There is nothing in the text to suggest that ἄτη is transferable, and that, as a result of one man's refusal of λιταί, ἄτη may affect another man. The text is quite positive that the refuser of Λιταί and the one dogged by Ἄτη will be the same person. Wyatt[60] and Thornton[61] are mistaken in supposing that ἄτη affects Patroclus as a result of Achilles' refusal of the λιταί of the ambassadors. Patroclus' ἄτη (*Il.* 16. 685) is his own affair: the association of Λιταί and Ἄτη in the allegory does not rule out independent operations by Ἄτη on her own initiative. Arieti[62] thinks that when Achilles refuses the embassy, he is in the grip of Ἄτη resulting from his act of hybris in almost killing Agamemnon and his hybris in prolonging his anger by asking Thetis to arrange with Zeus for the Greeks to fare badly in the fighting in his absence. All this is supposed to amount to hamartia, but there is nothing in the text to support the theory that Achilles is affected by ἄτη in book 9. Certainly, for Snell,[63] personal decisions do not arise in the Homeric poems: Homeric man does not attribute his powers to himself, and even in a choice between alternatives, the gods intervene. The human agent is nevertheless responsible.[64] Snell's work on decision is developed by Petersmann,[65] who shows that the poet of the *Iliad* is interested in what is decided, but not in how a decision is reached. No single factor is given as the reason for Achilles' decision to reject the embassy: he thinks Agamemnon has

---

[59] Another daughter of Zeus, Δίκη, behaves in much the same way, when, in the role of one falsely judged, she complains to Zeus to obtain vindication, Hesiod, *Op.* 256–62. This passage, like *Il.* 1. 22–51, deals with a king going against the wishes of his entire people. Stallmach (1968: 87–8) explains the double nature of Ἄτη as the damage one does, and the damage one suffers in consequence of rejecting Λιταί. See also Aubriot (1984).

[60] (1982: 253).

[61] (1984: 135).

[62] (1988: 4).

[63] (1982: 16–22; 1st pub. 1955).

[64] Lloyd-Jones (1971: 10).

[65] (1974).

deceived him (*Il*. 9. 371–5) but he does not say why. He might consider that awarding a prize and then taking it away again amounts to deception, or the reference to deception might be explained by the fact that Achilles regards the embassy as a whole as a μῆτις.

The constellation of the limping gait and squinting glance of the Λιταί, the designation of the embassy as a μῆτις (*Il*. 9. 93; 423), the presentation of Agamemnon's terms by the arch-trickster, Odysseus, and Achilles' retort, with its allusion to the man who says one thing and conceals another in his heart (*Il*. 9. 312–13), all add up to the impression that the embassy is not at all the deferential approach it might appear, but a μῆτις or devious plan (to manipulate Achilles into implicitly conceding Agamemnon's superiority), which is not only objectionable in itself, but which will have unfortunate consequences for the recipient if refused. In other words, the λιταί of the embassy are part of an attempt to manipulate Achilles to which it would be perfectly reasonable for Achilles to object, were it not for the consequences of rejection. The ambassadors' appeals to friend-ship are deviously combined with attempts to outmanoeuvre Achilles and with thinly disguised threats. Agamemnon's offer is dreamed up on *his* terms, without any negotiation with Achilles. The offer is put to Achilles on a 'take it or leave it' basis by Agamemnon's agents, with the implication 'if you leave it, so much the worse for you'. It is an attempt to buy Achilles off and control him at the same time. Of course the ambassadors refrain from indicating that acceptance will mean Achilles has conceded Agamemnon's superiority: instead they lay heavy emphasis on the other side of the question: if Achilles refuses, he will have rejected the λιταί of his comrades in arms, to whom he owes loyalty. In terms of the αἶνος, rejection of the λιταί of the ambassadors will anger the Λιταί themselves, who will seek retribution from Zeus: he will send Ἄτη, with unpleasant, if unspecified, consequences. The combination of gifts and entreaties, the ambassadors say, resembles the honours shown to a god (*Il*. 9. 498–501, 603). 'Come for the bribe' (*Il*. 9. 602) is an appeal to venality to which anyone might object—but refusal of the bribe constitutes a rejection of λιταί, and is likely to be punished. The λιταί confront Achilles with a double bind, a choice of evils: to give in to their veiled menace, or not to give in, and face the consequences. Confronted with such alternatives, there is no right decision for Achilles to make, and his dilemma is akin to dilemmas in tragedy. He makes his decision on grounds of honour, and pays heavily for it.

Achilles objects to Phoenix acting as an agent for Agamemnon in the matter of the embassy, but none of these factors is identified as *the* reason for rejecting the embassy. His reasons for rejecting it have been variously discussed: according to Griffin,[66] although the compensation offered meets the demands of the heroic code, Achilles' passionate nature prevents him from accepting the embassy. In Schein's[67] view, Achilles is disillusioned with fighting Agamemnon's cause, since, whether one does a great deal or nothing, the rewards are the same, and it all ends in death: Redfield[68] indicates that Achilles senses that the ambassadors' attempts to effect a reconciliation between himself and Agamemnon display their loyalty to Agamemnon rather than himself. Everything they say confirms his impression of isolation from his community. Redfield's view is supported by οὐδέ τί σε χρὴ τὸν φιλέειν, 'nor should you love him' (*Il.* 9. 613–14). Achilles' reasons for refusing the embassy are not clearly explained as resulting from some outside agency such as ἄτη, rather as Agamemnon's reasons for refusing the pleas of Chryses are not clearly explained as the result of anything in particular.

The use of personification for abstract concepts as observed in the αἶνος of the Λιταί is unusual in Homer, although it is not unknown.[69] Personification is more common in Hesiod, where it occurs in paraenetic contexts:[70] since the *Iliad* consists mainly

---

[66] (1980: 74).

[67] (1984: 104–6).

[68] (1975: 103).

[69] Δεῖμος (Terror) *Il.* 4. 440; Φόβος (Fear) *Il.* 4. 440; Ἔρις (Strife) *Il.* 4. 440; 5. 518; 11. 3, 73; 18. 535; 20. 48; Κήρ (Death) *Il.* 18. 535; Φύζα (Rout) *Il.* 9. 2; Ὄσσα (Rumour) *Il.* 2. 93. For a discussion of personified abstracts in Homer and their association with cult, see Stallmach (1968: 88 n. 160). For abstracts as gods see M. L. West (1966: 33–9). Reinhardt (1960b: 23–7) discusses the personified abstracts in Hesiod, and organizes them into a family tree.

[70] *Op.* Ἔρις (Strife) 11, 16, 28, 804; Πειθώ (Persuasion) 73; Ἐλπίς (Hope) 96; Αἰδώς (Shame) 200; Νέμεσις (Nemesis) 200; Δίκη (Justice) 213, 220, 256, 275, 283, 413; Ἄτη (Delusion) 216, 231; Ὅρκος (Oath) 219, 804; Εἰρήνη (Peace) 228; Λιμός (Hunger) 230, 302; Αἰδώ (Shame) 324; Ἀναιδείη (Shamelessness) 324;

of narrative, it does not often require the abstract concepts frequent in wisdom literature. The speeches in the embassy have a paraenetic element[71] to which the personified abstractions of Λιταί and Ἄτη are entirely appropriate. The αἶνος is certainly not incompatible with the *Iliad* as a whole,[72] and Sheppard regarded it as essential to the formal pattern of the poem.[73] Aubriot[74] explains the squinting and lameness of the Λιταί as expressive of their ability to look forward and back, and certainly the αἶνος appears to apply both to the past test of Agamemnon's ability to respond to λιταί, and to the coming test of Achilles' flexibility when confronted with λιταί. The Λιταί are deeply ambiguous: they may look as if they are on their last legs,[75] they may not be very quick off the mark, but their habit of requesting the dispatch of Ἄτη in pursuit of whoever rebuffs them reveals the paradoxical strength and terrifying menace underlying their apparent weakness. Their ambiguity, their spiteful retaliation born of resentment at the rebuff of their ostensibly deferential appeals, means that, although they

Δώς (Give) 356; Ἅρπαξ (Snatch) 356; Ἀμηχανίη (Hardship) 496; Πενίη (Poverty) 497.

[71] See Diller (1962: 53–4) for the paraenetic aspect of the αἶνος of the Λιταί (*Il.* 9. 502–12) and the image of Zeus' two jars (*Il.* 24. 527–33). Agamemnon uses the image of Ἄτη (*Il.* 19. 91–133) not in a paraenetic sense, but to clarify the psychological condition which he claims excuses his conduct. See also Griffin (1995: 133).

[72] Dodds (1951: 6): the Λιταί passage could be a Mainland idea, taken over (to Ionia) along with the Meleager story. Page (1959: 301–3) suggests the ideas of human responsibility and divine retribution are alien to, and incompatible with, the *Iliad*. Long (1970: 133 n. 40) follows Page.

[73] Sheppard (1922: 70, 79): cf. Thornton (1984: 116 n. 17).

[74] (1984: 22–3).

[75] Vernant (1981: 235–56) discusses the exceptional (and disturbing) qualities associated with limping. The tyrannical aspect of deformity is epitomized in the figures of Oedipus and Richard III. On tyrants and deformity, see also Ogden (1997: 86–94, 97, 103). The limping gait of the personified Λιταί perhaps calls attention to their double nature, rather as the feet of Hephaestus are the visible sign of his μῆτις: see Détienne and Vernant (1978: 242–52, 272). On the links between power and deformity, see Ogden (1997: 22, 36). Both the poet (*Il.* 9. 93) and Achilles (*Il.* 9. 423) refer to the embassy as a μῆτις. It is both appropriate and ironical that the compensation promised to Achilles by Athene (*Il.* 1. 213–14) should be offered in the context of a μῆτις. Athene did not promise Achilles that he would be pleased with the compensation when it came, and this kind of fulfilment of the letter, but not the spirit of an offer is typical of divine promises.

appear in confusingly different focuses at different stages in the poem, all their qualities, strong and weak, beneficial and minatory, are simultaneously present: the abstract expression of their double nature is apparent in the αἶνος of book 9, but we have already seen the retaliatory malice of rejected λιταί illustrated in the Chryses episode in book 1, long before.

7.1.7. Agamemnon's rejection of λιταί (prayers) from Chryses

The first incident in the *Iliad* is the arrival in the Greek camp of Chryses, the ἀρητήρ, the one who prays,[76] carrying στέμματα, garlands, of Apollo on a golden sceptre to indicate that he is under the protection of the god he serves.[77] Thornton[78] treats his approach to the Greeks as the first supplication of the *Iliad*, although Chryses neither performs nor makes allusion to the ritual gestures of the suppliant. He does not lay down his sceptre with the στέμματα as a suppliant would,[79] and his approach to the Greeks is rightly absent from Gould's list of supplications. The old man λίσσετο πάντας Ἀχαιούς, | Ἀτρεΐδα δὲ μάλιστα δύω, 'besought all the Greeks, especially the two Atreidae' (*Il.* 1. 15–16), praying for their success in taking Troy and their safe return, if only they would accept his ransom and give back his daughter (*Il.* 1. 17–21). He concludes with an invitation to the Greeks to accept his ransom showing reverence (ἀζόμενοι) to Apollo (*Il.* 1. 21). In the terms of the αἶνος, ὃς μέν τ' αἰδέσεται κούρας Διὸς ἆσσον ἰούσας | τὸν δὲ μέγ' ὤνησαν, 'who reverences the daughters of Zeus as they come near | him do they greatly bless' (*Il.* 9. 508–9), Chryses is praying for the benefit of the Greeks if they will respect his λιταί, with a slight menace that Apollo will be his avenger in the event of refusal.[80] The whole army wants to αἰδεῖσθαι, reverence,[81] his

---

[76] Kakridis (1980: 64) draws attention to the paradoxical power conferred on Chryses by his function.

[77] Griffin (1980: 26) takes the στέμματα to indicate that Chryses is a suppliant. However, the term for a suppliant's branch is ἱκετηρία, not στέμμα. Chryses keeps hold of his στέμματα, whereas the ἱκετηρία should be handed to, and accepted by, the person supplicated: see Burkert (1979: 44).

[78] (1984: 113).

[79] Delatte (1951: 442).

[80] Kakridis (1980: 61–76). See Kirk (1985–90: i. 55 ad *Il.* 1. 17–21): an insult to Chryses will be an insult to Apollo himself.

[81] αἰδώς is the proper reaction in such contexts: see Cairns (1993: 115).

request, and only Agamemnon stands out against it, sending the old man away with contemptuous threats and hostile words. It is significant that the term αἰδεῖσθαι is used in this context for respecting the priest who makes the λιτή, and later in the αἶνος of the Λιταί, for reverencing the Λιταί themselves. When rebuffed, Chryses prays to Apollo that the Greeks may τείσειαν, pay the penalty (*Il.* 1. 42) for rejecting his prayers: the same verb, ἀποτίνω, is used for the man who rejects Λιταί in the αἶνος.[82] Apollo responds immediately to Chryses' retaliatory prayer, running down from Olympus with deadly arrows clanking in his quiver (*Il.* 1. 44–6). He stations himself at a distance from the Greek ships and begins to shoot plague arrows at the mules and dogs of the Greek army, later turning his aim on the Greeks themselves (*Il.* 1. 48–52).

It is important to remember that the λιταί of Chryses to the Greeks and the Atreidae are a new beginning of the kind envisaged in *Il.* 9. 508–12: they are not λιταί of repentance or to obtain reparation,[83] but rather attempts to alter a course decided or embarked upon.[84] We should not imagine, with Benveniste, that all λιταί are consequent on an earlier offence, or that they are necessarily intended to make reparation for offences against the gods, or to obtain reparation for an outrage. Benveniste suggests the Greeks have affronted the priest of Apollo by abducting his daughter, and for this affront the god is exacting payment.[85] The idea makes no sense at all: there is nothing in the text to suggest that Chryses regards the outrage to himself as the abduction of his daughter any more than Priam regards the killing of Hector as an outrage against

---

[82] ἵνα βλαφθεὶς ἀποτείσῃ, 'so that he may come to grief and pay the penalty' (*Il.* 9. 512).

[83] See n. 52 above.

[84] To reverse the fate of someone in enemy hands: see Table C, 4.

[85] 'This λιτή of Chryses' is a demand for reparation': Benveniste (1973: 502; 1st pub. 1969), cited by Chantraine (1968: ii. 644 s.v. λίσσομαι). In his attempts to reconcile λίσσομαι with Latin *litare*, 'to obtain a favourable omen' with the extended sense 'to propitiate a divinity', Benveniste overlooks the asyndeton at *Il.* 9. 507–8, and conflates the two incidents envisaged in the αἶνος, so that *all* λιταί are seen in the context of offering or obtaining reparation. It is manifestly ridiculous to associate the idea of reparation with the Greeks' request to Achilles to eat (λισσόμενοι δειπνῆσαι) (*Il.* 19. 304), but Chryses certainly prays to Apollo to obtain reparation for the rebuff he has suffered from the Greeks (*Il.* 1. 37–42).

himself,[86] because the abduction of daughters and the killing of sons are to be expected in war. If the Greeks have affronted Apollo, and the god is exacting payment, it is not easy to explain why the priest, who is supposed to be the injured party, is the only one to be offering anything (ἀπερείσι᾿ ἄποινα, *Il.* 1. 13) in the way of compensation. The λιτή of Chryses is not a demand for reparation for the outrage of his daughter's abduction, but an attempt to alleviate the sufferings of war for his daughter and himself by having her returned to his protection. His prayer, conditional on the return of his daughter, for the Greeks to succeed in sacking Troy and returning home safely (*Il.* 1. 18–19), is an offer of a reciprocal favour, not a demand for reparation. He offers a ransom, which should be enough to secure her safe return, and which the Greek army urges Agamemnon to accept (*Il.* 1. 22–3).[87] When Agamemnon refuses his request Chryses certainly does demand reparation, when he asks Apollo for the Greeks to pay the penalty for his tears (*Il.* 1. 42).

Agamemnon's reasons for refusing to accept Chryses' ransom and release the girl are not explained until we learn (*Il.* 1. 112–13) that he likes Chryseis, and is unwilling (*Il.* 1. 118) to give her up because he does not want to be the only one of all the Greeks without a prize.[88] Quite apart from wanting to retain his prize, Agamemnon seems to enjoy gratuitously humiliating the old man whose social standing is so far beneath his own that the king would have no compunction in arranging for physical injury to be inflicted on Chryses, were it not for the emblems of Apollo which he carries (*Il.* 1. 28).[89] When Redfield describes

---

[86] Although he foresees destruction for his city and himself as a result of it (*Il.* 22. 42, 60–71).

[87] Priam will make a similar λιτή (plea), but in a context of supplication (λάβε γούνατα, 'he clasped his knees', *Il.* 24. 478) and in his case successful, to ransom the body of Hector from Achilles to save the corpse from mutilation and permit proper funerary honours. For the theme of the old father attempting to recover his child, see Sheppard (1922: 207–9); Whitman (1958: 259–60); Trypanis (1977: 18–19). For verbal echoes between Chryses' approach to the Atreidae and Priam's supplication to Achilles, see Macleod (1982: 33–4).

[88] For a brief discussion of Agamemnon's reasons for refusing to give up Chryseis, see Whitman (1958: 157); Taplin (1992: 60–4); Redfield (1975: 94).

[89] On the humiliation of Chryses, see Kakridis (1971: 130–1; 1980: 67–9); Redfield (1975: 94).

Agamemnon's rejection of Chryses' request for the return of his daughter as 'uncaused',[90] he must mean that all Agamemnon's reasons for refusing to accept the ransom are internal: no outside force is compelling him, but only his own nature.[91] There is nothing to suggest that at the moment of refusal, Agamemnon is the puppet of retaliatory ἄτη, although he soon will be.

Very shortly after sending the old man away, the Greeks hold an assembly to discuss the plague afflicting them, at which Calchas, the seer, advises that Chryseis must be given back to her father, Chryses, ἀπριάτην ἀνάποινον, unbought, unransomed, and that a hecatomb must be taken to Chryse (*Il.* 1. 99). What Agamemnon was asked to concede in the first instance in exchange for ransom, he is now forced to give up without ransom, and with the additional expense to himself of a hecatomb to Apollo: all this after the army has suffered the depredations of the plague. This pattern of refusing to make a concession in exchange for gifts, only to reach a point later where one must concede it anyway, but at a time when the gifts are no longer on offer, and after great loss and suffering, is, of course, the pattern of Meleager's reaction to the approaches made to him in the paradigm of book 9, and the pattern of Achilles' reaction to the approaches from the embassy and Patroclus, and to the eventual death of Patroclus. The Chryses episode is a 'Vorspiel', a 'Vorbereitung',[92] presenting in miniature a rehearsal of the elements of Achilles' quarrel with Agamemnon, his rejection of the offer of gifts in return for coming back to fight alongside the Greeks, only to find himself having to rejoin the battle anyway (gifts or no gifts) to avenge Patroclus. In compliance with Calchas' instructions, Odysseus is sent to escort Chryseis back to her father together with a hecatomb for Apollo (*Il.* 1. 309–11): on receiving back his daughter, Chryses prays to Apollo to ward off the plague, ἀεικέα λοιγόν (*Il.* 1. 456) from the Greeks, and the episode pans out in

[90] Redfield (1975: 94).

[91] Contrary to the arguments of Snell (1982: 16–22; 1st pub. 1955); see 7.1.6 and p. 203 above.

[92] 'Vorspiel': Schadewaldt (1966: 144, 148, 150; 1st pub. 1938) (Motivdoppelung in miniature of anger, dishonour, disaster, and expiatory reconciliation, 'Vorbereitung', Exposition). There is a kind of 'Nachspiel' too in the quarrel of Antilochus and Menelaus at the funeral games: see 4.5 above.

the festive atmosphere of the sacrifice and paean to Apollo (*Il.* 1. 472–4).

Chryses' role has corresponded exactly to the pattern expressed in abstract terms in the αἶνος of the *Λιταί*: his initial λιταί for the return of his daughter offered a reciprocatory prayer for the benefit of the Greeks (*Il.* 1. 18–19); when his λιταί were refused, he prayed (ἠρᾶθ', *Il.* 1. 35; εὐχόμενος, *Il.* 1. 43) for vengeance for the slight (*Il.* 1. 41); punished by the plague, the Greeks had to return Chryseis; his λιταί granted at last, Chryses prays for the benefit of the Greeks (who have lost by the delay: his original prayer was for them to sack Troy (*Il.* 1. 19), whereas now (*Il.* 1. 456) he prays (εὔχετο, *Il.* 1. 450; εὐχόμενος, *Il.* 1. 457) for their rescue from the plague, ἀεικέα λοιγόν). With this prayer for an end to the plague, the active role of Chryses is concluded.

7.1.8. *Agamemnon's affliction by* ἄτη *(delusion)*

So far, we have seen rejected λιταί followed by retaliatory prayers requesting (and obtaining) the punishment of the one who rejected them, and λιταί heeded followed by prayers for the benefit of the person(s) who has/have heeded them.[93] But the ἄτη consequent[94] on Agamemnon's rejection of the λιταί of Chryses is yet to be considered. As the priest of Apollo, Chryses appeals when rebuffed for vindication to Apollo, who champions his priest by sending the plague: when the girl has been returned to her father, and Apollo himself has been placated by a hecatomb, there is nothing to suggest that Apollo's anger against the Greeks on account of their treatment of Chryses continues. That should be the end of the matter, but it is not the end at all. Agamemnon, as we all know, having rejected Chryses' λιταί goes on to compensate himself, against the advice of Nestor, by appropriating Briseis, Achilles' prize. The sequence of Agamemnon's actions is significant: Agamemnon rebuffs Chryses and soon after, at the assembly, threatens to take Briseis to make good his loss. Only when Chryseis has been returned to her father, and Apollo pacified, does Agamemnon carry out his threat to take Briseis. Since Apollo has

---

[93] In illustration of *Il.* 9. 508–9.
[94] If it is consequent: see Yamagata (1991) and n. 95 below.

been pleased with the hecatomb (*Il.* 1. 474), he is clearly not the cause of Agamemnon's fulfilment of his threat: the force which drives Agamemnon to threaten at the assembly, and then to carry out the threat by taking the girl, alienating Achilles in the process, is always described as ἄτη (*Il.* 1. 412 = *Il.* 16. 274; see also *Il.* 9. 115; 19. 88) which, according to Agamemnon (*Il.* 19. 87), emanated from Ζεὺς καὶ Μοῖρα καὶ ἠεροφοῖτις Ἐρινύς: 'Zeus, Destiny, and the Fury that walks in darkness'. The αἶνος describes Λιταί retaliating against those who rebuff them by asking Zeus to send Ἄτη against the cause of their resentment. Although in book 1 we have not yet heard the αἶνος, it is not unreasonable to suppose, although it is impossible to prove, that when we eventually do hear it, Agamemnon is retrospectively seen as the victim of ἄτη sent by Zeus in response to rejected λιταί (of Chryses), and that it is the influence of ἄτη which causes him to requisition Briseis for himself.[95]

7.1.9. The λιταί (prayers) of Chryses rejected by Agamemnon and championed by Achilles

Agamemnon takes Briseis from Achilles rather than taking the prize of one of the other Greeks as he at first threatens (*Il.* 1. 137–9) because Achilles emerges as a kind of champion of the old man's attempts to recover his daughter: he takes over the part initially filled by Chryses in requiring from Agamemnon a concession he does not want to make. At the assembly in book 1 it is Achilles who proposes consulting Calchas to discover the reason for the plague (*Il.* 1. 62–7) and Achilles who proposes the return of Chryseis (*Il.* 1. 127), which Calchas says is the only way to secure an end to the sickness (*Il.* 1. 97–100). The proposal to return Chryseis is not exactly a λιτή originating

---

[95] For Yamagata (1991), the ἄτη which caused Agamemnon to take Briseis is entirely unconnected with Chryses' appeal, and quite inexplicable in moral terms. It is impossible to prove that Agamemnon is dogged by ἄτη sent by Zeus at the request of the rejected λιταί of Chryses, but the reverse is also true. The view of Taplin (1992: 52) that 'the poet issues a challenge of evaluation to the audience by not spelling out the morals of Agamemnon's treatment of Chryses and his great dispute with Achilleus' seems mistaken in view of the poet's care to indicate that Agamemnon is out on a limb in his treatment of Chryses: the whole army wanted to ransom Chryses' daughter (*Il.* 1. 22–3). 'Agamemnon rejected prayers in book 1 and is now suffering for it: Achilles has been warned': Griffin (1995: 133 ad *Il.* 9. 502–14).

from Achilles; rather, Achilles is taking up the λιταί of Chryses, and in his turn, he is slighted by Agamemnon, who threatens to compensate himself for his loss by commandeering Achilles' own prize, Briseis. Agamemnon is in the wrong,[96] as we see when Athene promises Achilles compensation for the slight (*Il.* 1. 212–14): she agrees with Achilles (*Il.* 1. 211, 214) that Agamemnon is guilty of ὕβρις. She forbids Achilles direct retaliation (*Il.* 1. 210–11), so he resorts to indirect means, asking his mother, Thetis, to arrange with Zeus for Agamemnon to suffer for slighting him (*Il.* 1. 401–12), pretty much as the rejected Λιταί go back to Zeus and ask for Ἄτη to pursue the cause of their resentment until he is harmed and ἀποτείσῃ, pays the penalty (*Il.* 9. 511–12). Zeus ponders how he might τιμήσειε, honour, Achilles and cause losses among the Greeks (*Il.* 2. 4). He sends a baneful Dream to Agamemnon, which causes him to believe (*Il.* 2. 6–36) that he is on the verge of taking Troy: by *Il.* 2. 111, Agamemnon publicly admits his ἄτη[97] and is soon told the reason for it by Thersites:

> ὃς καὶ νῦν Ἀχιλῆα, ἕο μέγ' ἀμείνονα φῶτα
> ἠτίμησεν· ἑλὼν γὰρ ἔχει γέρας, αὐτὸς ἀπούρας

who even now dishonoured Achilles, a far better man than he;
for he took his prize and keeps her, he took her away himself.

(*Il.* 2. 239–40)

But no one speaks in support of Thersites and his reproach is regarded as insubordinate and unacceptable,[98] so nothing is

---

[96] At least, he gives the impression of being more in the wrong than Achilles, as demonstrated by Schadewaldt (1966: 144–5 n. 3; 1st pub. 1938).

[97] Stallmach (1968: 45 n. 40) considers the ἄτη referred to in *Il.* 2. 111 to have no connection with the references to the Ἄτη of Agamemnon in books 1, 9, and 19, which deal with his shortcomings towards Achilles and their consequences, but he forgets that the false Dream which brought ἄτη to Agamemnon was sent by Zeus ultimately at the request of Thetis, for some redress in the matter of Agamemnon's shortcomings towards Achilles. She supplicated Zeus to send ruin on the Greeks when Achilles asked her to arrange for this, so that Agamemnon would become painfully aware of his error in failing to respect Achilles' claim to his own prize, Briseis: see Stallmach (1968: 57–8).

[98] 'Malicious': Kirk (1985–90: i. 72 ad *Il.* 1. 185). Thersites' name seems to be derived from θάρσυνω and θάρσος (boldness or impudence). He says what the rank and file of the army would say if they dared. It is not really fair to describe his words as malicious, and nobody says the same of Nestor when he echoes Thersites' summary of the situation (*Il.* 9. 109–11).

done to mend the quarrel with Achilles until Agamemnon
again admits his ἄτη (*Il.* 9. 17–25 = *Il.* 2. 110–18),[99] and receives

[99] In his private conversation with Nestor, Agamemnon admits his troubles
are due to the quarrel he began with Achilles (*Il.* 2. 375–8). To the trusted
group of γέροντες, elders, who advise him to send the embassy, Agamemnon
will privately admit his personal responsibility: ἀλλ' ἐπεὶ ἀασάμην φρεσὶ
λευγαλέῃσι πιθήσας, 'but since I was out of my mind, confident in my wretched
wits' (*Il.* 9. 119); cf. ἀλλ' ἐπεὶ ἀασάμην καί μευ φρένας ἐξέλετο Ζεύς, 'but since I
was out of my mind, and Zeus took away my wits from me' (*Il.* 19. 137).
Hainsworth (1993: 73) ad *Il.* 9. 119–20 indicates how Agamemnon does not
help his case with Achilles by rejecting the communal gift-giving proposed by
Nestor (*Il.* 9. 112–13 and 10. 212–13). The emphasis on divine agency as the
cause of ἄτη (*Il.* 19. 137) is to exculpate Agamemnon in a public assembly:
see Stallmach (1968: 34). Athenaeus, 1. 11a quotes a plus-line inserted by
Dioscurides, a pupil of Isocrates: ἢ οἴνῳ μεθύων ἤ μ' ἔβλαψαν θεοὶ αὐτοί (either I
was drunk with wine, or the gods themselves harmed me) (*Il.* 9. 119a). This
refers, as Dioscurides himself says, to Achilles' insult, οἰνοβαρές (heavy with
wine) (*Il.* 1. 225). Dioscurides, who thought drunkenness equal to madness, is
quoted by a later writer of the same name whose work, Περὶ τῶν ἡρώων καθ'
Ὅμηρον βίου, is mentioned without an author's name in the epitome of the first
two books of Athenaeus, and in the *Suda* under a bowdlerized title with the
author given as Dioscurides. See also *FGrH* 594. 8 (18): the date of this
younger Dioscurides is estimated by Susemihl (1892: 351, 554) as around 100
BC, which brings us into the time of the grammarian Dioscurides of Tarsus,
who came from a Stoic family, and who has been identified by Keil (1895:
441–2 n. 2) with the author of Περὶ τῶν ἡρώων καθ' Ὅμηρον βίου. The work of
the later Dioscurides is dependent upon (*a*) Aristarchus' exegesis of Homer:
see Weber (1888: 124–9); (*b*) the Stoic interpretation of Homer: see Weber
(1888: 139–46); (*c*) the body of Peripatetic λύσεις: see Weber (1888: 146–56).
Weber (1888: 150–1) argues that the later Dioscurides, Plutarch, and Porphyry
were all using the same material in their discussions of drunkenness, and that
the material derived from the λύσεις of the Peripatetics. Apthorp (1980: 99)
and Hainsworth (1993: 73–4 ad *Il.* 9. 119–20) refer to Wilamowitz, who considered *Il.* 9. 119a might well be genuine, and suffered expurgation in the
post-Homeric paradosis: 'Es ist schwer zu sagen, ob der Dichter seinen
Helden mit der eigenen Trunkenheit rechnen liess . . . oder erst ein Rhapsode
darauf kam. Dass ich das letztere nicht zuversichtlich behaupte bewirkt die
zimperliche Streichung von 458–61, einerlei wer sie vornahm': Wilamowitz
(1920: 66 n. 2). Bolling (1925: 54–5) found *Il.* 9. 119a insufficiently shocking to
warrant expurgation, but Van der Valk (1963–4: i. 485–6) rejected the line on
the grounds that Agamemnon is hardly likely to forget his position to such a
degree that he attributes his errors to drunkenness. (Cf. Griffin (1977: 47 and
n. 51).) Against Van der Valk (1964) and Griffin (1977) is the link between
quarrels and drink established in the quarrel of Agamemnon and Menelaus at
the drunken assembly after the fall of Troy (*Od.* 3. 137–51). An association
between ἄτη and drink is evidenced by the ἄτη afflicting the drunken Eurytion
(*Od.* 21. 297). See also Ch. 4, n. 26 above. Two views were taken on offences

the advice of Diomede and Nestor to send the embassy. Achilles has allied himself with the rejected λιταί of the old man: like Chryses and the Λιταί, he too is slighted in the first instance, but as a result of retaliatory λιταί (to Zeus, through his mother, Thetis), his antagonist is hounded by ἄτη, and eventually suffers harm and pays the penalty, as Agamemnon will later admit (*Il.* 9. 118) in the knowledge that Zeus ἔτεισε, recompensed, Achilles.

7.2. ACHILLES' REJECTION OF λιταί (PRAYERS) FROM THE EMBASSY

7.2.1. Captatio benevolentiae: *quarrels with authority*

The αἶνος of the Λιταί is the centrepiece of Phoenix's speech, which must attempt to soften the indignant refusal provoked in Achilles by the long speech in which Odysseus recounted Agamemnon's offer of terms for Achilles' return to the fighting. Phoenix must also try to avert Achilles' threat to depart the following morning for home, taking Phoenix with him if he will go (*Il.* 9. 427–9).[100] It is preceded by a kind of *captatio benevolentiae* in which Phoenix describes an incident from his own past, not dissimilar to Achilles' quarrel with Agamemnon.[101]

> ὡς ἂν ἔπειτ' ἀπὸ σεῖο, φίλον τέκος, οὐκ ἐθέλοιμι
> λείπεσθ', οὐδ' εἴ κέν μοι ὑποσταίη θεὸς αὐτὸς   445
> γῆρας ἀποξύσας θήσειν νέον ἡβώοντα,
> οἷον ὅτε πρῶτον λίπον Ἑλλάδα καλλιγύναικα,
> φεύγων νείκεα πατρὸς Ἀμύντορος Ὀρμενίδαο,
> ὅς μοι παλλακίδος περιχώσατο καλλικόμοιο,

committed while drunk: Aristotle refers to (a) τὴν συγγνώμην . . . ὅτι δεῖ μεθύουσιν ἔχειν μᾶλλον (the allowance one should make the more for the intoxicated) in his account of how (b) Pittacus doubled the penalty for offences committed when drunk, because more offences were committed by the drunk than by the sober (*Ath. Pol.* 1274[b]19–20). See also Aristotle, *Rh.* 1402[b]12; Diogenes Laertius, 1. 76; Plutarch, *Mor.* 155f.

[100] Scodel (1982) considers Phoenix's speech a partial success, in that it prevents Achilles from leaving by presenting Phoenix's own choice of departure from the scene of his quarrel with his father as an ignominious one.

[101] The similarities between the stories of Phoenix and Meleager, and the situation of Achilles are discussed by Scodel (1982).

τὴν αὐτὸς φιλέεσκεν, ἀτιμάζεσκε δ᾽ ἄκοιτιν,   450
μητέρ᾽ ἐμήν· ἡ δ᾽ αἰὲν ἐμὲ λισσέσκετο γούνων
παλλακίδι προμιγῆναι, ἵν᾽ ἐχθήρειε γέροντα.
τῇ πιθόμην καὶ ἔρεξα· πατὴρ δ᾽ ἐμὸς αὐτίκ᾽ ὀϊσθεὶς
πολλὰ κατηρᾶτο, στυγερὰς δ᾽ ἐπεκέκλετ᾽ Ἐρινῆς,
μή ποτε γούνασιν οἷσιν ἐφέσσεσθαι φίλον υἱὸν   455
ἐξ ἐμέθεν γεγαῶτα· θεοὶ δ᾽ ἐτέλειον ἐπαράς,
Ζεύς τε καταχθόνιος καὶ ἐπαινὴ Περσεφόνεια.
τὸν μὲν ἐγὼ βούλευσα κατακτάμεν ὀξέϊ χαλκῷ·
ἀλλά τις ἀθανάτων παῦσεν χόλον, ὅς ῥ᾽ ἐνὶ θυμῷ
δήμου θῆκε φάτιν καὶ ὀνείδεα πόλλ᾽ ἀνθρώπων,   460
ὡς μὴ πατροφόνος μετ᾽ Ἀχαιοῖσιν καλεοίμην.
ἔνθ᾽ ἐμοὶ οὐκέτι πάμπαν ἐρητύετ᾽ ἐν φρεσὶ θυμὸς
πατρὸς χωομένοιο κατὰ μέγαρα στρωφᾶσθαι.
ἦ μὲν πολλὰ ἔται καὶ ἀνεψιοὶ ἀμφὶς ἐόντες
αὐτοῦ λισσόμενοι κατερήτυον ἐν μεγάροισι,   465
πολλὰ δὲ ἴφια μῆλα καὶ εἰλίποδας ἕλικας βοῦς
ἔσφαζον, πολλοὶ δὲ σύες θαλέθοντες ἀλοιφῇ
εὑόμενοι τανύοντο διὰ φλογὸς Ἡφαίστοιο,
πολλὸν δ᾽ ἐκ κεράμων μέθυ πίνετο τοῖο γέροντος.
εἰνάνυχες δέ μοι ἀμφ᾽ αὐτῷ παρὰ νύκτας ἴαυον·   470
οἱ μὲν ἀμειβόμενοι φυλακὰς ἔχον, οὐδέ ποτ᾽ ἔσβη
πῦρ, ἕτερον μὲν ὑπ᾽ αἰθούσῃ εὐερκέος αὐλῆς
ἄλλο δ᾽ ἐνὶ προδόμῳ, πρόσθεν θαλάμοιο θυράων.
ἀλλ᾽ ὅτε δὴ δεκάτη μοι ἐπήλυθε νὺξ ἐρεβεννή
καὶ τότ᾽ ἐγὼ θαλάμοιο θύρας πυκινῶς ἀραρυίας   475
ῥήξας ἐξῆλθον, καὶ ὑπέρθορον ἑρκίον αὐλῆς
ῥεῖα, λαθὼν φύλακάς τ᾽ ἄνδρας δμῳάς τε γυναῖκας.
φεῦγον ἔπειτ᾽ ἀπάνευθε δι᾽ Ἑλλάδος εὐρυχόροιο,
Φθίην δ᾽ ἐξικόμην ἐριβώλακα, μητέρα μήλων,
ἐς Πηλῆα ἄναχθ᾽. ὅ δέ με πρόφρων ὑπέδεκτο,   480
καί μ᾽ ἐφίλησ᾽ ὡς εἴ τε πατὴρ ὃν παῖδα φιλήσῃ
μοῦνον τηλύγετον πολλοῖσιν ἐπὶ κτεάτεσσι,
καί μ᾽ ἀφνειὸν ἔθηκε, πολὺν δέ μοι ὤπασε λαόν·
ναῖον δ᾽ ἐσχατιὴν Φθίης, Δολόπεσσιν ἀνάσσων.

So then dear child, I would not wish to be left
apart from you, not even if god himself were to promise   445
to strip off my age and make me young and flourishing,
as when first I left Hellas of the fair women,
fleeing the reproofs of my father Amyntor, the son of Ormenos,
who was exceedingly angry with me on account of his fair-haired
    concubine,

to whom he habitually made love himself, and habitually dishonoured
    his wife,   450
my mother. But she always used to entreat me by my knees
to lie with the concubine first, so that she would become hostile to the
    old man.
I obeyed her and did it: the moment my father knew,
he called down many curses and invoked the hateful Furies
that he would never set on his knees a dear son   455
got by me, and the gods accomplished his curses,
Zeus under the earth and the dread Persephone too.
It occurred to me to kill him with the sharp bronze
but some one of the immortals checked my rage, who put into my
    heart
the gossip of the people and the many reproaches of men,   460
that I would not like to be called a parricide among the Greeks.
Then was the passion in my breast not at all restrained
to dwell in the palace of my angry father.
True that many of my kinsmen and cousins about me
there where I was entreated me and kept me in the halls,   465
and they slaughtered many fat sheep and shambling cattle with
    crumpled horns,
and many pigs teeming with fat were stretched
to singe over the flame of Hephaestus,
and a great deal of wine was drunk from the jars of the old man.
They slept close about my person for nine nights in succession   470
And they changed the guard as they kept watch, nor was the fire
ever quenched, one under the porch of the well-fenced court,
another in the vestibule, before the doors of my chamber.
But when the tenth dark night came for me
then I broke the closely fitted doors of my chamber   475
and got out, and I vaulted over the fence of the court
easily, escaping the notice of the guards and serving women.
Then I was on the run through Hellas of the broad dancing-places,
and came to Phthia of the rich ploughland, the mother of flocks,
to Lord Peleus, who received me kindly   480
and loved me as a father loves his son,
an only son of tender age and heir to many possessions,
and he made me rich and granted me a numerous people
and I dwelt at the furthest edge of Phthia, ruling over the Dolopes.

                                       (*Il.* 9. 444–84)

In this incident, Phoenix quarrelled with an authority figure
(his father) over a concubine. At the request (supplication:
λισσέσκετο γούνων, 'besought him by his knees' (*Il.* 9. 451)) of

his mother, he made love to his father's concubine, so that her affections would be alienated from the older man: his father knew, and cursed his son with sterility (*Il*. 9. 452–6).[102] Despite the pleas of his kinsfolk, λισσόμενοι him to remain, and although he was closely guarded (*Il*. 9. 465), Phoenix escaped and fled away from his own community, never to return.

According to Rosner,[103] Phoenix is partly exonerated since he seduced the concubine to preserve his mother's honour. I am not sure that taking his mother's part helps his moral position (in Homeric terms) at all, since excessive loyalty to the mother's οἶκος is a kind of refusal to grow up (reflected in Phoenix's punishment). It also subverts the absolute loyalty owed by a son to his father.[104] This loyalty is explored in the Herodotean account[105] of the hostility between Periander and his son, Lycophron, arising from Lycophron's realization that Periander had killed his mother. Enraged by his son's attitude, Periander told him that though he was the son of Corinth's βασιλεύς, king, he had chosen a vagrant life by opposing his father (Herodotus, 3. 52. 4). Lycophron is banished to Corcyra, and ignores his father's request that he return. His sister is sent to intercede with him: she says many τὰ μητρώια διζήμενοι τὰ πατρώϊα ἀπέβαλον, 'seeking after their mother's clan, have thrown away their father's clan/their inheritance' (3. 53. 4). This is very much what Phoenix does. Negative qualities such as disorder, pollution, and danger are associated in Greek thought with women:[106] the attribution of these qualities to women helps to define the male role.[107] In the light of such negative qualities, siding with the female against the male is unwise.

[102] With the effect that Phoenix will never replace his father as a sexual male: see Sourvinou-Inwood (1988: 172 n. 47).

[103] (1976: 316).

[104] For father–son loyalty see *Il*. 4. 477–9 = *Il*. 17. 301–3; Sophocles, *Ant*. 639–47; Andocides, 1. 74; Harrison (1968: 70–81); Lacey (1968: 116); Dover (1974: 273–5); Vickers (1973: 112–19); Sourvinou-Inwood (1989: 144). On women as subverters of kinship solidarity, see Gould (1980: 52–8, and esp. n. 123). The problem seems to be that women are essential to the continuity of the οἶκος, but as wives, their loyalty is felt to be to their paternal οἶκος, and not to that of their husbands, to which they are perceived to be a permanent threat.   [105] Discussed by Sourvinou-Inwood (1988).

[106] See Gould (1980: esp. 57–8); Du Boulay (1974: 104).

[107] See Pembroke (1967).

Different scholars interpret the details of Phoenix's auto-biography in different ways, relating them either to Achilles' situation in the *Iliad* or to the story of Meleager, which itself makes reference to the story of Achilles. For Ebel,[108] Phoenix's imprisonment by his kin is reminiscent of Achilles' self-imposed imprisonment, and Phoenix 'supplicated' by his kin refers to the present 'supplication' being made to Achilles by the embassy. Lohmann[109] points out similarities between the stories of Phoenix and Meleager, so that Meleager nursing his anger in the palace after being cursed by his mother, Althaea, repeats, with slight variation, the motif of Phoenix nursing his anger in his father's palace, after being cursed by his father, Amyntor. Bannert[110] discusses these parallels and shows how the net of references to χόλος in the stories of Phoenix and of Meleager is linked to the account of Achilles' quarrel with Agamemnon. Rosner[111] emphasizes the similarities between Phoenix's quarrel with his father over a concubine, and Achilles' quarrel with Agamemnon over a concubine. In both stories, murder is considered as a possible retaliation for the humiliation suffered, but in both cases it is averted by a god. For Heubeck[112] the closest correspondence between the stories of Phoenix and Achilles is this motif of contemplating murder as revenge, so that *Il.* 9. 458 ff. refers back to *Il.* 1. 188 ff. For Rosner, the gifts bestowed on Phoenix by Peleus are an allusion to the gifts offered to Achilles by Agamemnon, and the bad 'authority figure' of Agamemnon is echoed in the bad 'authority figure' of Amyntor. Schlunk[113] is surely mistaken in finding a connection between Phoenix appropriating his father's concubine and Agamemnon appropriating Briseis, since this association would ignore the power situation in the two episodes. (Agamemnon is powerful, and Phoenix is not.)

Sourvinou-Inwood[114] discusses the kind of father–son hostility described by Phoenix, centring on the father's second wife or surrogate wife: she uses the examples of Periander and Lycophron; Theseus and Hippolytus; Phoenix; and Tenes. Father–son hostility involves the son's failure to replace his father, and his permanent desertion of the home community.

[108] (1972: 87–8).   [109] (1970: 268–9).   [110] (1981).
[111] (1976).   [112] (1984: 134–5).   [113] (1976).
[114] (1979; 1988; 1991).

The hostility always begins from the son, or is represented by the father as beginning from him. Another kind of father–son hostility is found to centre on excessive loyalty to the mother's οἶκος, prejudicing the relationship with the father. While the relationships in the Agamemnon–Achilles hostility are not equivalent to those discussed by Sourvinou-Inwood, there are still remarkable reverberations between the events of book 1 and the stories of Phoenix and Lycophron. A junior, less kingly man, Achilles, acts as spokesman for the whole community of the army against the king, proposing to deprive a senior of his concubine/surrogate wife. The king, Agamemnon, retaliates by depriving the spokesman of *his* concubine, demoting him in sexual terms, rather like Phoenix, whose sexual demotion is complete and permanent. The aggrieved Achilles suffers isolation from his community, and considers leaving altogether, very much as Lycophron was initially isolated and then banished to Corcyra, where he continued to nurse his anger against his father. Phoenix is isolated, and leaves his home community permanently. The intercession of the ambassadors to Achilles is very like that of Lycophron's sister for her brother to return to Corinth, and like the requests to Phoenix from his relatives not to leave his community. The Agamemnon–Achilles hostility, unlike father–son hostility, is eventually resolved.

The parallels between the incident from Phoenix's past and Achilles' situation are striking: Phoenix left, rejecting λιταί that he should remain, rather as Achilles is threatening to leave, rejecting the λιταί of the ambassadors λισσόμενοι that he stay. The discrepancies between Phoenix's story and Achilles' situation in the poem are also significant: Achilles had quarrelled with an authority figure (Agamemnon) about a concubine, but in Achilles' case, the authority figure took the concubine away from her owner, whereas in Phoenix's case, the authority figure was deprived of (the affections of) his own concubine, when Phoenix made love to her. Phoenix's quarrel was with his father, but Agamemnon is not Achilles' father, and has no real paternal claims on his loyalty and compliance. By rejecting the offer of marriage to one of Agamemnon's daughters, Achilles has rejected Agamemnon even as a father-in-law.

7.2.2. The authority of surrogates

The implication that Agamemnon is to Achilles what Amyntor is to his son, Phoenix, is clearly false,[115] but it introduces the idea of paternal rights and authority vested in one who is not really the true father. This is an unpleasant idea which pervades Phoenix's speech, as we shall see. Four lines (*Il.* 9. 458–61)[116] reveal that Phoenix would have killed his father, but was prevented by the intervention of a god, who put into his mind the thought that if he killed his father, he would be called a parricide. The whole incident, with its divine intervention preventing the murder, is remarkably close to what happens in

---

[115] In the view of Scodel (1982), Phoenix makes Agamemnon parallel both his bad father (Amyntor) in Hellas, and his good (surrogate) father (Peleus) in Phthia.

[116] The lines appear as a quotation only in Plutarch, *Mor.* 26f. *Il.* 9. 461 is cited again at *Mor.* 72b; 9. 459 and the first half of 9. 460 are cited at *Cor.* 32, where it is said that Aristarchus ἐξεῖλε, 'deleted', them, φοβηθείς, 'in fear'. Bolling (1925: 120–2, with bibliography) argues against Plutarch's conclusion. In Heubeck's (1984: 135) view, the parallel with Achilles' desire to kill Agamemnon is certainly very close. Van der Valk (1963–4: i. 483) indicates that the lines supply motivation for Phoenix's flight. Cairns (1993: 51 n. 13) argues that the fear of δήμου φάτιν, 'what people say' (*Il.* 9. 460) is entirely Homeric, although Griffin (1995: 130 ad *Il.* 9. 458–61) indicates that public opinion, although a major concern (as at *Il.* 6. 350–1; 22. 105–6), is nowhere else so expressed in the *Iliad*. Apthorp (1980: 91–9) treated the lines quoted by Plutarch as 'a variation on the homicide and flight theme' (for which see Schlunk 1976) and rightly indicated that without these lines, the parallels between Phoenix's autobiographical episode and the main narrative of the poem are very tenuous (as is evident from the disagreement on where the parallels lie: see 7.2.1 above). Apthorp's conclusions on the passage are agnostic: the language, style, and sentiment are compatible with authenticity, but that is no justification for assuming it. S. West (1982: 84) offers, as an analogy for Plutarch's quotation of lines absent from the manuscript tradition, *SH* 534. 29, a line from Matro's Ἀττικὸν Δεῖπνον which seems to parody a Homeric verse, although no trace of the line parodied is found in the tradition. The 'vanished' line seems to have been another reference to an assault on someone which was prevented by the intervention of a god. She goes on to suggest that the lines quoted by Plutarch were known also to the interpolator (see Goold 1970) of *Aen.* 2. 567–88 (on Venus' intervention to prevent Aeneas from unleashing his wrath on Helen). Austin (1964: 217–19, with bibliography) argues for the genuineness of *Aen.* 2. 567–88). Janko (1992: 27–8) argues that Aristarchus omitted *Il.* 9. 458–61 because they were absent from manuscripts he preferred, probably unreliable emended texts: he concludes 'They are good enough to be genuine'. Van der Valk (1963–4: i. 483–6) accepts the lines as genuine.

book 1 where Athene intervenes to prevent Achilles from
killing Agamemnon. The similarity of the two episodes (even in
the terms used: ἦε χόλον παύσειεν, 'or would check his rage' (*Il.*
1. 192): τις ἀθανάτων παῦσεν χόλον, 'one of the immortals
checked my rage' (*Il.* 9. 459)) diverts attention from the dis-
parate relationships of the agents in each. Phoenix is a son who
almost kills his father, and Achilles almost kills Agamemnon,
but while Agamemnon may be an authority figure, he is not
Achilles' father. The offer he makes to Achilles in the embassy
would, if accepted, make him Achilles' father-in-law. A father-
in-law may exercise a claim on his son-in-law, especially if he
has given a great deal with his daughter, but relationships by
marriage are not valued in the same way as the father–son relationship. From what we learn of Achilles' relationship with his
father (he values him so highly that his father's death would be
the only cause of grief he could envisage (*Il.* 16. 15–16)), it
seems most improbable that Achilles would ever contemplate
killing him. In inviting Achilles to identify with him as one who
avoided parricide only out of concern for public opinion,
Phoenix is almost asking for an adverse reaction.[117]

Phoenix, although he received entreaties to stay from his kin
λισσόμενοι (*Il.* 9. 465), and despite the fact that he was closely
guarded (*Il.* 9. 471), broke out of the θάλαμος, the chamber in
which he was confined, to flee from his father's house and his
community for a life of exile (*Il.* 9. 475–8).[118] The example of

---

[117] For the absolute revulsion felt by the Greeks towards parricide, see
Parker (1983: 124). Burkert (1983: 74–82; 1st pub. 1972) is more tolerant.
Certainly, in making Agamemnon the parallel to both Amyntor (Phoenix's
bad real father) and to Peleus (his good surrogate father), Phoenix has been
trying to present him to Achilles as an authority figure who has been bad, and
will now (if Achilles accepts the terms offered) be good. But Achilles will be
speaking of his father, whom he wants to choose a wife for him (*Il.* 9. 394) and
from whom he will receive possessions (*Il.* 9. 400) (this is the transfer of
wealth *inter vivos*, discussed by Redfield (1975: 111–12), such as must have
occurred between Laertes and Odysseus), so the invitation to regard
Agamemnon as an authority figure and as a munificent father-in-law is
doomed to failure. Brenk (1986: 81–3) discusses what he takes to be Phoenix's
miscalculation in taking the line that Agamemnon will be a father-figure for
Achilles, but a father-in-law is not a father, and Phoenix seriously under-
estimates the strength of Achilles' attachments to his father and home.

[118] Cf. Meges, who went away to Dulichium when he was angry with his
father (*Il.* 2. 629).

Phoenix's ignominious flight from the scene of the quarrel for a life without κλέος (glory) is aimed at preventing Achilles from leaving the scene of his quarrel with Agamemnon for the life without κλέος he has been contemplating (*Il.* 9. 415).[119] Achilles, who has on two occasions (*Il.* 1. 169–70; 9. 428–9) threatened to depart from the scene of his quarrel with Agamemnon, is even now being entreated to stay by the best of the Achaeans who have been sent to entreat (λίσσεσθαι) him (*Il.* 9. 520): if he goes, he will be leaving the army of the Greeks, never to return. But this is not at all the same thing as leaving one's father's house and community, as Phoenix did. If Achilles leaves the army to return to Greece, he will be reject- ing the life of an exile, which Phoenix chose, and returning home to his father, who will shower him with wealth and choose his bride for him, prerogatives which Achilles recog- nizes as his father's (*Il.* 9. 394–400), but not as Agamemnon's (*Il.* 9. 378–92). Phoenix describes how he fled from Hellas and came to Peleus as a fugitive; he received from him a kingdom on the borders of Phthia, becoming a wealthy man and lord of the Dolopes (*Il.* 9. 478–84), a situation which would carry an obligation towards the patron who had conferred on him this wealth and position.[120] Agamemnon would be establishing a very similar relationship with Achilles, were Achilles to accept the wealth and position offered in the terms extended for Achilles' return to battle.[121] In leaving his father's house to

---

[119] Scodel (1982: 133–4); Griffin (1995: 128–9 ad *Il.* 9. 447 ff.).

[120] Fugitives were frequently homicides or other criminals who had been obliged to leave their home communities to avoid becoming the victims of vengeance. See Leaf (1900–2: ii. 570–1 ad *Il.* 24. 480, 482): 'a homicide exiled from his own land and taking refuge with a chieftain among whose retainers he will enrol himself in return for sustenance and protection'. On Medon (*Il.* 13. 694–7 = *Il.* 15. 333–6); Lycophron (*Il.* 15. 430–9); Phoenix (*Il.* 9. 447–95); Epeigeus (*Il.* 16. 570–6); Tlepolemus (*Il.* 2. 661–70), all exiled for murder, see Strasburger (1954: 29–31). Phoenix entertains the idea of parricide, although he is prevented from committing it. His story is a 'variation on the homicide and flight theme', see Schlunk (1976: 199–209). Cf. Bellerophon, falsely accused of adultery, and accordingly banished (see 5.5.3).

[121] Achilles twice refers to Agamemnon's public appropriation of Briseis, which dishonoured Achilles as if he were an ἀτίμητος μετανάστης, a wanderer of no account (*Il.* 9. 648 = *Il.* 16. 59). See Leaf (1900–2: i. 418) ad *Il.* 9. 648 for the lack of honour of the μετανάστης; cf. Wace and Stubbings (1962: 434); and Adkins (1972: 14–15): 'the wanderer without *time* (*Iliad* IX 648) who has no

become an exile, Phoenix became dependent on the generosity of strangers: by a strange and convoluted logic, he is now presenting this option of 'inclusion in the sphere of others'[122] as highly desirable for Achilles. Phoenix rejected λιταί to stay in his own community, fled from the scene of the quarrel, and chose inclusion in the sphere of others: he is asking Achilles to assent to λιταί (to stay at the scene of the quarrel, away from his own community), and choose inclusion in the sphere of others.

Phoenix's attitude towards departure from the scene of the quarrel with the authority figure is quite inconsistent: he wants to present the choice of departure/exile as simultaneously a bad thing, and a good thing. It was a bad thing in the case of his own departure from Hellas, in that it was an irrevocable choice involving the rupture of the succession from father to son[123] (but the same will not be true of Achilles' departure from Troy, if he chooses to leave), and a good thing, in that he became rich through the generosity of a stranger, Peleus, who offered Phoenix the love a father gives his son (*Il.* 9. 481–2). By his assertion that Peleus loved him as a father loves his son, Phoenix is offering his own relationship with Peleus as an illustration (*Il.* 9. 284) of Agamemnon's promise (*Il.* 9. 142–3) that he will treat Achilles as he treats his own son, Orestes. Phoenix is trying to argue for the preference of surrogate relationships over real ones: he is attempting to persuade Achilles to give his loyalty to Agamemnon (as both an authority figure and a future father-in-law), rather than return to his own father, Peleus.[124]

position and no possessions, nowhere to lay his head save by favour of some others, and no means of securing his own continued existence. He may be harmed with impunity', like the fugitive Phoenix, who is a wanderer dependent on Achilles' father. A migrant dependent on Agamemnon for patronage, and watching the appropriation of Briseis, would hardly feel secure in the enjoyment of his wealth: rather, he would be in constant fear of having it taken back again, on some caprice. Agamemnon's established record on the reappropriation of booty distributed does not render his offer to Achilles of more booty, however lavish, an attractive prospect, since he appears to reserve the right to take it away again when it suits him.

[122] Redfield (1975: 16).

[123] For the importance of the father–son relationship, involving the transfer of status and property, see Redfield (1975: 110–13).

[124] Rosner (1976: 318) and Finley (1980: 269) go so far as to suggest that Phoenix is trying to persuade Achilles to accept adoption. While this is quite an extreme view, it looks very much as if Phoenix is inviting Achilles to con-

Phoenix goes on to widen the scope of substitute relationships: lacking a son of his own, he dandled the baby Achilles on his knees, cutting up his meat[125] and allowing him to dribble down his shirt, since the child would eat for no one else:

καί σε τοσοῦτον ἔθηκα, θεοῖς ἐπιείκελ' Ἀχιλλεῦ,   485
ἐκ θυμοῦ φιλέων, ἐπεὶ οὐκ ἐθέλεσκες ἅμ' ἄλλῳ
οὔτ' ἐς δαῖτ' ἰέναι οὔτ' ἐν μεγάροισι πάσασθαι,
πρίν γ' ὅτε δή σ' ἐπ' ἐμοῖσιν ἐγὼ γούνεσσι καθίσσας
ὄψου τ' ἄσαιμι προταμὼν καὶ οἶνον ἐπισχών.
πολλάκι μοι κατέδευσας ἐπὶ στήθεσσι χιτῶνα   490
οἴνου ἀποβλύζων ἐν νηπιέῃ ἀλεγεινῇ.
ὡς ἐπὶ σοὶ μάλα πόλλ' ἔπαθον καὶ πόλλ' ἐμόγησα,
τὰ φρονέων, ὅ μοι οὔ τι θεοὶ γόνον ἐξετέλειον
ἐξ ἐμεῦ· ἀλλὰ σὲ παῖδα, θεοῖς ἐπιείκελ' Ἀχιλλεῦ,
ποιεύμην, ἵνα μοί ποτ' ἀεικέα λοιγὸν ἀμύνῃς.   495

And I made as much of you, godlike Achilles,   485
loving you from my heart, since you never wanted with anyone else
either to go to the feast or to eat in the palace
before I set you on my knees
and fed you, cutting you the first piece of meat and holding wine to
    your lips.
And many a time you soaked the shirt on my breast   490
dribbling wine in your troublesome infancy.
So I went through a lot with you, and took a great deal of trouble,
thinking on the fact that the gods would never bring about a child for
    me
got from me. But I made you my son, godlike Achilles,
so that one day you would ward off unseemly destruction from me.

(Il. 9. 485–95)

sider a relationship which renders him subordinate to Agamemnon, and which would prejudice his relationship with his true father, not least in the matter of his marriage.

[125] Cf. *Od.* 16. 442–4, where the infant Eurymachus is set on Odysseus' knee and fed by him. Phoenix emphasizes (*Il.* 9. 488) setting the baby *on his knees*, harking back to the language of his father's curse, μή ποτε γούνασιν οἶσιν ἐφέσσεσθαι φίλον υἱὸν | ἐξ ἐμέθεν γεγαῶτα, 'that he should never set on his knees a son born from me' (*Il.* 9. 455–6), and emphasizing that Achilles became the son Phoenix never had. In asking Achilles for the favour of returning to battle, Phoenix needs to establish that Achilles is under an obligation to him. The obligation arises from having been Achilles' tutor. This detail may be an invention by the poet, since other versions make Chiron the tutor of Achilles: see Braswell (1971: 22 n. 3).

In alluding to this past intimacy, Phoenix implies that Achilles is in the position of a surrogate son to him (*Il.* 9. 494–5) and has a corresponding obligation to defend him. Phoenix's language:

ἵνα μοί ποτ' ἀεικέα λοιγὸν ἀμύνῃς

so that you would ward off unseemly destruction from me

(*Il.* 9. 495)

closely resembles that used by Priam in describing the troubles of an aged father in the absence of his son:

οὐδέ τίς ἐστιν ἀρὴν καὶ λοιγὸν ἀμῦναι

nor is there anyone to ward off war and destruction.

(*Il.* 24. 489)

It is a son's duty to defend his father in old age,[126] and Phoenix, in attempting to establish his position as a family friend who made Achilles the substitute for the son he never had, is implying that Achilles has a duty to defend him (and if it means he defends the rest of the Greeks as well, that is, for the moment, incidental). Because of his special, almost paternal[127] relationship with Achilles, Phoenix feels able to offer advice in his own persona, whereas others who offer advice feel constrained to attribute it to the addressee's father,[128] even if it sounds as if it has been invented and put into his father's mouth for the immediate occasion.[129]

---

[126] *Il.* 24. 488–9, 540–2. Hesiod, *Op.* 185–8; see also Vickers (1973: 113). For discussion of Achilles' anxiety (*Od.* 11. 494–7; cf *Il.* 19. 334–7), that the aged Peleus may be driven out by usurpers, for lack of a son to defend him, see Edwards (1985: 53–7).

[127] Lohmann (1970: 249–50): as Peleus loved Phoenix like a son, so Phoenix loved Achilles like a son: this is the significance of τοσοῦτον, thus much (*Il.* 9. 485). (It does not necessarily refer, as Lohmann suggests, to καί με ἀφνειὸν ἔθηκε, πολὺν δέ μοι ὤπασε λαόν, 'and he made me rich, and made me leader over many' (*Il.* 9. 483), since there is no evidence that Phoenix was in a position to treat Achilles in this way.)

[128] For other examples of a father's advice, see *Il.* 5. 197–200; 6. 207–11. Hainsworth (1993: 306–7 ad *Il.* 11. 782) indicates how the motif could be varied by citing not what the father had said, but what he would say if he knew how badly he was being let down (e.g. *Il.* 7. 125).

[129] As in Odysseus' speech (*Il.* 9. 252–9), Nestor 'reminds' Patroclus (*Il.* 11. 785–90) that Menoetius told him he should offer guidance to Achilles, and goes on to suggest the kind of advice Patroclus should be giving: he should encourage Achilles to fight (but this is not plainly expressed), or, if Achilles has some reason not to, Patroclus should ask for his armour to wear on the

7.2.3. Advice from a surrogate

After carefully establishing his right to offer such advice,
Phoenix counsels Achilles to control his anger (*Il.* 9. 496): even
the gods permit themselves to change their minds (*Il.* 9. 497);
men λισσόμενοι can deflect them with prayers and sacrifices (*Il.*
9. 499–500); and their ἀρετή τιμή τε βίη τε, 'quality, honour,
and force', are even greater (*Il.* 9. 498), so there is no need to
worry about appearing indecisive if one changes one's mind in
response to λιταί. The αἶνος of the Λιταί (quoted 7.1.6 above),
with its personification of the abstract concepts of Λιταί and
Ἄτη, is followed by a bridge passage, underlining the relevance
of the αἶνος.[130] Like the one who reverences the Prayers and is
benefited by them in 508–9 of the αἶνος, Achilles too should
permit honour to the daughters of Zeus,

> ἀλλ', Ἀχιλεῦ, πόρε καὶ σὺ Διὸς κούρῃσιν ἕπεσθαι
> τιμήν, ἥ τ' ἄλλων περ ἐπιγνάμπτει νόον ἐσθλῶν.
> εἰ μὲν γὰρ μὴ δῶρα φέροι, τὰ δ' ὄπισθ' ὀνομάζοι   515
> Ἀτρεΐδης, ἀλλ' αἰὲν ἐπιζαφελῶς χαλεπαίνοι,
> οὐκ ἂν ἔγωγέ σε μῆνιν ἀπορρίψαντα κελοίμην
> Ἀργείοισιν ἀμυνέμεναι χατέουσί περ ἔμπης·
> νῦν δ' ἅμα τ' αὐτίκα πολλὰ διδοῖ, τὰ δ' ὄπισθεν ὑπέστη,
> ἄνδρας δὲ λίσσεσθαι ἐπιπροέηκεν ἀρίστους   520
> κρινάμενος κατὰ λαὸν Ἀχαιϊκόν, οἵ τε σοὶ αὐτῷ
> φίλτατοι Ἀργείων· τῶν μὴ σύ γε μῦθον ἐλέγξῃς
> μηδὲ πόδας· πρὶν δ' οὔ τι νεμεσσητὸν κεχολῶσθαι.

But permit, Achilles, you too, honour to attend on the daughters of
Zeus
which bends the resolve of other noble men.

battlefield (*Il.* 11. 790–801). Phoenix says he was charged by Peleus (*Il.* 9.
438–43) to teach Achilles μύθων τε ῥητῆρ' ἔμεναι πρηκτῆρά τε ἔργων, 'to be a
speaker of words and a doer of deeds'. For discussion of these conversations in
Phthia before the start of the war, see Willcock (1977: 46–9). Finley (1980) discusses Phoenix and Patroclus as Achilles' mentors at Troy, but he mistakenly
elevates the claims of father-substitutes to the status of rights. I think he is also
mistaken in regarding Patroclus as a father-substitute to Achilles: their relationship is one of colleagues. Both fathers, Peleus and Menoetius, are said to
offer instructions to their sons, and the advice Menoetius wants his son to give
to Achilles (because Patroclus is older than Achilles) is described as παραίφασις
ἑταίρου, the advice of a comrade (*Il.* 11. 793).

[130] Phoenix would not have been able to say these things to Achilles without
the vehicle of the αἶνος: see Reinhardt (1960b: 37–8).

For if the son of Atreus were not offering gifts, and promising others
   for the future,   515
but continuously remained swollen with choler,
I would not bid you to cast aside your anger
and defend the Greeks, although they are in need.
But now at the same time he is willing to give many straightway, and
   promises others later,
and he has sent the best men to entreat you,   520
picking out from the Greek army those who are
the dearest of the Greeks to you. Do not you expose to contempt
   either their words
or their coming. Before it was not a matter for indignation that you
   were angry.

$$(Il. 9. 513–23)$$

Phoenix would not ask Achilles to return if Agamemnon were
not offering gifts and promising more at the fall of Troy (*Il.* 9.
515–19),[131] but since he is offering them and has sent the best of
the Achaeans to entreat (λίσσεσθαι) (*Il.* 9. 520–1), Achilles
should not dishonour either what they say, or the fact that they
have come (*Il.* 9. 522–3), but emulate the one who reverences
the Λιταί when they come near (*Il.* 9. 508–9). Until the arrival
of the ambassadors λισσόμενοι (like the Λιταί which apply a cure
after Ἄτη (*Il.* 9. 507)), it was not a matter for indignation,
νεμεσσητόν, that Achilles was angry (*Il.* 9. 523) but now it is, or
will be if his anger continues, since even a god would allow
himself to be persuaded by such an approach: Achilles will be
honoured like a god[132] if he comes for the gifts. To hold out for

___

[131] Lohmann (1970: 253) athetizes *Il.* 9. 515–23 on the grounds that they
destroy the sequence: the gods are persuadable by sacrifice and prayers (*Il.* 9.
497–501); heroes are similarly persuadable by gifts and words (*Il.* 9. 524–6);
we should now pass effortlessly to the individual example, introduced by
μέμνημαι (*Il.* 9. 527), of Meleager. The trouble with this idea is that Meleager
is an individual example of a hero who was *not* persuaded by gifts, and who
held out for rather a long time before he allowed himself to be persuaded by
words. Hainsworth (1993: 130 ad *Il.* 9. 524–605) points out that Artemis, as
she appears in the Homeric story of Meleager, is not particularly amenable to
persuasion. *Il.* 9. 515–23 are quite logical as they stand, because the individual
persuaded by gifts and words is to be not Meleager, but Achilles: Phoenix
makes clear that the gifts and entreaties which have now been introduced into
the business should persuade Achilles as they would persuade the heroes of *Il.*
9. 524–6. Even the gods can be persuaded with gifts and prayers (*Il.* 9.
497–501): Phoenix is implying 'how can you hold out for more?'

[132] ἶσον γάρ σε θεῷ τείσουσιν Ἀχαιοί, 'for the Greeks will honour you like a

more, Phoenix implies, would be to seek to overstep human limitations.[133]

7.2.4. The paradigm of Meleager

As a kind of counterweight to the incident from his own past, his quarrel with an authority figure about a woman, Phoenix goes on, after the αἶνος which forms the centrepiece of his speech, to tell the story of Meleager, a hero who might have fought at Troy, but who was dead before the expedition set sail (*Il.* 2. 642):

---

god' (*Il.* 9. 603): cf. οἵ σε θεὸν ὡς | τείσουσ', 'who will honour you like a god' (*Il.* 9. 302–3). Odysseus' earlier advice, supposedly from Peleus, is also relevant: ληγέμεναι δ' ἔριδος κακομηχάνου, ὄφρα σε μᾶλλον | τίωσ' Ἀργείων ἠμὲν νέοι, ἠδὲ γέροντες, 'desist from mischief-plotting strife, so that both young and old of the Argives may honour you the more' (*Il.* 9. 257–8).

[133] Achilles will suffer as a result of rejecting the λιταί of the ambassadors, as we know. For discussion of whether he is morally wrong to reject the embassy, see Lloyd-Jones (1971: 18–19): the ambassadors think they *ought* to persuade Achilles, and Achilles seems to agree with them when he says that Ajax's speech is in accordance with his own θυμός (*Il.* 9. 645). Adkins (1971: 9) points out that Achilles could not yield to Agamemnon in book 1 without being δειλός and οὐτιδανός: Rowe (1983: 263) argues that when proper compensation is offered, to give ground would involve nothing more than Poseidon's concession to the superior status of Zeus (*Il.* 15. 211). At *Il.* 15. 203 Poseidon is advised to yield because the minds of the noble are flexible: στρεπταὶ μέν τε φρένες ἐσθλῶν. If Achilles is inflexible, he ceases, according to Rowe, to be ἐσθλός (noble). However, Rowe forgets that at *Il.* 9. 471, the context which deals with Achilles, it is not men, but the gods who are described as ἐσθλοί. Crotty (1994: 33) believes shame should limit Achilles' thirst for vengeance and render him content with the compensation offered, following Ajax's analogy with acceptance of compensation even from the killer of a brother or child (*Il.* 9. 632–6); cf. Fisher (1992: 179): Achilles' trouble is an over-readiness to tolerate the misfortunes of others in pursuit of his quarrel with Agamemnon. In terms of the αἶνος of the Λιταί, Achilles is wrong to reject the λιταί of the ambassadors on behalf of the Greeks. He is overconfident that the gods will continue to support him even after they have fulfilled their promise to make things go badly for the Greeks, so that Agamemnon will become aware of his mistake in dishonouring Achilles. The kind of impasse reached in the quarrel between Agamemnon and Achilles is reflected in the scene on the shield of Achilles showing a murderer saying that he can repay everything, while the dead man's relative refuses to accept anything (Andersen 1976): see also Muellner (1976: 105–6) and 3.3.1 above. The refusal to accept compensation can be understood as a matter of honour: Bourdieu (1955: 216).

οὕτω καὶ τῶν πρόσθεν ἐπευθόμεθα κλέα ἀνδρῶν
ἡρώων, ὅτε κέν τιν᾽ ἐπιζάφελος χόλος ἵκοι·   525
δωρητοί τε πέλοντο παράρρητοί τ᾽ ἐπέεσσι.
μέμνημαι τόδε ἔργον ἐγὼ πάλαι, οὔ τι νέον γε,
ὡς ἦν· ἐν δ᾽ ὑμῖν ἐρέω πάντεσσι φίλοισι.
Κουρῆτές τ᾽ ἐμάχοντο καὶ Αἰτωλοὶ μενεχάρμαι
ἀμφὶ πόλιν Καλυδῶνα καὶ ἀλλήλους ἐνάριζον   530
Αἰτωλοὶ μὲν ἀμυνόμενοι Καλυδῶνος ἐραννῆς,
Κουρῆτες δὲ διαπραθέειν μεμαῶτες Ἄρηϊ.
καὶ γὰρ τοῖσι κακὸν χρυσόθρονος Ἄρτεμις ὦρσε,
χωσαμένη ὅ οἱ οὔ τι θαλύσια γουνῷ ἀλωῆς
Οἰνεὺς ῥέξ᾽· ἄλλοι δὲ θεοὶ δαίνυνθ᾽ ἑκατόμβας,   535
οἴῃ δ᾽ οὐκ ἔρρεξε Διὸς κούρῃ μεγάλοιο.
ἢ λάθετ᾽ ἢ οὐκ ἐνόησεν· ἀάσατο δὲ μέγα θυμῷ.
ἡ δὲ χολωσαμένη δῖον γένος ἰοχέαιρα
ὦρσεν ἔπι χλούνην σῦν ἄγριον ἀγριόδοντα,
ὃς κακὰ πόλλ᾽ ἔρδεσκεν ἔθων Οἰνῆος ἀλωήν·   540
πολλὰ δ᾽ ὅ γε προθέλυμνα χαμαὶ βάλε δένδρεα μακρὰ
αὐτῇσιν ῥίζῃσιν καὶ αὐτοῖς ἄνθεσι μήλων.
τὸν δ᾽ υἱὸς Οἰνῆος ἀπέκτεινεν Μελέαγρος,
πολλέων ἐκ πολίων θηρήτορας ἄνδρας ἀγείρας
καὶ κύνας· οὐ μὲν γάρ κ᾽ ἐδάμη παύροισι βροτοῖσι·   545
τόσσος ἔην, πολλοὺς δὲ πυρῆς ἐπέβησ᾽ ἀλεγεινῆς.
ἡ δ᾽ ἀμφ᾽ αὐτῷ θῆκε πολὺν κέλαδον καὶ ἀϋτήν,
ἀμφὶ συὸς κεφαλῇ καὶ δέρματι λαχνήεντι,
Κουρήτων τε μεσηγὺ καὶ Αἰτωλῶν μεγαθύμων.
ὄφρα μὲν οὖν Μελέαγρος ἀρηΐφιλος πολέμιζε,   550
τόφρα δὲ Κουρήτεσσι κακῶς ἦν, οὐδ᾽ ἐδύναντο
τείχεος ἔκτοσθεν μίμνειν πολέες περ ἐόντες·
ἀλλ᾽ ὅτε δὴ Μελέαγρον ἔδυ χόλος, ὅς τε καὶ ἄλλων
οἰδάνει ἐν στήθεσσι νόον πύκα περ φρονεόντων,
ἤτοι ὁ μητρὶ φίλῃ Ἀλθαίῃ χωόμενος κῆρ   555
κεῖτο παρὰ μνηστῇ ἀλόχῳ, καλῇ Κλεοπάτρῃ,
κούρῃ Μαρπήσσης καλλισφύρου Εὐηνίνης
Ἴδεώ θ᾽, ὃς κάρτιστος ἐπιχθονίων γένετ᾽ ἀνδρῶν
τῶν τότε—καί ῥα ἄνακτος ἐναντίον εἵλετο τόξον
Φοίβου Ἀπόλλωνος καλλισφύρου εἵνεκα νύμφης·   560
τὴν δὲ τότ᾽ ἐν μεγάροισι πατὴρ καὶ πότνια μήτηρ
Ἀλκυόνην καλέεσκον ἐπώνυμον, οὕνεκ᾽ ἄρ᾽ αὐτῆς
μήτηρ ἀλκυόνος πολυπενθέος οἶτον ἔχουσα
κλαῖεν ὅ μιν ἑκάεργος ἀνήρπασε Φοῖβος Ἀπόλλων—
τῇ ὅ γε παρκατέλεκτο χόλον θυμαλγέα πέσσων,   565
ἐξ ἀρέων μητρὸς κεχολωμένος, ἥ ῥα θεοῖσι

πόλλ' ἀχέουσ' ἠρᾶτο κασιγνήτοιο φόνοιο,
πολλὰ δὲ καὶ γαῖαν πολυφόρβην χερσὶν ἀλοία
κικλήσκουσ' Ἀΐδην καὶ ἐπαινὴν Περσεφόνειαν,
πρόχνυ καθεζομένη, δεύοντο δὲ δάκρυσι κόλποι,   570
παιδὶ δόμεν θάνατον· τῆς δ' ἠεροφοῖτις Ἐρινὺς
ἔκλυεν ἐξ Ἐρέβεσφιν, ἀμείλιχον ἦτορ ἔχουσα.
τῶν δὲ τάχ' ἀμφὶ πύλας ὅμαδος καὶ δοῦπος ὀρώρει
πύργων βαλλομένων· τὸν δὲ λίσσοντο γέροντες
Αἰτωλῶν, πέμπον δὲ θεῶν ἱερῆας ἀρίστους   575
ἐξελθεῖν καὶ ἀμῦναι, ὑποσχόμενοι μέγα δῶρον·
ὁππόθι πιότατον πεδίον Καλυδῶνος ἐραννῆς,
ἔνθα μιν ἤνωγον τέμενος περικαλλὲς ἑλέσθαι
πεντηκοντόγυον, τὸ μὲν ἥμισυ οἰνοπέδοιο,
ἥμισυ δὲ ψιλὴν ἄροσιν πεδίοιο ταμέσθαι.   580
πολλὰ δέ μιν λιτάνευε γέρων ἱππηλάτα Οἰνεὺς
οὐδοῦ ἐπεμβεβαὼς ὑψηρεφέος θαλάμοιο,
σείων κολλητὰς σανίδας, γουνούμενος υἱόν·
πολλὰ δὲ τόν γε κασίγνηται καὶ πότνια μήτηρ
ἐλλίσσονθ'· ὁ δὲ μᾶλλον ἀναίνετο· πολλὰ δ' ἑταῖροι   585
οἵ οἱ κεδνότατοι καὶ φίλτατοι ἦσαν ἁπάντων·
ἀλλ' οὐδ' ὣς τοῦ θυμὸν ἐνὶ στήθεσσιν ἔπειθον,
πρίν γ' ὅτε δὴ θάλαμος πύκ' ἐβάλλετο, τοὶ δ' ἐπὶ πύργων
βαῖνον Κουρῆτες καὶ ἐνέπρηθον μέγα ἄστυ.
καὶ τότε δὴ Μελέαγρον ἐΰζωνος παράκοιτις   590
λίσσετ' ὀδυρομένη, καί οἱ κατέλεξεν ἅπαντα
κήδε', ὅσ' ἀνθρώποισι πέλει τῶν ἄστυ ἁλώῃ·
ἄνδρας μὲν κτείνουσι, πόλιν δέ τε πῦρ ἀμαθύνει,
τέκνα δέ τ' ἄλλοι ἄγουσι βαθυζώνους τε γυναῖκας.
τοῦ δ' ὠρίνετο θυμὸς ἀκούοντος κακὰ ἔργα,   595
βῆ δ' ἰέναι, χροῒ δ' ἔντε' ἐδύσετο παμφανόωντα.
ὣς ὁ μὲν Αἰτωλοῖσιν ἀπήμυνεν κακὸν ἦμαρ
εἴξας ᾧ θυμῷ· τῷ δ' οὐκέτι δῶρ' ἐτέλεσσαν
πολλά τε καὶ χαρίεντα, κακὸν δ' ἤμυνε καὶ αὔτως.

So too we hear about the famous deeds of men of old
when furious anger came over someone: 525
they were amenable to gifts and open to persuasion in words.
I remember this story from long ago, nor is it recent,
how it was: I will tell it among you who are all friends.
The Couretes and the Aetolians staunch in battle were fighting
around the city of Calydon and they were slaying one another,   530
the Aetolians defending lovely Calydon
but the Couretes eager to sack it for Ares.

For Artemis of the golden throne stirred up evil for them,
angry that Oeneus did not offer the first fruits of his orchard
to her. The other gods partook of hecatombs,   535
but to the daughter of Zeus alone he did not perform them.
Either he forgot, or he never thought of it, but he erred greatly in his
    heart.
But she was angry, the divinely born pourer of arrows,
and stirred up to forage a wild boar with savage tusks
which kept on doing much damage ravaging the orchard of Oeneus.
It hurled many tall trees on the ground, torn up   541
roots and all, flowers of the apples and all.
Meleager, the son of Oeneus, slew it,
gathering many hunting men from many cities
with their dogs. For it would not be subdued by a few men,   545
it was so big, and it set many men on the sorrowful pyre.
And she made a great confusion and uproar about it
about the head and shaggy hide of the boar,
between the Couretes and the great-hearted Aetolians.
As long as Meleager, dear to Ares, was fighting,   550
so long did it go badly for the Couretes, nor were they able
to remain outside the wall, although they were many.
But when Meleager assumed his anger, which swells the heart
in the breast of others too, even though they think wisely,
surely angry at heart with his dear mother, Althaea,   555
he lay beside his wedded wife, the fair Cleopatra,
the daughter of Marpessa of the fair ankles, daughter of Euenos,
and Idas, who was the strongest of mortal men
at that time—and indeed he drew his bow against lord Phoebus Apollo
for the sake of his bride of the fair ankles.   560
Her father and her lady mother in the palace then
always called her by the name Alcyone, since for her sake
her mother mourned having the lot of the plaintive kingfisher
because Apollo, the far shooter, snatched her away—
beside her he lay brooding on his grievous anger   565
enraged by the curses of his mother, who prayed to the gods
grieving much for the murder of her brother,
and many times she cudgelled the bountiful earth with her hands
calling on Hades and lovely Persephone,
going right down on her knees, her bosom drenched with tears,   570
to give death to her son: and the Fury who walks in darkness,
whose heart is relentless, heard her from the depths of Hell.
Soon the din and thud was in the air around the gates
of the towers under assault. The elders of the Aetolians

were entreating him (and they sent the best priests) 575
to come out and defend them, promising him a great gift:
wherever the plain of lovely Calydon was richest,
there they bade him take a very beautiful estate
of fifty acres, half of it vineyard,
and half open arable land of the plain to be ploughed. 580
The old man, the horseman, Oeneus, entreated him again and again,
standing on the threshold of the high-roofed chamber,
rattling the panelled doors, supplicating his son by his knees:
again and again his sisters and his lady mother entreated him,
but he refused all the more. And again and again his companions,
who were the closest and dearest to him of all: 586
but not even so did they persuade the heart in his breast,
until at last his chamber came under heavy bombardment, and the
     Couretes
were climbing on the towers and they were setting fire to the great
     city.
And at that point, of all times, his fair-girdled wife entreated Meleager
in tears, and she listed for him all the sufferings 591
as many as there are for men whose town is captured.
They kill the men, and fire turns the city to ashes,
and strangers carry off the children and deep-girdled women.
And she swayed his passion as he heard the sad story, 595
and he went to go, and he put his shining armour on his body.
And so he warded off the evil day from the Aetolians,
after yielding to his passion. But for him they no longer made good
their many and delightful gifts, but he warded off evil all the same.

(Il. 9. 524–99)

Meleager's father, Oeneus, the king of Calydon, sacrificed first-
fruits to all the gods, but omitted Artemis, either because he
forgot, or because it never crossed his mind at all (*Il.* 9. 537).
Artemis was angry,[134] and sent a boar to ravage the crops.
Meleager killed it, and gave the spoils to Atalanta, but his relatives reappropriated them.[135] The quarrel over the spoils[136]
resulted in a battle between the Aetolians of Calydon and their

---

[134] Artemis' anger at the slight of Oeneus' neglect resembles Apollo's anger
at Agamemnon's treatment of his priest, Chryses, in book 1: see Lord (1967:
243); Petzhold (1976: 154–5 n. 33).

[135] Apollodorus, 1. 8. 2–3.

[136] Swain (1988: 271–6; esp. 274): the audience is expected to associate the
quarrel over spoil in the story of Meleager with the quarrel between
Agamemnon and Achilles over spoil in book 1.

neighbours, the Couretes. As long as Meleager fought in defence of Calydon, the Couretes were unable to hold a position outside the walls of the city (*Il.* 9. 551–2),[137] but Meleager, in defending Calydon, killed one of his mother's brothers (possibly more than one).[138] Meleager's mother cursed her son and prayed for his death: outraged, the hero retired from the battle and lay beside his wife in his bedchamber, refusing to respond to the increasingly urgent appeals of the succession of visitors who entreated him to return and fight in their defence. First came the priests (sent by the elders) with the offer of a rich estate; then Meleager's father, followed by his mother and sisters, then his dearest friends. At last, when the Couretes had scaled the towers and were setting fire to the town, and even the chamber where Meleager lay with his wife, Cleopatra, was under bombardment, Cleopatra, in tears, enumerated to him the sufferings of the inhabitants of a captured city, and moved him by her appeal. Meleager took up arms and saved the city, but, as Phoenix tells the tale, his fellow-citizens no longer cared

[137] Achilles reminds Odysseus (*Il.* 9. 352–3) that as long as he, Achilles, was fighting, Hector had no desire to fight away from his wall.

[138] *Il.* 9. 567 mentions one anonymous brother, but Sch. A ad *Il.* 9. 567 (from Aristonicus) (= Erbse (1969–88: ii. 521), 567d¹) says there may be more brothers, and other scholiasts to 567 interpret κασιγνήτοιο φόνοιο as generic: κασιγνητικοῦ; Sch. A ad *Il.* 9. 567 (from Herodian) (= Erbse (1969–88: ii. 521), 567a) (at this same reference, the D-scholia list Althaea's brothers as Iphiclus, Polyphantes, Phanes, Eurypylus, Plexippus): ἀδελφικοῦ; Sch. A ad *Il.* 9. 567 (from Didymus) (= Erbse (1969–88: ii. 521), 567c¹). The two murdered brothers are named as Clytius and Procaon: Sch. T ad *Il.* 9. 567 (= Erbse (1969–88: ii. 521), 567b). Most accounts refer to two brothers: Bacchylides, 5. 128–9 gives their names as Iphiclus and Aphares: Apollodorus, 1. 8. 3, τοὺς μὲν Θεστίου παῖδας ἀπέκτεινε, 'he killed the sons of Thestius', but no names are given. The two brothers of Althaea who appear on the gable of the temple of Athene at Tegea are named by Pausanias as Prothous and Cometes (Pausanias, 8. 45. 6) but it does not follow that these were the ones killed by Meleager, and Pausanias might be mistaken in taking them for the sons of Thestius. In Hyginus, 244. 1, and Lactantius Placidus on Statius, *Theb.* 2. 481 and 4. 103, the brothers killed are Plexippus and Agenor. For fuller discussion, see Robert (1920: 89 n. 6). The relationship of maternal uncle to nephew is one of patronage: see Pembroke (1965). On the significance of killing one's maternal uncle (an authority-figure), see Bremmer (1983: 178–86). There is nothing in the Homeric account to suggest that the murdered uncle(s) fought on the side of the Couretes and lived in Calydon: Bacchylides, 5. 132–5 and 149–51 is the first to suggest they did; see March (1987: 36–7).

to award him gifts.[139] Meleager is an example of a hero who laid
aside his anger, as Achilles is being asked to do, but the point of
telling this story to Achilles is to urge him not to follow the
example of Meleager too exactly:[140] he should return to fight
now, and for the gifts; he should not, like Meleager, return at
the very last moment, when the offer of gifts is past. If he
delays, he may well succeed in defending the Greeks, but he
will not receive the same honour as if he had accepted the gifts
(*Il.* 9. 604–5). The story of Meleager is not told to illustrate the
αἶνος of the Λιταί, since we hear nothing of any visitation by
ἄτη after Meleager's repeated refusal of the λιταί of his earlier
visitors.

The first part of the story (*Il.* 9. 529–49) which tells how the
quarrel between the Aetolians and Couretes arose, is highly
compressed, suggesting the tale is familiar to the audience, but
the second part, dealing with Meleager's anger, is far more
detailed, and is not told elsewhere, except in sources influenced
by the Homeric account.[141] The story as it is told in the *Iliad* is
fairly closely analogous to Achilles' circumstances in book 9:
like Meleager, Achilles has had a quarrel over division of spoils,
as a result of which he will not fight for his community; like
Meleager, he remains shut away with a single companion; and
like Meleager, Achilles receives visitors who offer him gifts if
only he will lay aside his anger and fight in their defence.[142]

[139] Phoenix's version of Meleager's story recalls the account of Bellerophon
by Nymphis of Heraclea summarized by Plutarch (*FGrH* 432 F 7= Plutarch,
Mor. 248d): a wild boar ravaged the territory of Xanthus until Bellerophon
killed it. When he received no reward for this, he turned to Poseidon and
cursed the people of Xanthus. The land was covered in salt and the soil
became barren. Bellerophon was finally moved by the prayers of the women,
and asked Poseidon to avert his anger. For a more sensational version, in
which a wave engulfs Lycia, and Bellerophon is shamed (by the women lifting
their skirts at him) into abandoning his anger, see Plutarch, *Mor.* 248a–b.

[140] The story is told to Achilles as an αἶνος, to convey a warning in a diplomatic way: cf. *Od.* 14. 459–509, Hesiod, *Op.* 202–12: Macleod (1983: 170).
However, since Meleager rejects the λιταί of so many visitors, he is not the
most logical illustration of the heroes of old, who were, Phoenix says, δωρητοί
. . . παράρρητοί τ᾽ ἐπέεσσι, 'open to gifts . . . and to persuasion by words' (*Il.* 9.
526).

[141] Willcock (1964: 151).

[142] The parallels between the stories of Meleager and Achilles are discussed
by Lord (1967: 243) (anger of Artemis/anger of Apollo); Whitfield (1967: 99);
Lohmann (1970: 260–1) (the story of Meleager is closely paralleled by the

Phoenix presents Meleager as an example of someone who was offered the opportunity of laying aside his quarrel in return for gifts: he passes up the gifts, but the time eventually comes when he has to do the thing for which the inducements were offered, only by now they are no longer on offer.[143] In simple terms, he is presented with the opportunity of doing something in return for an inducement: he refuses the inducement, only to find he has to do as he was asked anyway, but without the inducement. We have already seen this happen to Agamemnon, who initially refused to accept a ransom to return Chryseis to her father, but was compelled to return her without receiving a ransom, to avert the plague sent by Apollo: now it is happening to Meleager in Phoenix's story, and we are, by implication (*Il.* 9. 524–5), being invited to consider the possibility of it happening to Achilles (as it surely will). Phoenix invites Achilles to avoid this eventuality by taking the opportunity of returning immediately and enriched by the gifts (*Il.* 9. 602–3).

7.2.5. Meleager's story adapted: from competing disloyalties to ascending scale of affection

The story of Meleager as told by Phoenix has attracted a great deal of scholarly attention; more, in fact, than any other secondary narrative in the poems.[144] This is because two other versions of the story exist which differ radically from the

situation in the *Iliad* at the end of book 8); Rosner (1976) (quarrel over concubine, murder attempt). Bannert (1981: 69–94) also gives a number of parallels (produced by references to χόλος and λίσσεσθαι) between the story of Phoenix's youth and the Meleager story; the story of Phoenix's youth produces a first evocation of the idea of wrath leading to disaster; the anger of Phoenix's father is akin to the anger of Meleager's mother.

[143] Crotty (1994: 52) takes the story of Meleager as a warning against ἔλεος, pity: 'You will ultimately fight out of *eleos* for those dearest to you, and if you wait until that happens, you will fight without compensation. Better to fight now and name your price.' This is quite close to the mark, but Meleager eventually fights, not only out of *eleos* for Cleopatra, but also out of necessity (see 7.2.7 below).

[144] For full modern bibliography, see Bremmer (1988) (but he is overconfident that the Homeric account of the story of Meleager is drawn from a pre-existing epic source); see March (1987). Homer did not invent Meleager, but surely invented many of the details of the story about him in book 9 in order to achieve parallels with the situation of Achilles.

The Paradigm of Meleager

Homeric version, whose form appears to be determined by the need for a parallel to Achilles' situation. In one of these versions, Meleager is killed by Apollo.[145] The other version[146] concerns a woman who finds herself in possession of a stick,[147] which is the life-token of her son. When the mother finds that

[145] The ancient evidence for this version is Pausanias, 10. 31. 3 quoting [Hesiod], fr. 25, 12–13 M–W (cf. *Katabasis of Peirithous*, fr. 280, 2 M–W), and the *Minyas*, fr. 3 Davies (1988: 144) (= fr. 5 Bernabé (1988: 138)). Willcock (1964: 153–4) discusses three papyrus fragments of versions where Apollo kills Meleager. Bremmer and March are convinced that these epic accounts were the source for the Homeric account of the story of Meleager (see also Howald (1924: 408); Kraus (1948: 11); Von der Mühll (1952: 177 n. 49)). It is true that Meleager's death at the hands of Apollo makes a good parallel for Achilles' death at the hands of Apollo (*Il.* 21. 275–8) (or Apollo and Paris (*Il.* 19. 416–17; 22. 359–60) but the poet may well have been simultaneously aware also of the versions mentioned in n. 148, and have chosen to exploit the reverberations of both stories, without giving an account of either. It is important to remember that Homer reveals nothing about Meleager's death, beyond the information that his mother prayed for it, and the Fury in Hades heard her prayer (*Il.* 9. 571–2).

[146] Thought by Kakridis (1949: 127–48) to have its origins in a folk-tale dealing with death by sympathetic magic: a woman, approaching the end of her child-bearing years, and having lost all her earlier children, is determined to keep her present child. When the child is three days old, the mother pretends to be asleep so that she can listen to the pronouncements of the Fates, who always visit on the third day after the birth of a child. The first Fate says the child will be handsome, the second says he will be rich, and the third, who is malevolent, says he will last only as long as the stick burning in the hearth is not consumed. The Fates vanish, the mother rushes out of bed, quenches the stick, wraps it in a cloth, and keeps it in a chest, protecting it as the life-token of her son.

[147] The stick removed from the fire to save the baby's life in the 'folk-tale' version of the story of Meleager bears a close resemblance to accounts of the baby Achilles seized from the fire by his father, Peleus, when his mother, Thetis, was burning out his mortal parts: Apollodorus, 3. 13 6; Sch. Aristophanes, *Nu.* 1068; both Sch. Apollonius Rhodius, 4. 816 (= Hesiod, *fr.* 300 M–W) and Lycophron, *Alexandra* 176–8 also mention the alternative method of dropping babies into basins of water to see if they are mortal. See also Sch. Tzetzes ad Lycophron, *Alexandra* 178; Ptolemaeus Chennos in Westermann (1843: 195). The motif of snatching the baby off the fire to frustrate attempts to burn out the mortal parts is found also in *h. Cer.* 239–62: for discussion see Richardson (1974: 237–8) on 237 ff. and Lord (1967: 246). The motif may be connected with the practice of putting on the fire a baby thought to be a changeling: the fairies always rescue the changeling and return the mortal baby, Frazer (1921: ii. 311–17); Ulster Folk and Transport Museum archive recording c76.43 (transcribed in UFTM Archive: Field Transcripts, vol. ii).

her son (Meleager) has killed her brothers in defence of
Calydon, she throws the log on the fire and Meleager falls down
dead as the stick is consumed.[148] The story is found in a number
of ancient sources.[149] In these versions, Meleager has no warn-

[148] Despite Bremmer (1988: 45–6) (who thinks it no earlier than the 6th
cent. BC), and March (1987: 43), this story of the stick is generally accepted as
the oldest version of Meleager's death: see Willcock (1964: 152 n. 1). For the
view that the folk-story of Meleager's death by burning the stick was heavily
adapted by the poet of the *Iliad*, who introduced the motifs of the mother's
curse, the hero's anger and withdrawal from battle in response to the curse,
and the culmination of a series of requests in the request of the hero's wife, to
make Phoenix's version of the story of Meleager resemble the story of
Achilles, see Willcock (1964: 152 n. 5), where he lists Robert (1920: 91);
Drerup (1921: 66); Bethe (1925: 11); Schadewaldt (1966: 141 n. 4; 1st pub.
1938); Noé (1940: 72–83); Von der Mühll (1952: 176). More recently, see
Heubeck (1974*b*: 533); Petzhold (1976: 153–5); Swain (1988). The compres-
sion of the narrative at *Il.* 9. 529–49 and its allusive style has led to the conclusion that the poet must be abbreviating an already existing poem well
known to the audience: see Willcock (1964: 149 n. 1); Swain (1988). The close
resemblance of the story of Meleager's anger in Phoenix's version to the
Iliadic account of Achilles' anger has led to the view that this hypothetical epic
of Meleager is the model for the *Iliad*: see Willcock (1964: 152 n. 4), where he
lists Finsler (1924: 39–42); Howald (1924: 409); Sachs (1933: 20) (the μῆνις of
Achilles is modelled on the μῆνις of Meleager). Some go further and argue that
this hypothetical *Meleagris* ended with Meleager's death at the hands of
Apollo: Willcock (1964: 152 n. 3), lists Howald (1924: 408); Kraus (1948: 11);
Von der Mühll (1952: 177 n. 49). More recently, see March (1987: 40);
Bremmer (1988: 44, 48–9). However, there is no evidence that the Homeric
audience derived its familiarity with the background to Meleager's story from
an earlier fixed epic poem. While we know of other versions of the story of
Meleager (see n. 149), there is nothing to confirm a version earlier than
Homer's which included the motifs of the mother's curse or the series of
requests to the hero, as suggested by Kraus (1948: 17 and 21). It is quite likely,
given the poet's habit of inventing mythological details attested nowhere else
to amplify correspondences to his immediate context, as argued by Willcock
(1964; 1977) and Braswell (1971), that the mother's curse, the hero's anger,
and the succession of requests concluding with that of the wife, were all introduced into the story of Meleager as allusions to the story of Achilles.

[149] Phrynichus, *Pleuroniae*, *TGF* i, *frr.* 5 and 6, quoted Pausanias, 10. 31. 4;
Bacchylides, 5. 136–55; Aeschylus, *Ch.* 603–12; Diodorus Siculus, 4. 34 (tells
the Homeric version, and gives the story of the Fates and the stick as an alternative account); Ovid, *Met.* 8. 445–525; Dio Chrysostom, *Or.* 67. 7; Apollodorus, 1. 8. 2–3; Hyginus, *fab.* 171; Antoninus Liberalis, 2. (Μελεαγρίδες);
Lactantius Placidus on Statius, *Theb.* 2. 481; Bode (1834: i. 46–7, no. 146);
Tzetzes Sch. ad Lycophron, 492 (Meleager's mother was told her son would
be unharmed as long as a leaf she bore with him remained unharmed. When
she learned of the death of her brothers, she burned the leaf, and Meleager

ing of his mother's intentions towards him, she just burns the stick and that is the end of the matter: the hero dies. Because the mother does not curse her son, he does not react to the malign intent demonstrated in the curse by withdrawing in anger from the fighting, he receives no succession of visitors offering him gifts if he will only lay aside his anger and return, and there is no dramatic final appeal from the hero's wife, his sole companion throughout the duration of his anger when, in tears, she pleads with her husband to avert the imminent destruction of the whole community.

The point of Meleager's story in the *Iliad* is that he was eventually persuaded to abandon his anger, but received nothing when he did: to achieve a closer correspondence to Achilles' situation, the sympathetic magic of the stick is dispensed with, and the motif of the hero's anger provoked by his mother's curse, is introduced, along with the string of visitors whose pleas to the hero to abandon his anger are rejected. Another addition is the eventual persuasion of the hero by his wife.[150] The wife, the hero's sole companion in nursing his anger, is closely modelled on Patroclus, Achilles' sole companion in nursing his anger, so closely that she is given a new name, Cleopatra, which is Patroclus reversed.[151] The new name presents her in the paradigm as a mirror image of Patroclus:

died); Malalas, *Chron.* 6. 21 tells how Meleager's mother bore an olive twig at the same time as her baby, and an oracle was given to Meleager's father that the child would last as long as its leaves. The father later burned the leaves, and the young man died. The motif of the life-token, the stick, as it occurs in the versions of the Meleager story used by Bacchylides and Ovid, deals with a kind of immortality or invulnerability; the hero will die only if the stick (or whatever happens to be the life-token) is destroyed, rather as Siegfried is invulnerable except where the leaf clung to his back as he bathed in the dragon's blood (*Niebelungenlied*, trans. A. T. Hatto (Penguin, 1984: 121), discussed by Janko (1992: 409) ad *Il.* 16. 777–867), or as Achilles in the later tradition is invulnerable except at his heel, by which his mother held him in the waters of the Styx (Statius, *Ach.* 1. 269; Hyginus, *fab.* 107). This kind of immortality or invulnerability is rather a mixed blessing, and the heroes who enjoy it often find themselves more mortal or vulnerable than their fellows, for whose destruction no precise directions are given. For further discussion, see Appendix D.

[150] For discussion of the introduction of the motif of the hero's anger into the Meleager story (for an epic of Meleager, his mother's anger would suffice), see Bethe (1925: 10–11); Heubeck (1974b: 533); Petzhold (1976: 154–5 n. 33).

[151] Eustathius, *Il.* 775. 64–6.

her real name is Alcyone.[152] A series of visitors makes its appearance in the Homeric version, all with some claim on the hero: they all beg him to lay aside his anger, and he eventually lays it aside for Cleopatra. This series of claims on the hero (paralleled in the claims of the visitors to Achilles) gives the clue to the particular suitability of the story of the stick to this kind of adaptation.

The folk-tale versions of the hero with the life-token seem in many cases to explore competing loyalties to him, or more accurately, competing disloyalties, arising from the question, which of the successive guardians of the hero's life-token, the

---

[152] Howald (1924: 411) saw in Kleo-patra the model for Patro-klos, since he took the story of Meleager as the prototype for the story of Achilles. Oehler (1925: 16) (followed by Schadewaldt (1966: 140; 1st pub. 1938); Theiler (1970: 41 n. 61; 1st pub. 1947) rightly reversed this position: although the name of Meleager's wife was Alcyone, Phoenix gave her the name Cleopatra in imitation of Patroclus, as a device to underline the parallel between Meleager's wife and Patroclus. Kraus (1948: 17) argues that the similarity would be missed in verbal delivery, and in any case, to make Patroclus assume a position parallel to Meleager's wife would be an Aristophanic vulgarism. Howald (1946: 132) concedes the comedy, but maintains his original contention. Kakridis (1949: 29–31) argues against any deliberate parallel between the names of Patroclus and Cleopatra, on the grounds that such play on names is unknown in the Homeric epics, but see Lendle (1957: 117–21) for a list of etymologies and puns from Homer to Aeschylus; Pfeiffer (1968: 4 with n. 5), where he cites L. P. Rank, *Etymologiseering en verwante Verschijnselen bij Homerus*, diss. Utrecht (1951: 35 ff.) (word-play in about fifty names in the *Iliad* and *Odyssey*); Podlecki (1961: 125–33) and Schein (1970: 73–83) on the play Οὖτις/μῆτις of *Od.* 9. 366–7, 369–70, 408. See also Fenik (1968: 101) on χερσίδαμας (*Il.* 11. 423) and Ἱππόδαμας (*Il.* 20. 401). On word-play with Hector's name, see Erbse (1961: 178 n. 31): Ἕκτωρ, Hector, boasts that he will ἐξέμεν, preserve, the city). It is important to remember the complete absence of the hero's anger, his wife, and the series of visitors from the non-Homeric versions of the story of Meleager: we have no evidence for a wife in the version where Meleager dies at the hand of Apollo, nor in the version which has him die when the stick is burnt. These details might well have been introduced into the story of Meleager by the poet to achieve a closer fit with details of the story of Achilles' anger and the string of visitors who entreat him to abandon it: see n. 148 above. Although Willcock (1964: 150 n. 4) rejects the parallel Patro-klos, Kleo-patra as an improbable theory, Lohmann (1970: 260) argues most convincingly in its favour, because the poet persistently employs mirroring, and such remodelling is typical of his work. (The parallel is accepted by Theiler (1970: 41 n. 61); Boskos (1974: 30–1); Nagy (1979: 105); Bremmer (1988: 41); Redfield (1975: 105) (Cleopatra foreshadows Patroclus); and Griffin (1995: 135–6, 138).)

stick, will be the one to burn it. These concerns are closely akin to the issues explored in the motif of the ascending scale of affection, a motif used in Phoenix's version of the story of Meleager in place of the competing loyalties of the guardian(s) of the stick in the folk-tale.

7.2.6. *The ascending scale of affection*

The motif of the ascending scale of affection was first discussed in connection with the paradigm of Meleager by Kakridis,[153] who explains the scale as a series of persons, each of whom stands higher in the hero's affection than the last. This series of persons may be approached by the hero for some favour, as when, for example, Admetus approaches both his mother and his father to die in his place: when they have both refused, he approaches his wife, Alcestis, who agrees to die instead of her husband. A succession of individuals may approach the hero to obtain some favour from him, as indeed the ambassadors are trying to persuade Achilles to fight to defend them, or as the series of visitors received by Meleager tries to persuade him to give up his anger and fight in their defence. In other cases, one person must be selected from all those who have a claim on the hero's affections, as happens in the case of Intaphernes' wife, who rescues her brother in preference to both her son and her husband.[154] It is not always desirable to be selected: the modern Greek ballad of the bridge of Arta requires the master-builder to select a victim to be walled up in the bridge to make it stand: he chooses his wife.[155] The motif may also be employed in cases where someone does for one person what he or she would do for no other, as when Antigone says she would not have defied the state to bury a husband or a son, but only her brother.[156]

Kakridis treats the ascending scale of affection as a motif of great antiquity, borrowed by the poet from the repertoire of popular tradition, and he argues for its persistence by adducing a series of modern Greek ballads in which he observes the use of the scale.[157] In these modern examples, the highest place in

---

[153] (1949: 19–20, 28–33, 34, 39, 49–53, 159–64).
[154] Herodotus, 3. 119.
[155] Politis (1958: 89); Beaton (1980: 120–4).
[156] Sophocles, *Ant.* 905–12.
[157] Kakridis (1949: 152–64, esp. 160).

the scale of affection is reserved for the spouse, leading Kakridis to infer two typical sequences for the arrangement of the persons in the scale: a shorter sequence of three groups, and a longer sequence of five groups:

3. husband/wife	5. husband/wife
—	4. brothers and sisters
—	3. father
2. parents	2. mother
1. friends	1. friends.

The order of persons addressing requests to Meleager in Phoenix's story is as follows:

5. wife
4. dearest friends
3. mother and sisters
2. father
1b. priests (offer gifts)
1a. elders (do not visit, but send priests).

It will be clear that we have here a scale of the kind discussed by Kakridis, but not the order established by him as 'traditional'. The friends have been promoted[158] and the eccentric order of those approaching Meleager is invented to reflect the order of those approaching Achilles.[159]

7.2.7. Λιταί (prayers) to Meleager in ascending scale of affection

That the figures λισσόμενοι Achilles to lay aside his anger (Nestor, Odysseus, Phoenix, Ajax (Patroclus)) are arranged in an ascending scale of affection becomes clear only through the paradigm of Meleager and the correspondences between the

[158] On the promotion of the friends, see Kakridis (1949: 22–3); Nagy (1979: 104–6).

[159] Lohmann (1970: 258–9). The motif of the scale is traditional, but the arrangement of figures in the scale used by Phoenix is the invention of the poet (Schadewaldt 1966: 87, 140; 1st pub. 1938). It is not a modification of a scale found in any previously existing epic of Meleager (see Noé (1940: 76–7)): there is no evidence for the appearance of any ascending scale of affection in any story of Meleager before the Homeric account, and the poet may be responsible for introducing this motif into the story. For discussion of the claims represented in the 'scale' in Phoenix's version of the story, see Noé (1940: 76–7), and Petzhold (1976: 157–61).

visitors to Meleager and the approaches made to Achilles in the embassy. As Phoenix proceeds through the series of entreaties to Meleager, beginning with the claims of the wider community and proceeding through those of family obligations, we become aware of a hierarchy of moral obligations (like those in n. 254 below) which could be expressed an an ascending scale. The elders λίσσοντο, entreated (*Il.* 9. 574), sending the noblest priests to convey their λιταί and offer their gift of a wealthy estate, a τέμενος. Meleager's father, Oeneus, supplicated his son (γουνούμενος) as he rattled the doors of the chamber from which he was excluded. The hero's sisters and mother ἐλλίσσονθ', but all the more Meleager refused. Even the friends who were κεδνότατοι καὶ φίλτατοι ἁπάντων, 'most cared-for and dearest of all' could not persuade him, and only when the enemy were actually setting fire to the town did Cleopatra persuade Meleager by her pleas and laments (λίσσετ' ὀδυρομένη, *Il.* 9. 591), as she enumerated the κήδεα, troubles, of the citizens. In terms of the scale, she succeeds where all others have failed because she appeals to her husband's instinct to care for his wife[160] and children. She has been closer to Meleager through the whole course of his anger even than the friends who were otherwise the κεδνότατοι of his visitors.

In fairness it should be indicated that other factors are at work in Meleager's situation in addition to the claims tested in the ascending scale of affection. Cleopatra's successful appeal should not be dissociated from those of her predecessors: her appeal is the culmination of 'an ascending intensity of moral pressure'.[161] Cleopatra's effectiveness is due at least in part to her perfect timing: she describes the sufferings of the inhabi-

---

[160] In pressing his point that Cleopatra is at the top of Meleager's scale of affection, Kakridis presents her as a self-interested woman whose husband is blind to her unpleasant qualities: she is 'motivated by the egotism of self-preservation' (1949: 60); '(her) entreaties bring about the immediate death of her husband' (1949: 30)—but there absolutely is no evidence for this, and we hear only that Meleager was not rewarded for saving the town (*Il.* 9. 598–9); her appeal comes only when most of the defenders of Calydon have been killed (1949: 25)—but again, the text does not say so, and Meleager *did* save the town: ὡς ὁ μὲν Αἰτωλοῖσιν ἀπήμυνεν κακὸν ἦμαρ, so he warded off the evil day *from the Aetolians Il.* 9. 599, suggesting on the whole that the community survived. For discussion of the motivation attributed to women entreating, see Appendix E.

[161] Hainsworth (1993: 138) ad *Il.* 9. 574, 581, 585, 590.

tants of a captured city when the sack is virtually in progress, and the city is already on fire (*Il.* 9. 589). At this stage, if the succession of visitors is not to become meaningless, and Meleager's anger with his mother irrelevant, the hero must be persuaded to abandon his wrath immediately, since he, and Cleopatra will suffer together with his mother and the rest of the inhabitants unless the sack is prevented.

7.2.8. Correspondences between λιταί *(prayers) to Meleager in ascending scale of affection and* λιταί *to Achilles*

The approaches to Meleager correspond closely to the approaches made in books 9 and 16 to Achilles: the correspondences are far closer than either Kakridis or even Lohmann suspected.[162] In Phoenix's account, the γέροντες λίσσοντο, the elders entreated (*Il.* 9. 574) Meleager, and sent the ἱερῆας ἀρίστους, the best priests to him (*Il.* 9. 575), to convey the offer from the γέροντες of a sizeable gift. The γέροντες of the paradigm correspond broadly to the γέροντες Ἀχαιῶν, the elders of the Greeks (*Il.* 9. 89) whom Agamemnon gathers in his tent at Nestor's instigation, for the council at which the decision is taken to send the embassy. In a narrower sense, Nestor himself (who is nothing if not a γέρων) corresponds to the Aetolian γέροντες, since he was the first to entreat Achilles to lay his anger aside: αὐτὰρ ἔγωγε | λίσσομ' Ἀχιλλῆι μεθέμεν χόλον, 'but I | entreat Achilles to let go his anger' (*Il.* 1. 282–3), and was responsible for arranging the embassy. Of course, the τέμενος, the estate, which the elders offer to Meleager (*Il.* 9. 577–80), corresponds to the gifts offered by Agamemnon to Achilles (*Il.* 9. 122–56, 264–98), and Odysseus, the spokesman for Agamemnon's offer, corresponds to the ἱερῆας ἀρίστους, the best

---

[162] Kakridis (1949: 22–4) makes Meleager's ἑταῖροι correspond to Ajax, Phoenix, Odysseus; he makes Cleopatra correspond to Patroclus. His identification of Meleager's ἑταῖροι with the whole embassy is consistent with *Il.* 9. 641–2, but the close fit between Nestor and the Calydonian elders; Odysseus and the Calydonian priests (both of whom offer gifts); Phoenix (who claims Achilles as a kind of surrogate son) and Meleager's father suggests an interpretation where the ἑταῖροι of Meleager correspond only to Ajax, who asserts the claims of friends. My interpretation of the parallels is given below at the end of this section. For Lohmann (1970: 258–60), the γέροντες correspond to Agamemnon; the priests correspond to Odysseus; Oeneus corresponds to Phoenix; the ἑταῖροι correspond to Ajax; Cleopatra corresponds to Patroclus.

priests. The next person to entreat Meleager is his father, Oeneus, whose appeal is a supplication, as we have seen (γουνούμενος, *Il.* 9. 583).[163] Achilles' father is not at Troy, but Phoenix, who entreats Achilles next after Odysseus, attempts to establish a rather dubious quasi-paternal claim over Achilles, whom he claims to have made his surrogate son (*Il.* 9. 494). In this way Phoenix equates himself with Oeneus in the paradigm. (The questionably paternal relationship of Phoenix towards Achilles is not the only questionable aspect of his appeal: if Oeneus, the hero's father, is shown supplicating Meleager, and Phoenix in the embassy appears as the parallel to Achilles' father, then perhaps the father-parallel to some extent invites us to infer that Phoenix, like Oeneus, is supplicating, although Phoenix makes none of the ritual gestures of supplication, either verbally, or in fact. If the father-parallel really is an invitation to infer that Phoenix is supplicating, then Phoenix is attempting to establish the obligation incumbent on the one supplicated without engaging at all in the ritual of supplication: it is not for nothing that the poet, and Achilles, call the embassy a μῆτις (*Il.* 9. 93, 423), since so many aspects of it are not what they seem.)[164] There are no parallels, in the approaches made by the Greeks to Achilles, to Meleager's mother and sisters, who are the next to try their influence over Meleager after his father,[165] and they complete the approaches from Meleager's

---

[163] Gould (1973: 80 n. 39).

[164] Reinhardt (1961: 230–2) links the μῆτις of the embassy with the sense of deception expressed by Achilles (*Il.* 9. 370–7). The only reason for the embassy is the fix in which the Greeks find themselves: Agamemnon has no genuine desire for reconciliation.

[165] There is a school of thought which considers that their appearance in the scale of approaches to Meleager leads Achilles to expect a direct approach from Agamemnon: Schadewaldt (1966: 141 n. 4; 1st pub. 1938); Boskos (1974: 29–30, 80–5); Crotty (1994: 57). The reasoning is something like this: because Meleager's anger was the result of his mother's curse, and his mother appears in the scale entreating him to return, Achilles, whose anger is the result of his quarrel with Agamemnon, is led to expect a direct appeal from Agamemnon. Achilles is aware that Agamemnon is far too arrogant ever to make in person an approach involving the physical contact of supplication: οὐδ᾽ ἂν ἔμοιγε | τετλαίη κύνεός περ ἐὼν εἰς ὦπα ἰδέσθαι, 'nor would he dare, although he is a dog [i.e., although he has no shame], to look me in the face' (*Il.* 9. 372–3). If he were less arrogant, Agamemnon could, in theory, make a supplication involving physical contact, but given the personalities involved and the personal animosity between the two men, such an approach is improbable

blood relatives. The next entreaties to Meleager come from his dearest friends, οἵ οἱ κεδνότατοι καὶ φίλτατοι ἦσαν ἁπάντων, 'who were most cherished and dearest to him of all' (*Il.* 9. 586): their entreaties correspond to those of Ajax. When the case of the embassy appears to be lost, Ajax asserts the claims of friendship with even greater emphasis than that employed by Odysseus and Phoenix. Ajax argues that Achilles is unreasonable in refusing to accept compensation, when any other man would accept it even for a more serious offence,[166] such as the murder of a brother or a child. Ajax appeals to the obligations of a host towards his guests: σὺ . . . αἴδεσσαι δὲ μέλαθρον, 'you . . . respect your own roof' (*Il.* 9. 640).[167] He insists on the close relationship between Achilles and the ambassadors: μέμαμεν δέ τοι ἔξοχον ἄλλων | κήδιστοί τ' ἔμεναι καὶ φίλτατοι ὅσσοι Ἀχαιοί, 'we claim to be far above all the dearest and the closest to you out of all the Greeks' (*Il.* 9. 641–2), rather as the friends who approached Meleager were the dearest to him of all his friends.[168]

until external factors (the need to avenge Patroclus) bring about their reconciliation in book 19. Priam displays a complete absence of arrogance when he supplicates Achilles for the return of Hector's body, but even though Achilles has killed Hector, there is not the same kind of personal rancour between Priam and Achilles as between Agamemnon and Achilles.

[166] On the point of compensation accepted even for murder, see Schlunk (1976: 205–6). The issue of compensation is raised again at *Il.* 18. 497–507, with (see Andersen 1976: 15–16) oblique reference to the compensation offered to Achilles. *Il.* 24. 480–1 indicate that the payment of compensation was not always an option: on migration to avoid blood vengeance, see *Il.* 15. 332–6, 430–2; 16. 570–4 and the discussions of Strasburger (1954: 29); Apthorp (1980: 96); Gagarin (1981: 6–19). Part of the μῆτις of the embassy may well lie in the reversal of the normal roles: the murderer who goes into exile is subordinate to the host who protects him, but Achilles, the injured party, will find himself subordinate, as son-in-law, to the offender, Agamemnon, if he accepts the compensation offered (see 7.2.2 above).

[167] For discussion of αἰδώς (respect) for one's own house, and the obligation to show αἰδώς among friends, see Cairns (1993: 92–4). On the very real obligation of Achilles to respond favourably to the claims of his friends, see Sinos (1980: 39–44) and Motzkus (1964: 58 and 60).

[168] The ambassadors are φίλτατοι (dearest) to Achilles: *Il.* 9. 198, 204 (Achilles speaking); 522 (Phoenix speaking); 642 (Ajax): the friends of Meleager are φίλτατοι (dearest) to him: *Il.* 9. 586. For discussion, see Sinos (1980: 40–5).

7.2.9. Rejection of λιταί *(prayers) and slight concession*

In the story of Meleager, λίσσομαι or λιτάνευω (pray, entreat) are repeatedly used of the appeals to Meleager to lay aside his anger and fight,[169] suggesting that these appeals are to be regarded as λιταί (prayers). The same verbs are used of the approaches of the embassy to Achilles, and these too may be considered λιταί. Meleager was obdurate in refusing the appeals of the γέροντες (elders), the priests, his father, his mother and sisters, and his friends. Achilles is less obdurate than Meleager, although he refuses outright to make any concession to Odysseus' speech, which restates Agamemnon's offer of terms for Achilles' return to battle while simultaneously attempting to establish certain other claims on Achilles. In describing Meleager's refusal of the appeals from Oeneus and the closest friends, Phoenix offers an analogy for the potential refusal by Achilles of his own plea and that of Ajax after it. In fact Achilles concedes a little to Phoenix, in that, far from leaving Phoenix alone, a prospect Phoenix dreads, Achilles says he will keep him with him, so that Phoenix does not return to the army with the other ambassadors. Having told Odysseus that he will sail for home the next morning, taking Phoenix with him, if he wants to leave (*Il.* 9. 427–9), Achilles' response to Phoenix is that the two of them will consider in the morning if they want to leave (*Il.* 9. 618–19). To Ajax, who wanted to be one of his κήδιστοι and φίλτατοι, closest and dearest,[170] Achilles concedes a little more: he will not leave in the morning, but will stay, although he will not return to the fighting until Hector has reached the ships of the Myrmidons and set fire to them: only then will he check Hector (*Il.* 9. 650–5). This is not an outright refusal in response to λιταί, and it is certainly an advance on his response to Odysseus, but it is not much of a concession for the embassy to take back to the army.[171]

---

[169] *Il.* 9. 574, 581, 585, 591.

[170] On the promotion of the friends, see Kakridis (1949: 22–3); Nagy (1979: 104–6).

[171] On Achilles' concessions see Whitman (1958: 190–2); Schadewaldt (1966: 135; 1st pub. 1938). Interestingly, Odysseus reports only the worst-case scenario, Achilles' threat to depart the following morning (*Il.* 9. 428–9, 682–7): for discussion see Janko (1992: 310).

7.2.10. Cleopatra and Patroclus: the last correspondence of the paradigm

As we saw, the motif of the ascending scale of affection (concluding with the pleas of the hero's wife) is absent from those versions of the Meleager story not modelled on the Homeric version. In Phoenix's story, the appeals to Meleager culminate in those of his wife, Cleopatra. When the bedchamber in which they are lying is under bombardment, and the enemy are in the process of scaling the towers and setting fire to the town, then Cleopatra, lamenting, entreats her husband, and by her account of the horrors inflicted on the population of a captured town, persuades him to go into battle and save the town. The hero's wife of the Homeric version has her counterpart in Patroclus, who, also in tears, approaches Achilles when the requests of the embassy have long since failed. Like Cleopatra, Patroclus succeeds in his request. The paradigm of Meleager and the embassy to Achilles give us the following correspondences, suggested by verbal echoes and similar actions:

Meleager		*Achilles*
Cleopatra (Alcyone)		Patroclus
dearest friends (κεδνότατοι, φίλτατοι)		Ajax (κήδιστοι, φίλτατοι)
sisters and mother		—
Oeneus (father)		Phoenix (surrogate father)
priests	*offer gifts*	Odysseus
elders	*send embassy*	Nestor.

The series of λιταί made to Achilles by the Greeks in ascending scale of affection is underlined and highlighted by the introduction into the story of Meleager of a closely corresponding series of figures making λιταί in ascending scale of affection to Meleager.

7.3. THE PARADIGM OF MELEAGER BREAKS
DOWN

7.3.1. The request altered

It seems most probable that Meleager's scale is an invention by the poet to provide a parallel for the scale of Achilles. The figure at the top of Meleager's scale, Cleopatra, is so closely modelled on Patroclus, that her name is a mirror-image of his; her real name is Alcyone.[172] This manufactured scale of Meleager's, designed to mirror closely the scale of approaches to Achilles as we have so far observed it, is a deceptive device by which the poet misleads his audience into thinking that the return of Achilles will resemble the events of the paradigm of Meleager. In terms of the positive application of the paradigm in book 9, Achilles should return to the battle in response to the request of the person he loves best, without material inducement, and just as the enemy are firing the town/ships.[173] Patroclus makes his request to Achilles just before the Trojans fire the ship of Protesilaus[174] (*Il.* 16. 122–4): the Trojans are coming close to the ships of the Myrmidons, and if the paradigm of book 9 were strictly applicable to the events of book 16, Patroclus' request to Achilles would be (like that of Cleopatra to Meleager) that he return to the fighting, and Achilles would return at this point. But Patroclus does not ask Achilles to return to the fighting, and Achilles does not return: it becomes clear that the paradigm has been something of a false trail, like the false predictions and other misdirections which create an expectation which is then frustrated, heightening the impact and significance of what happens instead.[175]

All the λιταί addressed to Meleager in the paradigm were consistent pleas for him to return to the fighting and defend the population of Calydon: Cleopatra's request was the same as those which had earlier been rejected by Meleager. But the request of Patroclus, when it comes, is not the same as the

---

[172] See n. 152 above.

[173] Whitman (1958: 191) thinks the paradigm of Meleager, contrary to its purpose, has the effect of clarifying for Achilles his unformulated intention to fight only at the last minute and without receiving any gifts.

[174] Which has been fought over since *Il.* 15. 705.

[175] On false predictions and misdirections, see Morrison (1992).

earlier request of the ambassadors that Achilles should return
to the fighting and defend them. Instead, Patroclus asks to be
allowed to enter the battle himself, wearing Achilles' armour
and leading the Myrmidons.[176] Certainly, Nestor urges
Patroclus not simply to rouse Achilles to fight, but if Achilles
has some reason, such as a prophecy, which prevents him from
fighting, then he, Patroclus, should go into battle in the armour
of Achilles (*Il.* 11. 794–8). When Patroclus announces his
intention to stir Achilles up to fight (*Il.* 15. 402), he repeats to
Eurypylus (with an appropriate change in a verb) (*Il.* 15. 403–
4), Nestor's suggestion (*Il.* 11. 792–3) that the advice of a
comrade might be enough to persuade Achilles (to fight). However, when Patroclus reaches the point of making his request to
Achilles, he never voices the request for Achilles to return in
person, discounting the possibility of persuading his friend (*Il.*
16. 29, 34–5).[177] Instead he tactfully mentions the possibility
first considered by Nestor (*Il.* 11. 794–5) of a prophecy preventing Achilles from fighting (*Il.* 16. 36–7: cf. *Il.* 11. 794–5)
and passes immediately to the second strategy proposed by
Nestor (*Il.* 11. 796–803) of requesting to be allowed to return to
the fighting himself, wearing the armour of Achilles, so that the
Trojans may be deceived into thinking that he is Achilles
(*Il.* 16. 38–45 approx. = *Il.* 11. 796–803).[178] It is true that an
implicit appeal to Achilles to return in person may be read into
the idea that even if the doctors can heal the wounded Greeks,

> σὺ δ' ἀμήχανος ἔπλευ, Ἀχιλλεῦ.
> μὴ ἐμέ γ' οὖν οὗτός γε λάβοι χόλος, ὃν σὺ φυλάσσεις,   30
> αἰναρέτη· τί σευ ἄλλος ὀνήσεται ὀψίγονός περ,
> αἴ κε μὴ Ἀργείοισιν ἀεικέα λοιγὸν ἀμύνῃς;

> but there is nothing to be done about you, Achilles.
> I hope this rage you are storing up does not get hold of me,   30

---

[176] Sinos (1980: 42) demonstrates that Patroclus recognizes Achilles' obligation to his φίλοι at a time when Achilles does not.

[177] On the importance given to the figure of Patroclus by the poet of the
Iliad, see Janko (1992: 313–14, with bibliography).

[178] Sch. bT ad *Il.* 16. 41 (= Erbse (1969–88: iv. 167), 41c), followed by
Janko (1992: 318) ad *Il.* 16. 21–45, are mistaken in saying that cowardice is
imputed to Achilles by the suggestion that a prophecy might prevent him from
fighting. Nestor and Patroclus are tactful in respecting this possibility, and
elsewhere (*Il.* 4. 381, discussed 5.3.2 above) fighting without due regard for
the signs sent by the gods is simply regarded as imprudent.

accursedly brave: what other man born in a later age will have any
   benefit from you,
if you do not ward off sheer destruction from the Argives?

(Il. 16. 29–32)

But the cause (of Achilles returning in person in book 16) is
already thought to be lost, and the direct imperatives of the
requests of the ambassadors,[179] and of the request Patroclus
succeeds in making asking to return in the armour of Achilles
(*Il.* 16. 38, 40), are significantly missing. If the request Patroclus manages to put to Achilles were not slightly different from
the request consistently put by all the ambassadors of book 9, to
return in person to the fighting, Achilles might have recollected
the paradigm. As it is, since Cleopatra, the person finally able
to affect and move Meleager, puts the same request to her
husband as all the others who had earlier sought and failed to
persuade him, while Patroclus' request is different from the
requests already received from the ambassadors, Achilles fails
to associate the approach of Patroclus, who (of all the Greeks at
Troy) is closest to him, with the approaches of the ambassadors
or with the paradigm of Meleager. He sees no connection
between Meleager's favourable response to Cleopatra's request,
and his own favourable response to Patroclus.

7.3.2. Beyond the paradigm: λιταί (prayers) not signalled by the paradigm

The consistency of the requests put to the hero is not the only
point in which the paradigm of Meleager diverges from the
situation of Achilles. Cleopatra is the last of a series of persons
who all request Meleager to return to the fighting and he
responds positively to her after refusing all the others. Since
Cleopatra is the last of the visitors entreating Meleager, we
would expect Patroclus to be the last person to make a request
of Achilles, if the paradigm is designed to fit Achilles' circumstances. However, the λιταί of Patroclus are certainly not the
last addressed to Achilles: long after Achilles' scale of parallel
and surrogate equivalents to Meleager's scale has been completed, Priam supplicates him (*Il.* 24. 478, 570) λισσόμενος
entreating him (*Il.* 24. 485) to exchange the corpse of Hector

---

[179] *Il.* 9. 247, 251, 260, 302, 496, 513, 600, 602–3.

for ransom. Priam's appeal is based on an evocation of the piti-
ful desolation of Achilles' own father, bereft of his son's
support in his old age (*Il*. 24. 486–9). Obviously, Priam's plea is
very different from both the requests of the ambassadors that
Achilles should return to the fighting, and from the request of
Patroclus to be allowed to return in Achilles' armour (the point
at which the factor of consistency disappears from the series of
requests to Achilles), but in the requests of Patroclus and
Priam, as in the requests of the embassy, we are still dealing
with λιταί. Since Priam's appeal is the last addressed to
Achilles, since he appeals to Achilles' affection for his real
father (not the surrogate father of the embassy), and since
Achilles earlier gives a hint (*Il*. 16. 14–16) that his father's
death really would be a cause for grief, it is clear that even after
the correspondences between the series of visitors to Achilles
and the series of visitors to Meleager in the paradigm are
exhausted, a further claim on Achilles' affections is explored
and tested, the claim of the true father. In fact the name, Cleopatra, at the top of Meleager's scale, and the name Patroclus, to
which Cleopatra is a parallel, look forward to the last and
strongest claim on Achilles' affections, that of the father.[180] The
sequence of λιταί addressed to Achilles must be extended to
include Priam's appeal to Achilles' affection for his father:

  6. father (Priam appeals to pity for Peleus)
  5. Patroclus
  4. Ajax
  3. Phoenix (surrogate father)
  2. Odysseus (offers gifts)
  1. Nestor.

The expectation created by the early mention of the father in
the series of persons approaching Meleager, with a correspond-
ingly early mention of the surrogate father (Phoenix) in the
series of persons approaching Achilles is that Cleopatra's
eventual success in persuading Meleager to fight, will be

---

[180] It is not necessary to go as far as von Scheliha (1943: 247), who believes
Patroclus is the invention of Homer, and named 'the glory of his father'
because he is made famous by Homer. Nagy (1979: 102–5) associates the
'glory of ancestors' conveyed by both names, Patroclus and Cleopatra, with
Achilles' choice of κλέος from the alternatives of κλέος (fame) and νόστος
(return) confronting him.

matched by a similar success on the part of Patroclus in persuading Achilles to fight. This expectation is a false clue, set up only to be frustrated, giving heightened significance to the final test on Achilles' affections, the claims of the father-figure represented by Priam. We shall return to the claims of Priam in due course.

7.4. THE αἶνος OF THE Λιταί (ALLEGORY OF THE PRAYERS) APPLIED TO ACHILLES

As we saw earlier, Achilles' intransigent response to the speech of Odysseus offering Agamemnon's terms for reconciliation so alarms Phoenix that he tells him the allegory of the Λιταί: the man who graciously yields to Λιταί (Prayers) when they approach is benefited by them, but the one who harshly rejects them is dogged, at their request, by Ἄτη (Delusion) until he suffers harm and pays the penalty. Although Achilles yields a little to Phoenix, and a little more to Ajax, the embassy is a failure: Achilles shows no sign of helping the Greeks in their emergency. He refuses the λιταί of the ambassadors, in that he refuses the reconciliation and compensation offered by Agamemnon, and refuses the claims on his loyalty and friendship of his comrades-in-arms. There is no doubt that he suffers harm in the loss of Patroclus—it is hard to imagine how anyone could suffer more than Achilles when he recognizes his own part in Patroclus' death. But is Patroclus' death the penalty for rejection of the embassy? If it is, then does the αἶνος of the Λιταί work in Achilles' case? Are the events leading to Patroclus' death the result of ἄτη[181] affecting Achilles' judgement?

7.4.1. The beginning of disaster for Patroclus

From the prow of his ship, Achilles watches the rout of the Greeks: at a word from him, Patroclus emerges from the tent, ἶσος Ἄρηϊ, κακοῦ δ' ἄρα οἱ πέλεν ἀρχή, 'equal to Ares, and it was

---

[181] Patzer (1972: 45) distinguishes three stages in the 'Verblendung' of Achilles: (1) μῆνις; (2) rejection of compensation (here he is in company with Arieti (1988: 4)); (3) sending Patroclus into battle in place of himself. For the reasons why Achilles is not afflicted by ἄτη in (1) and (2) see 7.1.6 above.

the beginning of disaster for him' (*Il.* 11. 604).[182] Achilles tells him how the Greeks will soon cluster at his knees, entreating (λισσόμενοι), and sends Patroclus to ask Nestor if the wounded man he has been watching was really Machaon (*Il.* 11. 609–12), an errand Patroclus performs without a word. This errand provides the justification for Patroclus' visit to Nestor, providing the occasion for Nestor to remind Patroclus of all the instructions Menoetius is supposed to have given him about offering good advice to Achilles (*Il.* 11. 785–9) before the expedition sailed for Troy. It is impossible to say what makes Achilles watch the battle, or what makes him send Patroclus to Nestor to enquire about Machaon, although it would be easy to supply subjective inferences about Achilles' fascination to discover the effect of his absence from the battle, and to gloat over the full horror of the rout. Alternatively, he might be genuinely concerned for the Greeks, and unable to suppress his interest in their welfare. All we know is that he anticipates some further approach from the Greeks, but instead of waiting for it, he sends Patroclus to make enquiries. It is absolutely clear, however, that the beginning of Patroclus' troubles is his obedience to a word from Achilles, a word which causes him to be exposed to the influence of Nestor.

7.4.2. *Departure from instructions*

Nestor is able to work on Patroclus' sympathy with information on the wounded Greeks (*Il.* 11. 658–64: see 4.4 above). The very long account he gives of his own exploits in the Pylian Wars demonstrates the full effectiveness of one hero (himself)[183] in an emergency. Nestor's account of his almost single-handed heroics in the Pylian Wars is offered to Patroclus as a pattern for similar single-handed heroics by a hero entering the

[182] On the comment of Sch. A ad *Il.* 11. 604 (from Aristonicus) (= Erbse (1969–88: iii. 238), 604b), that the fate of Patroclus is linked with the plan of Zeus, and that the completion of this plan follows closely upon the fulfilment of the foreshadowing of Patroclus' fate, see Duckworth (1931: 325–6 and 336); on Sch. bT ad *Il.* 11. 604 (= Erbse (1969–88: iii. 238), 604c), on the creation of interest in Patroclus' fate without detriment to the later account of it, see Duckworth (1933: 8 n. 19).

[183] On Nestor's speech as a paradigm to influence Patroclus, see Pedrick (1983) and 4.4. above.

battle now. That hero might be Achilles, if Patroclus can persuade him, and the most desirable eventuality would indeed be Achilles' entry into battle at this point. After remarks on Menoetius' injunction to Patroclus to give good advice to Achilles, Nestor concludes with the advice he wants Patroclus to offer: Patroclus should first attempt to persuade Achilles to return in person, but if there is some reason why he cannot, Patroclus should then ask for Achilles' armour and weapons for his own use, in an attempt to deceive the Trojans into thinking Achilles has returned to battle. Patroclus departs, again without a word in reply, intending to return to Achilles (*Il.* 11. 805) but he is deflected from his purpose through meeting the wounded Eurypylus, whom he agrees to treat along with other wounded Greeks,

> ἀλλ' οὐδ' ὥς περ σεῖο μεθήσω τειρομένοιο

but not even so will I leave you when you are distressed.

(*Il.* 11. 841)

This is the thin end of the wedge. Patroclus spends ages in the tent of Eurypylus (while the Greeks rally with the help of Poseidon in book 13, and Zeus is distracted from the battle by the Διὸς ἀπάτη (deception of Zeus) of book 14; Poseidon is withdrawn by Zeus in book 15 and Apollo is permitted to help the Trojans), not emerging until the Trojans are rushing at the wall round the ships (*Il.* 15. 395): then, repeating Nestor's words to him earlier (on the possible good effects of a friend's advice) (*Il.* 15. 403–4 = *Il.* 11. 792–3), he hurries away to Achilles with the intention of rousing him to battle (*Il.* 15. 402). He next appears in tears standing beside Achilles, to describe the distress of the Greeks and ask to go into battle wearing Achilles' armour, so that the Trojans will be fooled into thinking he is Achilles (*Il.* 16. 41–5 approx. = *Il.* 11. 799–803). Patroclus' folly in asking for his own death is underlined by the comment of the narrator:

> Ὣς φάτο λισσόμενος μέγα νήπιος· ἦ γὰρ ἔμελλεν
> οἷ αὐτῷ θάνατόν τε κακὸν καὶ κῆρα λιτέσθαι.

So he spoke, entreating, the great fool. For he was certainly about to entreat for evil death and destruction for himself.

(*Il.* 16. 46–7)

(Authorial intrusion is so rare that it is always highly significant.) Achilles provides the initial impetus to Patroclus' trouble by dispatching him to Nestor to make enquiries: from the moment Patroclus arrives among the Greeks, his sympathies are engaged by their predicament. Nestor manipulates Patroclus into acting in the interests of the community,[184] so that he requests to enter the battle himself, wearing the armour of Achilles. As a result of Nestor's influence, Patroclus is manoeuvred into imitating Nestor's example in the Pylian Wars, and saving the Greeks in their present emergency. Patroclus will die while he is imitating the pattern of Nestor's example, and his death will precipitate Achilles' return to battle.

When Patroclus arrives in Nestor's tent, he is under the influence of Achilles, but he is so affected by Nestor's calculated stratagems that when he leaves the tent he has fallen completely under the influence of Nestor.[185] He first departs from Achilles' instructions when he is on the point of returning to him (*Il.* 11. 805) but meets the wounded Eurypylus, and allows his sympathy for his companions to distract him from Achilles' business (*Il.* 11. 838–41). The second departure from Achilles' advice will be on the battlefield, and will be fatal. Achilles urges Patroclus to enter the battle (*Il.* 16. 126–9) but warns him to return when he has driven back the Trojans from the ships: he is not to pursue them to Troy since he might fall victim to Apollo (*Il.* 16. 87–94). The instructions Patroclus receives from Achilles run counter to the example of Nestor's heroics which Patroclus has already been invited to consider. Patroclus is under the influence of Nestor, whose example in the Pylian Wars he is imitating: Patroclus will pursue the Trojans back to Troy, as Nestor chased the Epeians to Bouprasion (*Il.* 11. 754–9) and Hector will kill Patroclus with Apollo's help. Patroclus goes into battle wearing the armour of Achilles, and the Trojans think he is Achilles (*Il.* 16. 278–82). He arrives as Achilles told Ajax he would himself return (*Il.* 9. 650–3), just when a Greek ship has been fired (*Il.* 16. 122–3). Patroclus, as long as he follows the instructions given him by Achilles, is

---

[184] On the claims of the community, see Sinos (1980: 42–6).

[185] For discussion, see Reinhardt (1961: 258–64).

successful in driving back the enemy,[186] but instead of returning to Achilles, as instructed, he imitates the example of Nestor
in pursuit of the Eleians, and pursues the Trojans back to the
walls of Troy. The narrator comments καὶ μέγ᾽ ἀάσθη, and he
erred greatly (*Il.* 16. 685).[187] Patroclus three times runs up the
revetment of the fortification wall, and is chased away by
Apollo (*Il.* 16. 702–5), but on his fourth attempt, Apollo
commands him to fall back (*Il.* 16. 707). After three further
rushes on the enemy (*Il.* 16. 784) Apollo strikes Patroclus (*Il.*
16. 791), ἄτη seizes him (*Il.* 16. 805),[188] and he becomes an easy
prey for Euphorbus and Hector.[189]

7.4.3. Achilles dominated by obsession

The death of Patroclus resolves the impasse reached in the plot
as a result of Achilles' refusal to accept compensation and
return to the fighting. Patroclus dies because Nestor's influence
causes him to show concern for the Greeks: Achilles is concerned only for Patroclus, but realizes this only when it is too
late. His reluctance to accept the compensation offered by
Agamemnon through Odysseus is understandable, but his preoccupation with Agamemnon's insulting behaviour in book 1
leads him to reject the embassy, thereby neglecting the claims
of the community of the Greek army on his assistance. When
Achilles has rejected the embassy and the claims of the Greeks
on his friendship, Nestor manoeuvres Patroclus into responding to the claims of the Greeks instead. The effect of Nestor's

---

[186] The theory that Patroclus, as a θεράπων (squire), is Achilles' ritual substitute, is based on a shaky Hittite etymology that θεράπων is derived from a
supposed Hittite term *tarpan-: see van Brock (1959), cited by Chantraine
(1968: i. 430–1, s.v. θεράπων). Nagy (1979: 292–3) and Sinos (1980: 33) accept
this idea and take the view that a θεράπων becomes vulnerable as soon as he
abandons the identity for which he functions as a ritual substitute.

[187] Bannert (1988: 42–3) attributes the ἄτη which causes Patroclus to depart
from Achilles' instructions to being encouraged by his victory over Sarpedon.

[188] There is nothing to suggest that ἄτη is transferable, affecting a man as a
result of another's action: see 7.1.6. above. Thornton (1984: 123, 135) thinks
Patroclus falls victim to ἄτη here as a result of Achilles' rejection of the
embassy. Patroclus has departed from Achilles' instructions and is acting on
his own initiative.

[189] For discussion of 'three times . . . but on the fourth . . .' see Bannert
(1988: 40–57): for this passage, 42–4.

influence is first observed when Patroclus, sent to enquire after
the sufferings of the Greeks, stays behind to help them instead
of returning to the angry Achilles. When Patroclus goes on to
comply with Nestor's instruction that he ask to go to the assistance of the Greeks, Achilles, far from considering the risk to
Patroclus if he fights alone, thinks a little more about the insult
to his honour (*Il.* 16. 52–9). He combines his warnings to
Patroclus to restrict himself to driving back the Trojans from
the ships with the anticipation of the return of Briseis and
handsome presents (*Il.* 16. 85–6), both suddenly desirable, now
that no one is offering anything, and the ships are in danger.[190]
When the ship of Protesilaus has been set on fire (*Il.* 16. 122–3),
he urges Patroclus to go out and fight. In effect, Achilles wants
Patroclus to take his place in fulfilling his promise to Ajax,
whose speech was based so firmly on the claims of the closest
friendship (*Il.* 9. 642), that he would return to the fighting
when the Myrmidons' ships were fired (*Il.* 9. 650–5). In
response to Patroclus' request to be permitted to go and fight[191]
Achilles himself refers to this promise:

$$\mathring{\eta}\tau o\iota \ \mathring{\epsilon}\phi\eta\nu \ \gamma\epsilon$$
$$o\mathring{\upsilon} \ \pi\rho\grave{\iota}\nu \ \mu\eta\nu\iota\theta\mu\grave{o}\nu \ \kappa\alpha\tau\alpha\pi\alpha\upsilon\sigma\acute{\epsilon}\mu\epsilon\nu, \ \mathring{a}\lambda\lambda' \ \acute{o}\pi\acute{o}\tau' \ \mathring{a}\nu \ \delta\grave{\eta}$$
$$\nu\mathring{\eta}\alpha\varsigma \ \mathring{\epsilon}\mu\grave{a}\varsigma \ \mathring{a}\phi\acute{\iota}\kappa\eta\tau\alpha\iota \ \mathring{a}\mathring{\upsilon}\tau\acute{\eta} \ \tau\epsilon \ \pi\tau\acute{o}\lambda\epsilon\mu\acute{o}\varsigma \ \tau\epsilon.$$

although I intended, at any rate,
that I would not put an end to my anger before, but when
the din of battle and the war actually reached my ships.

(*Il.* 16. 61–3)

In fact Achilles does not break his word about his entry into
battle, since Hector does not get as far as the ships of the
Myrmidons: the only ship set alight is that of Protesilaus. In his
prayer to Zeus before sending out Patroclus, Achilles accepts
(*Il.* 16. 236–7), that the original request (made by Thetis,
τίμησόν μοι υἱόν, 'honour my son for me' (*Il.* 1. 505)) has been
granted, and Zeus has honoured him, but now he has a further
request, this time a double-barrelled one.[192] Zeus is to make

---

[190] Cf. *Il.* 9. 589, 598–9.

[191] *Il.* 16. 61–3 refers back to *Il.* 9. 650–5: ἔφην (*Il.* 16. 61) is a sign of
weakening resolve: see Sch. A ad *Il.* 16. 61 (from Aristonicus) (= Erbse (1969–
88: iv. 175), 61d) and Janko (1992: 323–4 ad *Il.* 16. 61–3).

[192] See Janko (1992: 348 ad *Il.* 16. 233–48): Achilles' claim that Zeus has
honoured him and hurt the Greeks echoes Chryses' claim (*Il.* 1. 453) that

Patroclus as valiant alone as when he fights alongside Achilles, and to bring him back unscathed, with all his armour and companions. Zeus grants only the first half of the request (*Il.* 16. 250). Zeus has already fulfilled the promise he made to Thetis to honour Achilles, so Patroclus' repetition of

γνῷ δὲ καὶ Ἀτρεΐδης εὐρὺ κρείων Ἀγαμέμνων
ἣν ἄτην, ὅ τ᾽ ἄριστον Ἀχαιῶν οὐδὲν ἔτεισεν

so that even the son of Atreus, wide-ruling Agamemnon
may recognize his folly, when he honoured the best of the Achaeans
   not at all

(*Il.* 16. 273–4 = *Il.* 1. 411–12)

and his intention that he and the Myrmidons will honour Achilles (*Il.* 16. 271), do not augur well. Zeus has discharged his promise to honour Achilles, Agamemnon has recognized his folly (*Il.* 9. 15–22; 116) even if Achilles has never heard him say that he has, but now Achilles wants more.

   Patroclus is killed by Hector, and in the course of his extravagant mourning for Patroclus, Achilles regrets his failure to defend him:

αὐτίκα τεθναίην, ἐπεὶ οὐκ ἄρ᾽ ἔμελλον ἑταίρῳ
κτεινομένῳ ἐπαμῦναι

Let me die soon, since I was not going to defend my companion
when he was killed.

(*Il.* 18. 98–9)

Sinos[193] argues that Thetis misinterprets his words, taking them as a generalization about the virtues of defending one's companions, instead of a specific reference to *the* companion, Patroclus, whom Achilles failed to defend:

ναὶ δὴ ταῦτά γε, τέκνον, ἐτήτυμον οὐ κακόν ἐστι
τειρομένοις ἑτάροισιν ἀμυνέμεν αἰπὺν ὄλεθρον.[194]

this is surely true, child, it is no bad thing
to ward off sheer destruction from one's companions when they are
   distressed.

(*Il.* 18. 128–9)

Apollo has honoured him and hurt the Greeks, but Achilles will not intervene himself to end the troubles of the Greeks, as Chryses intervened to end the plague.

---

[193] Sinos (1980: 43).
[194] Cf *Il.* 18. 841.

Thetis may be referring to the claims of the community so far
neglected by Achilles: but for his part, he could live with
neglecting the other Greeks; what really troubles him is his
irreversible neglect of *the* companion,[195] Patroclus, who in place
of Achilles, lost his life for the sake of the community. Achilles
has had three opportunities to lay aside his anger voluntarily, in
response to λιταί,[196] and each time refused to do so, accompanying his refusal on two occasions with a rehearsal of his
grievance against Agamemnon. On the fourth occasion he no
longer has any choice: Phoenix had told him δάμασον θυμὸν
μέγαν, 'subdue your great passion' (*Il.* 9. 495); Achilles seems to
echo this advice in saying that he returns to battle after
Patroclus' death θυμὸν ἐνὶ στήθεσσι φίλον δαμάσαντες ἀνάγκῃ,
'subduing the passion in our breast by necessity' (*Il.* 18. 113).
Patroclus would not have died as he did if Achilles had not
rejected the embassy. The embassy sought to influence Achilles
through the offer of compensation and through asserting the
claims of friendship. Although it meets with refusal, the
embassy succeeds in arousing Achilles' interest in such
approaches, so that, despite implied warnings that the embassy
is doing him extraordinary honour, unlikely to be repeated (*Il.*
9. 302, 601–5), he looks forward (*Il.* 11. 609–10; 16. 85–6) to a
more satisfying and enhanced version of the embassy. The
paradigm of Meleager might have illustrated for Achilles how
unrealistic a prospect this is. Nothing but his anger prevents
him from fighting, he tells Patroclus (*Il.* 16. 50–3) in response
to diplomatic suggestions that prophecy or a divine message
may be the reason why he refrains from battle (*Il.* 16. 36–7).[197]
Something blinds him to the dangers inherent in Patroclus'
request to be permitted to wear the armour of Achilles and to
fight alone. He bitterly regrets his failure to defend Patroclus,
whose death was the result of a number of factors, and not least
Nestor's manipulation, which caused Patroclus to show a concern for his comrades not shared by Achilles.

[195] See *Il.* 18. 80–1.

[196] *Il.* 1. 282–3 (Nestor); the embassy of book 9; Patroclus' appeal in book
16. These are not marked by τρὶς μέν . . . τρὶς δέ . . . ἀλλ' ὅτε δὴ τὸ τέταρτον . . .
and Bannert (1988: 40–56) does not discuss them in his 'Dreimal als
Szenenmarke'.

[197] See n. 178 above.

7.4.4. Achilles punished by the visitation of ἄτη (delusion)

If Patroclus' death results from Achilles' rejection of the embassy, is Achilles affected by ἄτη in the events leading up to it? Achilles is never, in so many words, said to be affected by ἄτη. He seems to agree (*Il.* 17. 270) with Agamemnon's explanation of his appropriation of Briseis as the work of ἄτη (*Il.* 19. 88, 134–8). Something makes Achilles send Patroclus to enquire after the wounded Greeks, and something causes him to ignore the dangers to his friend, and send him, instead of going in person, to keep the promise made to Ajax in book 9. Whatever causes Achilles to act in this way is not unconnected with his anticipation of a more gratifying overture than the embassy in book 9: this anticipated approach is to feature supplication, as well as compensation and the return of Briseis. This fresh attempt at conciliation becomes, in Achilles' mind, his due, and he is to receive it with no effort on his part. The prospect drives all other thoughts from his mind, so that on both the occasions between the embassy and Patroclus' death when the action shifts to Achilles, he alludes to the more satisfactory delegation he hopes to receive (*Il.* 11. 609–10; 16. 85–6), although in each case, the mention of his obsession is quite inappropriate to the circumstances.

The death of Patroclus causes Achilles to see in a new light his preoccupation with satisfaction for Agamemnon's slight to his honour (*Il.* 18. 104). The gifts are offered again, and greeted with indifference (*Il.* 19. 147–8, 200–2). Briseis is returned, but first Achilles will wish she had died on the day he sacked Lyrnessus (*Il.* 19. 59–60). Agamemnon makes an apology (characteristically self-aggrandizing and self-exculpatory) (*Il.* 19. 86–138) and Achilles changes the subject (*Il.* 19. 148). In comparison with the loss of Patroclus, the obsessions which have so engrossed Achilles become utterly trivial. He has allowed, or been driven to allow, his mind to be occupied by something which turns out to have no significance, and to take risks with the person most precious to him in pursuit of it. His obsessions, when they become reality, bring no satisfaction. Whatever causes Achilles to send Patroclus to make enquiries, whatever causes him to permit his friend to fight alone, whatever causes the obsession with a new embassy to develop in

Achilles' mind, this force remains unspecified. Obviously, everything that happens is attributable to the plan of Zeus, and that is the explanation offered by Yamagata.[198] But we saw that the αἶνος of the Λιταί may be taken to apply even to the case of Agamemnon in book 1, even though Agamemnon never hears the warning contained in the αἶνος. Since the αἶνος is addressed to Achilles, it is even more likely to apply to him than to Agamemnon. The forces working on Achilles certainly produce the kind of mental blindness (to everything but the obsession) observed in Agamemnon in book 1, where his only concern is that he must not be without a prize, preferably the one he started with. The isolation of Agamemnon's position against the whole army is repeated in Achilles' complete isolation, once he has permitted Patroclus to act on his sympathy with the community of the army and return to battle. The forces causing Achilles to act as he does certainly bring him to grief: he suffers harm and pays the penalty for his self-aggrandizing obsession. This is the kind of work done by ἄτη, even if Achilles is never explicitly described as its victim.

7.5. HECTOR AND THE ASCENDING SCALE OF AFFECTION

7.5.1. The ascending scale of affection in book 6

Kakridis has argued that Hector too is the recipient of a series of requests in ascending scale of affection when he goes into Troy to deliver Helenus' message to Hecuba (*Il.* 6. 84–98).[199] Helenus' message is that Hecuba and the other old ladies of Troy should dedicate a robe to Athene with the promise of a hecatomb if she will check the murderous career of Diomede. In Troy Hector meets with a series of women, all of whom attempt to deflect him from his business with some request: Hector refuses them all in turn, gives them all instructions, and tells them what he is going to do next. To the Trojan women who meet him at the Scaean gate, asking for news of their sons, brothers, and husbands on the battlefield, Hector responds only with the collective instruction to pray to all the gods in

---

[198] Yamagata (1991: 15).   [199] Kakridis (1949: 49–64).

turn (*Il.* 6. 241–2). He arrives at the palace of Priam where his mother comes to meet him, bringing with her his most beautiful sister, Laodice. Hecuba surmises that his purpose in coming into the city must be to pray to the gods, and tries to persuade him to drink some wine first, and pour a libation, but Hector refuses, objecting that it would be improper to pour libations in his present state, spattered in blood and gore from the battlefield. He gives his mother Helenus' message to go with the other old ladies to the temple of Athene and promise sacrifice if the goddess will put a stop to the career of Diomede, and then tells her what he will do himself: he is going to visit Paris, to rouse him up to fight again. The message from Helenus was Hector's reason for coming back to Troy, but now that it is delivered, Hector does not immediately return to the fighting, but visits Paris and Helen in their bedchamber, then goes to look for his own wife and child. The danger posed by Diomede's murderous career is temporarily forgotten. In the apartments of Paris, his interview with his brother-in-law over, Hector's attention is engaged by an apparently repentant Helen, who is very free with self-reproach (*Il.* 6. 344–8) and abuse of her husband (*Il.* 6. 350–3). She attempts to detain Hector in conversation in her own quarters,[200] but while he acknowledges the claims of her affection for him: μή με κάθιζ', Ἑλένη, φιλέουσά περ, 'Don't ask me to sit down, Helen, although you love me' (*Il.* 6. 360), Hector refuses to be delayed by her, asserting that his θυμός (passion) urges him to return to the battle, where the Trojans are hard-pressed as a result of his absence. He asks Helen to hurry Paris along to the fighting,[201] saying that he himself is going to see his οἰκῆας;[202] his wife, Andromache, and his baby son, since he does not know, once

[200] Arthur-Katz (1981: 29) detects sexual overtones in Helen's invitation to Hector, but offers no evidence for them.

[201] Paris has been in his bedchamber since Aphrodite deposited him there when she rescued him from the duel with Menelaus (*Il.* 3. 380–2). The absence of a hero from the battlefield is so usually attributable to χόλος that Hector automatically makes it the reason for Paris' absence (*Il.* 6. 326): see Willcock (1956–7: 23–4). For other withdrawals from battle because of anger, see Bethe (1925: 4); Willcock (1964: 152–3 n. 6).

[202] On the relationship between οἰκεῖος and φίλος, see Chantraine (1968: ii. 782 and 1206), s.v. οἶκος B and φίλος, where he cites Benveniste (1973: 273–88; 1st pub. 1969).

he enters the battle, whether he will live to return to them, or whether he will die on the field (*Il.* 6. 365–8).

Hector's encounter with Andromache on the tower, the ὁμιλία, is one of the most famous scenes in Homer. It employs the motif of the ascending scale of affection not once, but three times (*Il.* 6. 410–28, 429–30, 450–4). The motif will not be used again until the embassy to Achilles. Andromache prefaces her request that Hector stay on the tower to direct the fighting, by an outline of what it would mean to her to lose him (*Il.* 6. 407–10): since her own city was sacked, and her father and brothers were killed, she has no one to shield her but Hector. He is father, mother, brother, and husband to her. In her anxiety not to lose him,[203] she asks Hector to fight defensively (*Il.* 6. 433–9) and to remain on the tower, commanding the army from there, out of pity for herself and their child. Hector says he loves her above all others: more than the Trojans, more than Hecuba and Priam, more than his brothers (*Il.* 6. 450–5). The relationships he rehearses are exactly those just mentioned by Andromache (*Il.* 6. 413–29), but Hector still rejects her appeal in favour of the principle of heroism. For Lohmann, it is not Andromache who occupies the highest position in Hector's ascending scale of affection, but the overriding heroic principle, always to be first in battle.[204] This view is temporarily invalidated for the few minutes when Astyanax succeeds, but only momentarily, in making his father lay aside the warrior's helmet.[205] The power of the son to sway his father is highly significant, and underlines the importance of the father–son relationship which is of primary interest to the poet, as we shall see. Redfield[206] discusses Hector's conflict of loyalties: his loyalty to his city as its leading warrior requires him to be ready to die: his loyalties to his city as Priams's heir and to the members of his household both require him to survive, to look forward to another day. Hector *could* opt for caution and fight as a defender without putting his personal safety at risk, since

[203] The motives ascribed to women entreating are discussed in Appendix E.

[204] Lohmann (1988: 42). When he has kissed and dandled the baby on his arm, Hector prays that his son may be πατρὸς . . . πολλὸν ἀμείνων, 'much better than his father' (*Il.* 6. 479) at killing: 'bloodier than him', trans. M. Longley, 'The Helmet', *Ghost Orchid* (London, 1995), 38.

[205] Schadewaldt (1965: 223; 1st pub. 1944).

[206] (1975: 123–4).

the future of his community depends on his personal survival. Instead he chooses to privilege his role as the leading warrior of his city, betraying his obligation to survive. Interestingly, Hector's reasons for his priorities are the dictates of his θυμός (passion) (*Il.* 6. 444),[207] and the requirements of αἰδώς (shame) (*Il.* 6. 442). Cairns[208] explains how this combination of αἰδώς and θυμός indicates a personal choice. The ὁμιλία (meeting of Hector and Andromache) is a turning point: Hector rejects the role proposed by Andromache, of cautious defender of Troy, in favour of heroic action in pursuit of glory (*Il.* 6. 441–6). Small wonder the women mourn him as he leaves the city for the battlefield, for the course he has chosen, as Andromache knows (*Il.* 6. 407–10), and as Hector himself acknowledges (*Il.* 6. 464–5), will lead to his death. Sophocles might have had this in mind when he made Andromache's appeal to Hector the model for Tecmessa's appeal to Ajax before his suicide.[209]

7.5.2. The approaches to Hector and Meleager compared

The approaches to Hector explored in book 6 culminate in Andromache's appeal to her husband to fight defensively and not to court danger in the pursuit of glory. This makes a logical conclusion to the previous requests, all of which sought to detain Hector within the protective safety of the city walls, delaying his return to the battlefield. There is a kind of consistency in the requests put to Hector, since they all attempt to deflect him from the pursuit of heroism. In concluding with his wife, the series of approaches to Hector in book 6 resembles that explored in the paradigm of Meleager,[210] to which it displays certain other correspondences:

Hector		*Meleager*
Andromache	wife	Cleopatra
Helen		dearest friends
Hecuba and Laodice		mother and sisters

---

[207] Something Achilles will be told to control (*Il.* 9. 496). Hector is motivated by θυμός (passion) at *Il.* 6. 361.

[208] (1993: 80–1). See also Redfield (1975: 115–19).

[209] See Reinhardt (1979: 20–2; 1st pub. 1933).

[210] The two episodes display verbal echoes in the terms for spouse: ἄκοιτις (*Il.* 6. 374), used of Andromache; παρακοίτης (*Il.* 6. 430) used of Hector; παράκοιτις (*Il.* 9. 590) used of Cleopatra.

father

priests

women of Troy

elders

The approaches to Hector, like those to Meleager, begin with members of the local community, progress through family members and close friends, and conclude with his wife. The women who entreat Hector in book 6 also mourn him, both at the end of book 6 when he has rejected their requests, and in book 24, where Andromache, Hecuba, and Helen each sing a dirge.[211] Hector provides no κῆδος, care for his dependants: instead, they must provide κῆδος for him, in the form of mourning. In her dirge for Hector, Andromache uses the image of the fate of the wives and children in a captured city:

ἀλόχους κεδνὰς[212] καὶ νήπια τέκνα,
αἳ δή τοι τάχα νηυσὶν ὀχήσονται γλαφυρῇσι,
καὶ μὲν ἐγὼ μετὰ τῇσι.

the cherished wives and the infant children
who will soon be carried off in the hollow ships,
and I among them.

(*Il.* 24. 730–2)

Andromache had earlier used this same image to describe the destruction of her own community by Achilles (*Il.* 6. 414–26) and entreated Hector to save Astyanax and herself from such a fate (*Il.* 6. 431–2). Her husband's failure to heed her advice means the image must become reality for Andromache and for the women and children of Troy. Such a fate for the women and children of Calydon is averted in the paradigm of Meleager by Cleopatra's successful use of the same image of the fate of the inhabitants of a captured town to awaken her husband's instinct to take care of them (*Il.* 9. 594).[213]

---

[211] *Il.* 24. 725–45, 748–59, 762–75.

[212] See Chantraine (1968) and Frisk (1954–70), s.v. κεδνός for possible association with κήδομαι, care for: cf. κεδνότατοι (*Il.* 9. 586); κήδιστοι (*Il.* 9. 642).

[213] Cleopatra describes the κήδεα of those whose city is captured: the men are killed, the city is destroyed by fire, strangers lead off the children and the women. Κήδεα are here troubles in the sense of being objects of care or concern: the word is related to κήδομαι, 'care for'. By describing the dangers faced by the children and wives of the citizens, Cleopatra succeeds in awaken-

7.5.3. Further requests to Hector

Long after we might have thought that the exploration of Hector's scale of affections was exhausted, we find two further appeals made to him, this time by Priam and Hecuba (*Il.* 22. 33–91). The import of their requests is the same as that of Andromache in book 6:[214] Hector should retreat within the protection of the city walls and not court heroism and death by remaining outside to face the lethal single combat with Achilles. To add to the intensity of the situation, Achilles is storming across the plain, visible to Hector and to Priam and Hecuba as they make their appeal. As we saw earlier (7.1.4), the appeals of his parents to Hector are λιταί in the context of supplication. Andromache outlined in her appeal in book 6 the consequences of Hector's death for herself and their child, and Priam paints a comparable picture of the consequences for himself and for the city of Troy if Hector persists in throwing away his life in the impending single combat with Achilles.

The consistency of Priam's supplication in book 22 with the earlier requests put to Hector in book 6 means that the claims on his affections are once more being tested in terms of this same requirement by Hector's community that he preserve his life and survive as the city's defender. This time we are looking at the claims of his parents, and of his father in particular. I am not suggesting that Hector loves Andromache less than he loves Priam and Hecuba: that could never be, since Hector himself is made to say that he is more concerned for her than for anyone else, and he specifically includes Priam and Hecuba (*Il.* 6. 451) among the list of people for whom he is less concerned than he is for Andromache. However, the effectiveness of the supplication of Priam and Hecuba is tested after the request of Hector's wife, the person he loves best. Priam and Hecuba certainly have no more success with their request than Andromache with hers. Priam's λιταί to Hector in a context of supplication after the closure of the series of requests made in ascending scale of affection in book 6 anticipate the λιταί of Priam in the context of

ing Meleager's instinct to care for them by fighting for them. Cleopatra's relationship to Meleager by marriage, κῆδος, succeeds in achieving what even the κεδνότατοι of friends cannot.

[214] For the association of the speeches in book 6 with those in book 22, see Beck (1964: 71–92); Kakridis (1971: 72–4).

his supplication to Achilles in book 24 after λιταί in ascending scale of affection to Achilles (those of Nestor in book 1, of the embassy in book 9, and Patroclus in book 16). Priam's supplication of Achilles asserts the claims of Achilles' father, Peleus, on his affections. Priam is the genuine, as opposed to the surrogate, father-figure at Troy, and he is used to test the claims of the genuine father on the affections of both, his own son, Hector, and of Achilles. He describes himself as ἐπὶ γήραος οὐδῷ, 'on the threshold of old age', in his appeal to Hector (*Il.* 22. 60) and uses the same phrase of Peleus in his appeal to Achilles (*Il.* 24. 487). Priam's claims on Hector are obviously paternal, but in his dealings with Achilles he asserts his claims in terms of his role as an aged father confronting old age deprived of the support of his (dead) son, as Achilles' father, Peleus, must confront old age deprived of the support of his son (who is fighting at Troy).[215] The significance of the claims of the father as the last test on a hero's affections will be discussed below. For the moment, the order in which claims on Hector's affections are tested is as follows.

---

[215] See Macleod (1982: 134) ad *Il.* 24. 542 for Achilles as the link between the sufferings of Peleus and Priam. Achilles neglects his own father and causes suffering to Priam by killing his sons. Crotty (1994: 24–41) explains the inability of warriors to respond to their fathers' demands for pity as resulting from their father having been the very person who taught them to feel the αἰδώς which drives them to fight. The conflicting demands of the father (for pity and protection in old age, *and* for displays of pitiless brutality on the battlefield) are epitomized in Priam's request to Hector not to fight Achilles (*Il.* 22. 38–76) and in Hector's prayer for Astyanax (*Il.* 6. 476–81). The mutually irreconcilable demands made by a father may help to explain why Hector concentrates on the shame he would feel if he had to face his followers and people, and chooses to ignore Priam's pleas to consider the fate which awaits him if Hector is killed, and why Achilles is able to respond to the claims of a father when they are represented by Priam. Priam's plea to Achilles is based on a genuine father–son relationship, as opposed to the surrogate relationship Phoenix claimed with Achilles, but Priam is not Achilles' father, and has not urged on him the kind of brutality Hector desires in his own son, Astyanax (*Il.* 6. 480–1). For a son, a father may be the embodiment of mutually conflicting demands, as Priam probably is for Hector. However, according to the αἶνος of the Λιταί (allegory of the Prayers), Hector's refusal of his father's λιταί must result in affliction by ἄτη (delusion).

Priam (and Hecuba)   (father (and mother))
——*ascending scale of affection stops here* (*Il.* 6. 450–4)——
Andromache   (wife)
Helen
Hecuba and Laodice   (mother and sister)
Trojan women

Hecuba appears twice in this series, since she makes a request to Hector in book 6 to stay and drink wine and pour a libation (*Il.* 6. 258–60) and a second request to him in book 22 to come within the protection of the city walls (*Il.* 22. 84–5). In book 6 she is the primary agent of the appeal, and her daughter, Laodice, who accompanies her, says nothing. Meleager's mother and sisters made an appeal together, but we are not told whether Meleager's sisters ever said anything in the course of it. In book 22, although Hecuba is the last to speak to Hector, her plea forms a unity with that of Priam, as indicated by the duals:

"Ὣς τώ γε κλαίοντε προσαυδήτην φίλον υἱὸν
πολλὰ λισσομένω

So *they two, lamenting, addressed* their son,
with many entreaties.

                        (*Il.* 22. 90–1)

The appeals of Priam and Hecuba in book 22 constitute an appeal from parents,[216] and the lion's share of the talking is done by Priam, the father.

7.5.4. *The nature of requests to Hector*

The motif of the ascending scale of affection is employed to test the claims on the affections of Hector, as well as on those of Meleager and Achilles, but the requests addressed to Hector in the ascending scale are not uniformly and undeniably classifiable as λιταί (prayers). None of the requests addressed to Hector

---

[216] Rather as Andromache and Astyanax make a unified appeal to Hector in book 6. Hector thinks of them as a unit when he tells Helen he is going to see them (*Il.* 6. 366). The emotional eloquence of Andromache's appeal in book 6 is associated with Astyanax's appeal by gesture (his terrified recoil from his father in the war-helmet (*Il.* 6. 467–70)), and the pattern is repeated in the eloquence of Priam in book 24 coupled with Hecuba's appeal by gesture (exposing the breast).

by the women in book 6 is associated with part of λίσσομαι (pray, entreat), none is described as a λιτή, nor are there any references to the rituals of supplication in book 6.[217] The women of Troy attempt to delay Hector with requests for news of their kinsmen on the field, both Hecuba and Helen attempt to delay his return to the mêlée, and the expression of their tactics of delay takes the form of undifferentiated petitions. Significantly, Hector asserts his own immediate plans when he refuses to comply with their requests (*Il.* 6. 280–1, 365–6, 492–3), establishing a pattern of refusal to deviate from the course on which he has decided. Andromache, and later (in book 22), his parents ask Hector to fight defensively, not to take unnecessary risks with his life. The requests of his parents are λιταί in the context of supplication: Andromache's request, although not called a λιτή, is an attempt to deflect Hector from his chosen course of heroism, and shares with the λιταί to Meleager and Achilles we have been examining the attempt to alter someone else's course of action. Obviously, their passionate concern for his safety stems from the intimacy and affection of their relationships with him, but they also want him to protect himself so that he will survive and continue to defend them. In a sense, they are asking him to look after everyone's interests, his own, as well as theirs, in protecting his life, but Hector himself does not view the situation in the same light as Andromache, Priam and Hecuba, and Polydamas. Andromache envisages the consequences of losing Hector, who represents the last support sustaining her position in a society not her own: if Hector is killed, she has no kin to whom she could return as a widow with an orphaned child (*Il.* 6. 407–9, 413–30).[218]

Priam and Hecuba look even deeper into the abyss than Andromache at this point: conscious of the danger awaiting

---

[217] Unless the Pythagorean idea that one's wife is a suppliant (DK 58C 4–5; Iamblichus, *VP* 18. 84; [Aristotle], *Oec.* 1344^{a}10) holds good for the Homeric poems. If it does, then Andromache's appeals to Hector in book 6 are appeals from a suppliant.

[218] She repeats these concerns at *Il.* 22. 484–506 and 24. 725–8. Her picture of the orphaned Astyanax driven away from the subscription feast by the farmers who have contributed to it is an unlikely prospect for the noble prince of the royal house of Troy, but entirely in keeping with the peasant communities of the 8th cent. and later: see Strasburger (1953: 108–9).

Hector if he carries through his intention of fighting Achilles in single combat, they address passionate λιταί to him[219] in the context of a supplication which appeals to αἰδώς by references to generative parts of their own, his parents', bodies. Priam describes the consequences of the fall of Troy which will follow hard upon Hector's death: his sons killed, his daughters dragged away, the children thrown on the ground in the carnage, the mistreatment of women by the conquerors, and his own corpse ravaged by the dogs he had fed at table. At *Il.* 22. 74 Priam imagines the dogs ravaging the grey head, the grey beard, and the privy parts of an old man who has been slaughtered: all these parts of the body are highly significant in the context of supplication. The mutilation of Priam's corpse, foreseen at *Il.* 22. 66–71 has been described as a symbol of the overthrow of civilization:[220] this is what is at issue when Priam begs Hector not to meet Achilles alone. Hecuba reinforces Priam's appeal, attempting to evoke αἰδώς and pity by the exposure of her breasts, an appeal to respect her maternity. She warns Hector of the more immediate consequences if he is killed by Achilles, who will permit no funeral, nor will the women be able to mourn him.[221] Hecuba fears that Hector will be eaten by the dogs, and that the χυτὴ γαῖα, the funerary monument he fore-saw for himself (*Il.* 6. 464) when he chose his present reckless course during the ὁμιλία with Andromache, will certainly not cover him after a hero's funeral in climax to a glorious career. Priam and Hecuba attempt to appeal to Hector's αἰδώς, one of the forces by which he is motivated, but not even their references to life-giving parts of their own bodies, or their descriptions of the bodies of father and son left shamefully unburied, a prey for the dogs, are sufficient to persuade his θυμός (*Il.* 22. 78), and so their appeals are doomed to failure.

---

[219] λισσόμενος (*Il.* 22. 35), of Priam: πολλὰ λισσομένῳ (*Il.* 22. 91), of both.

[220] Segal (1971*b*: 33–4).

[221] On the significance of ἔτι (*Il.* 22. 86), see Loraux (1990: 60–1): Hecuba has always been conscious that she will have to mourn Hector, and now even that is being taken from her. Sourvinou-Inwood (1981: 31–2) discusses the importance of funeral to 'good' death.

7.5.5. *Hector's responses*

Hector's responses to the appeals of his wife and to the λιταί and supplication of his parents could not appear more different. To Andromache, Hector confesses his awareness that the Trojans are all doomed:

εὖ γὰρ ἐγὼ τόδε οἶδα κατὰ φρένα καὶ κατὰ θυμόν·
ἔσσεται ἦμαρ ὅτ᾽ ἄν ποτ᾽ ὀλώλῃ Ἴλιος ἱρὴ
καὶ Πρίαμος καὶ λαὸς ἐϋμμελίω Πριάμοιο.

for well I know this in my mind and heart;
there will be a day when holy Ilion will perish
both Priam and the people of Priam of the good ashen spear.

(*Il.* 6. 447–9)

Andromache will be dragged off into slavery to serve foreign masters, for lack of a husband such as Hector to prevent it (*Il.* 6. 463): Hector seems aware that he will not survive until the fall of Troy, and hopes he will be dead and buried, with a hero's honours (*Il.* 6. 464) before the dreadful day. Andromache shares his awareness of impending disaster: φθίσει σε τὸ σὸν μένος, 'your strength will destroy you', she says (*Il.* 6. 407), although she asserts her will and her entreaties against it. She too knows it would be preferable to die rather than face what is coming (*Il.* 6. 410–11).

Although Hector tells his wife he is more concerned for her than for anyone else, he makes no concession to her pleas, because he is concerned (αἰδέομαι) how he will appear to the Trojans, if, like a base man, he shuns the war (*Il.* 6. 442–3). His θυμός urges him to fight in pursuit of glory (*Il.* 6. 444). He imagines how τις,[222] someone, will point out Andromache as the wife of Hector when the Trojan women are enslaved (*Il.* 6. 459–61). Cairns[223] has shown that Hector is motivated by personal choice and conditioning: the course he adopts is the one for which his life has prepared him, the only one of which he is capable. Hector's choice could be a mistake, it is certainly not much help to Andromache, and it reveals the limitations of Hector's imagination, but it does not result from a callous dis-

[222] Hector imagines what τις may say at *Il.* 6. 459–62, 479; 7. 87–91, 300–2; 22. 106. On such 'potential' τις-speeches as the inner voice of the speaker, see de Jong (1987*b*: esp. 177–8).

[223] Cairns (1993: 78–83); cf. Schadewaldt (1965: 220–1; 1st pub. 1944).

regard for his wife. The shared consciousness of doom, and the shared amusement at Astyanax's terror of his father's helmet (*Il.* 6. 471) argue for a real sympathy between husband and wife, apparent also in Andromache's swoon when first she sees her husband dead and mistreated (*Il.* 22. 466–72), but Hector has no comfort to offer her, beyond the idea that his destiny is inescapable, and that he will not be killed before his time (*Il.* 6. 487–9). Despite his compassion for his wife, Hector retreats to the certainties of the traditional roles, beyond which his imagination cannot reach: Andromache must return to her weaving (*Il.* 6. 490–2) after her expedition[224] to the walls, and he will return to the battle.

Hector is the victim of the same anxieties in book 22 as he waits outside the city walls to meet Achilles. His father fails to persuade his θυμός (*Il.* 22. 78): it was Hector's θυμός (passion) which urged him to return to the battle at *Il.* 6. 361 and 6. 444. Even when Hecuba joins her appeal to that of Priam, Hector's θυμός remains inexorable (*Il.* 22. 91). As far as Hector is concerned, it is no longer possible for him to re-enter Troy, since he cannot contemplate the loss of face resulting from the justified reproaches of Polydamas,[225] whose advice he has ignored (*Il.* 22. 99–102). Polydamas consistently argues for defensive strategy, rather like Andromache in book 6, but Hector insists on pursuing an offensive strategy. Once again, Hector is concerned for his reputation with others:

αἰδέομαι Τρῶας καὶ Τρῳάδας ἑλκεσιπέπλους

I feel shame before the Trojans and the Trojan ladies in their trailing gowns

$$(Il. 22. 105 = Il. 6. 442)$$

and imagines what τις, someone, lower down the social scale than himself (*Il.* 22. 106),[226] may say about him. What he

---

[224] A maenadic expedition (*Il.* 6. 389): for discussion of Andromache's two frenzied rushes to the city wall and their relationship to the destruction of her household, see Seaford (1994: 330–8) and cf. Arthur-Katz (1981: 30). The presentation of a robe to Athene is a collective progress to the acropolis prescribed by Helenus through Hector for the old women of Troy: Andromache's despair drives her in the opposite direction, to the limits of the city.

[225] On the warnings and advice of Polydamas, see 7.5.7 and 7.5.8 below, and Bannert (1988: 71–81): rather like the imaginary voice of τις, Polydamas is the voice of Hector's own, unexpressed thoughts.

[226] Cf. κακὸς ὥς, 'like a base man': *Il.* 6. 443.

imagines they will say is that he has destroyed the army (*Il.* 22.
107). Hector is aware that he has done something terrible, and
his anticipation of the coming reproaches heightens his consciousness of his past mistakes.[227] Rigid obedience to the
promptings of his θυμός in preference to any other advice, and
to the heroic values instilled by his conditioning, leads Hector
to fail his city and his community. He knows he has failed,
but he cannot face the public discussion of his failure. He
certainly wavers, considering, and rejecting, the possibility of
negotiating terms with Achilles for the return of Helen and the
property taken with her (*Il.* 22. 111–21), but finally prefers
to rely once more on the heroism which he has insisted on
pursuing, despite the repeated advice of his community.[228] The
fight with Achilles will almost certainly end in the death of
Hector, thus enabling him to avoid facing the public disgrace of
which he is so painfully aware, and if, by some chance, Achilles
should be the one to perish, Hector's past mistakes would be
redeemed.

It has already been demonstrated that Hector makes a
personal choice[229] to disregard Andromache's pleas that he fight
as a defender: it is his choice to privilege his desire for personal
glory as a warrior over his obligation to survive and protect his
community. One might wonder what alternative there is for a
leader in a defensive war but to do his best to fight back against
the attacker, but one must remember that it is possible to fight
as a defender without taking suicidal risks. A defender on
whose survival the city depends must first and foremost take
care to survive: he is not going to be much use to the city if he
goes out and gets killed in a blaze of glory as Hector thinks he
might: μέγα ῥέξας τι καὶ ἐσσομένοισι πυθέσθαι, 'when I have
achieved something great, for future generations to learn of' (*Il.*
22. 305). What would be gained if Hector retreated within the
walls as his parents request, and did not face Achilles? Would

---

[227] Cairns (1993: 82).

[228] Fenik (1978: 81–5) demonstrates that Hector entertains two strategies to
evade fighting Achilles: either re-entering Troy, or negotiating terms. His
decision to fight is taken for lack of any other course, and is not a firm one,
since Hector runs away (*Il.* 22. 81–2), something he earlier (*Il.* 18. 306–7) said
he would never do. On the intimacy of the exchanges Hector imagines
between Achilles and himself, see Crotty (1994: 85–7).

[229] Cairns (1993: 80–1) and 7.5.1 above.

this not lead to a miserable siege, or even to Achilles storming the city? These questions do not really arise, because they are outside the poem and the tradition. It is not absolutely clear why so much importance is attached to retreating within the walls (*Il*. 18. 266–79; 22. 56–8, 99–102) and to fighting from the defences of the walls (*Il*. 6. 431–4; 22. 84–5). Certainly ancient art shows the defenders of cities under siege attacking their beseigers from within the safety of the walls.[230] That, surely, is the point of fortifications: Andromache and Hector's parents are not unreasonable to advise their use. Hector achieves nothing by disregarding their advice. The point at issue is surely Hector's repeated refusal to heed advice which is not to his liking from members of his community.[231] The defender of a community must respect the advice of that community, especially when he himself is not good at strategy. Polydamas (*Il*. 13. 727–8) warns Hector that his military prowess causes him to think he excels in planning (βουλῇ) as well, but this is certainly not the case (*Il*. 13. 729–34). Hector cannot allow himself to be told what he does not want to hear (*Il*. 12. 231–50; 18. 285–96). Hector's plan to spend the night in the plain against the advice of Polydamas (*Il*. 18. 297–304) is deluded: the poet expressly says in his own voice that the Trojans applauded Hector's plan because Athene had taken away their wits (*Il*. 18. 311). Hector owes it to his family, who will pay the price of his mistakes, and to Polydamas, the seer who under-stands both the future and the past (*Il*. 18. 250 and see 7.5.8 below), not to try to know better than they do. Hector's refusals to listen to advice will have disastrous consequences. Hector complies with none of the requests put to him in ascending scale of affection in book 6, and in response to the λιταί of his parents, he says not a word, but completely ignores them.[232]

---

[230] See for example, the silver siege rhyton from Mycenae: Karo (1930: i. 106–8 and figs. 35 and 39; 1933: ii, pl. 122); BM 123–53, a Phoenician silver dish from Amathus, showing a city under siege, illustrated in Edwards (1991: 205, fig. 2).

[231] In addition to his failure to retreat within the walls and fight from them, he ignores advice to practise caution (*Il*. 12. 61–79, 216; 13. 726–47): all dis-cussed by Redfield (1975: 143–53).

[232] On the absolute obedience owed to parents see Dover (1974: 274).

7.5.6. Is Hector's rejection of λιταί (prayers) punished by the visitation of ἄτη (delusion)?

Hector receives and rejects a series of requests in ascending scale of affection, and goes on to reject the λιταί of his parents. In the terms of the allegory of the *Λιταί*, those who reject λιταί are prone to suffer from ἄτη. We have seen Agamemnon admit to his affliction by ἄτη after rejecting the λιταί of Chryses, and it would be reasonable to consider whether Hector appears as the victim of ἄτη after his disregard of the λιταί of his parents in book 22, or indeed, whether he manifests symptoms of ἄτη after his failure to comply with any of the requests put to him in ascending scale of affection in book 6.

Schadewaldt believed in an ἄτη-stricken Hector,[233] but he did not connect the ἄτη he supposed in him with his rejection of λιταί or requests, regarding it rather as part of the plan of Zeus. This plan began as Zeus' intention to fulfil his promise to Thetis (*Il.* 1. 509–10, 528) by making the Greeks lose, so that, in order to recover Achilles and his fighting strength, the Greeks will be obliged to recompense and honour (*Il.* 2. 3–4) the offended hero. Zeus employs some rather questionable methods to achieve his purpose, instilling false confidence through omens, prophecies, and direct communications delivered by divine messengers. He also exploits the tendency of mortals to overlook the full implications of his messages, and to fail to notice the limitations set on his promises. These tactics are employed against both Greeks and Trojans. Zeus lets out details of his plan in short instalments, but avoids any

---

[233] Schadewaldt (1966: 108, 156; 1st pub. 1938) is probably right that Hector is the victim of ἄτη, but as indicated by Dawe (1967: 99) he is never explicitly said to be the victim of ἄτη. Hector refers to his own ἀτασθαλία (*Il.* 22. 104): see Stallmach (1968: 58 n. 80). Finkelberg (1995: 16–21) distinguishes between errors ascribed to ἀτασθαλία (folly) and errors ascribed to ἄτη (delusion). The former, in her view, are preceded by a clear warning not to proceed with that particular course of action: it is rational, and comes from within. Ἄτη is associated with lack of foreknowledge and failure to consider the consequences. It comes from outside and is irrational. In Finkelberg's view (1995: 23), ἀτασθαλία is presented as the main cause of Hector's fall. Finkelberg may be right to describe the *interior* forces at work *in* Hector as ἀτασθαλία, but we should not neglect the considerable *exterior* forces at work *on* him to delude and deceive him. For association of ἄτη with ἀπάτη (which certainly affects Hector, as he says at *Il.* 22. 299) see Stallmach (1968: 40).

discusssion of the first step he takes. The evil Dream he sends to Agamemnon to delude him into thinking he is on the verge of capturing Troy (*Il.* 2. 8–15), has already been discussed (7.1.9) in terms of ἄτη sent by Zeus at the request of rejected Λιταί to punish the cause of their resentment. But Zeus sends the Dream as the first step in his plan to force the Greeks to honour Achilles when they have suffered heavy losses by the ships.[234] Ζεύς με μέγα Κρονίδης ἄτη ἐνέδησε βαρείη, 'Zeus, the son of Cronos, bound me in heavy ἄτη' (*Il.* 2. 111), says Agamemnon on realizing he has been duped by Zeus: ἄτη is both Agamemnon's punishment for rejecting the λιταί, and an instrument employed by Zeus against Agamemnon in the fulfilment of his plan.

7.5.7. *Hector's delusions and the plan of Zeus*

Redfield[235] discusses three major errors made by Hector after his visit to Troy: the first is his promise (*Il.* 8. 489–541) of victory for the following day; the second his refusal to withdraw the army within the walls (*Il.* 18. 243–313); the third his refusal to avoid Achilles by withdrawing within the walls (*Il.* 22. 25–130). Hector is never described in so many words as the victim of ἄτη, but he grows overconfident[236] in interpreting signals and messages sent by Zeus, and fails to appreciate the circumscribed nature of the success he is granted. The process by which he is led to suffer from overconfidence begins almost as soon as he returns to battle after refusing to agree to the requests of the women he met in book 6:[237] on the strength of an

---

[234] This is why it is impossible to dissociate Agamemnon's ἄτη in books 1, 9, and 19, which has to do with his misguided dealings with Achilles, from the Ἄτη resulting from the Dream sent by Zeus.

[235] (1975: 128–59).

[236] These are the symptoms of madness displayed by Hector: Γοργοῦς ὄμματ' ἔχων ἠδὲ βροτολοιγοῦ Ἄρεος, 'with the eyes of Gorgo or of Ares, bane of men' (*Il.* 8. 349); μαίνεται, 'he rages' (*Il.* 8. 355); κρατερὴ δέ ἑ λύσσα δέδυκεν, 'violent madness has come over him' (*Il.* 9. 239); λύσσαν ἔχων, 'in madness' (*Il.* 9. 305) (on λύσσα, see Lincoln (1975)); ἀφλοισμὸς δὲ περὶ στόμα γίγνετο, τὼ δέ οἱ ὄσσε | λαμπέσθην βλοσυρῇσιν ὑπ' ὀφρύσιν, 'foam gathered round his mouth, and his eyes blazed under his beetling brows' (*Il.* 15. 607–8). They may relate to his overconfidence, and the manipulation by Zeus which causes it.

[237] Shortly after he has rejected the appeals of the women in book 6 the verb μαίνομαι (to be mad) begins to be used of Hector: *Il.* 8. 355; 9. 238; 15. 605, 606; 21. 5.

assurance from his brother, Helenus,[238] that he has heard the gods say that Hector is not yet fated to die, Hector challenges the Greeks to provide a champion to fight him in single combat. Hector concludes his challenge with boastful words (*Il.* 7. 87–91) which caused the scholiasts to censure him as a braggart.[239] Ajax is selected by lot to fight him, and Hector escapes alive only because the heralds intervene when it is getting dark to stop the duel (*Il.* 7. 274–82). No one had really expected Hector to survive (*Il.* 7. 307–10). Further misleading encouragement from Zeus comes in the form of a thunderbolt, frightening the horses of Diomede as they career in pursuit of the Trojans (*Il.* 8. 133–4), and in the three thunderclaps (*Il.* 8. 170) which lead Hector to boast that Zeus has assented to a Trojan victory. Zeus reveals, in the course of upbraiding Athene and Hera for their abortive attempt to go to the assistance of the Greeks, who have been driven back by Hector to the defences round their ships, that he will permit no impediment to Hector's victorious career until Achilles returns to the fighting to avenge the death of Patroclus (*Il.* 8. 473–6). Hector, encouraged by the successes already achieved, boasts[240] that, with the help of Zeus and the other gods, he will drive away the Greeks completely (*Il.* 8. 526–7). He adds a wish that he could be ageless and deathless all his days, and be honoured like Athene and Apollo (*Il.* 8. 538–40).[241] This wish looks remarkably like a desire to overstep human limitations, and Hector will soon say more in the same vein.

After the night of the embassy, Zeus works further on the already frenzied Hector. He sends Iris to him with a message: Hector should keep out of the fighting until Agamemnon is wounded, but then he will be able to push the Greeks back to their ships and be victorious until sunset (*Il.* 11. 186–94).

---

[238] Hector twice follows advice from Helenus and twice follows advice from Polydamas, and has success. He ignores Polydamas' first warning, and succeeds anyway. His failure is associated with failure to heed the second warning of Polydamas: see Bannert (1988: 78).

[239] Sch. T ad *Il.* 7. 90 (= Erbse (1969–88: ii. 243), 90b¹) looks forward to Hector's hope that he will die performing some great action (*Il.* 22. 305). See also Sch. b ad *Il.* 7. 90 (= Erbse (1969–88: ii. 243), 90b²).

[240] Redfield (1975: 138) offers three translations for εὔχομαι ἐλπόμενος: I claim my hope; I confidently boast; I hopefully pray.

[241] On Hector's aspirations, see Nagy (1979: 148–9).

Needless to say, it is not very long before Agamemnon is wounded (*Il.* 11. 252) and retreats (*Il.* 11. 280–4). The Trojans, with Hector among them, drive back the Greeks as far as the ditch round their defences for the ships. Polydamas advises Hector not to use horses and chariots to pursue the Greeks over the ditch (*Il.* 12. 110–15). Asius is caught in the snowstorm of boulders hurled by the two Lapiths, Polypoetes and Leonteus (*Il.* 12. 159–61) and complains of deception by Zeus, whom he holds responsible for his own overconfidence in the Trojan victory. He is killed (*Il.* 13. 389–93), and his fate illustrates the serious consequences of disregarding the advice of Polydamas. It is not very long before we find Hector too disregarding the advice of Polydamas and putting his faith in Zeus. An eagle appears with a snake in its talons, but the snake bites the eagle, and forces it to let go (*Il.* 12. 200–7). Polydamas interprets this as a warning not to pursue the Greeks as far as their ships (*Il.* 12. 216–20): he senses that his advice will be unwelcome, and offers it in an ingratiating manner (*Il.* 12. 211–14) as if familiar with Hector's royal temper. His anxiety is well placed, for Hector refuses (*Il.* 12. 238) to listen to his interpretation of the portent, since it is by no means what he wants to hear, and contradicts the more satisfactory (in Hector's terms) message received earlier from Zeus via Iris (*Il.* 12. 241–2). Hector accuses Polydamas of cowardice and threatens to kill him if he speaks in this way again (*Il.* 12. 244–50). In tragedy, this is how tyrants behave.

Poseidon's warning to the two Ajaxes to beware of Hector,

ὃς Διὸς εὔχετ' ἐρισθενέος πάϊς εἶναι

who boasts to be the son of Zeus, mighty in strength

(*Il.* 13. 54)

could be an exaggeration by Poseidon of Hector's desire (*Il.* 8. 538–40) to be honoured like Apollo and Athene, and it is certainly of a piece with Hector's behaviour in what is coming. When Polydamas advises the Trojans to withdraw temporarily from the ships, so that they can deliberate whether to fall on the ships or whether they should retreat from them (*Il.* 13. 740–4), Hector permits Polydamas to detain the other Trojans, but announces that he himself will go to meet the battle, returning when he has given orders to those who have advanced further

(*Il.* 13. 751–3). Although when Hector presses on, he finds many of the Trojans dead, including Asius, he does not pause to reflect that he, like Asius, is about to ignore Polydamas' advice. With the men rallied to Polydamas, Hector leads a fresh attack, and is warned by Ajax that his success is due to divine favour, which will soon be withdrawn: when it is, Hector will have to flee (*Il.* 13. 811–20). Ajax's speech is confirmed by a bird omen, which reminds us of the earlier bird omen interpreted by Polydamas (*Il.* 12. 214–27). Again Hector ignores the omen and threatens Ajax with being eaten by the dogs and birds. His threats are accompanied by an amplification of his wish:

> εἰ γὰρ ἐγὼν οὕτω γε Διὸς πάϊς αἰγιόχοιο
> εἴην ἤματα πάντα, τέκοι δέ με πότνια Ἥρη,
> τιοίμην δ' ὡς τίετ' Ἀθηναίη καὶ Ἀπόλλων.

would that I were the son of aegis-bearing Zeus
for all time, and that the lady Hera bore me,
and that I were honoured as Athene and Apollo are honoured.

(*Il.* 13. 825–7 (*Il.* 13. 827 = *Il.* 8. 540))

If Hector earlier (*Il.* 8. 540) wished to overstep human limitations, this is worse than ever.[242]

7.5.8. *Departure from the advice of Polydamas*

Further details of Zeus' plan are released when he wakes up in a towering rage, realizing that Hera has tricked him into making love and going to sleep afterwards to prevent him from influencing the battle. In the context of threatening Hera about what she has done, Zeus reveals to her that Hector is to drive the Greeks back to the ships, Achilles is to send Patroclus into battle, Patroclus will kill Sarpedon, and Hector will kill Patroclus. Achilles will avenge the death of Patroclus by killing Hector, and not long afterwards, Troy will fall (*Il.* 15. 62–71). Hera thus gains the information that Zeus has a plan which meets with her approval, and this is enough to secure her co-operation. It is Hera who, without Zeus' knowledge, sends Iris to instruct Achilles to arm and avenge Patroclus (*Il.* 18. 165–80), as Zeus acknowledges (*Il.* 18. 357–9). When Patroclus

---

[242] Janko (1992: 49–50 ad *Il.* 13. 54) also relates *Il.* 8. 539–40 to Poseidon's words at *Il.* 13. 54 as clear evidence of presumption on Hector's part.

has been killed, Zeus condemns Hector for taking the arms of
Achilles οὐ κατὰ κόσμον, 'as you ought not', from the corpse (*Il.*
17. 205) but he still gives Hector great strength and success for
the time being. Hector is so intoxicated[243] by his achievements
that he is in no mood to listen to the third warning of Polydamas when it comes. Polydamas speaks in a formal assembly,
and his speech is prefaced by some comments from the narrator
underlining his wisdom: Polydamas is the only one of the
Trojans who considers both the future and the past (*Il.* 18.
250); he is a companion of Hector, his equal in age, and his
superior at speaking (*Il.* 18. 251–2). We are told expressly that
he offers his advice ἐϋφρονέων, wisely (*Il.* 18. 253). Polydamas
warns that the situation has changed and Achilles will pose a far
more serious threat in battle than the other Greeks. He advocates returning into Troy for the night, and fighting in the
morning from the city's defences (*Il.* 18. 249–83). Hector is no
more disposed to tolerate this advice now than he was when
Andromache offered it (*Il.* 6. 431–4), retorting that he is enjoying the favour of Zeus (*Il.* 18. 293–4), and the army will spend
the night in the plain, and will fight by the ships on the following day (*Il.* 18. 298–304). If Achilles has returned to battle, so
much the worse for him (*Il.* 18. 305–6). The Trojans all
applaud Hector's speech because Athene has taken away
their wits (*Il.* 18. 310–11). The disapproving comments of the
narrator on the assembly's decision (*Il.* 18. 312–13) reinforce
the impression created by his approving comments before the
speech of Polydamas: to ignore Polydamas' advice is the beginning of disaster.

7.5.9. *Hector duped by the gods*

Hector proceeds to ignore the λιταί (*Il.* 22. 35, 91) of his parents
to return within the protection of the city wall (*Il.* 22. 56, 85)
and their warnings of the shameful consequences if he does not
(*Il.* 22. 60–71, 86–9). The audience is by now familiar with
advice to Hector as defender of the city (ὄφρα σαώσῃς | Τρῶας
καὶ Τρῳάς, 'so that you may rescue the Trojans and the Trojan
ladies' (*Il.* 22. 56–7)) to make use of the defences the city has to

---

[243] See Fenik (1968: 211) for discussion of the infatuation with success
which causes both Hector and Patroclus to miscalculate. In the case of
Patroclus, the miscalculation is described as ἄτη (*Il.* 16. 685).

offer,[244] and also familiar with his refusal to accept such advice because of his preoccupation with honour, shame, and what τις (someone) will say.[245] We saw mourning provoked by his intransigence towards Andromache (*Il.* 6. 499–502),[246] and Priam's gesture of pulling out his hair is also a mourning gesture (*Il.* 22. 77–8). Hecuba weeps and laments (*Il.* 22. 79). In his soliloquy[247] Hector chooses to face Achilles rather than the reproaches of Polydamas, whose advice he ignored, and the reproaches of the Trojan people, whom he failed through his overconfidence (*Il.* 22. 99–107). He recognizes the impossibility of his position even as he considers the option of negotiation: it is too late to discuss with the Greeks terms for the return of Helen and the property taken with her (*Il.* 22. 114–18): the time for all that was the fiasco of the duel between Paris and Menelaus in book 3. Achilles is interested in vengeance, not negotiation. No sooner has Hector realized the gravity of his mistakes than the illusory hope reasserts itself, that the coming fight with Achilles will somehow be a contest on equal terms (*Il.* 22. 130), but then he runs away, unable to sustain the decision he has taken,[248] as Achilles advances (*Il.* 22. 136). For three circuits of the wall (*Il.* 22. 165) Apollo gives him strength to flee (*Il.* 22. 204), but on the fourth Zeus weighs the κῆρες (deaths) of Achilles and Hector (*Il.* 22. 208–11): Hector's goes down, and Apollo deserts him (*Il.* 22. 213). Athene instantly begins to deceive Hector, assuming the form of his brother, Deiphobus (*Il.* 22. 226–7). She even tells him Priam and Hecuba λίσσονθ' . . . γουνούμενοι, 'besought suppli-

---

[244] *Il.* 6. 431–4; 18. 266–83; 22. 56, 84–5.

[245] Honour: *Il.* 6. 446; 7. 91; shame: *Il.* 6. 442; what τις (someone) will say: *Il.* 6. 459–65; 7. 87–91. Hector once more anticipates what τις will say at *Il.* 22. 106.

[246] This mourning is followed by preparation of clothing and a bath, as if for the dead: see Seaford (1994: 339).

[247] On the superficial resemblances between the soliloquies of Odysseus (*Il.* 11. 404–10), Menelaus (*Il.* 17. 91–105), Agenor (*Il.* 21. 553–70), and Hector (*Il.* 22. 98–130), see Hentze (1904: 26–9): he argues for a closer relationship between the soliloquies of Agenor and Hector, since both express irresolution in apparent contradiction of the resolve suggested by the narrator. On Agenor and Hector, Hentze is followed by Petersmann (1974: 154–7).

[248] On the shallow roots of Hector's decision to fight Achilles, see Fenik (1978: 81–5). His role as blameless defender of a bad cause is tarnished with the guilt of his own mistakes.

cating' her/Deiphobus to remain within the walls (*Il.* 22. 239–42), a falsehood which can only heighten Hector's awareness that they have just made a similar appeal to him to return within the protection of the walls.[249] Hector fully recognizes that he has been duped (*Il.* 22. 299) when he asks his brother for a second spear, only to find Deiphobus is no longer there (*Il.* 22. 294–5). He realizes then that the gods are calling him to death. As he lies dying, with Achilles' spear in his neck, it is Hector's turn to supplicate, λισσόμενος:

λίσσομ' ὑπὲρ ψυχῆς καὶ γούνων σῶν τε τοκήων,
μή με ἔα παρὰ νηυσὶ κύνας καταδάψαι Ἀχαιῶν,
ἀλλὰ σὺ μὲν χαλκόν τε ἅλις χρυσόν τε δέδεξο   340
δῶρα τά τοι δώσουσι πατὴρ καὶ πότνια μήτηρ,
σῶμα δὲ οἴκαδ' ἐμὸν δόμεναι πάλιν, ὄφρα πυρός με
Τρῶες καὶ Τρώων ἄλοχοι λελάχωσι θανόντα.

I beseech you, by your life, and by your knees, and by your parents,
do not allow the dogs to devour me by the ships of the Achaeans,
but accept bronze and gold enough   340
the gifts which my father and my lady mother will give,
and give my body back home, so that
the Trojans and the wives of the Trojans may grant me the rites of fire
   when I am dead.

(*Il.* 22. 338–43)

His request is for burial, but he meets with the same intransigence from Achilles that he himself displayed towards such requests, and the last thing he hears said to him is that the dogs will eat him (*Il.* 22. 354).

Hector's errors and delusions are certainly a part of the plan of Zeus, but that does not mean that they are determined on no other level. The audience is free to decide whether to regard them, in the light of the αἶνος of book 9, as attributable to ἄτη resulting from his rejection of the series of requests made to him in book 6, and from his rejection of the λιταί of his parents,

---

[249] Richardson (1993: 130 ad *Il.* 22. 214–47) comments (against Sch. bT ad *Il.* 22. 231 (= Erbse (1969–88: v. 314), who think it is inappropriate, ἄτοπον, for the goddess to deceive Hector) that the Homeric gods regularly use deception to bring doom, as in cases of ἄτη. Sophocles' portrayal of the deception of Ajax by Athene when he has refused all appeals, including those of his wife, is inspired by Athene's deception of Hector when he has refused all appeals, including those of his wife.

just as they are free to decide whether there is any connection between Agamemnon's ἄτη and his rejection of the λιταί of Chryses. Hector begins to be misled immediately after refusing the requests put to him in book 6: in book 7 he is assured by his brother Helenus, who has overheard a conversation between Athene and Apollo, that his time has not yet come to die (*Il.* 7. 52–3), which leads to his boastful challenge (*Il.* 7. 87–91). It is worth noting that Athene and Apollo do *not* say Hector's time has not yet come to die.[250] From this beginning Hector's confidence that he enjoys divine favour builds up and culminates in Athene's impersonation of Deiphobus when Hector has rejected the λιταί of his parents, suggesting that the deceptions are not unconnected with his rejection of the entreaties addressed to him. When Agamemnon is the victim of such deceptions, he attributes them to ἄτη. If we accept this connection, the αἶνος of the Λιταί may be taken to apply not only to Achilles and Agamemnon, but also to Hector. The connection cannot be proved conclusively, but the reverse is also true. Those who reject any link between Hector's delusions and his rejection of entreaties must find a different explanation for their repeated juxtaposition. Of all the characters in the main action of the *Iliad*, the motif of the ascending scale of affection is used to explore competing claims on the affections of only Hector and Achilles. Hector rejects all appeals made to him in book 6, and goes on to reject those of his father: he becomes the victim of divine deception. In the terms of the αἶνος,

> ὅς μέν τ᾽ αἰδέσεται κούρας Διὸς ἆσσον ἰούσας,
> τὸν δὲ μέγ᾽ ὤνησαν καί τ᾽ ἔκλυον εὐχομένοιο.

who reverences the daughters of Zeus when they come near,
him do they greatly bless, and hear him when he prays.

> (*Il.* 9. 508–9)

Hector has not reverenced the daughters of Zeus, from whatever quarter they have approached him, and his last prayer, for burial, is not heard when he makes it. Now it is time to compare the responses of Achilles and Hector to the requests made to them in ascending scale of affection.

---

[250] See Kirk (1985–90: ii. 238 ad *Il.* 7. 52–3).

7.6. ACHILLES AND HECTOR CONTRASTED IN RESPONSES TO λιταί (PRAYERS)

7.6.1. Responses to λιταί (prayers) in ascending scale of affection

We have seen that requests in ascending scale of affection are addressed to both Achilles and Hector by members of their respective communities, and that after the closure of the ascending scales, each man receives λιταί from the father-figure, Priam. Achilles gives way to Priam and his λιταί, when Hector has already completely ignored him. Hector has yielded to none of the requests put to him by the women in book 6, not even that of Andromache to fight as a defender rather than seek glory and risk his life. Hector has gone on to take no notice of the λιταί of his parents not to throw away his life (and their defence), when his death in the duel with Achilles is a foregone conclusion. Achilles does not comply with the λιταί of the ambassadors to abandon his anger and fight to save his community, but by remaining at Troy he leaves open the possibility that he will fight eventually, and he even predicts that he will do this when the Myrmidons' ships are fired. Achilles makes some concessions to the ambassadors, and complies, disastrously, with the λιτή of Patroclus to be allowed to return to the fighting in Achilles' armour. Both men are granted their immediate desires, Achilles for the defeat of the Greeks in his absence, Hector for victory, but both become overconfident of continuing success, and both are finally conscious of disaster as a direct result of their actions. Zeus has long ago predicted that Achilles will kill Hector (*Il.* 15. 68), so the weighing of the κῆρες (deaths) at *Il.* 22. 209–13 is symbolic: it is not the moment of decision. Both men are already doomed when Zeus takes out his golden balance: Hector according to the prediction of Zeus just mentioned, and Achilles because, as Thetis indicates to him (*Il.* 18. 95–6), he is fated to die when he has killed Hector. Both men have accepted death, Achilles because he is determined to avenge Patroclus whatever the cost (this has been described as self-punitive), and Hector because he chose in book 6 to fight, not as a defender, but for glory, whatever the consequences. In his soliloquy (*Il.* 22. 99–130), he decides to stake everything on the outcome of this duel with Achilles.

When Zeus weighs the κῆρες of Hector and Achilles, an action
symbolizing the contrasts the poet has been exploring between
the two men, Achilles has a better record in giving way to λιταί
than Hector. In the matter of λιταί, Achilles has something of
an advantage over Hector, since Hector has already rejected the
λιταί of his parents. To ignore the wishes of parents is a serious
matter: the two sons of the seer Merops ignored their father's
warning not to fight at Troy, and the κῆρες γὰρ ἄγον μέλανος
θανάτοιο, 'the fates of black death led them (away)' (*Il.* 11. 329–
32). When Hector has ignored his father's warning not to fight,
his κῆρ goes down to Hades after Zeus has weighed it in his
golden balance (*Il.* 22. 213). On the other hand, Achilles'
responses to the λιταί of the true father-figure have not yet been
tested. Once Hector has refused the pleas of everyone who has a
claim on him, he really has no further possibility of conforming
to the prescriptions of the allegory of the Λιταί: there is no one
left for further exploration of his responses, and he must pay
the penalty for his complete refusal to make any concession to
the λιταί of anyone at all. Achilles, on the other hand, began in
the Chryses episode as the advocate of complying with λιταί.
The only terms to which his mind was completely closed were
those of Agamemnon in the embassy, and at the moment his
κῆρ is weighed against that of Hector, Achilles has already
suffered the loss of Patroclus in consequence of rejecting the
λιταί of the ambassadors and failing to defend his community.
Ironically, it was his compliance with the λιτή of Patroclus
which caused Achilles to lose Patroclus. He has even gone
through the motions of a reconciliation with Agamemnon. The
gods assure Priam that Achilles will respond graciously to the
λιταί of a father seeking the return of his child: Achilles long
ago advocated complying with such λιταί in the Chryses
episode (7.1.9 above). Priam reminds Achilles of the distress of
his own father in a desolate old age, deprived of the comfort of
his son, and Achilles, a stranger and an enemy, pities Priam[251]
when his own son refused to do so. Achilles' pity embraces not
only Priam, but the father he left behind in Phthia, who, for all
his wealth, is wretched in his old age, for lack of his son (*Il.* 24.
534–42).

---

[251] *Il.* 22. 74 approx. = *Il.* 24. 516.

7.6.2. The role of the father beyond the scale

The ascending scale of affection is used to explore the competing claims on the affections of both Achilles and Hector. They are the only figures in the primary narrative of the poem of whom the motif is used in fully developed form. As we saw, the introduction of the motif of the ascending scale of affection into the paradigm of Meleager alerts us to the use of the motif in the approaches to Achilles. The figures who address λιταί to Achilles in the embassy, Nestor, Odysseus, Phoenix, Ajax, and Patroclus, are not relatives, and are unusual among the instances of the motif in the *Iliad*. The figures in the scale of Hector are more usual, in that family members are included: in it we find the women of Troy; Hector's mother and favourite sister; Helen; Andromache and Astyanax. The series of approaches to both Achilles and Hector seem to end with the request of the person expressly said to be dearest to the addressee, in Hector's case, the request of Andromache, and in Achilles' case that of Patroclus. However, the series of requests do not end with either the requests of Andromache or of Patroclus, because after their requests further claims on the hero are explored, in both cases those of a father-figure.[252] In terms of response to λιταί, the *Iliad* explores the claims of the father on the son after all other relationships have been explored, and to some extent betrayed. Achilles' response to the λιταί of Priam for the return of Hector's body is exactly that advocated in the αἶνος of the Λιταί: Achilles graciously accedes to Priam's request, and treats his visitor with honour. Priam's nocturnal visit to the Greek camp to address λιταί to Achilles seems to repeat with corrections the nocturnal visit of the ambassadors to address λιταί to Achilles in book 9.[253] Above all, Priam is a real father, and reminds Achilles of the claims of Peleus, Achilles' real father:

μνῆσαι πατρὸς σοῖο, θεοῖς ἐπιείκελ' Ἀχιλλεῦ,
τηλίκου ὥς περ ἐγών, ὀλοῷ ἐπὶ γήραος οὐδῷ·

---

[252] This pattern of the final interview with the father, after the exploration of all other bonds, is found also in the series of recognitions of Odysseus in the *Odyssey*: for discussion, see Kakridis (1971: 151–63).

[253] On the echoes between the two episodes, see Macleod (1982: 34–5); Rutherford (1996: 36).

καὶ μέν που κεῖνον περιναιέται ἀμφὶς ἐόντες
τείρουσ' οὐδέ τίς ἐστιν ἀρὴν καὶ λοιγὸν ἀμῦναι.
ἀλλ' ἤτοι κεῖνός γε σέθεν ζώοντος ἀκούων   490
χαίρει τ' ἐν θυμῷ, ἐπί τ' ἔλπεται ἤματα πάντα
ὄψεσθαι φίλον υἱὸν ἀπὸ Τροίηθεν ἰόντα

be mindful of your father, godlike Achilles,
of such an age as I am, on the threshold of deadly old age:
perhaps those who dwell around him too
distress him, nor is there anyone to ward off harm and destruction.
But surely he, at any rate, when he hears of you alive,   490
rejoices in his heart, and he continues to hope every day
to see his beloved son returning from Troy

(*Il.* 24. 486–92)

whereas in the embassy, Phoenix is nobody's father, and can base his appeal only on a surrogate relationship: Achilles was like a son to him. The true father–son relationship is *the* relationship in terms of affection and obligation.[254] Achilles indicates this when he suggests that the death of one of their fathers could be the explanation of Patroclus' distress:

ἠέ τιν' ἀγγελίην Φθίης ἐξ ἔκλυες οἶος;
ζώειν μὰν ἔτι φασὶ Μενοίτιον, Ἄκτορος υἱόν,
ζώει δ' Αἰακίδης Πηλεὺς μετὰ Μυρμιδόνεσσι,   15
τῶν κε μάλ' ἀμφοτέρων ἀκαχοίμεθα τεθνηώτων.

or have you alone heard some message from Phthia?
In truth, they say that Menoetius, son of Actor, is still alive,
and Peleus, the son of Aeacus is alive among the Myrmidons.   15
We would be grieved for them if they died.

(*Il.* 16. 13–16)

The poet of the *Iliad* uses the exploration of the motif of the ascending scale of affection as a preface to heighten the impact

---

[254] Pausanias, 10. 28 describes Polygnotus' depiction of a man who was wicked to his father being strangled by Charon. He also describes the 'Dutiful men of Catana' who did not abandon their parents even when overtaken by a lava stream. On the importance of the father–son relationship, see Strasburger (1954: 24–6): the purpose of a father's existence is the life of his son. In his old age the father relies on his son to repay his care. The absence of lateral links in genealogies argues for the importance of the father–son relationship: see Thomas (1989: 191 n. 97). Dover (1974: 273) lists, in decreasing order of importance, the claims on the loyalty of an Athenian citizen: parents, kinsmen, friends and benefactors, fellow citizens, etc.

and underline the significance of the father–son relationship, the relationship most highly esteemed by his audience.

7.6.3. Conclusion

The motif of the ascending scale of affection in its developed form is used in the primary narrative of the *Iliad* in only the two cases of Hector and Achilles. Urgent requests, λιταί (entreaties, prayers) are addressed to both men by a series of figures who hope their claims on the hero will influence him to change his course of action and to protect his community. The motif of the ascending scale of affection is used to contrast Hector and Achilles in their responses to these requests and λιταί, a contrast which is further exemplified when their κῆρες (deaths) are weighed. At this point, both men have rejected the claims of their community on them, in favour of pursuing their own private concerns: Achilles has chosen to prolong his quarrel with Agamemnon, and Hector has chosen heroism and glory rather than the role of a defensive fighter. The final λιταί addressed to both men derive added intensity from their context in a supplication from a father-figure: Priam λισσόμενος (entreating) begs Hector to retreat inside Troy and not to throw away his life (and Troy's defence) in an engagement with Achilles in which Hector must perish. Hector rejects his father's entreaties, as he rejects all other requests and entreaties put to him by members of his community. Achilles pays for rejecting the λιταί of the embassy to protect the Greek community when he grants the λιταί of Patroclus to be allowed to enter the battle in place of Achilles. Patroclus is killed, and Achilles suffers terrible grief. Achilles is moved by Priam's λιταί (in the context of his supplication in book 24) for the return of Hector's body, because Priam bases his pleas on an appeal to Achilles to consider the predicament of his own father, Peleus. Achilles respects the pleas of a father: Hector does not.

The αἶνος of the Λιταί (allegory of the Prayers) indicates that whoever rejects Λιταί (Prayers) when they approach will be pursued by Ἄτη (Delusion) so that he will come to grief and pay the penalty. Achilles grants the λιταί of the father-figure, and survives, for the moment at least. The poem ends with mourning for Hector, who rejected the λιταί even of his father, and who suffered delusion by the gods and paid with his life as a result. The *Iliad* is built quite firmly on the motif of rejected λιταί: the λιταί of Chryses rejected by Agamemnon in book 1; the λιταί of the embassy rejected by Achilles in book 9; the requests of the women rejected by Hector in book 6 and the λιταί of Priam and Hecuba which Hector rejects in book 22. The correct pattern in response to λιταί is re-established when the gods ensure that the λιταί of the father-figure, Priam, for the return of his son's body are honoured by Achilles as the αἶνος of the Λιταί demands.

CEASEFIRE

I

Put in mind of his own father and moved to tears
Achilles took him by the hand and pushed the old king
Gently away, but Priam curled up at his feet and
Wept with him until their sadness filled the building.

II

Taking Hector's corpse into his own hands Achilles
Made sure it was washed and, for the old king's sake,
Laid out in uniform, ready for Priam to carry
Wrapped like a present home to Troy at daybreak.

III

When they had eaten together, it pleased them both
To stare at each other's beauty as lovers might,
Achilles built like a god, Priam good-looking still
And full of conversation, who earlier had sighed:

IV

'I get down on my knees and do what must be done
And kiss Achilles' hand, the killer of my son.'

Michael Longley, *Ghost Orchid*
(London, 1995: 39)

APPENDIX A

Approaches to Homer's Narratives

The first systematic work on secondary narrative in Homer is Oehler's study of mythological *exempla* in early Greek poetry, including Homer.[1] His introduction defines paradigm (model, plan, example) and discusses it as a technical term in rhetorical theory. Aristotle defines paradigm as an argument from induction,[2] and suggests that historical examples are particularly useful for political oratory.[3] He recommends the use of well-known events as sources for examples and praises Homer against Choerilus.[4] Archaic and mythical examples must have been common in rhetoric, because Apsines, the famous orator of the third century AD, complained about them:

χρὴ τὰ παραδείγματα γνώριμα εἶναι καὶ σαφῆ καὶ μὴ πάνυ ἀρχαῖα μηδὲ μυθώδη.

the paradigms must be well known and clear, and not exceedingly ancient or mythical.[5]

Josephus Rakendytes, the Byzantine rhetorician, recommends as good sources of examples the historians and chronicles, the Homeric epics, all poets, the *Library* of Apollodorus, Aesop's fables, and the historical books of the Old Testament.[6] The twenty-six items of Oehler's Homeric section cover a total of forty-six paradigms from Homer: twenty-one of these are from the *Iliad*. He groups the three examples concerning Diomede in his list, and the five paradigms he cites concerning Nestor. His discussion of the Meleager story covers the main points: alteration of an existing story; the curse of Althaea forgotten by the time she takes her place in the series of visitors entreating her son; Alcyone given the name Cleopatra to achieve a closer correspondence with Patroclus. The end of the Niobe story of *Iliad* 24 is not explicit on the subject of Niobe's petrifaction because that is not rele-

---

[1] Oehler (1925). Rhetorical theory on paradigm had been studied by Alewell in a dissertation submitted to the university of Kiel in 1913 (Oehler 1925: 3 n. 1), but I have not seen this dissertation.

[2] Aristotle, *Rh.* 1356ᵇ2, 1394ᵃ17.

[3] Aristotle, *Rh.* 1394ᵃ1–8.

[4] Aristotle, *Top.* 157ᵃ14–16.

[5] Apsines, *Art of Rhetoric* 1. 6. 6: Dilts and Kennedy (1997: 168, lines 19–20).

[6] Ἰωσὴφ Ῥακενδύτου, Σύνοψις Ῥητορικῆς 3 (Walz 1834: iii. 525).

vant to the purpose of the story, which is to encourage Priam to eat. A discussion of post-Homeric epic follows, and the paradigms are found to be used in the context of (1) warnings; (2) requests; (3) consolations; (4) wishes; (5) comparisons; (6) amplification (αὔξησις). The book also deals with paradigms in lyric and tragedy.

Rather surprisingly after this, Perry[7] claimed that Homer needed no justification for a digression 'other than the delight of his Greek audience in the story *per se*'. The view that digressions digressed was persistent: Auerbach declared that the 'digressions' of Homer are completely isolated from their context, intended to relax the tension and to make the listener forget what has just taken place.[8] However, the ancient attitude towards the past as a source of pattern was not forgotten, and van Groningen explained the use of historical events as paradigm, a pattern likely to be repeated in the present and future.[9] Austin uses the term 'digression' for subsidiary narratives: although digressions relate to the past, they are never irrelevant or ornamental, but instead display thematic and dramatic relevance to the structure of the whole poem. In his view, all digressions, even brief ones, and almost every reference to the past, even by the poet as narrator, are prompted by the desire to find paradigm in the past.[10] Austin's work is sensitive, brief, and accessible, with the added advantage of being free from jargon. His notes provide an excellent survey of past work on the subject.

Gaisser[11] is interested in digressions as evidence for the composition of the poems and for their relationship to each other: she is more concerned with their structure than with their subject matter and context, and she even isolates them from their context. She identifies fifty-one digressions (not always identical with Oehler's) to examine their structure and composition: twenty-three of the twenty-four digressions she examines from the *Iliad* are found to be cyclic in structure (based on ring composition), unlike those of the *Odyssey*: the more flexible structure of the digressions of the *Odyssey* suggests a later stage in the evolution of the epic style.

Hebel's[12] account of *Wiedererzählungen* collects the secondary narratives in the *Iliad* and *Odyssey* and discusses their literary function.

I have already mentioned in the introduction Willcock's work[13] on

---

[7] Perry (1937: 416).
[8] Auerbach (1953: 4).
[9] Van Groningen (1953: 31).
[10] Austin (1978: 71–6; 1st pub. 1966).
[11] (1969a). Her definition of digressions is quoted below.
[12] (1970).
[13] (1964; 1977).

the poet's readiness to invent details within the broad outline of a story used for paradigmatic purposes to achieve a closer fit with the material to which it is compared: others who have studied innovation for poetic purposes in mythical material include Gaisser, Braswell, Bremmer, and Andersen.[14] More recently, specific secondary narratives or paradigms in the *Iliad* have been studied by Lang, Andersen, and Scodel.[15] Morrison's study of Homeric misdirection explains how the expectations created in the audience through the paradigm of Meleager are not borne out by the events of the poem.[16]

A new development in Homeric studies is narratology, which derives from structuralism and formalism. It employs a complex terminology and a systematic approach to Homeric narrative. With its emphasis on who is speaking (the primary narrator or one of his characters), to whom (the narratee), and whose point of view is adopted (who is focalizing) at any point in the poem, it insists upon the variety and complexity of the presentation of the story and draws our attention to the devices used by the story's presenter to influence its reception.[17] The poet may also slip in judgements about actions: for example, the mistreatment of Hector's corpse is described as ἀεικέα (unseemly, *Il.* 22. 395 = 23. 24); the sacrifice of twelve Trojans on Patroclus' funeral pyre is described as κακά (evil, *Il.* 23. 176). De Jong[18] argues that ἀεικέα and κακά should be interpreted from the point of view of the characters involved and do not imply a moral judgement on the part of the poet. The description by the narrator of a character's point of view in the primary narrative is called 'embedded focalization', but it is admitted that it is not always possible to be certain that the poet is presenting the point of view of a character rather than that of the narrator. The comment that a character is νήπιος (foolish) is always addressed to the audience about the character, and always loaded, whether with pity or derision.[19] Patroclus' ignorance of the turn events are about to take is emphasized by calling him νήπιος when he entreats Achilles to lend him his armour and weapons (*Il.* 16. 46). Andromache is described as νηπίη (*Il.* 22. 445) when she prepares bath water for Hector, unaware that Achilles

[14] Gaisser (1969*b*); Braswell (1971); Bremmer (1988); Andersen (1990).

[15] Lang (1983); Andersen (1976; 1987); Scodel (1982; 1992).

[16] Morrison (1992: 119–24).

[17] The main exponent of narratology in the *Iliad* is de Jong (1987*b*). Richardson (1990) presents a narratological analysis of both the *Iliad* and the *Odyssey*. Accessible summaries of narratology may be found in Edwards (1991: 1–10) and de Jong in Morris and Powell (1997: 305–25).

[18] See de Jong (1987*b*: 138–9).

[19] Griffin (1986: 40).

has killed him.[20] Such devices often go unnoticed by the audience, although it will not fail to be influenced by them. We learn more about the poet's skill as narrator by having our attention directed to them. 'Straight' narratology like de Jong's has not strongly influenced my own approach to para-narrative in Homer, which, as I explain in the Introduction, grows largely out of the insights of Willcock and Kakridis, and from the general approach of Neo-analysis. The range of other past approaches to Homer's secondary narratives can, however, be usefully categorized from the stringently theoretical point of view of narratology: de Jong cites the following terms used by her predecessors to define them:[21]

(a) *digressions*[22]
   'anecdotes which describe action outside the time of the poem';[23]
   'the tales and episodes that interrupt the flow of the action to tell of events unconnected with the main story, and to give background information';[24]
   'stories that have only incidental relevance to the main narrative';[25]

(b) *paradigms*
   'a myth intended for exhortation or consolation';[26]

(c) *Wiedererzählungen*
   'Erzählungen die der Dichter als eigentlicher Erzähler des ganzen Epos einer handelnden Person innerhalb der Dichtung überträgt: diese Wiedererzählungen berichten Vergangenes, sei es, daß es aus dem unmittelbar zum Epos gehörenden Geschehen genommen, sei es von außen herangebracht ist';[27]
   (De Jong herself uses the term *external analepses* to describe (a), (b), and (c) above)[28]

(d) *mirror stories*
   'récit spéculaire (prospectif ou rétrospectif) renvoyant au récit/ à l'histoire (réelle/fictive)';[29]
   'prospective or retrospective stories which refer to something

[20] See de Jong (1987b: 66, 86).
[21] (1987b: 82–3).
[22] See 2.2.2 above.
[23] Austin (1978: 74; 1st pub. 1966).
[24] Gaisser (1969a: 2).
[25] Braswell (1971: 16).
[26] Willcock (1964: 142); see also 2.3.2. above.
[27] Hebel (1970: 5).
[28] De Jong (1987b: 160).
[29] Létoublon (1983b: 27).

told in the main story, and which are either true or fictitious relative to the facts of the main story'.[30]

On the subject of paradigms as mirrors, Andersen[31] explains how the mythological paradigms of the *Iliad* mirror or correspond to something in the main narrative, reflecting its elements with a different cast. The connection is established not through content, but through theme, as for example in the cases of Niobe and Priam, the loss of children, the question of eating, and the importance of burial; that is, the elements of the two stories mirror each other. In de Jong's view a large body of mythical material known to the poet and his audience can conveniently be quarried to provide the elements of such examples:

the speaker presupposes the stories, especially those of the remote past, which we call myths, to be known to his addressee, just as the (poet) presupposes them to be known to the (character to whom they are addressed in the poem) and ultimately the poet to his public.[32]

The categories to which digressions and similar material have been assigned in the past explore the relationship to the main narrative of material related by the characters of the poem, describing events beyond the poetic reality of the present, dealing generally with events from the past, and most often from the past outside the events of the poem. The broad category of para-narrative includes all these categories, but also covers those minor episodes of the main narrative which do not advance its progess, but are set beside its main events, offering miniature episodes for comparison with the major episodes.

---

[30] De Jong (1985: 5); see also Lohmann (1970: 183–212) and Reinhardt (1961: 79–81, 449) on paradigmatic mirroring.

[31] (1987: 8–9).

[32] De Jong (1987*b*: 161; see 81–90, 160–8).

APPENDIX B

The Nature of Homer's Text

I. ORAL COMPOSITION

Milman Parry demonstrated that the Homeric epics have many features in common with the living tradition of orally composed poetry of the former Yugoslavia, a tradition where each performance of a poem is recomposed by the *guslar* as he sings. Such poetry makes use of formulae, type-scenes, repetition, and traditional story shapes. Parry defined the formula as 'a group of words regularly employed under the same metrical conditions to express an essential idea'.[1] An example of such an essential idea might be Odysseus. If the poet wants to convey the essential idea Odysseus in the last seven syllables at the end of the hexameter, he will call him πολύμητις Ὀδυσσεύς (Odysseus of the many wiles) unless the word preceding ends with a short vowel requiring lengthening, in which case he will call him πτολίπορθος Ὀδυσσεύς (Odysseus, sacker of cities): the poet does not need other formulae to express the idea of Odysseus in the space ∪∪/−∪∪/− − and no others are found. The restriction of the system to a single formula to express an essential idea in any given metrical slot is known as formulaic economy. If the idea to be expressed in the same metrical space is Diomede, we will find ἀγαθὸς Διομήδης and κρατερὸς Διομήδης, and again the formula with the double consonant is required if we need to lengthen a preceding short vowel.[2] The poet is in fact composing in terms of metrical patterns, phrase patterns, and sentence patterns which he learns as part of his craft. Some of these are very old indeed,[3] going back at least to the fourteenth century BC; this is because the tradition tends to retain solutions to its metrical problems unless the formulae become incomprehensible or hopelessly unmetrical.[4] The metrical building blocks at the disposal of the poet include prefabricated line shapes such as

τὸν δ᾽ ἀπαμειβόμενος προσέφη πολύμητις Ὀδυσσεύς

him then answering there addressed Odysseus of the many wiles

[1] Parry (1971: 13).
[2] See Parry (1971: 38–52 and table 1).
[3] See Janko (1992: 10–11 and n. 10); Bennet in Morris and Powell (1997: 511–33).   [4] See Hainsworth (1993: 28–31).

where the pronominal object is found at the beginning of the line, the verb in the middle, and the subject at the end. Compare

τὸν δ' ἄρ' ὑπόδρα ἰδὼν προσέφη κρατερὸς Διομήδης

him then scowling there addressed the mighty Diomede[5]

which is essentially the same arrangement. The blocks can be bigger:

οἱ δ' ἐπ' ὀνείαθ' ἑτοῖμα προκείμενα χεῖρας ἴαλλον.
αὐτὰρ ἐπεὶ πόσιος καὶ ἐδητύος ἐξ ἔρον ἕντο

but they stretched forth their hands over the food lying ready before them.
But when they had driven out their desire for food and drink

is found three times in the *Iliad* and eight times in the *Odyssey*.[6]

As well as the formulae, traditional oral poetry tends to have standard descriptions of recurring scenes.[7] For example, Homeric heroes tend to put on the same items of equipment in the same order when arming for battle. The core of an arming scene appears in the description of Paris putting on his armour:

κνημῖδας μὲν πρῶτα περὶ κνήμῃσιν ἔθηκε
καλάς ἀργυρέοισιν ἐπισφυρίοις ἀραρυίας·
δεύτερον αὖ θώρηκα περὶ στήθεσσιν ἔδυνεν
*οἷο κασιγνήτοιο Λυκάονος· ἥρμοσε δ' αὐτῷ.
ἀμφὶ δ' ἄρ' ὤμοισιν βάλετο ξίφος ἀργυρόηλον
χάλκεον, αὐτὰρ ἔπειτα σάκος μέγα τε στιβαρόν τε·
κρατὶ δ' ἐπ' ἰφθίμῳ κυνέην εὔτυκτον ἔθηκεν
ἵππουριν· δεινὸν δὲ λόφος καθύπερθεν ἔνευεν·
εἵλετο δ' ἄλκιμον ἔγχος, ὅ οἱ παλάμηφιν ἀρήρει.

First, around his shins he placed greaves,
Fair ones, fitted with silver ankle pieces.
Secondly, he put on around his breast the corslet
*of his brother Lycaon, and it fitted him.
And about his shoulders he slung a silver-studded sword
of bronze, and then a shield, great and strong.
And upon his mighty head he set a well-wrought helmet
with horse-hair plume. And terribly the crest nodded from above.
And he took up his stout spear, which fitted in his grasp.

(*Il.* 3. 330–8)

With the exception of the line marked *, these lines form the core of a number of other arming scenes which the poet may ornament with variation, reflecting the importance of the hero arming or the

---

[5] These translations are hardly elegant, and are intended only to convey in English the layout of the words in Greek.

[6] The first of the two lines occurs three times more in the *Odyssey* and the second appears three times more in the *Iliad* and six times more in the *Odyssey*.　　　　　　　　[7] See Arend (1933).

significance of the moment of his arming. For example, the description of Achilles putting on the arms made for him by Hephaestus is
ornamented by lengthy description of each item as it is put on: St
Elmo's fire flashes from his shield and his helmet flashes like a star.
The protracted description emphasizes the momentous occasion of
Achilles' rearming to avenge Patroclus after so long an absence from
the battlefield. The poet will have in his mind the bones of many
descriptive passages which can be used with or without variation, as
the need arises. An example of such variation on an arming scene may
be observed in Hera's preparations before her seduction of Zeus (*Il.*
14. 164–223): her toilette is an amusing twist on an arming scene[8]
which would be particularly appreciated by an audience familiar with
the 'straight' model.[9]

Formulae can be moved, modified, expanded, and split to fit
various sentence patterns. Old formulae are constantly being replaced:
for example, μέλανος οἴνοιο is replaced by μελιηδέος οἴνου, Ἀπόλλωνος
ἑκάτοιο is replaced by ἑκηβόλου Ἀπόλλωνος. The basic poetical diction
and formular composition increased the powers of expression of a
gifted poet, whose compositions were constantly changing.[10] Quite a
high proportion of Homeric verse is non-formulaic, and in the hands
of a gifted poet, the non-formulaic proportion probably increases.[11]

The antiquity of the tradition of oral-formulaic poetry should not
be underestimated. The diction is artificial, with an earlier Aeolic
phase including some elements of Arcado-Cypriot, and a later Ionic
phase, perhaps to be dated around 800 BC when Ionian speakers
moved northwards into Chios and Smyrna.[12] Aeolic forms are
retained in the diction where they provide metrically indispensable
alternatives to the later Ionic forms. The metre of the poems, the
hexameter, is likely to date from at least as early as the fourteenth or
fifteenth century BC. Greek and Vedic poetry both employ systems of
quantitative verse, and the rules of their prosodies are similar,

---

[8] See Reinhardt (1961: 291).

[9] Fenik (1968: 73–4) discusses unusual aspects of Athene's arming scene at
Il. 5. 733–47: he relates ἐν δ᾽ Ἔρις, ἐν δ᾽ Ἀλκή, 'on it is Strife, on it is Might' (*Il.*
5. 740) to the description of Aphrodite's garment (*Il.* 14. 214–17): ἔνι μὲν
φιλότης, ἐν δ᾽ ἵμερος, ἐν δ᾽ ὀαριστὺς | πάρφασις (on it are sex and desire and
alluring endearment) but he says nothing about Hera's toilette as an arming
scene.

[10] For an accessible explanation of the formula, see Hainsworth (1993:
1–31); Russo in Morris and Powell (1997: 238–60).

[11] Edwards in Morris and Powell (1997: 269–70).

[12] Otherwise attributable to a southward movement of Aeolic poets from
Lesbos and Aeolic Cyme into the area of Ionic speech in Asia Minor: see
Janko (1982: 177–8; 1992: 15–17).

suggesting a common ancestry. Since the hexameter does not occur in
the Vedic tradition, it is most probably a Greek development within
the inherited tradition of quantitative verse.[13] The language of
Homeric epic preserves forms which were already archaic when
Linear B was being used to write Mycenaean Greek between the fourteenth and the twelfth centuries BC. For example, West[14] mentions
formulae which go back to the sonant r, a sound which in Mycenaean
developed into ro/or or ra/ar: to scan $- \cup \cup -$ at *Il.* 14. 78, νὺξ ἀμβρότη
must be restored to *nux amr.ta*: in Mycenaean *mr.* became *mro*, and
with a glide consonant *mbro*, altering the metrical shape of the word
entirely. A short syllable is used before βρ in the formula ἀσπίδος
ἀμφιβρότης, which must go back to *aspidos amphimr.tas*, the shield
that encircles a man, a shield in use before the fourteenth century.[15]
Similarly the placing of verbs in *tmesis* was already archaic in the
language of the tablets, as demonstrated by Horrocks.[16] The pre-
Mycenaean features of the language of Greek epic must have entered
the tradition at a time when they were current usage, and must have
been transmitted as part of the system of formulae.

2. WRITING

There is no reason to suppose that writing was not used to record the
composition of the *Iliad* and the *Odyssey*. We know of two systems of
writing Greek, and the Homeric tradition of poetry is older than the
earlier of these. Its language displays features which were already out-
moded in the Greek of the Linear B tablets:[17] these features can have
been preserved in the tradition only by oral transmission. The fresco
in the palace at Pylos which shows a singer accompanying himself on
the lyre[18] contributes to the impression of a tradition of poetry in
Mycenaean courts. Linear B is a complex system of ideograms representing whole words combined with syllabic signs written with a
stylus on clay tablets from left to right. Folded wooden tablets
recessed to take a coating of wax may also have been used for temporary records in Linear B, since such a pair of tablets is known from a
shipwreck of the fourteenth century off the southern coast of Asia
Minor.[19] So far there is nothing to suggest that the Linear B script was

[13] See West in Morris and Powell (1997: 233–7) and Bennet in Morris and
Powell (1997: 523–7).
[14] Morris and Powell (1997: 229, 234) and see also West (1988: 156–7).
[15] See West (1988: 157 n. 44).
[16] (1980).
[17] For survey with bibliography, see Janko (1992: 9–12).
[18] See Vermeule (1964: pl. XXX).
[19] Payton (1991).

ever used to record poetry. Linear B fell out of use when the palaces were destroyed at the end of the thirteenth century and the beginning of the twelfth.

The Greeks learned to write again from the Phoenicians, whose syllabary they modified to produce alphabetic writing including vowel sounds. Herodotus describes how the Ionians were taught writing by Phoenician settlers and adapted the writing for their own use, although they went on calling the letters Φοινικήια.[20] The medium used by the Phoenicians was again the folded wooden tablets, recessed to take a coating of wax on which one wrote with a stylus: longer texts might be written with pens on rolls of leather or papyrus. Papyrus does not survive well outside Egypt, but has left impressions on the clay sealings used to seal papyrus documents in other countries of the Mediterranean.[21]

The Phoenicians wrote from right to left, and many of the earliest Greek inscriptions follow their example. The earliest known example of alphabetic writing is a graffito on the side of a locally produced vase of 770 BC from tomb 482 at Gabii in Italy.[22] A complete hexameter is included in a graffito on the shoulder of a LG1B oenochoe from the Dipylon workshop in Athens. It reads

hoς νυν ορχεστον παντον αταλοτατα παιζει <u>τοτοδεκλλμιν</u>

he who of all the dancers performs most daintily . . .

The last twelve letters underlined above are written in a less skilful hand and seem to award the cup to the best dancer[23] in what must have been a public dancing competition with judges, such as we find in *Od.* 8. 258–65. Another prize, this time in a drinking competition in the Greek colony of Pithecusae in the bay of Naples, was a cup of about 730 BC imported from Rhodes and eventually buried with its owner around 720–10. It is inscribed from right to left with two lines of hexameter verse:

Νεστορος:ε[ιμ]ι:ευποτ[ον]:ποτεριο[ν]:
hoς δ' α⟨ν⟩ τοδε π[ιε]σι:ποτερι[ο]:αυτικα:κενον:
hιμερος:haιρεσει:καλλιστε[φα]νο:Αφροδιτης

I am the fair cup of Nestor
and he who drinks from this cup,
straightway shall the desire of fair-crowned Aphrodite seize him.[24]

---

[20] Herodotus, 5. 58.
[21] Powell in Morris and Powell (1997: 30 n. 54).
[22] See Peruzzi (1992).
[23] See Coldstream (1979: 298–9; 1st pub. 1977).
[24] See Coldstream (1979: 298, 300; 1st pub. 1977); Powell in Morris and Powell (1997: 23–4).

The competition seems to have required participants to cap the line written by the previous contestant. The first player begins with the assertion, this is the cup of Nestor, a humorous reference to the cup which only Nestor knows how to lift (*Il.* 11. 632–7).[25] The second participant, in a variant on the curse-formula which would run 'whoever steals this cup (will suffer something horrible)' issues a challenge: 'whoever drinks this cup . . .' and the verse is capped by the third contestant 'will become amorous'. A further graffito of eighteen letters arranged in three lines and scratched over the painted Geometric pattern on two joining fragments of an imported Rhodian bird-bowl was found at Eretria in 1977. The arrangement of the letters suggests that this inscription too was in verse, but unfortunately it has so far proved impossible to make sense of it.[26]

At its outset, alphabetic writing in Greece is associated not with commerce and a scribal class, but with poetry, and more precisely, with hexameter verse in epic diction. The symposiastic game evidenced by the 'cup of Nestor' from Pithecusae suggests a leisured, literate aristocracy. Its reference to Nestor, one of the heroes of the Homeric poems, suggests knowledge at least of the subject matter of the poems already spread over a wide area of the Mediterranean in the eighth century BC, although this does not necessarily mean that the persons responsible for the lines inscribed on the 'cup of Nestor' were familiar with a written text of the whole of the *Iliad* in the form in which we have it.

3. RECORDING

It looks very much as if the *Iliad* and the *Odyssey* might have been recorded in writing by means of dictation by the composer to a scribe. We have evidence of orally composed poetry recorded in this way from the modern tradition of the former Yugoslavia and from the ancient Near East. One of the Yugoslav *guslars* studied by Milman Parry was Avdo Međedović, an illiterate butcher and farmer born around 1870 in eastern Montenegro. He had learned his art as a poet and singer from others, in particular from his father, who had been strongly influenced by Ćor Huso, a singer of great reputation in his generation. Avdo had a repertoire of fifty-eight pieces: nine of these were recorded by Parry in 1935, and four more were written down to Avdo's dictation by Nikola Vujnović, Parry's assistant. One of these dictated songs, 'The Wedding of Meho, Son of Smail', was a master-

---

[25] For a Near Eastern parallel, see West (1997: 376).

[26] Johnston and Andriomenou (1989).

piece running to 12,311 lines. A published version of 2,160 lines had been written down in 1885 by F. S. Krauss from an 85-year-old singer, Ahmed Isakov Šemić, in Hercegovina and published in Dubrovnic in 1886. Hizvo Džafić read it five or six times in a reprinted version to Avdo, who expanded it by means of ornament and fullness of narrative. In 1950, when Avdo was in his eighties, he performed it again in a version of more than 8,000 lines. In 1935 Avdo also demonstrated his ability to perform and greatly expand a traditional song totally unfamiliar to him after hearing it only once from another singer, Bećiragić Meho.[27] The relationship between written text and oral transmission found in Avdo's performances closely resembles a wealth of evidence from the Near East suggesting that oral composition and dictation to an amanuensis were nothing unusual in the ancient world.

Gilgamesh appears to have been a real king of Uruk at some time during the third millennium BC. His legendary adventures became the subject of epic poetry, first in *Einzellieder* (separate, shorter songs) in Sumerian dating from the third Dynasty of Ur, perhaps from the time of king Shulgi (2075–2025 BC), who was instrumental in getting much current oral poetry recorded in writing. Texts of hymns with passages of narrative were also recorded at this time on clay tablets in cuneiform. An Akkadian poet of the First Babylonian Dynasty (19th–16th centuries BC) drew on the Einzellieder about Gilgamesh to create a full-length epic about him. In the Kassite period (second half of the sixteenth century to second half of the twelfth century BC) a revised text was made with a fixed format of twelve tablets (the twelfth is probably a later addition, and does not fit with the rest). This revision is associated with Sin-leqe-annini, a master scribe and incantation-priest at Uruk, who is generally understood to have produced the standard version of the first eleven tablets. The epic of Gilgamesh was translated into Hurrian and written versions of it have been discovered over a wide area of the Near East.

The Sumerian texts refer frequently to themselves as song and make liberal use of repetition, suggesting an oral medium of performance: they also refer to oral transmission of traditions about the past. The Sumerian poets meditated a poem before teaching it to a singer for performance or to a scribe for writing down. The Akkadian hymns and narrative poems contain internal evidence of oral performance and their opening lines 'Let me sing of . . .', 'I will sing of . . .' are followed by references to a song being heard. It is reasonable to assume both oral transmission and transmission in writing of the same work. Enheduanna, the daughter of Sargon of Akkad (2270–2220 BC),

[27] See Lord (1991: 57–71).

is associated with a revision of a collection of temple hymns: she says in her poem *Ninmesarra* that she composes at night and has the singer repeat the song next day at noon. Kabri-ilani-Marduk (ninth century, or first half of eighth century BC) also describes his work as both a song and a tablet: he composed at night and thought of his work in terms of both performance by a singer and recording by a scribe. A group of copiers of texts in Assur in the Neo-Assyrian period (beginning *c.* 1000 BC) were also singers and their library contained texts of poems which might be hundreds of years old.[28]

The medium of performance for the Homeric poems was still oral in the fourth century BC, long after the texts were fixed in a written form: rhapsodes recited Homer from memory and might also own a copy of the text which they studied before recitals.[29] By analogy with the singers of Assur who copied texts in the Neo-Assyrian and Late Babylonian periods, West[30] explains the 'wild' variants common in Homeric texts down to about 150 BC as the work of rhapsodes who knew the poems so well that they did not attend word-for-word to the exemplar they were copying. The many archaic forms they contain indicate that the poems were fixed in writing in the eighth century, before the time of Hesiod: there is no question of any major textual revision at the time of the Pisistratean recension, which might be no more than the acquisition by Pisistratus of a complete set of rolls making up a full text of the poems.[31]

It seems reasonable to conclude that contact with written epics in oral circulation in the Near East could have been the spur which led to the composition of the extended epics of the *Iliad* and the *Odyssey* by a traditional oral poet of exceptional brilliance, drawing on the many songs about the Trojan War in oral circulation, and dictating to a literate friend to enhance the prestige of an eighth-century ruler in Ionia.

[28] See West (1997: 63–7, 69, 590–606).
[29] See Xenophon, *Sym.* 3. 5–6; *Mem.* 4. 2. 10; Plato, *Ion* 530c.
[30] (1997: 601–2).
[31] See Janko (1992: 31).

APPENDIX C

The Meaning of the Exchange of Armour

I have tried to show that Glaucus tells Diomede the story of his grandfather, Bellerophon, to provide him with an illustration of *all* the consequences of heroic exploits performed under divine patronage. Divine patronage is capricious, Glaucus implies, and may at any time be withdrawn. One must consider the end of a career under divine patronage, and it may not be an enviable one. The reasons for divine hostility towards Bellerophon could not fail to present themselves to the audience's mind, despite their omission by Glaucus. Bellerophon's exploits, performed with divine assistance, led him to go too far: he attempted to ride to heaven and was thrown by his mount. Glaucus tries, and fails utterly, to convince Diomede of the dangers of the career on which he is presently embarked. Diomede's understanding of Glaucus' story is far from complete: his only response to Glaucus' genealogical paradigm is suddenly to recollect the ancestral guest-friendship between his grandfather and Bellerophon, whom Oeneus had entertained for twenty days,[1] when the two men had exchanged gifts. Oeneus gave Bellerophon a scarlet belt,[2] and Bellerophon gave his host a golden cup. Therefore, Diomede proposes, he and Glaucus should avoid each other in battle, and should exchange armour as a mark of their friendship. The exchange is unequal, since Diomede's bronze armour was worth nine oxen, and Glaucus' golden armour is valued at a hundred oxen (*Il.* 6. 235–6).

Early explanations of the unequal exchange may be summarized as follows: Glaucus, delighted to have Diomede's friendship, repeats the generosity of Bellerophon.[3] The exchange will ensure that the guest-friendship is recognized by both armies. Alternatively, the Greek emerges as victor from the exchange, for the gratification of the

---

[1] This entertainment of his grandfather by Diomede's family means Glaucus is indebted to Diomede: Martin (1989: 129).

[2] For another example of the gift of a ζωστῆρα φοίνικι φαεινόν, 'a belt shining with scarlet', see *Il.* 7. 305, where Ajax gives one to Hector, and receives a sword.

[3] Sch. bT ad *Il.* 6. 234 (= Erbse (1969–88: ii. 171), 234a); Porphyry ad *Il.* 6. 234 (= Schrader (1880: i. 98)).

audience.[4] Modern interpretations explain the exchange in one of two ways: Glaucus asserts his superiority by the magnificence of his gift, and the authorial intrusion (*Il.* 6. 234–6) indicates a society which no longer understands potlatch,[5] or alternatively, Glaucus is tricked into accepting a humiliating exchange for his golden armour.[6] He is glad to escape with his life.[7]

The authorial comment that Zeus took away the wits of Glaucus when he complied with this request, has been the subject of endless speculation.[8] Scodel points out that characters in the poem may say that Zeus has stolen someone's wits (often when the speaker himself is the one whose wits are gone) to explain actions so stupid that only the intervention of a god could make anyone do such a thing.[9] For example, at *Il.* 18. 311 the poet says that Athene makes the Trojans take Hector's mad advice to camp on the plain: no one in his right mind would adopt such a plan, and the Trojans' decision can only be explained by their not being in their right mind at the time (because Athene has taken away their wits). She rightly insists that when the poet says that Zeus removed Glaucus' wits, this must mean that Glaucus' action is inconceivably stupid, but she can find no reason why Zeus should wish to make a fool of Glaucus in this way.[10] Instead

---

[4] Sch. T ad *Il.* 6. 234 (= Erbse (1969–88: ii. 171), 234b[1]); Porphyry ad *Il.* 6. 234 (= Schrader (1880: i. 98)).   [5] Calder III (1984).

[6] Donlan (1989); Martin (1989: 127).

[7] Craig (1967); Willcock (1992).

[8] Kraus (1948: 9–10) compares the materialism with Phoenix's materialistic remark that Meleager fought without receiving the gifts (*Il.* 9. 598–9). Kirk (1985–90: ii. 191) takes Γλαύκῳ Κρονίδης φρένας ἐξέλετο Ζεύς, 'Zeus, the son of Cronos, took away the wits of Glaucus' (*Il.* 6. 234) as a *façon de parler*, arguing that Zeus would not do anything so trivial, especially to a friend of Sarpedon.

[9] Scodel (1992: esp. 75–6). The examples are as follows: (*a*) Paris: the gods must have destroyed (ὤλεσαν) Antenor's wits if he thinks Paris will give back Helen (*Il.* 7. 360); (*b*) Hector: the gods must have destroyed Polydamas' wits if he thinks the Trojans should not pursue the Greeks to the ships (*Il.* 12. 234); (*c*) Achilles: when Agamemnon took Briseis, Zeus took away (εἵλετο) his wits (*Il.* 9. 377); (*d*) Athene took away the Trojans' wits when they agreed to Hector's plan to camp in the plain (*Il.* 18. 311) against Polydamas' advice; (*e*) Agamemnon: Zeus took out (ἐξέλετο) Agamemnon's wits when he ἀασάτο and took Achilles' prize (*Il.* 19. 137); (*f*) Hector: Zeus harmed (βλάπτε) the Trojans' wits when they prevented Hector from fighting at the ships (*Il.* 15. 724).

[10] In her view, the speeches of Diomede and Glaucus offer different views of the gods and the extent to which mortals can rely on their help. The exchange of armour is an example of divine intervention which caps their verbal exchange, and shows how Zeus acts without clear motive on the mind of a character who has shown no previous inclination to act as Zeus causes him to act.

of looking for reasons why Zeus should wish to make a fool of Glaucus, it might be better to look again at the instances of the gods taking away, or damaging someone's wits. The idea is certainly associated with stupid behaviour, but the stupid behaviour arises from loss of control: no one who was in control of himself would behave so foolishly. Certainly, Agamemnon seems to think he was quite helpless against the workings of Ἄτη when Zeus took out his wits, and he offended Achilles (*Il.* 19. 136–7). Glaucus must have lost his wits (Zeus must have taken them), because otherwise he would never have agreed to the unequal exchange of armour with Diomede.

If Zeus deprives Glaucus of his wits so that he consents to exchange his golden armour for Diomede's bronze armour, he may make Glaucus look like a fool, but at the same time he extricates him from a dangerous situation in that the belligerence of Diomede is deflated when Glaucus acquiesces in the exchange.[11] Divine intervention to rescue a person overrides the normal processes by which that person operates. By depriving Glaucus of his wits in this situation, Zeus rules out any possible interference from Glaucus, so that he can rescue him by a means to which Glaucus would never have consented if he had had any control over the situation.

The significance of the exchange is different for Diomede. Diomede has been collecting the horses of Trojans, including those of Aeneas,[12] and now he stands to obtain a suit of golden armour, without killing the owner. These items may be flaunted to increase Diomede's prestige, and detract from that of their previous owners.[13] Immediately before the exchange, however, Diomede receives a

[11] The episode of Glaucus relating his genealogy and being rescued by divine intervention (which may do nothing for his prestige, but nevertheless, buys him his life) is comparable to Aeneas' account of his genealogy (*Il.* 20. 209–41) and his subsequent rescue by the intervention of Poseidon (*Il.* 20. 322–39).

[12] *Il.* 5. 323–7. He obtains the horses of Idaios and Phegeus after killing Phegeus (*Il.* 5. 25) and the horses of two sons of Priam, Echemmon and Chromios (*Il.* 5. 165). The passages are compared by Fenik (1968: 11–14, 24).

[13] Cf. *Il.* 17. 192, where Hector dons the armour of Achilles, stripped from the corpse of Patroclus. In the context of the exchange of armour, it is worth remembering *Il.* 8. 194–5, where Hector hopes to strip from Diomede the corselet made for him by Hephaestus: if he could obtain it, he could drive the Greeks away that very night. Whatever its material value, armour made by Hephaestus ought to be superior to anything of mortal manufacture, but in book 6 the poet says nothing about the divine provenance of Diomede's armour. For the time being in book 6 we are not to think of it as divine, or there would be some difficulty in maintaining that Glaucus lost his wits when he obtained the armour. Nothing is said in book 8 about the exchange of armour between Glaucus and Diomede.

warning, in the form of Glaucus' paradigmatic genealogy, of the dangers of placing too much confidence in the reliability of divine assistance.[14] The effect of this warning is outweighed by Zeus' intervention (*Il.* 6. 234) taking away the wits of Glaucus and inducing him to part with his golden armour.[15] Diomede is unaware of Zeus' part in his acquisition of the golden armour, but this further stroke of luck by divine agency, coming immediately after a run of success dependent on divine patronage and a warning against the dangers inherent in it, does not augur well for Diomede.

[14] Marshall (1990: 165–6) explains how luck, whether good or bad, is not necessarily desirable: in Thucydides, unexpected success is ominous and presages downfall through overconfidence.

[15] The incident suggests Diomede is beyond assistance, and certainly beyond the reach of any warnings. A more extreme, but analogous incident would be the story of how Polycrates of Samos was warned by Amasis, king of Egypt (Herodotus, 3. 40–3), that an unbroken run of good fortune generally ended in complete ruin. To avoid this, Polycrates was told he should immediately deprive himself of something he valued highly. Polycrates duly threw into the sea a ring which he prized. The ring was swallowed by a fish which was caught and presented to him as a gift. When Amasis learned how Polycrates recovered even what he had thrown away, he foretold a miserable end for him. Eventually Polycrates' greed and ambition enabled his enemies to lure him to Magnesia and murder him there (Herodotus, 3. 120–5). Amasis' warning to Polycrates concerns the danger of κόρος, satiety, or 'having too much', which was thought to lead to ὕβρις, arrogance, which in turn led to ἄτη, delusion, ending in disaster. This pattern of thought is frequent in Aeschylus and Herodotus. Polycrates readily understands the warning from Amasis, but his dangerous good fortune defies his attempt to induce a setback by throwing away his ring: his ruin is inevitable. Diomede, on the other hand, gives no indication of having registered the warning from Glaucus, and far from attempting to interrupt his run of good fortune, aspires positively to increase it by acquiring Glaucus' golden armour.

APPENDIX D

The Hero's Death by Destruction of a Life-Token

Knaack[1] compares Meleager's death by the sympathetic magic of burning the brand with Simaitha burning the laurel branch to destroy Delphis.[2] He traces Meleager's family through several generations closely associated with plants, through a passage from Hecateus:[3] Orestheus, son of Deucalion, came to the kingdom of Aetolia, where his dog gave birth to a root-crown. When it was planted, it grew into a magnificent vine, and Orestheus therefore called his son Phytion. His son, Oeneus, was named for the vine. Knaack suggests Meleager's association with the olive shoot, which is of a piece with the family association with plants, is older than the stick: as the link between kings and vegetation weakened, Meleager's olive twig withered into a stick. Burkert[4] and Bremmer[5] associate the ancestry of the stick story with the cult of Artemis Laphria at Calydon.[6] Meleager's death when the stick is burned is listed by Stith Thompson,[7] but the parallel he gives of Olgar the Dane[8] is not at all close to the story of Meleager. In the Icelandic *pattr* (short story) of Norna-gestr, the guest, or retainer of the Norns (Fates), the hero's life-token is not a stick but a candle, which is burnt when he is 300 years old.[9] It resembles the Turkish tale of Trakosaris (the Three-Hundred-Year-Old).[10] Many other stories exist of death by the sympathetic magic of burning a candle.[11] The

[1] (1894: 310–13).
[2] Theocritus, 2. 23–6.
[3] *FGrH* 1 F 15.
[4] (1985: 62–3; 1st pub. 1977).
[5] (1988: 45–9).
[6] See also Petropoulou (1993), who associates Phrynichus' (*TrGF* i. 74–5; 3F5–6) version of Meleager's death by burning in a sheet of flame as the stick is burned with the establishment of the cult of Artemis Laphria at Calydon, and with the Celtic fire-festival, Beltene.
[7] (1955–8: ii. 514–15; E 765 1 and 2).
[8] Hartland (1925: 204–5).
[9] Kershaw (1921: 14–37).
[10] Quoted in Kakridis (1949: 135), with other modern versions of the story (Kakridis 1949: 127–36).
[11] See Baughman (1966: D 2061. 2. 2. 6); Henderson (1879: 182–3) (from Hennock in Devonshire: so long as the candle burned, the victim would be in flames: when it expired, he would be dead); Hurston (1931: 406–7), an

idea of destroying a life-token to cause death may be related to invultuation or *envoûtement*, a form of murder by the maltreatment of an effigy or image representing the person to be destroyed.[12] It is worth differentiating, however, between stories like that of Norna-gestr, where the candle is the life-token from the time of birth, and stories such as those collected by Briggs (under the heading 'Meleager'), where a candle acquires the significance of a life-token.

American story of murder attempted by burning candles. However, the candles have assumed their significance only for the purposes of the spell: they were not life-tokens from the time of the victim's birth. To Baughman's list, add Briggs (1971: i. 45, 53, 68, 76–7): four stories from the British Isles of persons who incur an obligation to go with the Devil when the candle is burned out. In 1490 Johana Benet was called before the commissary of London for sorcery with a candle: 'sicut candelam consumit, sic debet homo consumere': Hale (1847: 20).

[12] For discussion of *envoûtement* , see Kittredge (1929: 29).

APPENDIX E

The Motivation Ascribed to Wives Entreating Husbands

Kakridis[1] inferred from the requests from women in book 6, and especially from that of Andromache, that women are represented by the poet as inhibiting the work of Hector[2] (and of men generally) by asserting their own claims over them. His inference has been followed by many others: 'all three [i.e. Hecuba, Helen, and Andromache] represent the same temptation . . . to turn his back on the terrible world of fighting and death, and linger in the delightful company of loving women and their plausible justifications'.[3] This school of thought subscribes to the absolute polarity of Hector's view (*Il.* 6. 490–3): women to the loom, men to the war, and fails to see that Andromache asks her husband to fight defensively, a perfectly creditable option, which would enable him to honour his commitments both to Troy and to her.[4] The extreme view taken by Hector is imitated in Shakespeare:

Andr. When was my lord so much ungently temper'd
    To stop his ears against admonishment?

---

[1] (1949: 50–2: cf. 1971: 71–2).

[2] Redfield (1975: 152–3) draws attention to the practical need for the Trojans to win before their city runs out of resources to bribe the allies.

[3] Griffin (1980: 6): cf. Schadewaldt (1965: 219–21; 1st pub. 1944); Schein (1984: 174–5); Scully (1990: 64–8). Rutherford (1996: 85) ('it is common for a woman to restrain a man from going out to battle') forgets Cleopatra, who sends Meleager out to fight. This causes him to see Helen's exhortations to Paris to fight (*Il.* 3. 432–6) as a reversal of the 'common motif' (of a woman restraining a man from going out to battle). In fact there are two motifs: the first is the figure, like Andromache in book 6 , or like Priam in book 22, who restrains a man from fighting; the second is the figure, like Oeneus or Cleopatra in the story of Meleager, who exhorts a man to fight. Another example of this second figure would be Aethra, who exhorts an initially reluctant Theseus to fight in the cause of the mothers of the Seven (Euripides, *Supp.* 306–31).

[4] Schmitz (1963: 140–58); Arthur-Katz (1981: 33). Crotty (1994: 50) is another sympathizer with Andromache, but indicates that her appeal to ἔλεος is doomed to failure, since it is contrary to the heroic code. The polarity of male and female worlds is well discussed by Bourdieu (1977: 72–95 (esp. 92–3) and 214–18).

Unarm, unarm, and do not fight today.
Hect. You train me to offend you: get you in.

(Troilus and Cressida, Act 5, Scene 3)

in representing her as attempting to prevent him from returning to battle at all (instead of asking him to command the army from the tower, stationing the troops at the weak point in the defences, as she does at *Il.* 6. 431–7), and Hector as 'the man who, on behalf of his family, must leave his family, so that his very defence of them becomes a betrayal'.[5] Andromache's attempts to persuade Hector to fight defensively are described by Kakridis as arising from 'the egotism of love'.[6] But there is more: Cleopatra urges Meleager to fight, Kakridis tells us 'for fear that she may become a slave: the egotism of self-preservation'.[7] There is clearly something wrong here, since the women are censured if they urge their husbands to fight, and censured if they do not, and whatever they do, they are motivated by egotism. There is nothing in the text to suggest that Andromache and Cleopatra are egotistical, and much to imply that the obstinacy of their husbands represents a threat to their communities.[8] To ascribe the motive of egotism to Andromache and Cleopatra is unjustifiable because it depends so heavily on personal interpretation. It would be better to compare attempts by women in Greek literature to restrain men. Compare Andromache remonstrating with Hector:

[5] Redfield (1975: 123); Schein (1984: 174).

[6] (1949: 60).

[7] The evidence for this inference depends on the interpretation of *Il.* 9. 592–4, which do not necessarily indicate that Cleopatra's appeal is motivated only by her own fear that she will be enslaved. We are not told what is in Cleopatra's mind as she describes the fate of a captured city, but only what she says. We are not in a position to judge her motivation.

[8] Similarly Griffin is not justified in comparing Andromache with Helen to 'prove' that Andromache cannot mean what she says to Hector in book 6: 'we see from Helen's contempt for Paris (who is lingering in the bedroom, rather than returning to the battlefield) and Andromache's love for Hector that what a woman really wants in a man is the strength to resist her and go out among the flying spears' (1980: 7). Griffin here fails to take any account of the differences in character between the two women, epitomized in the subject matter of their tapestries: Helen, the heroic woman, works into her web the battles of the Greeks and Trojans for her sake, whereas Andromache, the life-giving, life-sustaining wife and mother, works into her fabric a design of flowers: Segal (1971*a*: 40–1); Lohmann (1988: 60); cf. Arthur-Katz (1981: 24–6). Helen and Andromache are completely unlike each other, and there is no justification for the view that Andromache cannot really take the attitude she expresses in book 6 towards her husband's exploits on the battlefield because Helen does not share that attitude at *Il.* 3. 428.

δαιμόνιε, φθίσει σε τὸ σὸν μένος, οὐδ' ἐλεαίρεις
παῖδά τε νηπίαχον καὶ ἔμ' ἄμμορον, ἣ τάχα χήρη
σεῦ ἔσομαι

Poor wretch, your might will destroy you, nor do you even pity
your infant child, and me, ill-fated, who soon
will be widowed of you.

(*Il.* 6. 407–9)

with the chorus's attempt to restrain the fratricidal Eteocles:

μή τί σε θυμοπληθὴς δορίμαργος ἄτα φερέτω· κακοῦ δ'
ἔκβαλ' ἔρωτος ἀρχάν.

Let not wrathful Ate, raging with the spear carry you away. Cast out
the root of an evil passion.

(Aeschylus, *Th.* 687–8)

and with Tecmessa's attempt to restrain Ajax:

ὦ πρὸς θεῶν ὕπεικε καὶ φρόνησον εὖ

O, by the gods, yield and think straight.

(Sophocles, *Aj.* 371)

Andromache attempts to restrain Hector's rash course by emphasiz-
ing her dependence on him through her description of the sack of her
own city and the enslavement of her mother:

ἤτοι γὰρ πατέρ' ἁμὸν ἀπέκτανε δῖος Ἀχιλλεύς,
ἐκ δὲ πόλιν πέρσεν Κιλίκων εὖ ναιετάουσαν,　　　　　　415
Θήβην ὑψίπυλον· κατὰ δ' ἔκτανεν Ἠετίωνα,
οὐδέ μιν ἐξενάριξε, σεβάσσατο γὰρ τό γε θυμῷ,
ἀλλ' ἄρα μιν κατέκηε σὺν ἔντεσι δαιδαλέοισιν
ἠδ' ἐπὶ σῆμ' ἔχεεν· περὶ δὲ πτελέας ἐφύτευσαν
νύμφαι ὀρεστιάδες, κοῦραι Διὸς αἰγιόχοιο.　　　　　　420
οἳ δέ μοι ἑπτὰ κασίγνητοι ἔσαν ἐν μεγάροισιν,
οἱ μὲν πάντες ἰῷ κίον ἤματι Ἄϊδος εἴσω·
πάντας γὰρ κατέπεφνε ποδάρκης δῖος Ἀχιλλεὺς
βουσὶν ἐπ' εἰλιπόδεσσι καὶ ἀργεννῇς ὀΐεσσι.
μητέρα δ' ἣ βασίλευεν ὑπὸ Πλάκῳ ὑληέσσῃ,　　　　　　425
τὴν ἐπεὶ ἂρ δεῦρ' ἤγαγ' ἅμ' ἄλλοισι κτεάτεσσιν,
ἂψ ὅ γε τὴν ἀπέλυσε λαβὼν ἀπερείσι' ἄποινα,
πατρὸς δ' ἐν μεγάροισι βάλ' Ἄρτεμις ἰοχέαιρα.
Ἕκτορ, ἀτὰρ σύ μοί ἐσσι πατὴρ καὶ πότνια μήτηρ
ἠδὲ κασίγνητος, σὺ δέ μοι θαλερὸς παρακοίτης.　　　　　430

But certainly, godlike Achilles slew my father
 and sacked utterly the well-built city of the Cilicians,　　　　415
high-gated Thebe. He slew Eëtion,
but he did not strip his armour, for he abhorred that in his heart,
but he burnt him with his skilfully wrought armour
and constructed a mound over him, and the mountain-dwelling nymphs,

the daughters of aegis-bearing Zeus, planted elm-trees around it.   420
And the seven brothers I had in the palace
all went down to the house of Hades on a single day:
for swift-footed godlike Achilles killed them all
in charge of the shambling cattle and the white goats.
And my mother, who was queen under wooded Plakos,   425
when he brought her here with the other property,
he released her again, receiving a countless ransom,
and arrow-shooting Artemis struck her in the palace of her father.
But Hector, you are my father and my lady mother
and my brother, you are my youthful husband.   430
                                                        (*Il.* 6. 414–30)

Hector himself describes the sack of Troy and the slavery into which
Andromache will fall when he is not there to save her:

εὖ γὰρ ἐγὼ τόδε οἶδα κατὰ φρένα καὶ κατὰ θυμόν·
ἔσσεται ἦμαρ ὅτ’ ἄν ποτ’ ὀλώλῃ Ἴλιος ἱρὴ
καὶ Πρίαμος καὶ λαὸς ἐϋμμελίω Πριάμοιο.
ἀλλ’ οὔ μοι Τρώων τόσσον μέλει ἄλγος ὀπίσσω,   450
οὔτ’ αὐτῆς Ἑκάβης οὔτε Πριάμοιο ἄνακτος
οὔτε κασιγνήτων, οἵ κεν πολέες τε καὶ ἐσθλοὶ
ἐν κονίῃσι πέσοιεν ὑπ’ ἀνδράσι δυσμενέεσσιν,
ὅσσον σεῦ, ὅτε κέν τις Ἀχαιῶν χαλκοχιτώνων
δακρυόεσσαν ἄγηται, ἐλεύθερον ἦμαρ ἀπούρας·   455
καί κεν ἐν Ἄργει ἐοῦσα πρὸς ἄλλης ἱστὸν ὑφαίνοις
καί κεν ὕδωρ φορέοις Μεσσηΐδος ἢ Ὑπερείης
πόλλ’ ἀεκαζομένη, κρατερὴ δ’ ἐπικείσετ’ ἀνάγκη·
καί ποτέ τις εἴπῃσιν ἰδὼν κατὰ δάκρυ χέουσαν·
“Ἕκτορος ἥδε γυνή, ὃς ἀριστεύεσκε μάχεσθαι   460
Τρώων ἱπποδάμων, ὅτε Ἴλιον ἀμφεμάχοντο.”
ὥς ποτέ τις ἐρέει· σοὶ δ’ αὖ νέον ἔσσεται ἄλγος
χήτεϊ τοιοῦδ’ ἀνδρὸς ἀμύνειν δούλιον ἦμαρ.

For well I know this in my mind and in my heart:
there will be a day when holy Ilion will perish
and Priam, and the people of Priam of the good ashen spear.
But not so much does the anguish of the Trojans hereafter concern me,   450
nor of Hecuba herself, nor of lord Priam,
nor of my brothers, who would fall, many and noble,
in the dust at the hands of hostile men,
as much as yours, when one of the bronze-shirted Greeks
leads you off in tears, wresting away your day of freedom.   455
And then in Argos you would weave a web at the command of another woman,
and you would carry water from the spring Messeis or Hypereia,
resisting vigorously, and strong necessity will be upon you.
And one day some one may see you shedding a tear and say
‘This is the wife of Hector, who was always the best at fighting   460
of the horse-taming Trojans, when they fought around Ilion.’

So someone may say, and your anguish will begin anew
for lack of such a man to ward off the day of slavery.

(Il. 6. 447–63)

Like Andromache, the women of Thebes express their horror at the
prospect of slavery if Eteocles persists in his intention to fight his
brother, and their city falls to the Seven:

θεοὶ πολῖται, μή με δουλείας τυχεῖν.

Gods of my city, let me not meet with slavery.

(Aeschylus, *Th.* 253)

and Sophocles' Tecmessa likewise expresses fear of enslavement if
Ajax persists in his present course:

μή μ' ἀξιώσῃς βάξιν ἀλγεινὴν λαβεῖν
τῶν σῶν ὑπ' ἐχθρῶν, χειρίαν ἐφείς τινι.
ἦ γὰρ θάνῃς σὺ καὶ τελευτήσας ἀφῇς
ταύτῃ νόμιζε κἀμὲ τῇ τόθ' ἡμέρᾳ
βίᾳ ξυναρπασθεῖσαν Ἀργείων ὕπο
ξὺν παιδὶ τῷ σῷ δουλίαν ἕξειν τροφήν.
καί τις πικρὸν πρόσφθεγμα δεσποτῶν ἐρεῖ
λόγοις ἰάπτων, "ἴδετε τὴν ὁμευνέτιν
Αἴαντος, ὃς μέγιστον ἴσχυσε στρατοῦ,
οἵας λατρείας ἀνθ' ὅσου ζήλου τρέφει."
τοιαῦτ' ἐρεῖ τις· κἀμὲ μὲν δαίμων ἐλᾷ
σοὶ δ' αἰσχρὰ τἄπη ταῦτα καὶ τῷ σῷ γένει.

Don't require me to receive a painful report
at the hands of your enemies, yielding me up to the power of someone else.
For on the day you die and pass away and abandon me,
on that day think of me too,
snatched away by the Argives
with your son, to eat the bread of slavery.
And one of my masters will utter a bitter address,
assailing me with words, 'Look at the bedfellow
of Ajax, who was the strongest of the army,
What servitude she now enjoys in place of what happiness.'
That is the kind of thing someone will say. And the fate will wound me,
But these wicked words will be against you and against your family.

(Sophocles , *Aj.* 494–505)[9]

To indicate that Hector is the only hope of protection she has,
Andromache describes how her own community was sacked by
Achilles as quoted above. Tecmessa puts the same argument to Ajax,
he is her only hope, because he was the destroyer of Tecmessa's own
community:

---

[9] Sophocles, *Aj.* 500–5 are closely modelled on *Il.* 6. 459–63.

ἐμοὶ γὰρ οὐκέτ᾽ ἐστὶν εἰς ὅ τι βλέπω
πλὴν σοῦ. σὺ γάρ μοι πατρίδ᾽ ἤστωσας δορί,
καὶ μητέρ᾽ ἄλλη μοῖρα τὸν φύσαντά τε
καθεῖλεν Ἅιδου θανασίμους οἰκήτορας.
τίς δῆτ᾽ ἐμοὶ γένοιτ᾽ ἂν ἀντὶ σοῦ πατρίς;
τίς πλοῦτος; ἐν σοὶ πᾶσ᾽ ἔγωγε σῴζομαι.
ἀλλ᾽ ἴσχε κἀμοῦ μνῆστιν.

For I no longer have anything to look towards
except you. For you destroyed my native land with the spear,
and a different fate overtook my mother and my father
who begot me, mortal inhabitants of the house of Hades.
What native land would I have without you?
What wealth? For in you is all my safety.
But have some remembrance of me too.

(Sophocles, *Aj.* 514–20)[10]

Andromache attempts to persuade Hector to fight defensively rather
than rashly to pursue glory at the risk of his life:

ἀλλ᾽ ἄγε νῦν ἐλέαιρε καὶ αὐτοῦ μίμν᾽ ἐπὶ πύργῳ,
μὴ παῖδ᾽ ὀρφανικὸν θήῃς χήρην τε γυναῖκα·
λαὸν δὲ στῆσον παρ᾽ ἐρινεόν, ἔνθα μάλιστα
ἀμβατός ἐστι πόλις καὶ ἐπίδρομον ἔπλετο τεῖχος.
τρὶς γὰρ τῇ γ᾽ ἐλθόντες ἐπειρήσανθ᾽ οἱ ἄριστοι
ἀμφ᾽ Αἴαντε δύω καὶ ἀγακλυτὸν Ἰδομενῆα
ἠδ᾽ ἀμφ᾽ Ἀτρείδας καὶ Τυδέος ἄλκιμον υἱόν.

But come now, have pity, and stay here on the tower,
do not make your son an orphan and your wife a widow.
But station the war host by the fig-tree where the city
is especially vulnerable, and the wall may be scaled.
For three times at that point the best attempted it,
around the two Ajaxes and very famous Idomeneus
and around the Atreidae and the bold son of Tydeus.

(*Il.* 6. 431–7)

Tecmessa's attempts to restrain Ajax:

ὦ πρὸς θεῶν ὕπεικε καὶ φρόνησον εὖ.

O, by the gods, yield, and think straight.

(Sophocles, *Aj.* 371)

εὔφημα φώνει

Speak words of good omen.

(Sophocles, *Aj.* 591)

πρὸς θεῶν, μαλάσσου.

By the gods, give ground.

(Sophocles, *Aj.* 594)

[10] Cf. *Il.* 6. 411–31.

are more cavalierly dismissed by Ajax than Andromache's advice is dismissed by Hector:

μῶρά μοι δοκεῖς φρονεῖν
εἰ τοὐμὸν ἦθος ἄρτι παιδεύειν νοεῖς.

You seem to me to think stupid things
if you think you can even now educate my character.

(Sophocles, *Aj.* 594–5)

The women of Thebes, who conclude their attempts to advise Eteocles with:

πείθου γυναιξὶ καίπερ οὐ στέργων ὅμως

Be ruled by women though you like it not.

(Aeschylus, *Th.* 712)

are told:

οὐκ ἄνδρ' ὁπλίτην τοῦτο χρὴ στέργειν ἔπος

A man and a soldier must not acquiesce in this advice.

(Aeschylus, *Th.* 717)

These passages from tragedy are likely to be influenced by the Homeric model of Andromache's advice to Hector. In both plays the intransigence of the hero is associated with ἄτη and wrong-thinking. Eteocles and Ajax are blind to the irrational nature of their own actions, and regard irrationality as the sole preserve of women: Eteocles finishes as a fratricide and Ajax as a suicide. Ἄτη and wrong-thinking are attributed to Eteocles and Ajax when they reject the advice of the women under their protection, and a bad end awaits them: Hector's career in the *Iliad* seems to follow a similar pattern, since he also rejects the moderate position advocated by a woman.

Hector, as he tells Andromache, has always learned to fight in the forefront of the battle, ἀρνύμενος πατρός τε μέγα κλέος ἠδ' ἐμὸν αὐτοῦ, 'maintaining the great glory of my father[11] and of myself' (*Il.* 6. 446). This is done out of deference to public opinion:

αἰδέομαι Τρῶας καὶ Τρῳάδας ἑλκεσιπέπλους[12]
αἴ κε κακὸς ὣς νόσφιν ἀλυσκάζω πολέμοιο

---

[11] On the effect of the achievements of children on the standing of their parents, see Dover (1974: 246).

[12] On the repetition of this line at *Il.* 22. 105, see Fenik (1978: 84): avoidance of disrepute turns to shame already incurred by failure to follow the safer course advocated by Andromache. Hector incurs shame by his failure to protect his community (*Il.* 22. 107): this is why Erbse (1979: 15) is mistaken in thinking Hector's response to Andromache's arguments irrefutable.

Appendix E

I feel shame before the Trojans and the Trojan ladies in their trailing gowns
if, like a base man, I skulk away from the war

(*Il.* 6. 442–3)

and from personal choice. Kakridis, Griffin, etc. applaud what they
see as Hector's assertion of his superior understanding of war against
the woolly thinking of the women. The difficulties with their view are
(*a*) Hector knows before he starts that what he is doing is useless:
Troy will fall (*Il.* 6. 446–9) and her inhabitants will not be saved by his
pursuit of heroism and κλέος, and (*b*) Priam himself will in book 22
join his pleas to those of the women in book 6 in attempting to
dissuade Hector from his reckless course.[13] It is difficult to maintain
that Hector is fighting to maintain his father's great glory if his father
himself is urging him to desist. If the poet is out of sympathy with the
women, why should he make Priam, whom nobody would describe as
woolly-minded, take up their cause?[14] By his pursuit of heroics,
Hector makes his family suffer the humiliation of witnessing the mistreatment of his corpse, and he narrowly escapes the disgrace of going
unburied. In order to restore some semblance of honour to his family,
Priam is reduced to supplicating Achilles for the return of Hector's
corpse. The old man succeeds in dealing with his fear of entering the
Greek camp to recover the body, and by his demeanour earns the
respect of Achilles (*Il.* 24. 519–21) but Hector, whose obstinacy has
necessitated this display of courage from his father,[15] has quite
reversed the heroic ideal of protecting the father in his old age: his
father is obliged to protect him. Ironically, Hector's determination
to fight for the glory of his father (*Il.* 6. 446) results in Priam's
demonstration of his own heroism by his visit to the quarters of his
son's killer, where he must abase himself as a suppliant to recover
Hector's body for burial. In a poem exploring the consequences of
rejected λιταί, the correct pattern of compliance with their demands is
re-established in response to the λιταί of a father on behalf of his son.
The intervention of the gods to ensure that this time Achilles complies
with Priam's λιταί illustrates once more the αἶνος of the Λιταί, and
vindicates all those, including the women of book 6, whose pleas were
rejected earlier in the poem.

[13] The Trojan elders are in favour of giving back Helen (*Il.* 3. 159–60), and
Priam, despite his kindness to Helen (*Il.* 3. 162–5), swears an oath to return
her if Menelaus wins the duel against Paris (*Il.* 3. 250–91). Priam seems unable
to carry out his promise (*Il.* 7. 368–78), in the face of Paris' objections (*Il.* 7.
362–4).

[14] Priam may be seen as a representative of the non-combatant population
of women, children, and old men: Kakridis (1971: 68–75). On his soundness of
mind, see Achilles' tribute (*Il.* 20. 183).

[15] On Priam's courage, see Bowra (1952: 50); Kakridis (1971: 74).

REFERENCES

The following abbreviations are used:

AAHG	*Anzeiger für Altertumswissenschaft*
AJP	*American Journal of Philology*
AM	*Mitteilungen der deutschen archäologischen Instituts: Athenische Abteilung*
AU	*Der Altsprachliche Unterricht* (Arbeitshefte zu seiner Wissenschaftliche Begrundung und praktischen Gestalt, Stuttgart)
BCH	*Bulletin de Correspondance Hellénique*
BICS	*Bulletin of the Institute of Classical Studies*
BSA	*Annual of the British School at Athens*
CA	*California Studies in Classical Antiquity*
CJ	*Classical Journal*
CP	*Classical Philology*
CQ	*Classical Quarterly*
CR	*Classical Review*
CW	*Classical World*
GRBS	*Greek, Roman, and Byzantine Studies*
HSCP	*Harvard Studies in Classical Philology*
IF	*Indogermanische Forschungen*
JHS	*Journal of Hellenic Studies*
LCM	*Liverpool Classical Monthly*
OA	*Opuscula Atheniensa*
ΠΑΕ	Πρακτικὰ τῆς ἐν Ἀθήναις Ἀρχαιλογικῆς Ἑταιρείας
PCPS	*Proceedings of the Cambridge Philological Society*
RÉG	*Revue des Études Grecques*
RM	*Rheinisches Museum*
SO	*Symbolae Osloenses*
TAPhA	*Transactions of the American Philological Association*
WS	*Wiener Studien*
ZPE	*Zeitschrift für Papyrologie und Epigraphik*

ADKINS, A. W. H. (1960), *Merit and Responsibility: A Study in Greek Values* (Oxford).
—— (1969), 'Threatening, Abusing, and Feeling Angry in the Homeric Poems', *JHS* 89: 7–21.

ADKINS, A. W. H. (1971), 'Homeric Values and Homeric Society', *JHS* 91: 1–14.

——(1972), *Moral and Political Behaviour in Ancient Greece from Homer to the End of the Fifth Century* (London).

——(1975), 'Art, Beliefs, and Values in the Later Books of the *Iliad*', *CP* 70: 239–54.

ALDEN, M. J. (1993), 'An Intelligent Cyclops?', in *M. Παΐζη-Αποστολοπούλου* (ed.), Σπονδές στον Όμηρο (Μνήμη Ι. Θ. Κακριδή) (Ithaca), 75–95.

——(1997), 'The Resonances of the Song of Ares and Aphrodite', *Mnemosyne*, 50: 513–29.

ALEXIOU, M. (1974), *The Ritual Lament in Greek Tradition* (Cambridge).

ALLEN, T. W. (1912) (ed.), *Homeri Opera*, i–v.

ANDERSEN, Ø. (1976), 'Some Thoughts on the Shield of Achilles', *SO* 51: 5–18.

——(1978), *Die Diomedesgestalt in der Ilias*, *SO* suppl. 25 (Oslo).

——(1982), 'Thersites und Thoas vor Troia', *SO* 57: 7–34.

——(1987), 'Myth, Paradigm, and "Spatial Form" in the *Iliad*', in J. M. Bremer, I. J. F. de Jong, and J. Kalff (eds.), *Homer: Beyond Oral Poetry* (Amsterdam), 1–13.

——(1990), 'The Making of the Past in the *Iliad*', *HSCP* 93: 25–45.

APTHORP, M. J. (1980), *The Manuscript Evidence for Interpolation in Homer* (Heidelberg).

AREND, W. (1933), *Die Typischen Scenen bei Homer*, Problemata 7 (Berlin).

ARIETI, J. A. (1988), 'Homer's Litae and Atê', *CJ* 84: 1–12.

ARTHUR-KATZ, M. B. (1981), 'The Divided World of *Iliad* VI', in H. P. Foley (ed.), *Reflections of Women in Antiquity* (Philadelphia; repr. 1992), 19–44.

AUBRIOT, D. (1982), 'Remarques sur le personnage de Phénix et sur le Chant IX de l'*Iliade*', *Les Actes du Département d'Histoire des Idées du C. E. R. I. C.* (Amiens).

——(1984), 'Les Litai d'Homère et la Dikè d'Hésiode', *RÉG* 97: 1–25.

AUERBACH, E. (1953), 'The Scar of Odysseus', in *Mimesis: the Representation of Reality in Western Literature*, trans. W. R. Trask (Princeton; 1st pub. Berne, 1946), 3–23.

AUSTIN, N. (1978), 'The Function of Digressions in the *Iliad*', in J. Wright (ed.), *Essays on the* Iliad (Bloomington), 70–84 (1st pub. *GRBS* 7 (1966), 295–312).

AUSTIN, R. G. (1964) (ed.), Virgil, *Aeneid* II (Oxford).

AUTENRIETH, G. (1920), *Wörterbuch zu den Homerischen Gedichten*,

13th edn. with improvements by A. Kaegi (Leipzig).

—— (1984), *Homeric Dictionary*, trans. R. Keep (London; 1st pub. as *Autenrieths Schulwörterbuch zu den Homerischen Gedichten*, Leipzig, 1873).

AVERY, H. C. (1994), 'Glaucus, A God? *Iliad Z* 128–43', *Hermes*, 122: 498–502.

BANNERT, H. (1981), 'Phoinix's Jugend und der Zorn des Meleagros', *WS* 15: 69–94.

—— (1988), *Die Formen des Wiederholens bei Homer. Beispiele für eine Poetik des Epos*, *WS* Beiheft 13 (Vienna).

BARRETT, W. S. (1964) (ed.), *Euripides, Hippolytos* (Oxford).

—— (1974), 'Niobe', in R. Carden (ed.), *The Papyrus Fragments of Sophocles* (Berlin), 171–235.

BASSETT, S. E. (1934), 'The Ἁμαρτία of Achilles', *TAPhA* 65: 47–69.

—— (1938), *The Poetry of Homer* (Berkeley).

BAUGHMAN, E. W. (1966), *Type- and Motif-Index of the Folk-Tales of England and North America*, Indiana University Folklore ser. 20 (The Hague).

BEATON, R. (1980), *Folk Poetry of Modern Greece* (Cambridge).

BECK, G. (1964), *Die Stellung des 24. Buches der Ilias in der alten Epentradition* (Bamberg).

BENVENISTE, E. (1973), *Indo-European Language and Society*, trans. E. Palmer (London; 1st pub. as *Le Vocabulaire des Institutions Indo-Européennes*, Paris, 1969).

BERGK, T. (1872), *Griechische Literaturgeschichte*, i (Berlin).

BERNABÉ, A. (1988), *Poetae Epici Graeci: Testimonia et Fragmenta* (Leipzig).

BETHE, E. (1925), 'Ilias und Meleager', *RM* 74: 1–12.

BEYE, C. R. (1964), 'Homeric Battle Narrative and Catalogues', *HSCP* 68: 345–73.

BOARDMAN, J. (1993), *The Oxford History of Classical Art* (Oxford).

BODE, G. H. (1834), *Scriptores Rerum Mythicarum Latini Tres, Romae Nuper Reperti* (Cellis).

BOLLING, G. M. (1925), *The External Evidence for Interpolation in Homer* (Oxford; repr. 1968).

—— (1944), *The Athetized Lines of the* Iliad (Baltimore).

BÖLTE, F. (1934), 'Ein Pylisches Epos', *RM*, 83: 319–47.

BOSKOS, A. I. (1974), "Μελέαγρος-Ἀχιλλεὺς καὶ Φοῖνιξ", *Στάσινος*, 1 (Leucosia).

BOURDIEU, P. (1955), 'The Sentiment of Honour in Kabyle Society', in J. G. Peristiany (ed.), *Honour and Shame: The Values of Mediterranean Society* (London), 191–241.

—— (1977), *Outline of a Theory of Practice*, trans. R. Nice

(Cambridge; 1st pub. as *Esquisse d'une théorie de la pratique, précedée de trois études d'ethnologie kabyle*, Geneva, 1972).

BOWRA, C. M. (1930), *Tradition and Design in the* Iliad (Oxford; repr. 1950).

—— (1952), *Heroic Poetry* (London).

—— (1972), *Homer* (London).

BRASWELL, B. K. (1971), 'Mythological Innovation in the *Iliad*', *CQ* 21: 16–26.

BREMMER, J. (1983), 'The Importance of the Maternal Uncle and Grandfather in Archaic and Classical Greece and Early Byzantium', *ZPE* 50: 173–86.

—— (1988), 'La Plasticité du mythe: Méléagre dans la poésie homérique', in C. Calame (ed.), *Métamorphoses du Mythe Grec* (Paris), 37–56.

BRENK, F. E. (1986), 'Dear Child: The Speech of Phoinix and the Tragedy of Achilleus in the Ninth Book of the *Iliad*', *Eranos*, 84: 77–86.

BRIGGS, K. M. (1971), *A Dictionary of British Folk Tales* (London).

BÜHLER, W. (1960), *Die Europa des Moschos*, *Hermes* Einzelschriften 13 (Wiesbaden).

BUNDY, E. L. (1986), *Studia Pindarica* (Berkeley; 1st pub. 1962 (U.C. Publ. Cl. Phil. 18.1–2)).

BURKERT, W. (1979), *Structure and History in Greek Mythology and Ritual* (Berkeley).

—— (1983), *Homo Necans*, trans. P. Bing (Berkeley; 1st pub. Berlin, 1972).

—— (1985), *Greek Religion*, trans. J. Raffan (Oxford; 1st pub. as *Griechische Religion der archaischen und klassischen Epoche*, Stuttgart, 1977).

—— (1983), 'Oriental Myth and Literature in the *Iliad*', in R. Hägg (ed.), *The Greek Renaissance of the Eighth Century B.C.: Tradition and Innovation*, Skrifter utgivna av Svenska Instituet i Athen 4° 30 (Stockholm), 51–6.

CAIRNS, D. (1993), *Aidos* (Oxford).

CALDER III, W. M. (1984), 'Gold for Bronze: *Iliad* 6. 232–36', in K. J. Rigsby (ed.), *Studies Presented to Sterling Dow*, Greek, Roman, and Byzantine Monographs 10 (Durham, NC), 31–5.

CALHOUN, G. M. (1927), *The Growth of Criminal Law in Ancient Greece* (Berkeley).

CAMPBELL, M. (1991) (ed.), *Moschus, Europa*, Altertumswissenschaftliche Texte und Studien (Hildesheim).

CANTIENI, R. (1942), *Die Nestorerzählung im XI. Gesang der Ilias* (Zurich).

CAREY, C. (1980), 'Three Myths in Pindar', *Eranos*, 78: 143–62.

CARPENTER, T. H. (1986), *Dionysian Imagery in Archaic Greek Art* (Oxford).

CARTER, A. (1992), *Underwear, the Fashion History* (London).

CHANTRAINE, P. (1968), *Dictionnaire étymologique de la langue grecque*, i–ii (Paris; repr. 1980–90).

COLDSTREAM, J. N. (1979), *Geometric Greece* (London; 1st pub. 1977).

COLLARD, C., *et al.* (1995) (eds.), *Euripides: Selected Fragmentary Plays*, with introd., trans., and comm., i (Warminster).

CORLU, A. (1966), *Recherches sur les mots relatifs à l'idée de prière d'Homère aux Tragiques* (Paris).

CRAIG, J. D. (1967), 'χρύσεα χαλκείων', *CR* 17: 243–5.

CRAIK, E. M. (1980), *The Dorian Aegean* (London).

CROTTY, K. (1994), *The Poetics of Supplication* (Ithaca, NY).

CUNLIFFE, R. J. (1924), *A Lexicon of the Homeric Dialect* (London).

DANEK, G. (1988), *Studien zur Dolonie*, *WS* Beiheft 15 (Vienna).

D'ARMS, E. F., and HULLEY, K. K. (1946), 'The Oresteia Story in the *Odyssey*', *TAPhA* 77: 207–13.

DAVIDSON, O. M. (1980), 'Indo-European Dimensions of Heracles in *Iliad* 19. 95–133', *Arethusa*, 13: 197–202.

DAVIES, M. (1988) (ed.), *Epicorum Graecorum Fragmenta* (Göttingen).

DAWE, R. D. (1967), 'Some Reflections on Ate and Hamartia', *HSCP* 72: 89–123.

DEICHGRÄBER, K. (1952), *Der listensinnende Trug des Gottes* (Göttingen).

DE JONG, I. J. F. (1985), 'Iliad 1. 366–92: A Mirror-Story', *Arethusa*, 18: 1–22.

—— (1987a), 'The Voice of Anonymity; tis-Speeches in the *Iliad*', *Eranos*, 85: 69–84.

—— (1987b), *Narrators and Focalizers* (Amsterdam).

DELATTE, A. (1951), 'Le Baiser, l'agenouillement, et le prosternement de l'adoration (Προσκύνησις) chez les Grecs', *Bulletin de la Classe des Lettres et des Sciences Morales et Politiques*, Académie Royale de Belgique, 3: 423–50.

DÉTIENNE, M., and VERNANT, J. P. (1978), *Cunning Intelligence in Greek Culture and Society*, trans. J. L. Hassocks (Brighton; 1st pub. as *Les Ruses de l'intelligence*, Paris, 1974).

DIEHL, E. (1936) (ed.), *Anthologia Lyrica Graeca* (Leipzig).

DILLER, H. (1962), *Die Dichterische Form von Hesiods Erga* (Wiesbaden).

DILTS, M. R., and KENNEDY, G. E. (1997), *Two Greek Rhetorical Treatises from the Roman Empire. Introduction, Text and Translation of the Arts of Rhetoric attributed to Anonymous Seguerianus and to Apsines of Gadara* (Leiden).

DIMOCK Jnr., G. E. (1963), 'The Name of Odysseus', in C. H. Taylor Jnr. (ed.), *Essays on the* Odyssey (Bloomington), 54–72.

DINDORF, W. (1875–88) (ed.), *Scholia Graeca in Homeri Iliadem*, i–vi (Oxford).

DODDS, E. R. (1951), *The Greeks and the Irrational* (Berkeley).

DONLAN, W. (1989), 'The Unequal Exchange Between Glaucus and Diomedes in the Light of the Homeric Gift-Economy', *Phoenix*, 43: 1–15.

DOVER, K. J. (1974), *Greek Popular Morality in the Time of Plato and Aristotle* (Berkeley).

DRERUP, E. (1921), *Das Homerproblem in der Gegenwart* (Würzburg).

DU BOULAY, J. (1974), *Portrait of a Greek Mountain Village* (Oxford).

DUCKWORTH, G. E. (1931), 'Προαναφώνησις in the Scholia to Homer', *AJP* 52: 320–38.

——(1933), *Foreshadowing and Suspense in the Epics of Homer, Apollonius, and Vergil* (Princeton).

DÜNTZER, H. (1848), *De Zenodoti Studiis Homericis* (Göttingen).

EBEL, H. (1972), *After Dionysus: An Essay on Where We Are Now* (Cranbury, NJ).

EBELING, H. (1880–5), *Lexicon Homericum*, i (1885), ii (1880) (Leipzig; repr. Hildesheim, 1963).

EDWARDS, A. T. (1985), *Achilles in the* Odyssey (Meisenheim).

EDWARDS, M. W. (1987), *Homer, Poet of the* Iliad (Baltimore).

——(1991), *The Iliad: A Commentary*, v (Cambridge).

EICHHOLZ, D. E. (1953), 'The Propitiation of Achilles', *AJP* 74: 137–48.

ERBSE, H. (1961), 'Beobachtungen über das 5. Buch der *Ilias*', *RM* 104: 156–89.

——(1969–88), *Scholia Graeca in Homeri Iliadem*, i–vii (Berlin).

——(1979), *Ausgewählte Schriften zur klassischen Philologie* (Berlin).

——(1986), *Untersuchungen zur Funktion der Götter im homerischen Epos* (Berlin).

EWING, E. (1971), *Fashion in Underwear* (London).

——(1978), *Dress and Undress: A History of Women's Underwear* (London).

FENIK, B. (1964), Iliad *X and the 'Rhesus'. The Myth*, Coll. *Latomus* 73 (Brussels–Berchem).

——(1968), 'Typical Battle Scenes in the *Iliad*', *Hermes* Einzelschrift 21 (Wiesbaden).

——(1974), *Studies in the* Odyssey, *Hermes* Einzelschrift 30 (Wiesbaden).

FENIK, B. (1978) (ed.), *Tradition and Invention* (Leiden).

FINKELBERG, M. (1995), 'Patterns of Human Error in Homer', *JHS* 115: 15–28.

FINLEY, R. (1980), 'Patroklos, Achilleus, and Peleus: Fathers and Sons in the *Iliad*', *CW* 73: 267–73.

FINSLER, G. (1924), *Homer I: Der Dichter und seine Welt*, i. *Vorfragen. Homerkritik* (Leipzig).

FISHER, N. R. E. (1992), *Hybris* (Warminster).

FRAENKEL, E. (1950), *Aeschylus, Agamemnon*, edn. and comm. (Oxford).

FRANCIS, E. D. (1983), 'Virtue, Folly, and Greek Etymology', in C. A. Rubino and C. W. Shelmerdine (eds.), *Approaches to Homer* (Austin, Tex.), 74–121.

FRÄNKEL, H. (1975), *Early Greek Poetry and Philosophy*, trans. M. Hadas and J. Willis (Oxford; 1st pub. as *Dichtung und Philosophie des frühen Griechentums*, New York, 1951).

FRAZER, J. G. (1921) (ed.), *Apollodorus, The Library*, i–ii (London; repr. 1989).

FRAZER, R. M. (1989), 'The Return of Achilleus as a Climactic Parallel to Patroklos' Entering Battle', *Hermes*, 117: 381–90.

FRIEDLÄNDER, P. (1969), *Johannes von Gaza, Paulus Silentiarius, und Prokopios von Gaza* (Hildesheim; 1st pub. 1882).

FRISK, H. (1954–70), *Griechisches Etymologisches Wörterbuch* (Heidelberg).

GAGARIN, M. (1981), *Drakon and Early Athenian Homicide Law* (New Haven).

—— (1983), 'Antilochus' Strategy: The Chariot Race in *Iliad* 23', *CP* 78: 35–9.

GAISSER, J. H. (1969*a*), 'A Structural Analysis of the Digressions in the *Iliad* and the *Odyssey*', *HSCP* 73: 1–43.

—— (1969*b*), 'Adaptation of Traditional Material in the Glaucus-Diomedes Episode', *TAPhA* 100: 165–76.

GANTZ, T. (1993), *Early Greek Myth: A Guide to Literary and Artistic Sources* (Baltimore).

GOOLD, G. P. (1970), 'Servius and the Helen Episode', *HSCP* 74: 101–68.

GOULD, J. P. (1973), 'Hiketeia', *JHS* 93: 74–103.

—— (1980), 'Law, Custom and Myth: Aspects of the Social Position of Women in Classical Athens', *JHS* 100: 38–59.

GOW, A. S. F. (1950) (ed.), *Theocritus*, ed. with a trans. and comm. (Cambridge).

GRIESSMAIR, E. (1966), *Das Motiv der Mors Immatura in den griechischen metrischen Grabinschriften* (Innsbruck).

GRIFFIN, J. (1977), 'The Epic Cycle and the Uniqueness of Homer', *JHS* 97: 39–53.

GRIFFIN, J. (1980), *Homer on Life and Death* (Oxford).

—— (1986), 'Homeric Words and Speakers', *JHS* 106: 36–57.

—— (1990), 'Achilles kills Hector', *Lampas*, 23: 353–69.

—— (1995) (ed.), *Homer, Iliad IX*, ed. with an introd. and comm. (Oxford).

HAINSWORTH, B. (1993), *The Iliad: A Commentary*, iii (Cambridge).

HALE, W. H. (1847), *A Series of Precedents and Proceedings in Criminal Cases extending from the year 1475 to 1640 extracted from Act-Books of Ecclesiastical Courts in the Diocese of London* (London).

HALL, E. (1989), *Inventing the Barbarian* (Oxford).

HAMMOND, N. G. L. (1985), 'The Scene in *Iliad* 18. 497–508 and the Albanian Blood-Feud', *Bulletin of the American Society of Papyrologists*, 22: 79–86.

HANSEN, J. G. (1986), 'Die Blendung des Polyphem', *AU* 29: 61–74.

HARRISON, A. R. W. (1968), *The Law of Athens*, i. *The Family and Property* (Oxford).

HARTLAND, E. S. (1925), *The Science of Fairy Tales* (London).

HAUSRATH, A. (1970), *Corpus Fabularum Aesopicarum*, i. fasc. 1, rev. H. Hunger (Leipzig; 1st pub. 1940).

HAVERS, W. (1910), 'Zur Semasiologie von griech. ἄτη', *Zeitschrift für vergleichende Sprachforschung*, 43: 225–44.

HEBEL, V. (1970), *Untersuchungen zur Form und Funktion der Wiedererzählungen in Ilias und Odyssee* (diss. Heidelberg).

HEITSCH, E. (1965), *Aphroditehymnus, Aeneas und Homer, Hypomnemata*, 15 (Göttingen).

HENDERSON, W. (1879), *Notes on the Folk-Lore of the Northern Counties of England and the Borders* (London).

HENTZE, C. (1904), 'Die Monologe in den homerischen Epen', *Philologus*, 63: 12–30.

HEUBECK, A. (1974a), *Die Homerische Frage* (Darmstadt).

—— (1974b), review of H. Patzer, *Dichterische Kunst und poetisches Handwerk im Homerischen Epos* (Wiesbaden, 1972), in *Gnomon*, 46: 533.

—— (1984), 'Das Meleagros-Paradeigma in der Ilias', in *Kleine Schriften* (Erlangen), 128–35 (1st pub. in *Neue Jahrbücher*, 118 (1943), 13–20).

—— et al. (1988–92) (eds.), *A Commentary on Homer's Odyssey*, i–iii (Oxford).

HOFFMANN, W. (1954), *Lateinisches Etymologisches Wörterbuch* (Heidelberg).

HOFMANN, E. (1922), *Qua ratione ἔπος, μῦθος, αἶνος, λόγος et vocabula ab eisdem stirpibus derivata in antiquo Graecorum sermone (usque ad annum fere 400) adhibita sint* (Göttingen).

HOLST-WARHAFT, G. (1992), *Dangerous Voices* (London).

HOMMEL, H. (1969), 'Die Gerichtsszene auf dem Schild des Achilleus. Zur Pflege des Rechts in homerischer Zeit', in P. Steinmetz (ed.), *Politeia und Respublica: Beiträge zum Verständnis von Politik, Recht und Staat in der Antike. Dem Andenken Rud. Starks gewidmet*, Palingenesia ser. 4 (Wiesbaden), 11–38.

HOOKER, J. T. (1979), *Homer*, Iliad *III: Text with Introduction, Notes and Vocabulary* (Bristol).

——(1980), '*ΑΙΓΑΙΩΝ* in Achilles' Plea to Thetis', *JHS* 100: 188–9.

HOPE-SIMPSON, R., and DICKINSON, O. T. P. K. (1979), *A Gazetteer of Aegean Civilisation in the Bronze Age*, i. *The Mainland and Islands*, Studies in Mediterranean Archaeology 52 (Gothenburg).

HORROCKS, G. C. (1980), 'The Antiquity of the Greek Tradition', *PCPS*, NS 26: 1–11.

HOWALD, E. (1924), 'Meleager und Achill', *RM* 73: 402–25.

——(1946), *Der Dichter der Ilias* (Zurich).

HUIZINGA, J. (1970), *Homo Ludens* (London; 1st pub. Basle, 1944).

HUMBERT, J. (1960), *Syntaxe grecque* (Paris).

HURST, A. (1994), 'Un nouveau papyrus du premier hymne homérique: le papyrus de Genève 432', in A. Bülow-Jacobsen (ed.), *Proceedings of the 20th International Conference of Papyrologists, Copenhagen 23–9 August 1992* (Copenhagen), 317–21.

HURSTON, Z. (1931), 'Hoodoo in America', *Journal of American Folk-Lore*, 44: 317–417.

HUXLEY, G. L. (1969), *Greek Epic Poetry* (London).

JAHNKE, R. (1898) (ed.), *Lactantii Placidi qui dicitur Commentarios in Statii Thebaida et Commentarium in Achilleida* (Leipzig).

JAMISON, S. (1994), 'Draupadi on the Walls of Troy: Iliad 3 from an Indic Perspective', *CA* 13: 5–16.

JANKO, R. (1981), 'Equivalent Formulae in the Greek Epos', *Mnemosyne*, 34: 251–64.

——(1982), *Homer, Hesiod, and the Hymns* (Cambridge).

——(1986), 'The *Shield of Heracles* and the Legend of Cycnus', *CQ* 36: 38–59.

——(1992), *The Iliad: A Commentary*, iv (Cambridge).

JOHNSTON, A. W., and ANDRIOMENOU, A. (1989), 'A Geometric Graffito from Eretria', *BSA* 84: 217–20.

KAIBEL, G. (1878), *Epigrammata graeca ex lapidibus conlecta* (Berlin).

KAKRIDIS, J. T. (1949), *Homeric Researches* (Lund).

——(1971), *Homer Revisited* (Lund).

——(1980), *Προομηρικά, Ομηρικά, Ησιόδεια* (Athens).

KAKRIDIS, P. J. (1961), 'Achilleus' Rüstung', *Hermes*, 89: 288–97.

KARO, G. (1930–3), *Die Schachtgräber von Mykenai*, i–ii (Munich).

KEANE, M. (1988), *Loving and Giving* (London).

KEARNS, E. (1982), 'The Return of Odysseus: A Homeric Theoxeny', *CQ*, NS 32: 2–8.

KEIL, B. (1895), 'Die Rechnungen über den Epidaurischen Tholosbau', *AM* 20: 404–50.

KENNEDY, G. (1963), *The Art of Persuasion in Greece* (Princeton).

KERSHAW, N. (1921), *Stories and Ballads of the Far Past translated from the Norse (Icelandic and Faroese)* (Cambridge).

KIRK, G. S. (1962), *The Songs of Homer* (Cambridge).

—— (1985–90), *The Iliad: A Commentary*, i–ii (Cambridge).

KITTREDGE, G. L. (1929), *Witchcraft in Old and New England* (Cambridge, Mass.).

KLINGNER, F. (1940), 'Über die Dolonie', *Hermes*, 75: 337–68.

KNAACK, G. (1894), 'Zur Meleagersage', *RM* 49: 310–13.

KOPPERSCHMIDT, J. (1967), *Die Hikesie als dramatische Form* (Bamberg).

KRAUS, W. (1948), 'Meleagros in der *Ilias*', *WS* 63: 8–21.

KULLMANN, W. (1956), *Das Wirken der Götter in der Ilias. Untersuchungen zur Frage der Entstehung des homerischen 'Götterapparats'* (Berlin).

—— (1984), 'Oral Poetry Theory and Neoanalysis in Homeric Research', *GRBS* 25: 303–23.

LACEY, W. K. (1968), *The Family in Classical Greece* (London).

LANG, M. L. (1983), 'Reverberation and Mythology in the *Iliad*', in C. A. Rubino and C. W. Shelmerdine (eds.), *Approaches to Homer* (Austin, Tex.), 140–64.

ŁANOWSKI, G. (1947), 'La Passion de Daphnis', *Eos*, 42: 175–94.

LATACZ, J. (1975), 'Zur Forschungsarbeit an den direkten Reden bei Homer 1850–1970', *Grazer Beiträge*, 3: 395–422.

LATEINER, D. (1995), *Sardonic Smile* (Ann Arbor).

LATTIMORE, R. (1962), *Themes in Greek and Latin Epitaphs* (Urbana, Ill.).

LEAF, W. (1887), 'The Trial Scene in *Iliad* XVIII', *JHS* 8: 122–32.

—— (1892), *A Companion to the Iliad* (London).

—— (1900–2) (ed.), *The Iliad of Homer, edited with apparatus criticus, prolegomena, notes, and appendices*, i–ii (London).

LENDLE, O. (1957), *Die Pandorasage bei Hesiod* (Würzburg).

LESSING, H. (1880), *Laokoon*, ed. H. Blumner (Berlin; 1st pub. 1766).

LÉTOUBLON, F. (1980), 'Le Vocabulaire de la supplication en grec: Performatif et dérivation délocutive', *Lingua*, 52: 325–36.

—— (1983a), 'Défi et Combat dans l'*Iliade*', *RÉG* 96: 27–48.

LÉTOUBLON, F. (1983*b*), 'Le Miroir et la boucle', *Poétique*, 53: 19–36.
LEUTSCH, E. L. A., and SCHNEIDEWIN, F. G. (1958) (eds.), *Corpus Paroemiographorum Graecorum*, i–ii (Hildesheim).
LINCOLN, B. (1975), 'Homeric Lussa: Wolfish Rage', *IF* 80: 98–105.
LLOYD, G. E. R. (1966), *Polarity and Analogy: Two Types of Argumentation in Early Greek Thought* (Cambridge).
LLOYD-JONES, H. (1960), 'Three Notes on Aeschylus' *Agamemnon*', *RM* 103: 76–80; repr. in Lloyd-Jones (1990), 305–9.
—— (1971), *The Justice of Zeus* (Berkeley).
—— (1990), *Greek Epic, Lyric, and Tragedy* (Oxford).
LOHMANN, D. (1970), *Die Komposition der Reden in der Ilias* (Berlin).
—— (1988), *Die Andromache-Szenen der Ilias*, Spudasmata ser. 42 (Hildesheim).
LONG, A. A. (1970), 'Morals and Values in Homer', *JHS* 90: 121–39.
LONGLEY, M. (1991), *Gorse Fires* (London).
—— (1995), *The Ghost Orchid* (London).
LONSDALE, S. H. (1990), *Creatures of Speech: Lion, Herding, and Hunting Similes in the* Iliad, Beiträge zur Altertumskunde 5 (Stuttgart).
LORAUX, N. (1986), 'Matrem Nudam', *L'Écrit du temps* 11: 90–102.
—— (1990), *Les Mères en deuil* (Évreux).
LORD, A. B. (1991), *Epic Singers and Oral Tradition* (Ithaca, NY).
LORD, M. L. (1967), 'Withdrawal and Return', *CJ* 62: 241–8.
LUDWICH, A. L. (1884–5), *Aristarchs Homerische Textkritik*, i–ii (Leipzig).
LYNN-GEORGE, J. M. (1978), 'The Relationship of Σ 535–40 and *Scutum* 156–60 Re-examined', *Hermes*, 106: 396–405.
—— (1983), 'Epos: Word, Narrative, and the Iliad' (diss. Cambridge).
—— (1988), *Epos: Word, Narrative, and the* Iliad (London; shortened version of diss. Cambridge, 1983).
MCDONALD, W. A., and WILKIE, N. C. (1983), *Excavations at Nichoria in Southwest Greece*, iii. *Dark Age and Byzantine Occupation* (Minneapolis).
—— —— (1992), *Excavations at Nichoria in Southwest Greece*, ii. *The Bronze Age Occupation* (Minneapolis).
MCDOWELL, C. (1997), *Forties Fashion and the New Look* (London).
MACDOWELL, D. M. (1978), *The Law in Classical Athens* (London).
MCGLEW, J. F. (1989), 'Royal Power and the Achaean Assembly at *Iliad* 2. 84–93', *CA* 8: 283–95.
MACLEOD, C. (1982) (ed.), *Homer*, Iliad *XXIV* (Cambridge).
—— (1983), *Collected Essays* (Oxford).
MAFTEI, M. (1976), *Antike Diskussionen über die Episode von Glaukos und Diomedes im VI. Buch der Ilias*, Beiträge zur Klassischen Philologie 74 (Meisenheim).

MALTEN, L. (1925), 'Bellerophontes', *Jahrbuch des deutschen Archäologischen Instituts*, 40: 121–60.

MALTEN, L. (1944), 'Homer und die Lykischen Fürsten', *Hermes*, 79: 1–12.

MARCH, J. R. (1987), 'The Creative Poet', *BICS* suppl. 49 (London).

MARG, W. (1957), *Homer über die Dichtung. Der Schild des Achilleus*, Orbis Antiquus 11 (Münster).

MARSHALL, M. (1990), 'Pericles and the Plague', in E. M. Craik (ed.), *Owls to Athens* (Oxford), 163–70.

MARTIN, R. P. (1989), *The Language of Heroes* (Ithaca, NY).

MATTHEWS, V. J. (1974), *Panyassis of Halicarnassus, Mnemosyne* suppl. 33 (Leiden).

MERKELBACH, R. (1973), 'Ein Fragment des homerischen Dionysus-Hymnus', *ZPE* 12: 212–15.

MEULI, K. (1975), 'Herkunft und Wesen der Fabel: ein Vortrag', *Gesammelte Schriften*, ii (Basle), 731–56 (1st pub. as *Herkunft und Wesen der Fabel* (Basle, 1954)).

MORRIS, I., and POWELL B. (1997) (eds.), *A New Companion to Homer* (Leiden).

MORRIS, W. (1970), *News from Nowhere*, ed., J. Redmond (London; 1st pub. 1891).

MORRISON, J. V. (1992), *Homeric Misdirection: False Predictions in the Iliad* (Ann Arbor).

MOTZKUS, D. (1964), *Untersuchungen zum 9. Buch der Ilias unter besonderer Berücksichtigung der Phoinixgestalt* (Hamburg).

MOULTON, C. (1977), *Similes in the Homeric Poems*, Hypomnemata 49 (Göttingen).

MUELLNER, L. (1976), *The Meaning of Homeric Εὔχομαι through its Formulas* (Innsbruck).

MÜLDER, D. (1910), *Die Ilias und ihre Quellen* (Berlin).

MURRAY, G. (1960), *The Rise of the Greek Epic* (Oxford; 1st pub. 1907).

MYLONAS, G. E. (1953), 'Ἀνασκαφὴ Νεκροταφείου Ἐλευσῖνος', *ΠΑΕ*: 77–87.

MYLONAS-SHEAR, I. (1998), 'Seven Bronze Hinges', *JHS* 118: 187–9.

NAGY, G. (1979), *The Best of the Achaeans* (Baltimore).

NAUCK, A. (1926) (ed.), *Tragicorum Graecorum Fragmenta* (Leipzig).

——(1963), *Aristophanis Byzantii Grammatici Alexandrini fragmenta* (Hildesheim; 1st pub. Halle, 1848).

NOÉ, M. (1940), *Phoenix, Ilias und Homer* (Leipzig).

OEHLER, R. (1925), *Mythologische Exempla in der älteren griechischen Dichtung* (Aarau).

OGDEN, D. (1997), *The Crooked Kings of Ancient Greece* (London).

OGLE, M. B. (1911), 'The House-Door in Greek and Roman Religion and Folk-Lore', *AJP* 32: 251–71.

ONIANS, R. B. (1951), *The Origins of European Thought* (Cambridge).

OTTEN, H. (1953), 'Ein kanaanäischer Mythus aus Boğazköy', *Mitteilungen des deutschen Instituts für Orientforschung*, 1: 125–49.

PACK, R. A. (1965), *The Greek and Latin Literary Texts from Greco-Roman Egypt*, 2nd edn. (Ann Arbor; 1st pub. Ann Arbor, 1952).

PAGE, D. L. (1959), *History and the Homeric Iliad* (Berkeley).

PARKER, R. (1983), *Miasma: Pollution and Purification in Early Greek Religion* (Oxford; reissued 1996).

PARRY, A. (1971) (ed.), *The Making of Homeric Verse: The Collected Papers of Milman Parry* (Oxford).

PATZER, H. (1972), *Dichterische Kunst und poetisches Handwerk im homerischen Epos* (Wiesbaden).

PAYTON, R. (1991), 'The Ulu Burun Writing-Board Set', *Anatolian Studies*, 61: 99–106.

PEDRICK, V. (1982), 'Supplication in the *Iliad* and the *Odyssey*', *TAPhA* 112: 125–40.

——(1983), 'The Paradigmatic Nature of Nestor's Speech in *Iliad* 11', *TAPhA* 113: 55–68.

PEEK, W. (1955), *Griechische Vers-Inschriften* (Berlin).

PEMBROKE, S. (1965), 'The Last of the Matriarchs', *Journal of the Economic and Social History of the Orient*, 8: 217–47.

——(1967), 'Women in Charge: The Function of Alternatives in Early Greek Tradition and the Ancient Idea of Matriarchy', *Journal of the Warburg and Courtauld Institutes*, 30: 1–35.

PEPPERMÜLLER, R. (1962), 'Die Glaukos-Diomedes-Szene der *Ilias*. Spuren vorhomerischer Dichtung', *WS* 75: 5–21.

PERRY, B. E. (1937), 'The Early Greek Capacity for Viewing Things Separately', *TAPhA* 68: 403–27.

PERUZZI, E. (1992), 'Cultura greca a Gabii nel secolo VIII', *La Parola del Passato*, 47: 459–68.

PESTALOZZI, H. (1945), *Die Achilleis als Quelle der Ilias* (Erlenbach–Zurich).

PETERSMANN, G. (1974), 'Die Entscheidungsmonologe in den Homerischen Epen', *Grazer Beiträge*, 2: 147–69.

PETERSMANN, H. (1981), 'Homer und das Märchen', *WS* 15: 43–68.

PETROPOULOU, A. (1993), 'The Laphrian Holocaust and its Celtic Parallel: A Ritual with Indo-European Components?', *Grazer Beiträge* Supplementband, 5: 313–334.

PETZHOLD, K. F. (1976), 'Die Meleagros-Geschichte der Ilias', *Historia*, 25: 146–69.

PFEIFFER, R. (1968), *History of Classical Scholarship*, i. *From the*

332 *References*

Beginnings to the End of the Hellenistic Age (Oxford).

PITT-RIVERS, J. (1977), *The Fate of Shecham or the Politics of Sex* (Cambridge).

PODLECKI, A. J. (1961), 'Guest-Gifts and Nobodies in *Odyssey* 9', *Phoenix*, 15: 125–33.

POKORNY, J. (1959), *Indogermanisches Etymologisches Wörterbuch* (Bonn).

POLITIS, N. G. (1958), Ἐκλογαὶ ἀπὸ τὰ Τραγούδια τοῦ Ἑλληνικοῦ Λαοῦ (Athens).

PÖTSCHER, W. (1985–6), 'Homer, *Ilias* 24, 601 ff. und die Niobe-Gestalt', *Grazer Beiträge*, 12/13: 21–35.

POULSEN, F., and DUGAS, C. (1911), 'Vases archaïques de Délos', *BCH* 35: 350–442.

PRIMMER, A. (1970), 'Homerische Gerichtsszenen', *WS* 4: 5–13.

PRITCHARD, J. B. (1969) (ed.), *Ancient Near Eastern Texts relating to the Old Testament*, trans. W. F. Albright, H. L. Ginsberg, *et al.*, 4th edn. (Princeton; 1st pub. 1950).

RABEL, R. J. (1990), 'Apollo as a Model for Achilles in the *Iliad*', *AJP* 111: 429–40.

——(1991), 'Agamemnon's *Iliad*', *GRBS* 32: 103–17.

RADERMACHER, L. (1943), *Mythos und Sage bei den Griechen*, 2nd edn. (Brünn; 1st pub. 1938; repr. Darmstadt, 1968).

REDFIELD, J. M. (1975), *Nature and Culture in the Iliad: The Tragedy of Hector* (Chicago; expanded edn. Durham, NC, 1994).

REHM, R. (1994), *Marriage to Death: The Conflation of Wedding and Funeral Rituals in Greek Tragedy* (Princeton).

REINHARDT, K. (1960a), *Tradition und Geist: gesammelte Essays zur Dichtung* (Göttingen).

——(1960b), 'Personifikation und Allegorie', in *Vermächtnis der Antike, Gesammelte Essays zur Philosophie und Geschichtschreibung* (Göttingen), 7–40.

——(1961), *Die Ilias und ihr Dichter*, ed. U. Hölscher (Göttingen).

——(1979), *Sophocles*, trans. H. and D. Harvey (Oxford; 1st pub. Frankfurt, 1933).

RICHARDSON, N. J. (1974), *The Homeric Hymn to Demeter* (Oxford).

——(1987), 'The Individuality of Homer's Language', in J. M. Bremer, I. J. F. de Jong, and J. Kalff (eds.), *Beyond Oral Poetry* (Amsterdam), 165–84.

——(1993), *The Iliad: A Commentary*, vi (Cambridge).

RICHARDSON, S. (1990), *The Homeric Narrator* (Nashville).

ROBERT, C. (1920), *Die Griechische Heldensage*, 4th edn. (Berlin).

ROSNER, J. A. (1976), 'The Speech of Phoenix: *Iliad* 9. 434–605', *Phoenix*, 30: 314–27.

References 333

ROWE, C. J. (1983), 'The Nature of Homeric Morality', in C. A. Rubino and C. W. Shelmerdine (eds.), *Approaches to Homer* (Austin, Tex.), 248–75.

RUTHERFORD, R. (1996), 'Homer', *Greece and Rome* New Surveys in the Classics, no. 26 (Oxford).

SACHS, E. (1933), 'Die Meleagererzählung in der *Ilias* und das mythische Paradeigma', *Philologus*, 88: 16–29.

SCHADEWALDT, W. (1965), *Von Homers Welt und Werk*, 4th edn. (Stuttgart; 1st pub. Leipzig, 1944).

—— (1966), *Iliasstudien*, 3rd edn. (Berlin; repr. Darmstadt, 1987; 1st pub. Leipzig, 1938).

SCHEER, E. (1958) (ed.), *Lycophronis Alexandra* (Berlin).

SCHEFOLD, K. (1966), *Myth and Legend in Early Greek Art* (London; 1st pub. Munich, 1964).

SCHEIN, S. L. (1970), 'Odysseus and Polyphemus in the *Odyssey*', *GRBS* 11: 73–83.

—— (1980), 'On Achilles' Speech to Odysseus: *Iliad* 9. 308–429', *Eranos*, 78: 125–31.

—— (1984), *The Mortal Hero* (Berkeley).

SCHLUNK, R. R. (1976), 'The Theme of the Suppliant-Exile in the *Iliad*', *AJP* 97: 199–209.

SCHMITZ, A. (1963), 'La Polarité de contraires dans la rencontre d'Hector et Andromaque: *Iliade* VI 369–502', *Études Classiques*, 21: 129–58.

SCHOECK, G. (1961), *Ilias und Aethiopis* (Göttingen).

SCHRADER, H. (1880) (ed.), *Porphyrii Quaestionum Homericarum ad Iliadem Pertinentium Reliquias Collegit* (Leipzig).

SCHUBART, W., and WILAMOWITZ-MOELLENDORFF, U. (1907) (eds.), *Berliner Klassikertexte*, herausgegeben von der Generalverwaltung der Königlichen Museen in Berlin 5, no. 3 (Berlin).

SCHWABL, H. (1963), review of *Hésiode et son influence*, ed, K. Von Fritz, Fondation Hardt pour l'Étude de l'Antiquité Classique, Entretiens sur l'Antiquité Classique, VII (1962), in *AAHG* 16: 31–2.

SCODEL, R. (1982), 'The Autobiography of Phoenix: *Iliad* 9. 444–95', *AJP* 103: 128–36.

—— (1992), 'The Wits of Glaucus', *TAPhA* 122: 73–84.

SCOTT, J. A. (1912), 'Phoenix in the *Iliad*', *AJP* 33: 68–77.

SCULLY, S. (1990), *Homer and the Sacred City* (Ithaca, NY).

SEAFORD, R. A. (1994), *Reciprocity and Ritual* (Oxford).

SEGAL, C. (1971a), 'Andromache's Anagnorisis: Formulaic Artistry in *Iliad* XXII 437–76', *HSCP* 75: 33–57.

SEGAL, C. (1971b), 'The Theme of the Mutilation of the Corpse in the *Iliad*', *Mnemosyne* suppl. 17 (Leiden).

SEGAL, C. (1988), 'Nestor and the Honor of Achilles', *Studi micenei ed egeo-anatolici*, 13: 90–105.

SEILER, H.J. (1954), 'Homerisch ἀάομαι und ἄτη', in A. Debrunner, *Sprachgeschichte und Wortbedeutung*, Festschrift Albert Debrunner gewidmet von Schülern, Freunden und Kollegen (Berne), 409–17.

SEVERYNS, A. (1928), *Le Cycle épique dans l'école d' Aristarque* (Paris).

SHEPPARD, J. T. (1922), *The Pattern of the Iliad* (London).

SIDWELL, K. (1992), 'The Argument of the Second Stasimon of *Oedipus Tyrannus*', *JHS* 112: 106–22.

SINOS, D. S. (1980), *Achilles, Patroklos and the Meaning of Philos*, Innsbrücker Beiträge zur Sprachwissenschaft 29 (Innsbruck).

SLATKIN, L. (1991), *The Power of Thetis* (Berkeley).

SNELL, B. (1982), *The Discovery of the Mind in Greek Philosophy and Literature*, trans. E. T. Rosenmeyer (New York; 1st pub. Hamburg, 1955).

SOLMSEN, F. (1965), '*Ilias* Σ 535–40', *Hermes*, 93: 1–6.

SOURVINOU-INWOOD, C. (1979), 'Theseus as Son and Stepson', *BICS* suppl. 40 (London).

—— (1981), 'To Die and Enter the House of Hades: Homer, Before and After', in J. Whaley (ed.), *Mirrors of Mortality: Studies in the Social History of Death* (London), 15–39.

—— (1983), 'A Trauma in Flux: Death in the Eighth Century and After', in R. Hägg (ed.), *The Greek Renaissance of the Eighth Century B.C.: Tradition and Innovation*, Skrifter utgivna av Svenska Instituet i Athen 4° 30 (Stockholm), 33–48.

—— (1988), 'Myth and History: On Herodotus III 48 and 50–3', *OA* 17: 167–82.

—— (1989), 'Assumptions and the Creation of Meaning: "Reading" Sophocles' *Antigone*', *JHS* 109: 134–48.

—— (1991), *'Reading' Greek Culture: Texts and Images, Rituals and Myths* (Oxford).

STALLMACH, J. (1968), *Ate. Zur Frage des Selbst- und Weltverständnisses des frühgriechischen Menschen*, Beiträge zur klassischen Philologie 18 (Meisenheim).

STANFORD, W. B. (1947) (ed.), *The* Odyssey *of Homer* (London).

STANLEY, K. (1993), *The Shield of Homer: Narrative Structure in the Iliad* (Princeton).

STRASBURGER, G. (1954), *Die kleinen Kämpfer der* Ilias (Frankfurt).

STRASBURGER, H. (1953), 'Der soziologische Aspekt der Homerischen Epen', *Gymnasium*, 60: 97–114.

SUSEMIHL, F. (1892), *Geschichte der griechischen Literatur in der Alexandrinerzeit* (Leipzig).

SWAIN, S. C. R. (1988), 'A Note on *Iliad* 9. 524–99: The Story of Meleager', *CQ*, NS 38: 271–6.

SYNODINOU, K. (1987), 'The Threats of Physical Abuse of Hera by Zeus in the *Iliad*', *WS* 100: 13–22.

TAPLIN, O. (1980), 'The Shield of Achilles within the *Iliad*', *Greece and Rome*, 27: 1–21.

—— (1990), 'Constructing Agamemnon's Role in the *Iliad*', in C. Pelling (ed.), *Characterization and Individuality in Greek Literature* (Oxford), 60–82.

—— (1992), *Homeric Soundings* (Oxford).

TATE, J. (1929), 'On the History of Greek Allegorism', *CQ* 23: 142–54.

—— (1930), 'On the History of Greek Allegorism (contd.)', *CQ* 24: 1–10.

—— (1934), 'On the History of Greek Allegorism (contd.)', *CQ* 28: 105–15.

THEILER, W. (1970), *Untersuchungen zur antiken Literatur* (Berlin), 11–47 (1st pub. as 'Die Dichter der *Ilias*', *Festschrift für E. Tièche* (Bern, 1947), 125–67).

THIEL, H. VAN (1982), *Iliaden und Ilias* (Basel).

THOMAS, R. (1989), *Oral Tradition and Written Record in Classical Athens* (Cambridge).

THOMPSON, STITH (1955–8), *Motif-Index of Folk Literature*, i–vi (Copenhagen).

THORNTON, A. (1984), *Homer's Iliad: Its Composition and the Motif of Supplication*, Hypomnemata 81 (Göttingen).

TOUCHEFEU-MEYNIER, O. (1968), *Thèmes Odysséens dans l'art antique* (Paris).

Tragicorum Graecorum Fragmenta, i, ed. B. Snell (Göttingen, 1971); ii, ed. R. Kannicht (Göttingen, 1981); iv, ed. S. Radt (Göttingen, 1977).

TRYPANIS, C. A. (1977), *The Homeric Epics* (Warminster).

TSAGARAKIS, O. (1971), 'The Achaean Embassy and the Wrath of Achilles', *Hermes*, 99: 257–77.

VAN BROCK, N. (1959), 'Substitution rituelle', *Revue Hittite et Asianique*, 65: 117–46.

VAN DER VALK, M. H. A. L. H. (1963–4), *Researches on the Text and Scholia of the Iliad*, i–ii (Leiden).

VAN GRONINGEN, B. H. (1953), *In the Grip of the Past* (Leiden).

VAN LEEUWEN, J. (1912–13) (ed.), *Ilias: cum prolegomenis, notis criticis, commentariis exegeticis*, i–ii (Leiden).

VERMEULE, E. (1964), *Greece in the Bronze Age* (Chicago).

—— (1987), 'Baby Aigisthos and the Bronze Age', *PCPS* 33: 123–52.

VERNANT, J. P. (1981), 'Le Tyran boiteux', *Le Temps de la réflexion*, 2: 235–56.

—— and DÉTIENNE, M. (1967), 'La Métis d'Antiloque', *RÉG* 80: 68–83.

VICKERS, B. (1973), *Towards Greek Tragedy* (London).

VON DER MÜHLL, P. (1952), *Kritisches Hypomnema zur Ilias*, Schweizerische Beiträge zur Altertumswissenschaft 4 (Basel).

VON SCHELIHA, R. (1943), *Patroklos. Gedanken über Homers Dichtung und Gestalten* (Basle).

VON STEUBEN, H. (1968), *Frühe Sagendarstellungen in Korinth und Athen* (Berlin).

WACE, A. J. B., and STUBBINGS, F. H. (1962), *A Companion to Homer* (London).

WACKERNAGEL, J. (1916), *Sprachliche Untersuchungen zu Homer* (Göttingen).

WAGNER, R. (1891), *Epitoma Vaticana ex Apollodori Bibliotheca* (Leipzig; repr. Hildesheim, 1971).

WALZ, C. (1834), *Rhetores Graeci*, i–viii (Stuttgart).

WEBER, R. (1888), 'De Dioscuridis περὶ τῶν παρ' Ὁμήρῳ νόμων libello', *Leipziger Studien zur Classischen Philologie*, 11: 87–196.

WECKLEIN, N. (1918), *Über Zusätze und Auslassung von Versen im Homerischen Texte* (Munich).

WELCKER, F. G. (1857), *Griechische Götterlehre* (Göttingen).

WEST, M. L. (1966), *Hesiod, Theogony* (Oxford).

—— (1978), *Hesiod, Works and Days* (Oxford).

—— (1980), *Delectus ex Iambis et Elegis Graecis* (Oxford).

—— (1985), *The Hesiodic Catalogue of Women* (Oxford).

—— (1988), 'The Rise of the Greek Epic', *JHS* 108: 150–60.

—— (1997), *The East Face of Helicon* (Oxford).

WEST, S. (1967) (ed.), *The Ptolemaic Papyri of Homer*, Papyrologica Coloniensa, iii (Cologne).

—— (1982), 'Crime Prevention and Ancient Editors (*Iliad* 9. 458–61)', *LCM* 7: 84–6.

—— (1991), 'Herodotus' Portrait of Hecataeus', *JHS* 111: 144–60.

WESTBROOK, R. (1992), 'The Trial Scene in the *Iliad*', *HSCP* 94: 53–76.

WESTERMANN, A. (1843), *ΜΥΘΟΓΡΑΦΟΙ: Scriptores Poeticae Historiae Graeci* (Brunswick).

WHITE, J. (1984), *When Words Lose their Meaning* (Chicago).

WHITFIELD, G. K. (1967), 'The Restored Relation: The Supplication Theme in the *Iliad*' (diss. Columbia).

WHITMAN, C. H. (1958), *Homer and the Heroic Tradition* (Cambridge, Mass.).

WILAMOWITZ-MOELLENDORFF, U. VON (1920), *Die Ilias und Homer*, 2nd edn. (Berlin; 1st pub. 1916).

WILLCOCK, M. M. (1956–7), 'B 356, Z 326 and A 404', *PCPS* 184: 23–4.

—— (1964), 'Mythological Paradeigma in the *Iliad*', *CQ* 14: 141–54.

—— (1973), 'The Funeral Games of Patroclus', *BICS* 20: 1–11.

—— (1977), 'Ad Hoc Invention in the *Iliad*', *HSCP* 81: 41–53.

—— (1978–84) (ed.), *The Iliad of Homer*, i–ii (London).

—— (1983), 'Antilochus in the *Iliad*', in *Mélanges Edouard Delebecque* (Aix-en-Provence), 479–85.

—— (1992), 'Nervous Hesitation in the *Iliad*', in J. Pinsent and H. V. Hurt (eds.), *Homer 1987* (Liverpool), 65–73.

WILLIAMS, F. (1978), *Callimachus, Hymn to Apollo: A Commentary* (Oxford).

WOLF, F. A. (1985), *Prolegomena to Homer 1795*, trans. A. Grafton, G. W. Most, and J. E. G. Zetzel (Princeton).

WOLFF, H. J. (1946), 'The Origin of Judicial Litigation among the Greeks', *Traditio*, 4: 31–87.

WOODFORD, S. (1993), *The Trojan War in Ancient Art* (London).

WYATT, W. F. (Jnr.) (1982), 'Homeric Ἄτη', *AJP* 103: 247–76.

YAMAGATA, N. (1991), 'Phoenix's Speech—Is Achilles Punished?', *CQ*, NS 41: 1–15.

ZARKER, W. (1965), 'King Eëtion and Thebe as Symbols in the *Iliad*', *CJ* 61: 110–14.

ZIELINSKI, T. (1901), 'Die Behandlung gleichzeitiger Ereignisse im antiken Epos', *Philologus* Supplementband 8: 405–97.

INDEX OF PASSAGES CITED

GENERAL INDEX